The
Last Testament
of
Lucky Luciano

BOOKS BY RICHARD HAMMER

The Last Testament of Lucky Luciano (with Martin A. Gosch)

Playboy's Illustrated History of Organized Crime

The Court-Martial of Lieutenant Calley

One Morning in the War

Between Life and Death

The Last Testament of Lucky Luciano

MARTIN A. GOSCH
RICHARD HAMMER

Little, Brown and Company · Boston · Toronto

To my darling Chip, without whom this book could not have been written and who was there from the beginning.

M. A. G.

And to Arlene.
R. H.

LIBRARY OF CONGRESS CATALOGING IN PUBLICATION DATA

Gosch, Martin A
   The last testament of Lucky Luciano.

   1. Luciano, Charles. I. Hammer, Richard, joint author.
II. Luciano, Charles. III. Title.

Designed by Susan Windheim

*Published simultaneously in Canada
by Little, Brown & Company (Canada) Limited*

PRINTED IN THE UNITED STATES OF AMERICA

Introduction

Early in 1961, Charles "Lucky" Luciano made a decision. He was then sixty-three and more than half his life had been devoted to crime, much of it as the overlord of the organized underworld in the United States; he had been its ruler even during fifteen years of exile in Italy. But at that moment, his position, whatever it was, was shaky. His health was not good: he had already suffered a major heart attack. And now his life had been threatened by his onetime friends and associates back in America.

Luciano's decision was that his passing should not go unattended, that the portraits painted of him in the past, which he considered at least partially untrue and greatly distorted, should not be the only ones left behind. Someday, he wanted the truth, as he saw it, told about his life, about his ambitions and how he had achieved them, about his crimes, about those he had known and dealt with; it should be told not at that moment but later, when retribution could no longer fall upon him or most of those directly involved in his life.

It was the decision, perhaps, of a bitter man. For some months he had been directly involved in a proposed motion picture loosely related to the later years of his life. It was the first time, despite the entreaties of film producers through the years, that he had ever authorized such a project or cooperated on one. On February 18, he had read the script and approved it and given his word that he would do all he could to help in its making; in return, he was to receive $100,000 and a percentage of whatever profits the movie earned. He had taken two copies of the script that day and sent one to an actor in Hollywood he wanted to portray him, keeping the second copy for himself.

Within a few days, however, he had received very unsettling news. Tommy Eboli, then the caretaker for the underworld interests of Vito Genovese, who was serving a term in federal prison for narcotics conspiracy, arrived in Naples with orders from New York. The rulers of the American underworld had decreed that there was to be no picture.

Luciano had little choice but to accede. He called Martin Gosch, one of the authors of this book, the coauthor of the screenplay and coproducer of the projected film, and asked him to return to Italy from London, where Gosch had gone on the Luciano project. "Could you come down here?" Luciano said. "I have to talk to you, Marty."

Gosch knew that the request must, indeed, deal with something important, and he was just as certain that it must mean the movie deal was collapsing. "There's one thing I have to know," he said. "Is there anything wrong with the deal on the picture?"

"Oh, no. No, nothin's wrong with the picture. Everything's okay. But I gotta see you right away. I'll explain the whole thing when you get here."

By noon of the following day, February 26, 1961, Gosch was in Rome, had met Luciano at the Quirinale hotel. They did not stay there. Luciano took Gosch's luggage and drove him back to the airport, most of the trip in silence. At the airport terminal, they went to the mezzanine restaurant. Luciano ordered spaghetti *molto al dente*. Gosch drank tea and watched while Luciano ate slowly and deliberately. Halfway through the meal, Luciano looked up. "Marty," he said, "could you call off the picture?"

It was what Gosch had been expecting, but still it was a shock. "For chrissake, why? I don't understand this and until I do, I simply have no answer for you."

"Marty, I can't tell you. I think you gotta give up the picture."

Luciano spoke calmly, without emotion, and that distressed Gosch. "Charlie," he said, "you're supposed to be a man whose word is his bond. I've heard over and over, 'Charlie Lucky promises this,' 'Charlie Lucky says that,' 'Charlie Lucky guarantees.' You're so proud of always keeping your word and now you've broken it to me, someone you've told everyone you like so much. Didn't you tell me on the phone last night that there was nothing wrong? You lied to me, Charlie."

After a moment, in a strained voice, Luciano said, "Marty, I'm gonna let you read somethin'. I want to prove that you are the guy I trust and that I'm only doin' what I have to do." Luciano took a plain piece of white stationery, folded in half, from his inside jacket pocket, and handed it to Gosch.

"Dear Charlie," the note said. "We have decided that the picture you want to make is a bad thing at this time, for all the reasons you know. The Little Man would be very upset if you decided to go ahead. So you better not do it." The note was unsigned.

"How did you get this?" Gosch asked.

"A guy brought it to me from New York, a week ago."

From all Gosch had learned in recent months dealing with Luciano, he knew who the Little Man was — Meyer Lansky. Now he asked, "Why should Meyer Lansky want to scare me out of making *The Lucky Luciano Story?* For God's sake, he could read every word of that screenplay and not find one line that's remotely connected with him."

"I'm not talkin' about him scarin' you; I'm talkin' about guys gettin' killed. First, they'll kill me, then they'll kill you, and maybe a few other guys. I oughta know. These guys play rough."

"Do you mean to say that if I go ahead with this movie, a movie, that our lives are actually in danger?"

"Marty, I don't have to think about it. I can tell you. I know them. I'm as good as dead. And maybe you, too." Then Luciano paused for a moment. "Marty, would you be willin' to take down my whole life story?" Gosch was too stunned to reply. Luciano continued. "I mean it. I've been thinkin' about it for the last three days. I've reached the point where somebody has to know the truth about me. I want somebody to know my life."

Gosch and Luciano had come together to make a movie, a movie that was to be essentially fiction, and Gosch was not sure that he wanted to know any more about the exiled American racketeer.

But Luciano persisted. "Marty, I would like you to do it for me."

"Why me?"

"Because, like I told you before, you're the only person I trust who's not in the outfit."

"Why not Pat Eboli or someone who's really close to you? Let one of them know the facts."

"They ain't no writers."

"You want me to write your story?"

"Yeah. But I have to make one condition."

"You're playing games with me, Charlie."

"No, I swear to you, I'm not. The condition is only this. I'll give it all to you. I won't hold back nothin'. But you gotta promise you won't use it, no part of it, for ten years. And I mean ten years after I die."

"Oh, come on. Except for popping those nitro pills into your mouth every five minutes, you're in marvelous shape. You're taking care of your heart and nine chances out of ten you'll outlive me."

"No," Luciano shook his head. "If you have everythin' about my life, it'll be an annuity for you and Chip [Gosch's wife, Lucille]. I think you oughta do what I say. You don't have to answer me now, but I wish you would."

"Charlie, if I become your Boswell . . ."

"Who the hell is he?"

Gosch explained.

"Okay, you're my Mr. Boswell," Luciano said. "I appoint you officially. I just have one more condition to put on you. You can't use anythin' I'm gonna tell you if Tommy Lucchese is still alive, even if the ten years are up. He's one good friend I don't want to hurt."

"Listen," Gosch said, "right now you're angry. Some guy brought you a message; they're trying to stop the movie and they've been cutting off your money and threatening you. At this minute, you're sore at the world. Tomorrow morning, you may feel differently."

"No, Marty," Luciano said. "I gave a lotta thought to this. It's the way I want it."

Early that afternoon, on the mezzanine of the airport outside Rome, the deal was struck. For the next ten months, Luciano told in detail the story of his life to Martin Gosch, and Gosch was with him at the moment of his death.

What follows, then, is Luciano's own story, the leader's story of organized crime and how it came into being, grew and flourished. Parts of it may seem self-serving, and they may well be. Much of it is angry, scurrilous, even defamatory, but that is the way Luciano saw it. It is, in all, the story of an organization and of the man who made the decisions, who gave the orders.

Part One

Genesis
1897-1927

1.

"It ain't like I didn't remember Lercara Friddi. After all, I was nine years old when we left there in 1906. Even though I didn't set eyes on the place again for thirty-nine years, when I got outa jail and they sent me back there, to what was supposed to be my 'hometown,' it was like all my memories came back in a couple of minutes. There was the same stink of the sulfur mines outside of our village where my father used to work. There was the same kind of gray dust coverin' everythin', and I remembered how it used to get so deep into our clothes that our mothers couldn't wash it out. And there was the same smell. It was the smell of no money, the smell of bein' hungry all the time."

In that poor hillside village of unpaved streets set into the baked, arid interior of Sicily on November 24, 1897, Charles "Lucky" Luciano, christened Salvatore Lucania, was born, the third child and second son of Antonio Lucania and the former Rosalie Capporelli. He was his mother's favorite from the beginning, supplanting his older brother Giuseppe and sister Francesca, and never completely supplanted, when they arrived, by his younger siblings, Bartolo and Concetta.

"All the time we was growin' up, it seemed that all my old man ever talked about was going to America. We had a calendar that come from the steamship company in Palermo, which was where you got on the boat. My old man used to get a new one every year and hang it up on the wall, and my mother used to cross herself every time she walked past it. Sometimes we even went without enough to eat, because every cent my old man could lay his hands on would go into a big bottle he kept under his bed. It was his private bank and my mother would count it at the end of every month so we could figure how long it would take before we had enough to go to Palermo and make the boat."

The bottle was still not full enough in the spring of 1906, and "the idea of missin' the April sailin' again was practically eatin' my father alive. But there was a cousin in Lercara Friddi on my mother's side, by the name of Rotolo. He had some money from some houses he rented out. My old man was too proud to ask him for a loan. So my mother went to see him in secret and set the whole thing up for Rotolo to hand him a bag of money for the tickets, with a little bit to spare. My old man didn't find out what my mother had done for more than a year, not until after we was in America. Then he just put money aside and paid Rotolo back in less than two years."

In the teeming steerage of a creaking ship, in April of 1906, Antonio Lucania led his family, miserable, cold, seasick, to a world alien beyond all their visions. From the quiet, sparsely peopled, familiar ground of Lercara Friddi, where everyone knew everyone, where there were only friends and enemies and relatives, where everyone spoke the same language, where everyone was poor, they arrived in a place where it was a struggle to breathe the air, where there were so many people crowded into so little space that it was a fight just to walk on the sidewalks, where the streets and sidewalks were paved not with gold but with cement and tar, where the night was not dark and starlit but glowing almost like day with artificial light, where the noise made the ears ring, where everyone and everything were strange and terrifying.

It was to the polyglot Lower East Side of New York, below Fourteenth Street and far east near the river, that Antonio Lucania brought his family, to a tiny, dingy, dark flat in a decaying tenement, indistinguishable from the tenements on either side or anywhere in the neighborhood. It was a street, an area, not just of Sicilians, with their warmth and friendship and offers of aid, with their familiar ways. There were Neapolitans and Calabrians and other mainland Italians with their decipherable but still strange accents and customs, and there were the undecipherable, belligerent and hard-drinking Irish. But at least they were all Catholics. For there were also the bizarre, clannish and alien Jews, the anti-Christs the Church had always taught them to fear and avoid.

It did not take long for Antonio Lucania to perceive that he had exchanged the familiar poverty of Lercara Friddi not for a new world of riches but for a new and even more grinding poverty. His and his family's world was circumscribed, perhaps even more than it had been back in Sicily. They were limited by their inability to speak the language of this new country, by their unfamiliarity with its customs and mores. They had little knowledge of anything beyond their own street and neighborhood. And their lack of training left them ill prepared to cope with the social and economic realities. Antonio Lucania became a day laborer; though the pay was more than he could have dreamed of earning in Sicily, would have been enough there to provide luxuries, in the United States it provided a bare subsistence.

But he had turned forever from life in Sicily, had made his choice for a new life in America where there was, if nothing else, hope, especially for the children. He applied for and received citizenship as soon as possible, and under the laws then in effect, his wife and five minor children became United States citizens as well.

"As far as my mother and father was concerned, the best thing about America was the schools. They was free. Back in Lercara Friddi, we had only Catholic schools and you hadda pay to go to them." The five young Lucanias — quickly Americanizing their names so that Giuseppe became Joseph; Francesca, Fannie; Bartolo, Bart; and Concetta, Connie ("Me? I was the holdout, because I figured that if they started to shorten my name, I would be called Sal. Hell, that's a girl's name, and they wasn't gonna hang that on me") — were enrolled in Public School 19. "It wasn't easy to go to an American school and not know a goddamn word of English. Maybe, in my whole life, that was the worst time I ever experienced, the first couple years at P.S. 19." Salvatore was nine, the oldest kid in his class, forced to sit in the back of the room and ignored by his teachers until he could respond in English. It was an experience familiar to the children of almost all immigrants; some adjusted to it quickly, driven by a thirst for knowledge and what education could bring; others were almost narcotized, enveloped by bewilderment; still others, and Salvatore Lucania was one, resisted stubbornly and belligerently and turned to the streets. "All the other kids in my class was like little babies, but they could talk English and I didn't know what the fuck they was

5

sayin'. Maybe that's why I fought so hard to get outa school, out into the streets where a lotta people spoke Sicilian-Italian and they knew what I was sayin' and I could understand them. I picked up my English on the streets. That's the one thing I regret in my life more than anythin' else, that my grammar is lousy and I don't have too many good words and I talk with a New York accent."

During his five years of formal education, from the ages of nine to fourteen, first at P.S. 10 and later at P.S. 40, Salvatore Lucania, trapped by ignorance, resistance and greater age and size, watched with a kind of bitter envy the smaller, younger kids, especially the Jewish kids (against whose "corrupting" influence he was constantly warned at home and by the Church), avidly absorb the knowledge and lessons that escaped him, that seemed to soar through their brains to a region beyond his reach. But there was something he learned by watching them; it stayed with him through the years, overcame his suspicions and the inculcations of home and Church, and, unlike most of his Sicilian and Italian associates in later life, drew him to them and opened the way to friendship; they had brains, they were smart, they could prove extraordinary allies.

He was certain, though, that the "old broads," as he called his teachers (none of whom he could remember by name), had nothing to teach him. But almost without realizing it, he did learn a concept from them that he would eventually bend and distort for his own use. This was the time of union struggle for acceptance and power, and that struggle germinated and flourished on the Lower East Side where the only work available was in sweatshops at long hours and low pay. "Some of the mothers of guys I knew used to work on them sewin' machines, and if they got up to get a glass of water or open their mouths to breathe some air, some bastard foreman could fire 'em just like that." In such a climate, Samuel Gompers became a hero and his fledgling International Ladies' Garment Workers' Union a cause to be devoutly espoused. "The old broads in school was always hammerin' away about union. Of course, what they meant was Washington and Lincoln and the whole country. But to us, unions was somethin' that had to do with gettin' people a couple bucks more or a chance to work a few hours less, a chance to organize and become strong. I used those ideas in the twenties, with Lepke and Tommy Lucchese, when I figured out a way to organize the unions and take 'em over. Later, when the newspapers were callin' me the head of the labor rackets in New York, I used to wonder if my old teachers knew that they was the ones that taught me all the principles about organizing people."

In the classroom, Lucania's behavior only infrequently brought him into open conflict with authorities. That, perhaps, was because he was so rarely in the school. He became a chronic and persistent truant, appearing only to make what profit he could. Very early he had noticed that some of the older Irish and Italian kids were waylaying the younger and smaller Jewish kids on their way home from school, beating and robbing them. Lucania turned this to his profit. For a penny or two a day, he sold his protection to the potential victims. If they paid, they could be sure that their daily trips to and from school would be made in safety, for though young Lucania was never a giant, he was tough enough and old enough to make his promise of protection stick.

It was all part of the widening street world he was learning. In that world, he scrounged for money any way he could get it. Realizing early that "some people had money and some people didn't," he had determined that he was destined to be one of those who had it. He ran errands, carried packages from a neighborhood ice cream parlor, the grocery, for anyone who needed an errand boy. Soon he discovered there were easier ways; he branched out into pilfering whatever was lying loose.

But his was still a limited world, made narrow by Sicilian parental authority. The truant officer was often at the door of the Lucanias' flat, and those visits were invariably followed by a beating from his father. His mother tearfully pleaded with him to finish school, and he would promise that he would. (When he quit at fourteen, after the fifth grade, and got his working papers, he was sure that he had made good on that promise.) But the truancy persisted, and finally on June 25, 1911, the Board of Education took its ultimate stern measure: he was committed to the Brooklyn Truant School, to remain for four months.

"This first time I was locked up is like a fog to me. This was a place where you was supposed to learn that it was wrong not to go

7

to school. They worked our asses off, just doin' nothin'. And what a kid learns in that place is how to steal better, or how to pick pockets, all that stuff. When I came out after four months, I knew school and me was through. I also knew I hated Brooklyn. Even later, when I was runnin' things in Manhattan, I always managed to stay away from Brooklyn and let the guys over there play their own games without interference."

As he walked through the school gates, his father was waiting for him, to take him home. "We had a lot of trouble gettin' back to our neighborhood because Brooklyn was like a foreign country. We got lost on the El and it was almost dark by the time we reached home; it took us more than two hours. All durin' that time, my old man only talked about one thing — go back to school or get a job. I wasn't goin' back to school."

But the only jobs available were those of errand boy, and even those were not easy to come by. The neighborhood was filled with other boys his age, sons of immigrants, who had quit school, were ill educated, held menial jobs if they worked at all, and dreamed of riches, of someday making the big score. "My old man kept sayin' the neighborhood was gettin' worse, that there was gangs of young guys around my age who was knockin' off stores, grabbin' handbags from old ladies, stuff like that. He said every kid in the neighborhood was growin' up to be a crook.

"When I looked around the neighborhood, I found out that the kids wasn't the only crooks. We was surrounded by crooks, and plenty of them was guys who were supposed to be legit, like the landlords and storekeepers and the politicians and cops on the beat. All of 'em was stealin' from somebody. And we had the real pros, the rich Dons from the old country, with their big black cars and mustaches to match. We used to make fun of them behind their backs, but our mothers and fathers was scared to death of them. The only thing is, we knew they was rich, and rich was what counted, because the rich got away with anythin'. One time, we got a big prosciutto ham that was sent to my mother by a cousin in Lercara Friddi. We got all excited because it was the first package that ever come from home. My old man got out a hammer and opened up the crate, and there was this beautiful ham all wrapped up in burlap. We was ready to attack it right then, but my mother

8

said no, a prosciutto ham has to be hung up for a while so that the air could get at it and it wouldn't be too soft.

"The next day, a guy named Moliari knocked at our door after dinner. It was Tuesday, and he come to collect his dollar. He was a moneylender, the fat bastard, and he specialized in Sicilians. I think my old man had borrowed some money to buy a new bed for my sisters and he was about three or four weeks behind in payments. So Moliari come up with two guys to take back the bed. When he got a look at that prosciutto ham hangin' in the kitchen, the son of a bitch took it like it belonged to him and started to walk out. When he got to the door, he said to my mother somethin' like, 'I'll take this; you don't want your girls to sleep on the floor.' But I fixed that shitheel good. About two months later, we knocked off his apartment and we grabbed over four hundred dollars. That was the most expensive prosciutto the son of a bitch ever stole."

Out in the street, young Lucania, looked at by his contemporaries with some awe because he had served time, became the leader of a gang, his leadership reinforced by the lessons in crime he had learned during his four months in Brooklyn and could now teach his followers. His gang, of six to a dozen Sicilian friends, marauded through the Lower East Side. There was hardly a store or a lone pedestrian walking home at dusk safe from him or from scores of other gangs like his. But it was one thing to rob and steal and have some real money, and another to be able to use it. Lucania and his friends still lived at home, under stern and watchful eyes. Their fathers worked long hours, came home exhausted with only a few dollars each week, hardly enough to keep the family in food and shelter. They knew what things cost and what it took to earn money. To flaunt new clothes, new possessions on a delivery boy's pay, part of which was going to help the family, would do more than create suspicion; it would earn a beating or worse from fathers whose word was law in their own homes and whose morality was unbending.

To circumvent such parental suspicion and punishment, young Lucania developed a plan, using what he had learned from his teachers at school, whenever he was at school, about union. Unity meant sharing the work and the profits. So all the money they gained from their forays was put into a common pool to be shared

9

equally by all members of the gang, with the money hidden away, buried in vacant lots or other caches. Everyone wanted new clothes, for they were the outward signs of success. But new clothes meant trouble at home. Lucania decreed that new wardrobes would have to be acquired gradually, in such a way that suspicions at home and suspicions of patrolling police would not be aroused. When someone felt he needed a new pair of shoes, a new shirt, anything new, there would be a meeting of the gang at which the expenditure was put to a vote.

"I had a rule that every member hadda have a job, as a kind of front so he could explain how come he could buy new things. I let two Irish kids join because they had jobs and besides, they was nice fellows. One of them was a redheaded guy by the name of Willie Mulvaney, whose old man was a cop up in the Bronx. One time, Willie wanted a new pair of pants; he was still wearin' knickers because he was so little. So we had a regular meet and his request got turned down flat. Well, this dumbhead Willie Mulvaney takes the money anyway and buys himself the long pants and wears them home. His old man, Mulvaney the cop, kept a book on every penny Willie earned. When he found out that Willie didn't steal the pants from a store but actually paid for them, the shit hit the fan. There was about fifteen kids in my gang by that time, and we all got hauled to the police station on Fourteenth Street. It was like a circus. Our mothers and fathers, all our relatives was tryin' to talk at the same time, tryin' to explain to the sergeant that we was good boys who wouldn't do nothin' wrong. Everybody, that is, but my old man. He beat the crap outa me right there in the police station."

It was not long before the neighborhood became too small to contain Lucania and his friends. It was too poor; even the most successful job earned only a few dollars. And there was competition for those few loose dollars. There was the multitude of other young gangs. And there were the neighborhood branches of the old secret societies, the Mafia and the Camorra and the rest, brought over from the old country and terrorizing the immigrants who could not escape them, bleeding the neighborhood of everything beyond mere subsistence.

So, Salvatore Lucania began to look outside, uptown. To the

north, in Manhattan, was East Harlem, and there, in another Italian-Sicilian ghetto, other youths had their own monopoly. That territory was unfamiliar and the spoils there no greater than at home. But in between was the rest of the island of Manhattan where, they thought, were limitless riches. As Lucania looked north of Fourteenth Street into this realm of wealth, he began to perceive how its residents lived, what possessions they had. He dreamed that someday it would all be his, that he would control and own it, would walk its streets like a king in his own domain.

He was, of course, not alone with such ideas. Other gangs from the Lower East Side and from East Harlem had similar visions. They hit the middle of Manhattan from both ends, and though conflict was inevitable, it was held to a minimum because the territory was so vast and there was so much for all.

And midtown was a place where new friends could be made and new, if at first uneasy, alliances struck. "It happened at a movie theater in Times Square — I think it was called the Victoria. It was a Saturday night and some of my guys and me went uptown to see what the action was. We liked to go to the movies because them silent pictures had titles and they helped us learn English. Of course, we always sat in the balcony; it was cheaper and besides we could throw stuff down on the people in the orchestra and raise all kinds of hell. This particular night the manager threw us out, and at the same time he threw out some other guys who was sittin' on the other side of the balcony. One of the guys was a little bit older than us and he had an outfit called the 104th Street Gang. We got together and it turned out that this older guy was not from Sicily; he was a Calabrian from Cozenso. His name was Francesco Castiglia; later on, though, he got famous under the name of Frank Costello.

"The first time I heard him talk, I had to lean over to hear him, because his voice was very husky, like he had a cold. A lot of Italian kids talk like that. Their mothers wanted the best for them, and they thought the best was to get their tonsils and adenoids out the first time the kid's nose started to run. A lot of times, the doctor wasn't so good, or the knife slipped, and the kid always talked like he had a permanent sore throat after that. That's what happened to Frank."

11

Until he met Castiglia, young Lucania had always thought that intelligence was the sole preserve of Jews. But in Castiglia he discovered an Italian who seemed just as clever and perceptive, who had dreams for the future that paralleled Lucania's, and who combined it all with a certain surface polish and a deep-grained toughness; Castiglia then was rarely without a pistol and he was earning a reputation as a hardened hoodlum. The two became immediate friends and that friendship would last until the final years of Luciano's life.

If crime had become the main vocation of Lucania and his friends by the time they were fifteen or sixteen, some legitimate employment was still a necessity if they were to continue to live at home with their families; they were not yet making enough outside to do otherwise. Lucania moved from job to job as errand boy, and in 1914, when he was seventeen, went to work as a runner for the Goodman Hat Company on West Twenty-fourth Street. His job: delivering ladies' hats to Goodman's customers in shops and department stores around town. His wages: six dollars a week, a dollar more than the going rate. "It's a little hard to explain that one dollar a week more could make such a difference. But that was around 1914, and a dollar was a fortune. With my guys, that extra buck made me important, and I kinda liked the feelin'."

Goodman had raised the ante on Lucania because, like so many who met him throughout his life, Max Goodman was charmed by him, fell under a spell he seemed able to conjure almost at will. On one level, Lucania was a tough and vicious kid off the streets with little social conscience, with a barely concealed penchant for violence that led him, with little thought, to smash anyone and anything in his way. It was this side that his father discerned early and that convinced the older man that his son was, perhaps, beyond redemption. But there was another aspect, and he donned it whenever it suited his mood or need. It was this side that drew his mother, Goodman and hundreds of respectable people to him through the years, that helped them ignore or dismiss the hoodlum. They saw him with his mask of warmth, openness, almost naïve ambition; with them, he could be ingenuously eager to please and to emulate, reliable, thirsting for knowledge, willing to work hard, even at times selfless.

12

These were the qualities Max Goodman saw and became certain he could foster. Not only did he pay Lucania that extra dollar in wages, but often he would take the young man home with him after work, and not infrequently on a Friday afternoon to celebrate the Sabbath. With Goodman, Lucania saw another way of life, that of the Jewish middle class, which drew him and filled him with envy. The Goodman apartment in the West Forties was large and well furnished in the style of the immediate pre–World War I period, with comfortable overstuffed chairs and sofas covered in mohair, dark mahogany chests and tables; all his life he would remember the doilies and antimacassars that Mrs. Goodman crocheted and that lay across the backs and arms of chairs and sofas, on the tops of tables and chests. He would pick them up and stare at them, finger and examine them, put them down and return to them. And he began to realize what it meant to be not poor.

He began, as well, to get a sense of another side of the Jewish world that had always been alien to him, the religious side. On those Friday evenings when Max Goodman brought him home, he was part of the religious Sabbath festival, and he would watch with fascination as Goodman put the yarmulke on his head and spread the tallith across his shoulders to preside at the service at his own table. Mrs. Goodman would light the candles and Goodman would read the prayers, and then the dinner would be served, chicken-in-the-pot, chicken soup with matzo balls, noodle kugel, noodle soup, all the traditional Jewish foods. At first, he had expected, for he had always been taught, that it would all be barbaric, both the ceremonies and the food. Instead, he found it only a kind of happy family gathering and discovered that even some of the food was familiar; Jews ate spaghetti, though it was the wide kind and not garnished with garlic or tomato sauce; they liked ravioli filled with meat, though in a different shape from what his mother made, and they called it "kreplach." And so he began to understand that Jews were not all that different from the people he knew. (Later, he was a regular customer at Jewish delicatessens and later still, when in Italian exile, it was the taste of such food that he missed most.)

But none of his feelings for Goodman, nor any of the trust that Goodman placed in him, could deter Lucania from the road he had chosen. Still, success on that road eluded him. In the petty crimes he and his gang were committing, he was no closer to it than in his six-dollar-a-week daytime job. Some of his friends had already been picked up and sent to jail. His new friend from East Harlem, Frank Castiglia, was arrested in 1915 for possession of a gun, pleaded guilty, and was sent away for a year by a judge who told him: "You had a reputation for being a gunman and you certainly were a gunman in this particular case. You were prepared to do the work of a gunman." (Castiglia served ten months, avoided guns as much as possible thereafter, and was not convicted of another crime for nearly forty years.)

So far, Lucania himself had been lucky with the law; he had not been caught during robberies, muggings and the rest, though he was increasingly suspect and his constant nights out and the new things he sometimes sported brought him under suspicion at home. Against this was the realization that if he was going to make the kind of money he wanted in the field he wanted, if he was going to achieve the kind of power he dreamed of, he would have to take chances, bigger and more dangerous ones.

For some time he had been watching George Scanlon move through the neighborhood. "You couldn't miss Scanlon; he drove a big limousine and parked it wherever he wanted to — next to fire hydrants, even on the sidewalk — and nobody bothered him. He wore sharp clothes with wide stripes and he had a diamond ring on his pinky finger. He smelled like the United States Mint." But nobody ever held up George Scanlon; he was as safe as if he were surrounded by a troop of police, and perhaps he was. For Scanlon was the neighborhood narcotics pusher.

Scanlon's business was a relatively new one. It had been only about a decade since Congress had taken the first tentative steps to outlawing addicting drugs, with the passage of the Pure Food and Drug Act in 1906 and more stringent prohibitions in 1914 with the Harrison Act. Though the real clamp-down was yet to come, such laws had an insidious and unexpected effect. For decades, Americans had been seeking relief from a thousand real and imaginary ills by gulping Chief Raincloud's Indian Elixir and a hundred other patent medicines. If they brought none of the expected cures, they did something else: based on opiates or cocaine, they turned thousands into addicts. And so when such laws banning narcotics were passed, the addicts were forced by act of Congress and the New York State Legislature to seek drugs illegally, and to pay higher prices for them than ever before. A new breed of criminal rose to fill the demand, not just from pimps and prostitutes, the most notorious and well-publicized users, but from the addicted housewives deprived of their patent medicines.

Scanlon did his business in drugs right out in the open, unafraid of the police, since he was paying them for protection. Lucania "started to wonder how I could get to him to maybe take me on, so I could make a hunk of real money." The opportunity came one evening when Lucania was eighteen. Coming home from work at Goodman's, tired and dirty, he saw Scanlon's car parked in front of his house. He ran up the four flights to the flat, grabbed a dishrag from the kitchen, raced back down and started briskly polishing the pusher's car. In a few minutes, Scanlon appeared, watched until the job was done, and then tossed Salvatore Lucania a quarter.

Lucania handed the quarter back. "Here, you keep it. I just wanna talk to you for a minute." He told Scanlon he wanted to work for him. Scanlon asked what kind of a job he had; Lucania told him he was a delivery boy for a hat factory, that he carried packages all over town. "If I can deliver hats, then I can deliver other things," he said. Scanlon said maybe he'd give him a tryout the following week.

For the next months, Lucania combined his work for Goodman with his work for Scanlon, secreting Scanlon's narcotics in the hatbands of the ladies' bonnets he was delivering. Each morning he would set out carrying a dozen or so hatboxes to Goodman's customers, stopping off here and there to make a delivery to one of Scanlon's customers. There were no set wages for the work, just a handful of bills, a ten or a twenty, adding up in some weeks to as much as a hundred dollars; it would have taken him more than four months to earn that much from Goodman.

It looked like easy work for easy money. But it didn't last. Afterwards, he was convinced that one of his friends, jealous of his new affluence, had tipped off the cops. He was spotted on a number of occasions going in and out of a poolroom on East Fourteenth

Street, a hangout for addicts and pushers, and police kept close watch on him. Early in June of 1916, he was arrested outside that poolroom; in a hatband in one of Goodman's boxes was found a phial containing a half-dram of heroin.

On June 26, 1916, Salvatore Lucania pleaded guilty in New York Court of Special Sessions to unlawful possession of narcotics. In view of his previous committal to truant school, and despite a plea on his behalf by Max Goodman and a near-hysterical outburst by Rosalie Lucania, he was sentenced to one year at Hampton Farms Penitentiary. His father did not come to court.

After six months he was paroled, and he would not be convicted of another crime for twenty years, and during those years he would become the most notorious and powerful leader of organized crime in the United States.

2.

It was Christmas when the gates of Hampton Farms opened for him. The Salvatore was gone as his first name; from then on, he would be Charles, or Charlie, Lucania.

This time, he had been sent away for something he had done, and this time there was a cache of funds, however small, waiting for him. "But it wasn't worth it." Not that he was going to follow the advice of Goodman or the orders of his father to get a job and become an honest, hardworking citizen. It was just that "I made up my mind I was never gonna get caught again. I'd kill myself before they'd ever put me away again."

For his family, his arrest and conviction had been almost more than could be borne, a shame that saddened and bowed them. His father, who saw all his suspicions of the boy confirmed, felt that his son's hopes for the future were smashed. His mother, who like so many mothers saw the prodigal as her favorite, mourned and forgave. But while he was in prison, they had treated him as if he were dead; they did not come to visit despite his frequent written pleas.

It was Max Goodman who appeared at the prison to see the young convict, not once but several times. Goodman himself had come under suspicion as a result of Lucania's arrest with narcotics in the hatbands. Though he had cleared himself, it had been a terrifying experience for a man who was no longer young and resilient. "Why?" Goodman asked during a visit. "Why did you do this to me? Is this the thanks I get for being nice to you, for treating you like a son?"

Luciano remembered later that he started to cry as Goodman talked to him and that rarely in his life would he ever cry again. He had a deep affection for the man who had helped him, had revealed to him a world he had not before known even existed, who visited him in prison while his own family abandoned him, had been almost a surrogate father to him. At last, he said, "I wanted to make money."

"Money isn't the whole world," Goodman said.

"If you don't have it, it is."

"If you needed money, you should have come to me."

"If I came to you, you wouldn't've given it to me. I needed a new suit."

"I wear a new suit," Goodman said. "Why shouldn't you wear a new suit? The only thing is, people have to work for new suits." Then Goodman said, "Sal . . ."

"Don't call me Sal. From now on, my name's Charlie." In his mind, Sal was an effeminate name. During his first days at Hampton Farms, he had been called Sallie; it was, he was sure, a girl's name and it had led other convicts to attempt to assault him homosexually, attacks he had resisted violently. Charlie was more masculine and, henceforth, it would be his name.

"All right," Goodman said, "now we'll call you Charlie. I'm going to try to get you out of here. Only you must make me a promise that you will do everything they tell you to do here, and do it the best you can."

Then Goodman began a campaign, by letter and personal visits, to persuade parole authorities to release Charlie Lucania, promis-

17

ing to hire him back at his old job. It took six months for the campaign to succeed.

During those six months, Lucania lived by his word to Goodman and was a model prisoner. (Through the years, it would be one of his boasts that he had never broken his word to anyone, that his word was as good as a written contract, even better, since nothing involving him could ever be put down on paper.) "I scrubbed floors, I scrubbed walls, I cleaned out latrines, I scoured pots and pans. They had guards watchin' all of us young guys and we got the worst kind of work. They stood over us with rubber hoses and there was hardly a day when I didn't get a few solid whacks across the back. I had a bucket, some rags and a heavy brush and some kind of cleanin' liquid with lye in it. I hadda get down on my hands and knees and scrub the floors. When I'd get up at the end of the day, my knees'd be raw and bleedin' and they never got a chance to heal. Sometimes I'd make knee-pads out of a few rags, but when the guards seen what I was doin', they'd beat the shit outa me. Every single night I was too tired to eat, and even when I was starved, the food was so terrible that it was almost impossible to swallow.

"The worst part of them six months for me was that I didn't have no privacy, that I could never be alone. I hated the idea that there was no place where you could take a crap without fifty million guys watchin' you. How can a human bein' wipe his ass with all them guys watchin'?"

What came to Luciano's mind as he talked about the past was a movie. An inveterate moviegoer all his life, he constantly saw himself in films, drew allusions to his own life from them. "I seen a movie called *Oliver Twist*. It was written by some English guy by the name of Charles Dickens, and the young kid in that picture reminded me of myself, because they used to knock this little bastard around in the picture the way they did to me at Hampton Farms."

Then, into the snow, the slush, the mud of Christmas, 1916, Charlie Lucania walked out a conditionally free man. With nowhere else to go, with parole to restrict his movements, he returned to his family's home, to what at best was a tenuous situation.

He had been thin and wiry when he entered prison; he was

emaciated when he left, and his mother cried over him, fed him enormous portions of pasta. "It seemed like everybody in my family, even my brothers and sisters, come charging at me to 'reform,' to go back to work for Goodman. I knew they was ashamed of me in front of all their Sicilian friends, that everybody called me 'the bad one.' And you might think I committed murder because I changed my name to Charlie. My mother started to tell me about everybody in my family with the name Salvatore and what a great name this was and how I had no right to make it sound like somethin' dirty. In fact, she never gave up calling me Sal, and my father, when I told him, he just spit on the floor and walked out."

He was nineteen then, no longer a child but a man, and he had established his direction. "I began to realize that what I'd promised Goodman would make me nothin' but a crumb, workin' and slavin' for a few bucks, like all the other crumbs. I made up my mind that if I hadda wind up a crumb, I'd rather be dead."

But there was no need to be what he saw as a crumb. He was in demand, a more prestigious leader of a street gang with a term in prison behind him. He had gone to school there, learning the technique of bigger and more successful jobs, had begun to practice them and so was attracting the attention of the older gangsters in Little Italy, who began to approach him with offers to join their gangs. Occasionally he went with them on jobs, but the relationship was never close and he never considered himself a member of another group. He saw himself as a leader, not a follower taking orders from someone else.

And the suspicions of his father that Charlie Lucania had picked up the old threads grew, and the old man looked for evidence. It did not take him long to find it. Early in 1917, behind some socks in Charlie's drawer, he discovered an expensive gold belt buckle. Antonio Lucania said nothing to his son, merely went around the neighborhood the next morning and, about four blocks away, found a jewelry store that had been robbed; among the missing items, the gold belt buckle.

That night, the old man flung the buckle in Charlie's face and demanded, "Why did you have to steal a gold belt buckle? Is this the most important thing in your life?"

19

"I wanted it, so I took it," Charlie answered.

His father removed a heavy metal belt from his trousers and hit Charlie across the face with it, cutting his cheek, from which the blood dripped down his face. "I felt like hittin' him back then, but I didn't. It don't matter what happens, a Sicilian son never hits his old man." Charlie tried to stem the flow of blood with a kitchen towel as his father stood over him and roared, "You are not my son! You are only a thief and you cannot live in my house any more! Get out!"

Just at that moment, Rosalie Lucania came into the room. Charlie looked at her and said, "So long, Mom, I'm leavin'."

Instantly, she understood and started to pummel Antonio with her fists, screaming, "No, no, you cannot do this. I will not let you throw my Sallie out into the street." But the old man was adamant.

That night, Charlie Lucania was on his own. He moved into a cold-water flat in the West Twenties with a young friend from his gang, Frankie Coppola. They paid three dollars a week for a room with a sink, a one-burner gas plate, a brass double bed, a small round table, and for their clothes, some nails driven into one wall and six shelves bracketed into another. "In the beginning, it was like a palace to us, because it was our joint, the first time we lived away from home. The biggest thing for us was that now we had a place to bring broads and we didn't have to do those quickies in the whorehouses. Frankie and I would toss a coin to see who could use the place for the night while the other guy went for a walk; sometimes we didn't stay out late enough and we'd walk in on each other."

That sense of freedom lasted only a few weeks. The girls Lucania brought to the room began to talk about marriage and "I wasn't the kind of a guy who was lookin' for romance. There were too many things I wanted to do. The thing that made me realize that I still was goin' nowhere happened one night when our gang done a job down at the Battery. One of the guys, Willie Cioppi, had cased a warehouse near the fish market where a whole shipload of canned anchovies had just come in. Italians love anchovies and these was the best quality. We set the whole thing up; we had a wholesaler who was willin' to fence the stuff at half price, which would have meant over two grand for us. The only thing, Willie didn't case the job too good; he didn't know they had two night watchmen on weekends instead of one. Frankie Coppola got caught. The rest of us got away. It was Frankie's first offense, so he got off with probation on condition that he live with his folks and go back to school. That's what he did; he learned how to be a cabinetmaker and he stayed straight."

Now Lucania was completely on his own, and it was not easy. "Things was lousy; I had a good gang of guys but the jobs was scarce and a lotta times we had no money." He had, however, a place to turn for some help. His ties with his family had not been totally broken. He returned home at regular intervals for visits and free meals, though when his father was around, the atmosphere was always charged. And his mother would visit him in his room about once a week, bringing with her a jar of spaghetti sauce. She told him, "You don't know how to eat anybody's spaghetti sauce but mine." It, along with a big pot to cook spaghetti in, was a gift most appreciated, but a gift that presented problems. The single-burner gas plate required the deposit of a dime in a meter before it would work, and sometimes dimes were hard to come by. And then, with only a single burner, when the sauce was hot, the spaghetti was cold, and when the spaghetti was hot, the sauce was cold. "Once in a while, the woman who had the apartment next to my room, Mrs. Petracci, she owned the building, would let me use her stove. But when she was out or I didn't have no dimes, I went hungry."

Along with the spaghetti sauce, his mother came loaded with lectures and advice, particularly about the necessity of returning to school for an education that would prepare him to hold a decent job. "What are they gonna teach me in high school?" was his unvarying response. Well, if he wouldn't go back to school, then at least he ought to go back to work for Goodman.

Goodman, in fact, was persistent in his efforts to win Charlie Lucania back to honest labor. He sought him out and sought out his family. Early in 1917, it seemed that the campaign had succeeded. Goodman came to the Lucania home and told Antonio and Rosalie that Charlie had finally promised to return to work the next week. But Antonio Lucania was convinced that if Charlie had indeed made such a promise to Goodman, he had no intention of living up to it. That evening, Charlie appeared at the flat for the first time in several weeks, and he entered wearing a new suit, new shoes, a stylish hat and even a silk shirt. As the family gathered around the dinner table to eat Charlie's favorite dish, lasagna filled with meat, Antonio began to cross-examine his son about his new clothes. Charlie said that he had bought them out of his pay, that he was again working for Goodman, had been doing so for some weeks.

The lie, coming so soon after Goodman's visit, was final confirmation to Antonio that he had been right in throwing his son out of the house. He called Charlie a liar, almost triumphantly told of Goodman's visit. Rosalie started to sob. Charlie turned on her and said, "Oh, Ma, for chrissake, shut up."

"In my house, I had committed a mortal sin; I used Christ's name like a swear-word. But it was an even worse sin to tell your mother to shut up. My father got up very slow, with his eyes half-closed, then he leaned over the table and slapped me square across the face. Then, like in one movement, he picked up his whole plate of lasagna and threw it at me. This was a brand-new suit I had on, and the meat and the sauce and the cheese, the whole works, practically covered me from head to foot. Nobody said nothin'. My father just stood there and stared down at me, my mother was bawling, and my sisters and brothers was lookin' somewhere else. So, I got up and walked right out of the house. I didn't go back home for a long time, not for a lotta months, and then only during the daytime when my father was workin'. And the olive-oil stains never come outa that suit."

3.

By late in 1917, living by himself in his cold-water room, Charlie Lucania's goals seemed as elusive through crime as they would have been through honest work for Goodman. It was not easy to be a successful thief. Often the jobs he and his gang tried to pull, a robbery or a heist, yielded only a couple of dollars. The real profits went to the fence. And his face was becoming known, in his old neighborhood and his new one, and when he appeared almost anywhere, he was carefully watched.

But he kept telling himself that he had "plans," that he would make it, that it was only a matter of time. And indeed, the lines toward the future he believed was his were being set. His friend Frank Castiglia was out of jail, and they renewed their contact, became a close team. And soon they were joined by two younger tough kids from Lucania's old Lower East Side neighborhood, two Jewish kids with matching ambitions. Maier Suchowljansky had been born in 1902 in Grodno, Russia (then in the Polish Pale of Settlement), and had arrived in New York's ghetto in 1911, when he was nine, with his parents, a sister and a younger brother, Jake. In school, with the Americanized name of Meyer Lansky, he gulped knowledge insatiably and proved something of a prodigy in mathematics. Out in the streets, he just as insatiably drank in the knowledge available there, and though small for his age (even as a grown man, he was only a few inches over five feet), he was belligerent enough and good enough with his fists, with rocks, with any weapon to earn a reputation and to be avidly sought as an ally in any fight. With money needed at home, Lansky quit school after the eighth grade and went to work as an apprentice tool-and-die maker; he proved just as adept with his hands as with his mind; later, his friends would consider him a genius with a car, equaled only by his friend Charlie Lucania. Like Lucania, his aim was higher than skilled labor and he had few scruples to deter him.

Everywhere Lansky went, he was followed by a shadow, a boy four years his junior. Benjamin Siegel was a native American, his family having arrived on the Lower East Side from Kiev a few years before his birth. Even as a boy, he was tall and handsome, moving with a fluid grace and displaying an openness that beguiled victims and friends. "Everybody," Lucania would say, "loved Benny." And despite his youth, he won their grudging respect. Though Benny Siegel was not as smart as Lansky, he was even more fearless, willing to do anything, to take any chance to

23

prove that he had more guts than anybody else. He was the first to throw a punch in a fight, the first into a store or loft in a robbery. While some of the others were still a little leery about carrying a gun, Benny Siegel was rarely without one. He was, his friends would say, nuts, and so they called him "Bugsy" (though in later years, as he acquired a civilized veneer, no one called him that to his face, except for friends from the old days like Lansky and Lucania; he was Ben or Benny to everyone else).

"I first saw Lansky and Siegel long before I left home, when I used to grab pennies from the little Jewish kids for protection. I remember when I made Lansky the usual proposition. I was about a head taller than this midget, but he looked up at me without blinkin' an eye, with nothin' but guts showin' in his face, and he said, 'Fuck you.' Well, I started to laugh. I patted him on the shoulder and said, 'Okay, you got protection for free.' He just pulled away and yelled, 'Shove your protection up your ass, I don't need it!' Believe me, I found out he didn't need it. Next to Benny Siegel, Meyer Lansky was the toughest guy, pound for pound, I ever knew in my whole life, and that takes in Albert Anastasia or any of them Brooklyn hoodlums or anybody anyone can think of."

One of the things, besides ambition and guts, that drew Lucania and Lansky together, as it drew them to Costello, was an ability to keep their emotions in check. "We was like analyzers; we didn't hustle ourselves into a decision before we had a chance to think it out. Siegel was just the opposite, and I guess that's what made him good for us, because he would make his move on sheer guts and impulse."

That Lansky and Siegel were Jewish bothered Lucania hardly at all — though it bothered some of his Italian and Sicilian friends a great deal. There was more about the two to attract him than to repel him; the same ambitions, desires and intensity transcended religious differences.

It was a coming together that would dominate the face of organized crime, would change it radically from the sporadic, haphazard thing it was into a new and all-pervasive menace that would influence the social life of the United States far into the future. There was Charlie Lucania (a decade later, he would rename himself Charlie Luciano), tough, shrewd, a natural leader and organ-

24

izer, calm, with animal cunning and intelligence. There was Francesco Castiglia (soon to be called Frank Costello), suave, tough, intelligent, always figuring the angles. There was Meyer Lansky, tough, shrewd, circumspect, preferring the background where he could influence and manipulate others without their knowing it, considered by his friends a genius. And there was Benjamin "Bugsy" Siegel, tall, handsome, suave, tough, merciless, daring, a killer. All four were men with plans and a dream for the future. "We was," Luciano said, "the best team that ever got put together. We knew our jobs better than any other guys on the street. We was like the Four Horsemen of Notre Dame — except what would two Jewish guys be doin' at Notre Dame?"

It was during one of their first jobs together that Castiglia came upon his new name. "We was gonna break into a riverfront warehouse. Benny was gonna lead the way and take out the night watchman. When we was plannin' our move, Meyer sort of objected. The way he put it was, 'Why should the Jews, Bugsy and me, always go first and take all the chances, then everything gets split down the middle? After all, we've got two Italians, so why don't you guys take the same chances?'

" 'Whadda you mean, two Italians?' I said to him. 'We're one wop, one mick and two Jews, just like in the neighborhood.'

"Lansky stared at me like I was nuts. 'What're you talkin' about,' he said, 'one wop and one mick? Where's the mick?'

"I started to laugh and I pointed to Frank. I said, 'Him. He's Irish. Y'know, Frank Costello.' That's how Costello got his name. I remember we told this story so many times later on that lots of guys would sometimes call Costello, 'Hey, Irish.' And, of course, when we got up to our ears in New York politics, it didn't hurt at all that we had an Italian guy with us with an Irish name like Costello."

The coalition prospered. They had learned from failures to plan carefully and so their thefts, robberies, stickups grew bigger, the profits began to mount and their gangs expanded. "We had so much dough comin' in that it was hard to keep track of it. Even a good counter like Lansky got a little confused once in a while. We figured maybe it would be a good idea if we opened a bank account. There was a bank down on the Lower East Side, I think it was called the United States Bank, and Lansky's uncle knew one of the big shots. Frank went over to take a look at it, to see if that's where we should put our dough. While he was lookin' it over, he couldn't help but kinda case the joint a little bit, and he sees they only got one guard, an old guy who must've been about a hundred and four. So a couple of weeks later, instead of puttin' our money in the place, we take out over eight thousand bucks and got away clean. Meyer said, 'If that's the way they're gonna protect our dough, the hell with 'em.' "

Only one thing seemed now to stand in the way of their forward march. Not the police, for they were confident they would not be caught. In the spring of 1917, the United States went to war with the Central Powers. Siegel and Lansky were both too young for military service and Costello's throat trouble made him unfit. But Charlie Lucania was twenty, tough and trim — the ideal American fighting man.

But he had no intention of going to war; it would interrupt his plans. "I wasn't afraid that if I went to war I'd get killed or nothin' like that. But I knew goddamn well that if I went to Europe, by the time I got home it would be the end of me when it come to my outfit. So the war in Europe come at a bad time; for the first time, things was goin' great for me and my gang needed me a helluva lot more'n Uncle Sam. So we had a meet to figure out how to fix up my draft status.

"Bugsy Siegel started it off by saying, 'The only way we're gonna give up Charlie Lucania to Uncle Sam is if he'll give us General Pershing.' " Everybody thought that was a great joke, but when Siegel started callin' me 'Black Jack Lucania' I stopped them jokes. But it was Siegel who come up with the idea that kept me out of the army. He was just a punk kid, not even fourteen, but he knew more about broads than all of the rest of us put together. He said, 'There's only one thing that's gonna keep Charlie out of the army, and that's a good long dose of the clap.' And all my good friends agreed.

"I looked at them like they was out of their minds and told 'em the idea was out. But Frank Costello assured me that with a friendly doctor, a case of the clap could be a breeze and that he could keep the cure goin' until the war was over. And then

Lansky, the mathematical wizard, says, "I give five-to-two, the war won't last more than a year.' So I was outvoted, three to one.

"The only question was, where and how did I get the clap, because it ain't somethin' you buy in a store and we was all pretty much babes when it came to that kind of thing, except maybe Siegel. A couple days later, Siegel came over to my room and tells me he's got it all fixed up. 'A guy I know, Herbie Shapiro,' he says, 'just caught a dose of clap from a broad named Nora over at Jenny's,' which was a house at Sixteenth Street and Second Avenue.

"I told Benny, 'Thanks very much, but I changed my mind and you three guys can go fuck yourselves.' Just then Lansky came in and he says I'm lettin' down the partnership. I really got sore and I told him, 'What the hell, you're only a little shrimp. You ain't even got a prick half the size of Benny's. You don't give a shit about nooky; you're only interested in money, and that's why you're so anxious to keep me out of the army.'

"But it didn't do no good and they finally talked me into it. So that night I went over to Jenny's and I went up to a room on the second floor with this girl, Nora, who was really stacked, with red hair, and she wasn't a day over eighteen. All I could think of was what a terrible thing that a pretty girl like that was diseased. We get into the room and I'm too scared to move. Nora looks at me and she says, 'Come on, let's go. Take your clothes off. What're you here for?'

"Like an idiot, I say to her, 'I come here to get the clap.' Well, she picked up a lamp and threw it at me, and she comes at me with her nails a mile long, tryin' to cut my face to ribbons. I grabbed hold of her and tried to explain what it was all about. When I tell her that she's got the clap, she gets scared and says she's gotta get outa there and go see Jenny's doctor. Then she stops and says, 'But first I'm gonna take care of you,' and she starts to undress me. I was so nervous that I couldn't get it up. So she says, 'Don't worry, Charlie-boy,' and she pushes me down on the bed and starts to go down on me, and I'm wonderin' to myself if maybe I can get clap by mouth, which shows how much I knew. But when I'm good and ready and start to get off the bed, she grabs me and yells, 'Oh, no, you don't. You come here for it and you're gonna get it.' She was right. A week later I had it.

27

"If I'd known what it was gonna be like to get cured, I'd rather have run around the trenches in France with a bunch of krauts shootin' at me. I had to get treatments every other day for over a year by some doctor down on Tenth Street; I paid him plenty so he wouldn't report me to the health authorities. And what a treatment. He put a rubber tube with some kinda solution in it all the way up my pecker, and then he'd follow this with a round metal bar I think he called a 'sound.' He told me it'd help make the cure permanent so that my pecker would never close up again."

And so any worries about the war were behind him. If he were to be shot now, it would be on the streets of New York. Lucania and his friends rapidly expanded their activities during the war years; there was plenty of money around and they were determined to have their share. By the time the Armistice was signed in November 1918, they had organized a gang of more than twenty members, were ranging over the downtown area of Manhattan where Lucania, Lansky and Siegel had grown up and still lived, over the East Harlem terrain of Frank Costello, and into the wealth of midtown in between. They hit small banks, warehouses, stores, anyplace where there was loose money or loose goods that could be fenced. Siegel was always out in front, the man to take the risks. A favorite ploy was to send him into a jewelry store on pretense of looking for a gift for his mother, which gave him an opportunity to examine the merchandise, see where it was kept and how tight the security was. When the store was robbed, it was easy pickings.

In the ghettos, the pawnbrokers and moneylenders were natural targets, and if some of them got badly beaten, "it was their fault for keepin' so much money around," or for objecting to its loss. And then there were the bearded insurance men who toured the Jewish ghettos selling small policies and collecting dime and quarter premiums each week. "If all the nickels and dimes we took from them had been put into premiums, I'd own more than a million dollars' worth of life insurance today," Luciano said later.

As the profits piled up beyond their immediate needs, they sought ways to put that money to work. They knew that off-track betting was a protected business and they began to buy into established "books," even taking shares in several small ones in midtown. It was the beginning of what would become a gambling empire blanketing the nation. It was also a school in which they learned some important lessons: that there were some illegal activities the public not only did not frown upon, but actually encouraged; that with certain illegal activities, protection could be purchased from the police and other public officials, to insure continued operations and profits; that the opportunities in professional gambling were limitless and that, paradoxically, the operators could gain a certain status and power in society. They had only to look at Arnold Rothstein, the millionaire gambler and political fixer, to see how true that was.

"Ever since we was kids, we always knew that people could be bought. It was only a question of who did the buyin' and for how much. After all, we saw it everywhere around us — from the cop on the beat to the captain of the police precinct, from the ward heeler to some top politicians. We knew that most of them guys had their hands out. It was Frank Costello, a little bit later, who really opened the door to the whole business of buyin' influence and protection. He had the style and the class of a guy twice his age, and with that Irish-Italian name we hung on him, he was able to move into all circles. That's when we set up a private bank. Not a real bank. We called it our 'Buy-Money Bank.' It started with five grand and the pot was turned over to Costello to use any way he saw fit." Within a decade, the amount in the Buy-Money Bank — to corrupt those on the public payroll — had grown into millions of dollars. Costello started small and cautiously with this limited initial bankroll, putting cash into the hands of police and politicians in the districts where the group was buying into bookmaking operations, greasing the ward heelers who could use it to insure election victories by buying turkeys, cigars, medical treatment and more in exchange for votes.

Early in 1919, a new world suddenly opened. The keys to riches and a kind of shadowy respectability were handed to Charlie Lucania and his friends, and the door slid open easily, greased by the funds Costello had spread from the Buy-Money Bank. On January 16, the Eighteenth Amendment to the Constitution of the United States was ratified, to become the law of the land a year later. It banned the general manufacture, sale and transporta-

29

tion of intoxicating liquors and beers. Ten months later, on October 27, over the veto of President Woodrow Wilson, Congress passed the Volstead Act, amplifying and strengthening the language of the Prohibition amendment and setting up the federal machinery for its enforcement. The Woman's Christian Temperance Union had scored its long-sought victory; there would be no more public drinking in the United States.

But millions of Americans were not about to stop drinking. They would just have to look somewhere else than the old neighborhood saloon or package store for their booze. The Roaring Twenties were about to begin and the stars of the new era were about to take center stage.

4.

They were all Italians and Sicilians, most of them young, and they gathered in a favorite restaurant on Mulberry Street in Little Italy late in 1920 to toast a local boy who was making it big in Chicago. After an absence of more than a year, Alphonse Capone had come back to New York for a visit, to confirm the rumors of his success and to tell his friends that they, too, could share the wealth. When he had left the city, Capone had been only another small-time strong-arm man, with a violent temper backed by fists, a club and a gun he seemed always anxious to use, with two murders to his credit already and a third man he had brutally beaten in a Brooklyn barroom about to die in a hospital.

"Capone was three or four years younger than me, a guy with plenty of muscle and guts and a way of lookin' ahead. He'd done a couple jobs with me. When we found out through our contacts that the law was gonna throw the book at him, I sent word to him in Brooklyn and we arranged a meet in a dry-goods store on East Fourteenth Street that was owned by an aunt of Benny Siegel's. Capone walks into the back room, throws his arms around me and says, 'Hey, Cousin Charlie, what's goin' on?' Of course, he wasn't my cousin, but he always called me that. I said, 'I'll tell you what's goin' on; you gotta get the hell outa town and don't bother to pack.'

"Al's face fell so much his whole body sagged. It was the first and only time I ever seen him look scared. Maybe because I was the second guy in a couple of hours who'd told him the same thing, though I didn't know it at the time. The other guy was Frankie Yale [born Francisco Uale], who was the boss of the old Unione Siciliano. Al was workin' for him in one of his bars as a bouncer. I told Al not to worry, that I had it all arranged. I'd been in touch with Johnny Torrio out in Chicago and he was willin' to take Al on. I handed him two grand in small bills and told him to get right up to Grand Central and buy a ticket; he could get new clothes when he got to Chicago in a couple days. Capone got so emotional he almost started cryin'; then he hugged me again and kissed me right on the lips, like a Sicilian, and he left. Jesus Christ, he was no Sicilian, he was a Neapolitan, and I didn't like him kissin' me that way, but what could I do? The thing I found out later was that Frankie Yale had been in touch with Torrio, too, about Al, because he knew Torrio from way back when they was workin' together in Brooklyn before Torrio went to Chicago, and he'd done the same as me, settin' things up for Capone. So Al had two of us sponsorin' him when he went out there, which didn't hurt him none."

In Chicago, Capone became the strong and enforcing right arm of Torrio, sometimes called "Terrible John" or "The Fox," another man with visions of the profits that could come if crime were organized, of the opportunities opened up by Prohibition. When Capone arrived, however, Torrio was blocked from turning his vision into a reality by Big Jim Colosimo, then the ruler of vice and rackets in the notorious "Levee" district of the nation's second city. Despite the urgings of Torrio, his chief aide and his wife's cousin, Colosimo was satisfied with things as they were, had little interest in illegal liquor, did not see its future. He reluctantly permitted Torrio to move into bootlegging, but only in a small way.

But Torrio saw what Prohibition could bring to anyone perspicacious and daring enough. He was not to be blocked, just as he was determined not to be second man. On the surface a courtly, gentle man who always expressed an abhorrence of violence, he dealt with Colosimo's opposition and lack of vision in a final and sudden manner. For ten thousand dollars, he brought his old comrade, Frankie Yale, to Chicago and on May 11, 1920, Yale put a bullet in Jim Colosimo's head. The funeral was gargantuan, the model for all the Prohibition-era funerals that would follow. And when Jim Colosimo was laid to rest, Johnny Torrio was the boss, Al Capone was his aide, and the liquor and money poured in an unceasing fountain in Chicago.

Now, a year later, Capone had returned to New York for his visit, wearing a hand-tailored suit and diamond rings, a big cigar in his mouth, the veneer of power upon him. He sat at the head of the table in the Mulberry Street restaurant, drinking the best imported Italian wine, being toasted and toasting those around him. Late in the evening, the air redolent with smoke, heads heavy with drink, Capone raised his glass and pointed down the table to Charlie Lucania. "To my cousin Charlie," he shouted, "who's gonna be the King of Booze in New York."

Capone went back to Chicago, to his own vision of becoming the king of booze and all the rackets there. He left behind a Charlie Lucania already planning his next moves and determined to make Capone's prophecy come true. If he could do that, he was certain he would overshadow Capone and everyone else. For Chicago was only the second city; New York was the first, the biggest, where everything important happened. To be king in New York was to be supreme.

But the crown was elusive and there were other pretenders, some older and more experienced, and all equally determined. At that moment, Lucania and his partners were hardly grown men: he was only twenty-three, Lansky not yet twenty, Siegel still an adolescent; only Costello was past twenty-five. Their dreams and ambitions might be majestic, but their knowledge and experience were limited.

They were not men, though, to let opportunities pass, and soon they were joined by another, equally ambitious, young man who gave them the needed chance. His name was Giuseppe Antonio

Doto; he was born in a small town near Naples in 1902 and brought to the United States a few years later. (His father, in a moment of oversight, forgot to take out citizenship, and that would in later years return to haunt Doto.) By the time he was eighteen, he had become an adept thief and had adopted a new name, Joseph A. Adonis, which his friends later shortened to plain "Joe A." The Adonis was a natural for him. "I always thought of Joe as a kind of younger brother," Luciano said. "But I used to laugh at him. He was always lookin' in the mirror and combin' in his hair. Once I asked him, 'Who do you think you are, Rudolph Valentino?' He stared at me for a minute and then he said, very serious, 'For looks, that guy's a bum.'"

Adonis's entrance into the Lucania circle came one afternoon late in 1920. He called Lucania and met him at an ice cream parlor in Little Italy — both men had a passion for ice cream they would never lose. "We sat there eatin' big plates of spumoni and Joe said, 'Charlie, I know we never done no business together and I never like to ask a favor. But I need ten grand to make a whiskey buy down in Philly, and I'll cut you in for half.'"

The night before, Adonis had been in Philadelphia to see Frankie Genaro (later the world flyweight champion) box, and had met the promoter, Max "Boo-Boo" Hoff, who had introduced him to Irving Wexler, something of a bootleg power under the name "Waxey" Gordon. Adonis and Gordon struck up an immediate friendship, and before Adonis boarded the train back for New York, he had been offered a carload of 100-proof bottled-in-bond rye. But Adonis didn't have enough money to complete the purchase, and so he turned to Lucania for the needed additional ten thousand dollars. "I put my arm around Adonis's shoulder and told him to keep his money, that he'd just found himself a partner who'd put up all the dough. I called Costello, Lansky and Siegel and we got together an hour later. The four of us put up thirty-five grand in cash, and early the next morning Adonis and I headed out in my new car, a Marmon limousine." The trip to Philadelphia was only ninety miles, but the roads were mudholes and there were detours every ten miles. Before they had gotten halfway, Lucania turned around and returned to New York. The next morning they went to Philadelphia by train.

33

"That was the first time I ever ate in a dinin' car on a train. The tablecloths was so white the inside of the car looked like it was all covered with snow. It was the first time I ever ate corned beef hash for breakfast; it had a fried egg on top. Joe thought I was crazy; he had hot oatmeal, and I had two more orders of that hash. One time, I told my mother about that breakfast and she looked at me just like Joe A. did — they just didn't understand how to eat American."

As Adonis and Lucania ate, two men who looked like bankers sat down at the table with them in the crowded diner. Lucania could not keep his eyes off them. Even then, the veneer of money, manners and class fascinated and entranced him, made him realize his own social limitations, and made him determined to cultivate the same aura so that one day he could meet such people as equals. "They was really elegant, like old money, and I said to myself, 'That's for me.' Then I remembered that Joe and I was sittin' there carryin' guns and I got thirty-five grand in my pocket to buy booze with down in Philly, just so guys like them could pay through the nose for it."

The deal with Waxey Gordon, the first of many, was struck that afternoon, and Lucania and his friends were now bootleggers. In their new business, they could use all they had learned and practiced before, the strong-arm methods, the discipline of gang action, the quick strike; but this time their victim was not an individual. It was only a law, an unpopular one foisted upon the country by what Luciano always referred to as "them old flatchested broads of the W.C.T.U., who was even uglier than the schoolteachers." The profits were far greater than could ever have been realized by crimes against innocent persons and their property, and the penalties were far less, and the chances of ever paying those penalties almost minute.

With no honest citizen as a victim, the enforcers of the unpopular law could be persuaded to ignore it, especially if they could share in the profits of that deliberate ignorance. Protection could be purchased at all levels. "Within a year, we was buyin' influence all over Manhattan, from lower Broadway all the way up to Harlem, and even across the Hudson beyond the Palisades in Jersey."

34

Most of the money then, and for the next several years, was used, of course, to guarantee that there would be no interference with the bootlegging operations, and that those operations would have official protection. "When we made that first buy down in Philly, we almost hit the big time at the very beginnin', like we started at the top and kept goin' up from there. Of course, like in any big business, we hadda take care of the guys that could help us, so we greased the police and the politicians. It was all part of the overhead, just like any other business."

It did not take them long to realize that the demand for liquor was enormous and that they could sell all they could obtain, and more. And so "Lansky's Law" came into being. "It was no joke at first. Meyer was always readin' books about business, economics, things like that. One day, he shows me a library book and he's all excited about it." The book was *Making Profits*, written in 1915 by Professor William Taussig of Harvard University.

"Charlie," Lansky said, "there's somethin' very important in this book for us."

"Meyer," Lucania said, "I don't need you around to quote to me from library books."

"Will you please, for God's sake, listen. You always talk about how you want to learn new things; now, I want to explain something that's really important. This writer talks about a thing called the law of supply and demand. What he says applies to us right now. If you have a lot of what people want and can't get, then you can supply the demand and shovel in the dough. In other words, that's what we ought to do with whiskey — get plenty of it, good, uncut stuff right off the boat and then sell it at a high price to a bunch of people who don't have brains enough not to drink it."

That simple economic precept was quickly dubbed Lansky's Law, and it would be the rule by which organized crime would live, just as society outside was ruled by it.

To understand and accept a basic economic principle was one thing; to put it to work in the most efficacious way required some hard decisions, and the necessity to make those decisions became urgent when Waxey Gordon offered them three thousand cases of top-quality, uncut Scotch. Their future depended on making the right choice. They could strike for quick and big profits by cutting and watering down the Scotch until it was the cheap, barely drinkable rotgut served in the sleaziest speakeasies, a drink in which the original Scotch was an infinitesimal part. There would be no trouble selling the stuff and turning a huge profit, for the demand for liquor of any kind was unceasing. But if they took this road, they would have to pay a price: they would be tagged as purveyors of cheap booze and their clientele would be those in the lowest strata.

Or they could sell the Scotch as it was, uncut. They would still realize huge profits and at the same time they would win as customers the best speakeasies in midtown Manhattan and the most socially prominent private clients. Their reputation as big-timers, as class merchants, would be made; customers would flock to them, and these customers would be people with plenty of money. The choice was, then, really no choice for men whose eyes were on the top.

So they began meeting the demand for good-quality liquor in the best places in New York. And they began, too, moving in as the prime suppliers in another place where "we knew we could sell more whiskey than we'd ever be able to get our hands on if Prohibition lasted a hundred years." This was in the garment center. In the world of ready-to-wear clothes, the out-of-town buyers on their annual or semiannual trips to New York, with open checkbooks, were the bosses. The manufacturers knew it and rained upon them a torrent of free dinners at the best restaurants, the best seats at the top hit shows, anything and everything that would persuade them to sign the order blanks and fill out those checks. If the male buyers wanted pretty girls, then pretty girls they would have. If the female buyers wanted men, then gigolos were supplied, with manufacturers picking up the tab. "Most of the lady buyers were ugly and dyin' to get laid, and the garment district had more studs workin' nights than Paris ever had. But if you seen some of them dames, you'd have to admit the guys earned their money."

But, perhaps, what most of them wanted most of all were bottles of good Scotch. "If you was a manufacturer who could give somebody a case of real Scotch, you never had to worry about sellin' 'em dresses, especially if the head of the store back home got some of

36

it. So we helped the manufacturers unload millions of garments and they paid us through the nose for uncut bottles of Scotch 'right off the boat.' We never cheated 'em on quality, but I can't say the same for some of the clothes they made." It was, in fact, Luciano's view, expressed often, that there were no truly honest people in the world. "Everybody's got larceny in 'em, only most of 'em don't have the guts to do nothin' about it. That's the big difference between us and the guys who call themselves honest. We got the guts to do what they'd like to do only they're too scared to."

The more important Lucania and his friends became in bootlegging, the more complex their business became, and so, to meet the growing problems, the leaders began to devote more and more of their time to special interests. In addition to his bootlegging with the group and in association with the Irish bootleg king Big Bill Dwyer, and in addition to his gambling interests in East Harlem and elsewhere, Costello was assiduously cultivating his connections in official circles, so as to guarantee complete protection for his and his partners' interests. Lansky and Siegel formed what became known as the "Bug and Meyer Gang," experts in transportation, with no job too dangerous, no requirement too complex or difficult. They hijacked or rode shotgun as protectors against hijacking, depending upon the exigencies of the moment or the special demands of Charlie Lucania. Joe Adonis was spreading out into a multiplicity of rackets and was even spreading his territory from Brooklyn and Manhattan, where he was earning a name as a leader of the "Broadway Mob," into Fort Lee, New Jersey (where eventually he would buy a home and settle with his wife and family). And Charlie Lucania, in addition to his executive responsibilities in overseeing the operations, was devoting considerable effort to recruiting key personnel and forging new alliances.

In his old neighborhood, in Little Italy, Lucania found a young and ambitious hoodlum who was an obvious recruit and who rose rapidly to a position as a major aide in all Lucania's enterprises. A short, muscular man with a round face and a wide smile, a secretive manner and a willingness to use a gun with no mercy, his name was Vito Genovese. "I never really liked him, but he did have moxie. I figured that if this Vito had even a part of Meyer's

37

guts — remember, he was a little guy like Meyer — then I'd have a good man. When I first heard of him around the neighborhood, he was already makin' a rep for himself. He was livin' in a neighborhood where the Sicilians outnumbered everybody else ten to one; to us, anybody who didn't come from Sicily was a dirty foreigner, and that made it tough, especially for a little guy like Vito, who was born in some town near Naples. But he could fight like a son of a bitch. I didn't have to love him to use him. But I thought he'd be loyal. What a mistake! But I didn't find that out until many, many years later."

Through Joe Adonis, Lucania won the allegiance of Francesco Chiccio Scalise, a Sicilian who had settled in Brooklyn, and Frank "Cheech," as he became known, provided an avenue of communications into the Brooklyn underworld. And Scalise recruited a fellow Brooklyn mobster, Carlo Gambino. "Someday," Luciano would predict in 1961, "Gambino will be head of the whole outfit in the United States." From Brooklyn, too, came a recent arrival from Italy, only just released from the Sing Sing death house when his conviction for murder had been overturned on appeal and the witnesses against him had vanished. His name was Albert Anastasia, a slight corruption of the real family name, Anastasio, made to save his relatives embarrassment when Albert first ran into trouble with the law. Almost from their first meeting, he developed an intense loyalty to Lucania, who responded with considerable affection. "Y'know, Charlie," Anastasia once told him, "I'll betcha I'm the only loudmouthed bum you really like." Stocky and muscular, Anastasia was a violent man with few restraints; he could commit murder impulsively or by design — it meant little to him which — and so he developed naturally into the enforcer.

But the circle of friends, associates and allies was not limited to Italians. Lansky opened the lines of communication to a fellow Jew who was emerging as a major power in the garment-center rackets. One day he brought Louis Buchalter to meet Lucania and his friends at the private offices they maintained at the Claridge Hotel. "I took one look at him and all I could see was a guy with a fat face, a big head and so much muscle it was bulgin' out of his sleeves. Somethin' inside warned me that this guy was mostly strong-arm and very little brain. So I said to him, 'Listen, Lou . . .'

38

"He stopped me and said, kinda nice, 'You can call me Lepke.'

"I couldn't help it. I started to laugh. I said, 'What the fuck kinda name is that?' He got all red and embarrassed and he explained that when he was a kid his mother used to call him by a pet Jewish name, Lepkele. So from then on, we all called him Lepke. How can you not like a guy who always thinks about his mother?"

Though Lucania had little faith in Lepke's intelligence, he did admire the hoodlum's guts and cunning and ambition, and Lepke was a key to entrance into the garment center. He was, as well, smart enough to listen to suggestions when they could benefit him. During that initial meeting at the Claridge and during subsequent ones, Lucania, Lansky and the others talked to Lepke about what they saw as his wasteful and unsystematic efforts in the garment center. He was selling protection and using strong-arm methods — a bottle of acid, a stick of dynamite, a sudden fire, a couple of goons — to persuade recalcitrant manufacturers to pay up. But there had been little planned method to his operations. A simple blueprint was drawn up for him to concentrate initially on securing a firm hold over small and vulnerable shops, then using that as a base to move against bigger and tougher targets. In this way, the protection racket could be turned into an orderly business — based, of course, on such old techniques as the wedge and the persuader — that would prosper and spread like a spider web into every corner of the garment district and beyond. Lepke bought the plan and so became a member of the Lucania hierarchy. And with his buying of it, Lucania and his partners had a solid foothold for the marketing of liquor in the garment center, and something they would later use to infiltrate the entire industry.

Lansky had brought in one Jew, Lepke; Frank Costello brought in another, Arthur Flegenheimer. As "Dutch Schultz," he was an emperor in his own right, carving out a bootleg domain in the Bronx. Early in their careers, Lucania convened a meeting at the Claridge to discuss an affiliation with the Dutchman. "When Frank first brought up his name, Vito screamed, 'What the hell is this! What're you tryin' to do, load us up with a bunch of Hebes?' Before Benny or Meyer could even open their mouths, Frank

39

almost swung on him, and he said, very quiet, 'Take it easy, Don Vitone, you're nothin' but a fuckin' foreigner yourself.'

"The reason I remember that so clear is that two important things come out of it. Whenever anybody wanted to rub Vito's nose in it, they'd call him 'Don Vitone' to his face, or behind his back. And Vito never forgave Frank for remindin' him that he wasn't a Sicilian and couldn't ever really 'belong.' That prick Vito had a memory like an elephant and the patience of a lizard — and he waited thirty-five years for a chance to blast Frank's head off."

Despite Genovese's outburst, Lucania and Schultz forged their alliance of equals, of barons, in their own nonconflicting realms, and it lasted beyond Prohibition. And Genovese's hatred of Jews did not prevent Lucania and his partners from reaching another agreement with another Jew, Abner "Longie" Zwillman, emerging as one of the major bootleggers and racketeers in northern New Jersey, and Zwillman's partner, Willie Moretti. Two more different men would have been hard to find. Zwillman was quiet, soft-spoken, studious, a book-reader and a man who aspired to respectability. In his later years, he carried on a long love affair with motion picture star Jean Harlow. Moretti had already won a reputation in New Jersey as a killer, and he was, like Capone, rash and headstrong and a woman-chaser; this proclivity would eventually leave him with syphilitic brain damage that made him such an irresponsible talker that his death was considered a necessity.

And then there was another Jew, whose influence on Lucania, and on the whole world of organized crime, was incalculable. His name was Arnold Rothstein, the prodigal son of a respectable Jewish family. Rothstein had early in his life become a gambler and loan shark, and he was rumored to be the brains behind the notorious 1919 Black Sox scandal, the fixing of the World Series. Gambling was his real passion and he was able to satisfy it and his zest for travel simultaneously, crisscrossing the Atlantic in never-ending poker games aboard luxury liners.

Soon after the start of Prohibition, Rothstein turned for a time to bootlegging, and he was the man who gave Waxey Gordon his start. "What Arnold did was really very smart. Everybody knows that them guys in Scotland are tight and love money, so Rothstein made legit contracts with them and laid down big deposits so he would be guaranteed delivery. Then he went to Waxey Gordon to arrange for distribution of this liquid gold, with the condition that I should have first call on the buy. Naturally, I bought every drop of it."

But there was more that attracted Lucania and Rothstein. "He taught me how to dress, how not to wear loud things but to have good taste; he taught me how to use knives and forks, and things like that at the dinner table, about holdin' a door open for a girl, or helpin' her sit down by holdin' the chair. If Arnold had lived a little longer, he could've made me pretty elegant; he was the best etiquette teacher a guy could ever have — real smooth.

"I did lots of favors for Rothstein, too. I used to back him in poker games. We both made money. But he could spend it so fast just livin' that it even made my head spin, and I was a pretty good spender myself. All he hadda do was ask me for the dough he owed; I'd've sent it right over." On November 4, 1928, Rothstein was shot to death at the Park Central Hotel in Manhattan, where he resided. "All I knew about it was that he'd welshed on a bet. That was the rumor. Of course, the cops called me in and they grilled me, but I never knew who done it."

With the organization growing, with customers waiting in line for their good liquor, with business growing at an almost unbelievable pace, there was an urgent necessity to insure the sources of good whiskey. Much was being purchased in Canada, from men like Samuel Bronfman, later head of the Seagram Corporation and one of Canada's richest and most philanthropic citizens, but then, as Luciano noted, a man who "was bootleggin' enough whiskey across the Canadian border to double the size of Lake Erie." If there was no problem in lining up supplies in Canada, there were problems in getting them from the border to market, by truck. "Plenty of the goods was hijacked by other mobs, and we lost a lot more because the trucks would break down. In them days, hundreds of trucks was stranded all over the East Coast."

Even without the dangers and the mechanical troubles, there was never enough uncut whiskey, from Canada or Scotland, to fill the ever-increasing demand. It did not take Lucania and his friends long to realize that if the bottles looked the same, the

41

labels were identical, the quality high and the taste close, the customers would buy the booze wherever it was bottled and distilled and assume it was the real thing; and if sources close at hand could be found for such quality liquor, the market could be expanded. "I figured on account of that we had such a good contact in Philadelphia with Waxey Gordon, it was the place to make the move, for one reason: they had a lotta companies down there turnin' out pure grain alcohol." Without that alcohol, there could be no whiskey; with that alcohol, real whiskey could be cut and the result would still be pretty good whiskey that most drinkers couldn't tell from the real thing.

The manufacture of such alcohol was legally permitted in small quantities under a loophole in the Volstead Act. While consumption of alcoholic beverages for the general public was outlawed, liquor could still be drunk for medicinal purposes and purchased under a doctor's prescription. Somebody had to make it, and government licenses were handed out to a number of companies, several in Philadelphia. Such companies immediately became the target for underworld infiltration, and the legitimate owners usually capitulated without a murmur, either because threatened violence left them with no choice or because the acquisition of underworld partners meant sharply increased business and profits. In these distilleries, the alcohol, some unaged whiskey, and a little caramel for coloring could turn one bottle of Scotch or Canadian whiskey, American rye or bourbon into several bottles of the parent whiskey with little quality loss.

Lucania's interests and those of Gordon's merged, their friendship and cooperation growing as both became richer, as each became assured of the other's competence and trustworthiness, as they operated in noncompeting spheres. "I never had a real problem with Waxey Gordon from the day we met down in Philly. We shook hands and in about a half an hour, it was all settled — prices, splits of goods, profits, the whole deal." From that moment on, Lucania and his friends would buy their illegal liquor from Gordon and his friends, would arrange to have their own illegal liquor shipments cut, blended, rebottled and relabeled in Gordon's Philadelphia and south Jersey plants, and then would arrange delivery all along the East Coast.

Most in demand was Scotch. Before Prohibition, the Scottish distilleries sold their product for seventeen dollars a twelve-bottle case, F.O.B. Glasgow. Once Prohibition arrived, and the demand in the United States for Scotch soared, the distillers "didn't mind puttin' the squeeze on us, because they knew we was bootleggers and gangsters. And then they was only deliverin' the stuff to a point in the ocean outside the three-mile limit, that is if they was deliverin' it at all; lots of us, and Rothstein was the first, hadda charter our own ships to carry the Scotch to the three-mile limit. Then we hadda take all the chances of runnin' the goods in to shore in speedboats. That's how the name Rum Row and the rum-runners got started — runnin' the boats from Cuba with rum, or anythin' else we could buy and land."

By the time pure Scotch reached the American shore, the price to the bootleggers was somewhere around $2.20 a fifth. Some was sold directly to important customers at about $30 a fifth. The rest was cut in Gordon's plants, or plants established by Lucania and his partners. "We made what we called 'Scotch right off the boat,' and that original Scotch would bring us as high as a thousand bucks a case. That case cost us, if you forget the danger part of it, only around twenty-five bucks. But what the hell, we took all the gambles. That three miles of ocean was loaded with sharks — federal men, hijackers with speedboats. A guy could easily get killed at that time for a case of Scotch. And, of course, sometimes we'd lose a truck or even a whole shipment to the Feds or to some hijackers, and we'd have to write it off."

It was not enough just to get the Scotch and other whiskey to shore, nor was it enough in addition to control the grain alcohol with which to cut it. There had to be plants to cut it in, and there had to be bottles, looking exactly like the originals, to rebottle it. So they went into the bottle business. They needed labels identical to the original Johnnie Walker, Haig & Haig, Dewar's and the rest, so they went into the printing business, buying huge color presses and becoming major consumers of papers and inks. The bottles had to be stored in warehouses, so they went into the real estate business. The crates had to be shipped, so they became proprietors of sprawling trucking combines.

What none of them sensed initially was that they were not just

43

in the liquor business. When it was all put together, a relatively small group of men, led by Charlie Lucania, had forged an illegal empire that rivaled any legitimate one. "I'll bet in the days when me and my guys got our whiskey business together, we had a bigger company than Henry Ford. We controlled plants, warehouses, all kinds of manufacturin'; we had a fantastic shipping business, and our drivers hadda drive good and shoot straight. We had bookkeepers that Lansky used to watch over like a hawk, and these wasn't little guys with green eyeshades. These guys — and we even had plenty of girls as bookkeepers — was guys with photographic memories because not too much of their numbers ever got on paper. We had exporters and importers, all kinds of help that any corporation needs, only we had more. And we had lawyers by the carload, and they was on call twenty-four hours a day. Guys always told me later that I should've put my brains to runnin' a legit business and I'd have been a tremendous success. But I wouldn't've enjoyed it like what I was doin'."

5.

By 1923, at the age of twenty-six, foreign-born, as a child poor to the point of poverty, unable even to communicate then in the language of his new country, the self-educated Charlie Lucania was on top of a pyramid far grander than any of his earlier dreams. He had nearly reached the pinnacle predicted by Capone; if not the king of booze in New York, he was certainly close to the throne. Around him were his friends and allies, many of them rulers in their own limited spheres, and they accepted his leadership as the wisest course to the future.

Now a power in his own right, he began to attract overtures from his competitors, the major figures in the Italian underworld. At the dawn of Prohibition, their names — Giuseppe "Joe the

Boss" Masseria, Salvatore Maranzano, Ciro Terranova and others — were unknown outside the ghettos, except to certain policemen and politicians, some on their payrolls. They were older, had come to the United States as grown men, waxed in the tradition of the Mafia of their native Sicily, and never more than partially emerged from the traditions, closeness and security of the Little Italys.

To many Americans they often appeared, if they appeared at all, as outlandish and quaint men, not to be taken with complete seriousness; with their bulging bellies hanging over their pants, their thick thighs, their flowing mustaches, their somber, dated clothes, their old-country manner, their clannishness, their guttural and almost unintelligible accents, they seemed almost cartoon characters. Compared with the younger, more Americanized Charlie Lucania and his friends and allies, the old Dons remained for most of the nation, even for most New Yorkers, little more than shadowy figures about whom there were hardly even rumors.

"When Torrio knocked off Big Jim Colosimo in Chicago, Frank and I thought that'd help us. We figured it'd be like a sign to them old fat bastards in New York that some of the younger guys was movin' up. That's one time we was dead wrong, because we forgot how to read our own kind. Masseria, Maranzano, and all the rest of them pricks had been like kings. They ran everything in Little Italy." The old Dons had cornered the market and controlled the prices of all the necessities and luxuries of Italian life — olive oil, artichokes, cheese, the Italian lottery and all forms of gambling. "I remember once a neighbor of ours by the name of Forzano had a little penny-ante poker game in his kitchen once a week. Would you believe that them dirty Dons sent one of their boys to draw off a dollar a week from the pot, for expenses."

With the coming of Prohibition, the old Dons saw the opportunities just as did the younger men, and with their hold on the ghettos they had a built-in source of supply in the homemade stills that were a fixture in many an Italian household, and whose output could be sharply increased to supply a multitude of low-class speakeasies. Further, they began to move out of the ghettos to go after the bigger American market for illegal booze.

As they did so, they tried to eliminate competition, and one way was to take over some of their competitors. The first overture to Lucania came from Salvatore Maranzano, a major aspirant to American Mafia rule. "I always knew, I felt it in my bones, that someday this old bastard was gonna get in touch with me. But I always knew that no matter what that guy would offer me, I was gonna turn it down. When he first come to this country, right after the war, and I was just startin' out, that old shitheel would come around the neighborhood once in a while and hold up his hands, spread out like he was a Pope givin' the people on the street a blessin'. But Maranzano was a guy with plenty of education; he spoke five languages and he really knew a lotta culture. And me, just because I had no good schoolin', I made myself feel like dirt every time I had any contact with him. Of course, he helped."

But when the summons came, Lucania was flattered. "The meet took place in the back room of a small restaurant that used to be called Il Palermo, just off Minetta Street in Little Italy. When I walked into the room, Maranzano comes over to me with his arms up in the air — and there he goes, startin' that fuckin' Pope routine again. He puts his arms around me and he says that his name is Salvatore, like mine, that I'm his namesake, the 'young Caesar.' Then he starts quotin' Julius Caesar to me, in Latin, for chrissake. If he had somethin' nice to say to me, why the hell couldn't he have said it in English? So I told him that, and he started to laugh. And I'll never forget what he answered. He said, 'My son, words of praise are only meant for the great, and you will do great things.' Shit. I could've spit in his face.

"Then he said to me, 'I understand you now like to be called Charlie. Somehow, I find it difficult to think of you as anything but Salvatore. Tell me, my name was not good enough for you to keep? There is something about it which shames you?'

"I was just about to answer him and explain how I didn't like to be called Sallie. But he started to wave his right hand around, and on his pinky finger where most of them old Dons used to wear a diamond that would choke a horse, all Maranzano had was what they call a signet ring with his initials, 'S.M.' He held out his right hand and I really couldn't tell if he was pleadin' with me to change my name back, or all he wanted me to do was kiss his lousy ring. It was amazin' to me that the old man couldn't see that I was disgusted with him. He started to go on and on about how he'd been watchin' the things I was doin' and that he was very impressed with me, and he thought that I was brave and I had lots of brains and imagination. And then he threw in a zinger. He tells me he don't like the guys I'm associatin' with.

"So I said, 'Well, Don Salvatore, that's too bad. You're talkin' about friends of mine, and that ain't nice.'"

Maranzano retreated, told Lucania it was something they could talk about later. What he had in mind at this point was an offer. "The world is changing and there are new opportunities for those who are ready to reach out and seize them, who are ready to join forces with those who are stronger and more experienced. Come into my organization and I promise you that you will prosper along with it. I will make an important place for you, my son." Then Maranzano told Lucania to think about it before deciding.

But before Lucania left, Maranzano had one final bit of business. "He snaps his fingers and a waiter comes rushin' in to open a bottle of red wine, and pours out a little bit for the old guy to sample. I can see him smellin' the cork and rollin' the wine around in his mouth to check the flavor and all that crap. Then he waves his signet ring at the waiter and the guy pours out two glasses, and Maranzano says to me, 'My dear young man, we will conclude the ceremonies with a toast to our mutual good health, and it is symbolic that the gesture of our friendship and mutual understanding be made with the finest Sicilian wine. Here, Charlie Lucania, I wish you long life.' That was the way the guy always talked, and it used to drive me nuts. He raised his glass and I raised mine and shoveled out the same old long life, good health and all that, and then I drunk the wine. It was absolutely sour. With all his culture and five languages, that was one dago you could give piss or vinegar and he would've drunk it, as long as it was red and come from Sicily."

From that meeting, Lucania drove back uptown to the Claridge, telling his excited driver, who asked what had happened, "Nothin' much. He just don't like Jews, and he don't know a fuckin' thing about wine."

"The next day, I sent my driver, Gino, back down to Minetta Street with a message: to thank Don Salvatore for his very nice

47

offer and just to say that this wasn't the right time and we should sorta keep the door open. Along with the message, I sent a full case of a dozen quarts of the best twelve-year-old King's Ransom Scotch. I knew that he would get it right away that I was salutin' the health of the king. That goddamn case of pure Scotch meant over two grand to me, but it was worth even more just to show that old prick he wasn't no better than me when it come to doin' the right thing."

There had been no question in Lucania's mind that he would not accept Maranzano's offer, and his decision was based not alone on his feelings about the man. Maranzano's organization, like most branches of the Mafia at the time, was composed solely of Sicilians — in his case, natives of his hometown of Castellammare del Golfo, though he was willing to take other Sicilians as well. Even Neapolitans and mainland Italians from other areas were barred. Were Lucania to join Maranzano, no matter how important the capacity, it would mean breaking his ties with his closest friends, the Jews like Lansky, Siegel, Lepke and Rothstein, whom Maranzano despised, as well as the Calabrian Costello and the Neapolitans Genovese and Adonis. He was not about to abandon those valuable partnerships and friendships. "And it was just about the time that well-known people on the right side of society was gettin' to know who I was and to show me some respect. I loved it, and I wasn't gonna give that up to go with Maranzano, because I was sure I could make all the dough I ever wanted on my own."

In succeeding years, the wisdom of that decision became ever more apparent as success piled upon success in the bootleg racket. His empire was expanding, particularly across the Hudson River into New Jersey. "But not Brooklyn, never Brooklyn for me personally. That was like a foreign country, and it was okay with me to let it stay there, with my good friends Adonis and Scalise to keep me posted on what was goin' on." Along with Costello, Adonis and Lansky, he made private investments down the "Sawdust Trail" of roadhouses just beyond the Jersey Palisades, places they supplied with liquor and whose gambling rooms had sawdust on the floor; they lined the roads in Fort Lee just a ferryboat ride from the 125th Street pier across the Hudson.

And he was gathering the allies who could give him the extra needed firepower to turn back any challenge, allies he would have been forced to forget had he gone with Maranzano. He knew he could always depend upon Zwillman and Moretti to implement the strength of the Bug and Meyer Gang, and he had at his disposal the guns of Albert Anastasia and the forces of Dutch Schultz and Lepke.

He was, too, becoming a figure of note. His booze was the best and his customers the finest. He was providing all the whiskey to the most exclusive speakeasies in Manhattan and his liquor was drunk wherever society gathered, even at the private parties on Park Avenue and in the mansions and estates of Westchester County and Long Island.

What pleased him most was that some of his customers sought out his friendship. He developed a passion for golf and earned himself a low handicap during rounds at exclusive country clubs in the suburbs, where, of course, his liquor stocked the bars. The police and the politicians were more than polite to him, especially those whose pockets Costello lined regularly. He was fawned upon and catered to, and he discovered that money could buy almost anything and almost anyone.

And the gates of some of the most exclusive homes swung open to Charlie Lucania, and once inside, he was the center of attraction. "One of my big-shot customers was a guy in that Whitney family, the stockbrokers. He was a polo player and he invited me out to this tremendous estate he had in Manhasset, Long Island, to watch him play polo and also to supply the party he was givin' afterwards. All them society girls gathered around and asked me how we hijacked shipments and how sometimes we would shoot it out with the Feds, and stuff like that. They listened to me with their eyes wide open like I was some kind of movie star, like Douglas Fairbanks. I piled it on and they loved it.

"About four in the mornin', one of these broads, a really beautiful girl, dragged me away and made me drive her home in her car, which was a Locomobile about a block long. When we got to her old man's estate, we drove through the gates and there was about a mile of grass on both sides of the driveway. She reaches over and turns off the ignition, pulls me outa the car and practically made me screw her right there on the grass in the dark. And all the time we're doin' it, she's yellin', 'Hijack me! Hijack me!' "

So Charlie Lucania was becoming an increasingly familiar figure in all the right places, not just the homes of the rich but in the best nightspots in Manhattan. Almost every night, he toured them with a showgirl on his arm. He loved the scene, supplied the clubs with their liquor, and owned a piece of many. The girls were often those introduced to him by Joe Adonis, whose eye for beautiful women was already becoming a legend that would eventually put him in command of the home of beautiful showgirls, New York's Copacabana. "In the early days, Joe would fix me up with some dame from the Follies or George White's Scandals or the Vanities, and we'd make the rounds. That's how the rumors started about me and broads. I was long over the clap by then, but sometimes I'd go out with one of them girls and take her home without tryin' to lay her. The next day it was all over that Big Shot Charlie Lucania couldn't get it up. Actually, for a couple of years after the doctor told me I was cured, once in a while I'd get a pain in the groin or maybe my balls would hurt, and it would scare me to death. Let's say that some night I'd be with a beautiful girl and I'm dyin' to lay her, and I know I can, then all of a sudden I'd feel a pain and I'd be afraid that maybe if I screwed her, it might start the clap all over again. I know it was stupid. The doc explained it to me a thousand times, but it didn't do no good. I lost plenty of good tail that way."

Charlie Lucania had reached a plateau of great importance in his world. He wore good clothes. He mixed with honest people (and some just dishonest enough to render favors in exchange for payment). He was often in public, smiling, approachable and soft-spoken. He had learned well Arnold Rothstein's continuing lessons in manners. He had molded for himself the façade of a gentleman.

But that was the surface. There was another side. He was the boss of a gang, and not a boss who sat behind a desk just giving orders for others to carry out. He still carried a gun when a business trip demanded it; it would have been insane in his business not to, and not to be prepared to use it. Hijackings, and even many regular liquor shipments, were rarely peaceful affairs, especially when a shipment of quality liquor might be worth a hundred thousand dollars or more, and the hijacking could accomplish two purposes: getting the liquor to fill orders and at the same time seriously damaging a competitor. On most hijackings, shots were fired, blood was spilled and often someone was killed. "Did I ever kill anybody myself? That depends on how you look at it. If it means, did I ever pull the trigger and actually knock somebody off myself, then the answer is no. Nobody ever died from my gun. I managed to hurt a few people pretty bad, but no murder. On the other hand, if you look at it from the strict letter of the law, where an accessory or a guy who gives the orders to make a hit is just as guilty as the guy who pulls the trigger, then I guess I done my share."

It was a time when Lucania developed a supreme confidence in himself, in his own invincibility. He understood that one of the necessities of being in the rackets was to be subjected to an occasional arrest, and he would be brought to the nearest police station for questioning when some crime had been committed or when some public official wanted a little publicity as a scourge of the underworld and had howled too loudly about the crime in the streets of New York. The interrogations were rarely more than formalities; he would not be held long, and then the charges would be dropped, if, indeed, there had been any charges at all. His release was invariably accompanied by an apology for the inconvenience.

"When the fix was in, it was a breeze, nothin' to it. After all, that's what Costello and the Buy-Bank was makin' sure of. Most of the time, if I ever got picked up, it was because some precinct captain wanted to talk to me private about a raise in pay. Except there was one time, at Christmas in 1922." A large liquor shipment had landed the night before, and Lucania had gone down to the Jersey coast to supervise. On the way back to New York, he stopped off to meet with Willie Moretti, to collect twenty-five thousand dollars Moretti and Longie Zwillman owed as their share of the cost of the load. "I met Willie that afternoon in a diner on the outskirts of Jersey City. My car was loaded with presents for my whole family, and I promised my mother I'd be there for turkey dinner about four o'clock. She was makin' it special for me; she wanted to prove she could cook American. If I disappointed her, I knew my old man would murder me."

As Lucania and Moretti left the diner, two New Jersey state cops were waiting, "and I'm carryin' a gun on account of the job the night before. They took us all the way to the State Police Headquarters in Newark. In the back room, there's a guy in fancy uniform like a general. He gets up and shakes hands with Willie, and it turns out he's one of Willie's 'protectors.' He says, 'Gee, I'm sorry, Willie, but I'm going to have to book you for being with a man who's carryin' a gun.' Moretti just says, 'That's okay,' and I laugh and say, 'Boy, Lieutenant, am I glad you're a friend of Moretti's,' and he says, 'You bet I am.' Then he gives me a hard look and he says, 'But I'm not a friend of yours. You landed a lot of stuff in my state last night.'

"So I know what I gotta do; either I buy myself a new friend or it's gonna take me all night to get outa there, and it's almost four o'clock already and I can already hear my old man givin' the Sicilian jab about me to my mother. So the guy books us, which he hadda do, and then I paid him ten grand of Willie's money, and the charges was dropped and I got the hell outa there."

It was seven o'clock before Lucania reached his parents' home on the Lower East Side. "Nobody says a word; they're all lookin' at my father, and he's lookin' at this big turkey that's sittin' in the middle of the table, all cold and shriveled up like it's been out in the snow. I'm standin' there with an armful of Christmas presents, so I drop them on the floor and I say, 'These are for everybody,' and I hand my brother Bart an envelope with money in it and tell him, 'Give this to Pop when he ain't so mad,' and I turn around and walk out. My father didn't talk to me for another six months."

By 1923, so convinced was Lucania of the venality of the law and his own untouchableness that "I did somethin' I never done before or afterwards; I got money-hungry, like I wasn't already makin' a fortune, most of it from booze, but a lot from gamblin' and the jobs our boys would pull a couple of times a week that would leave us with a pile of jewelry and furs. Then I got greedy and I walked right into my own trap, like a goddamn fool."

In June of 1923, "Vito brought a guy to see me, name of Charley Lagaipa; they called him 'Big Nose Charley' because he was sniffin' the stuff he was sellin'. I told Vito, 'Don't tell me about it. I don't want to get mixed up with junk. Once is enough.' "

But Genovese told Lucania there was nothing to worry about. Lagaipa needed twenty thousand dollars to make a narcotics buy that would return a hundred and fifty thousand on the street. If Lucania would put up the money, he would get sixty per cent. It seemed without risk; the heroin was already packaged and Genovese said, "You can have some of it checked out over at Joe A.'s place in Brooklyn."

Lucania fell in with the plan, and almost immediately discovered how wrong his and Genovese's assessment had been. On June 5, 1923, he was arrested on Fourteenth Street with several packages of pure heroin in his pocket. "I must've been crazy, like a loose nut. I could've sent any one of fifty guys; like a jerk, I decided to take the stuff over to Joe A.'s myself."

His and Costello's contacts in the police department and with Prohibition agents were useless. The Narcotics Bureau was not for sale. "With one junk conviction already on my record, and with everybody knowin' my puss, it looked like I was goin' up for a long stay in the federal pen. I tried everythin'; I offered them three bastards anythin' they could name, but they wouldn't even look at me. For the first time I really had things goin' good and now my own greed was gonna chop my legs off."

When all his efforts at bribery and cajolery had been spurned, Lucania came up with another idea. It would cost him seventy-five thousand dollars at least, all the profits he had figured on making from the narcotics deal and more. "If I couldn't buy them guys, maybe I could hand 'em somethin' that would help me make a deal. When we got to the station, they let me make a telephone call. I didn't call my lawyer. I called my brother Bart, and I talked to him in Sicilian. I told him that I wanted him to do an errand, exactly like I explained, with no changes. I told him to go to a certain place in Little Italy and move a box, like a small trunk, made outa cardboard, from one place to another. He wasn't to look inside."

Then, for more than an hour, in the basement of a precinct, Lucania was interrogated by local and federal officers. Late in the afternoon, when he was certain that Bartolo had finished moving the box, Lucania suddenly told his questioners that he had a deal for them; if they would drop the narcotics charges, he would direct them to a trunk filled with pounds of pure heroin.

It was too good a deal to pass. Though Lucania was offering them no names, and no arrests would be made, they would be able to seize a large cache of heroin, taking it off the market, and they would be able to spread around the word (as they did) that Lucania was a stool pigeon. And so they agreed. He then told them to go to the basement of 164 Mulberry Street, and in a closet there, they would find a box filled with hundreds of packets of heroin. While Lucania waited in a cell, already booked on the narcotics charge, the agents piled into their cars and sped to Little Italy. Right where Lucania had said it would be, they found the box and the heroin. He was freed; the charges against him were dropped.

It was, he afterwards maintained, an expensive lesson. He was out his own investment and potential profits and "I give a good bundle to Big Nose Lagaipa because I blew his profits for him. What I found out later was that them guys only turned in half the haul, which means that the other half got back on the street and somebody not only got credit for pulling in Charlie Lucania but probably wound up with a good fifty grand for the stuff I already paid for.

"But the worst thing was that I got tabbed from then on as a guy who handled narcotics, and because it was me, I was called the Big Guy in the junk business. No matter what I tried to do, I could never lose that rep of bein' a junk dealer. Even my own guys believed it, even though I ran away anytime I ever got a proposition after that time."

6.

The narrow escape from a long prison term for narcotics was a shattering experience for Lucania. He was no longer convinced of his own invincibility and no longer so certain of his own eminence in the rackets and in society, even though his underworld friends congratulated him on his ingenuity in wiggling out of the charge.

But the authorities had publicized the arrest, and "I was really ashamed to face all the friends I made in society, guys I played golf with. All I could think about was how to get clean again in front of them legit people. Besides, for the whole summer I was bein' grilled every five minutes by the police, or else I hadda go and see a psychiatrist every day for two hours, which was one of the conditions they made when they dropped the charges. I didn't want to go out to make any deliveries up on Park Avenue; I wouldn't even go to the speaks, unless it was some joint that didn't have the better class of customers. I was like a hermit.

"Then, one day I got a telephone call from a Wall Street guy, Julie Bache. I not only supplied him but practically all of his customers, and I know he liked me." Bache had only one question: Had Lucania really been deeply involved in narcotics? "I told him that I was just a big enough idiot to be involved in one deal, and he told me he believed me and asked me to come down and see him one day soon."

The call from Bache seemed almost a signal. Adonis called that same day, demanded that Lucania accompany him that night to the Follies, with Adonis supplying the girls. Then Meyer Lansky showed up and told Lucania that he was taking him down to the East Side for a good Jewish dinner. "I started to laugh, and I said to Meyer, 'You didn't just come over here to buy me matzo balls and chicken soup. What's really on your mind?' "

What Lansky had in mind was for Lucania to start adapting "Lansky's Law" as the way to overcome the bad publicity and get himself back in everyone's good graces. "Right now," he said, "you want to impress a lot of people. Don't you know that this whole town is made up of nothin' but whores? Give 'em somethin' they want bad enough and they'll even buy horseshit and molasses."

"You mean you want me to give away our best Scotch?"

"Who's talkin' about business? There's a fight comin' up next month; a pair of tickets are harder to get than a good set of counterfeit plates. Don't that throw you an idea?"

On the night of September 14, 1923, there were 82,000 people

55

at the Polo Grounds in New York to watch heavyweight champion Jack Dempsey destroy his Argentine challenger, Luis Angel Firpo, the Wild Bull of the Pampas, in two rounds. That leading boot-legger, Charlie Lucania, so recently tarred by the stories of his narcotics involvement, was the third star of the evening. More than two hundred persons were his guests in high-priced ringside seats.

"I got a call from Philly right when I was talkin' to Meyer, from a guy by the name of Ben Gimbel; his old man was one of the founders of that big department store outfit, and Ben was about as old as me and a pretty good playboy; he used to come up to New York from Philly every other night; he had a lotta girls in the shows and we got to know each other. He was callin' to find out if I could get him two tickets to the Dempsey-Firpo fight, on account of he and his family was pretty good customers of ours, and of Waxey's down in Philly. But first he started to pooh-pooh all that newspaper crap about the drugs, and he wanted to make sure that I didn't take it too bad. I kinda liked the idea that a guy from such a well-known family didn't mind callin' me after everythin' that was said. In fact, later on I give him the tickets for free."

But the first problem was to round up enough tickets. "That night, after the Follies, who do I run into at Dave's Blue Room but Bill Corum, the famous sportswriter. I said, 'Bill, I need some seats for the Dempsey-Firpo fight.' He says to me, with the laugh, 'Would you like to have mine?' Of course, he was only kiddin', but I took him up on it and I said, 'As a matter of fact, I would — and all the rest of 'em in your row.' When he realized I was serious, he says, 'Jesus Christ, Charlie, you want me to get twenty tough newspaper guys to give up their front-row seats? Where the hell do you expect them to sit?' And I said to him, 'In the row behind me, the second row. But that ain't all, pal; I want another ninety pair in the first five rows. Do you think you can handle it? I don't give a shit what it costs, Bill, I gotta have all them seats.' I don't know how Bill done it, but two days later, I had all the tickets I asked for and where I wanted 'em. It cost me about twenty-five grand, and I never regretted it."

Together with Costello, Lansky and Siegel and his other friends, Lucania spread the word that he was going to invite a hundred people and their dates as his guests to the fight. "Within twenty-four hours, I was the most popular guy in the United States, and I was gettin' telephone calls from all over the country." Then lists were drawn of the people who could do them the most good, among their suppliers, politicians, police and other notables in all areas of society. The initial list ran to six hundred names, and since everybody on the list had to receive two tickets, that meant twelve hundred tickets. "What a job that was to cut that list down to a hundred pairs, includin' ourselves. There was a lot of guys who was pretty sore at bein' left off, but we hadda go with the best."

What concerned Lucania next was cutting the right image at what now was almost certainly going to be his night of triumph. "So I got hold of Arnold Rothstein and the next morning he picked me up and took me down to John Wanamaker's department store. Actually, I felt a little guilty, and I told Arnold that maybe I owed it to Ben Gimbel to go to his old man's store, but he said to me, 'No, Charlie. John Wanamaker's men's department has the stuff you need. I'm going to turn you into another Francis X. Bushman.''

At Wanamaker's, Lucania bought two or three of everything, his only argument with Rothstein over whether to buy suits ready-made or made to order. Lucania wanted his specially made, but Rothstein countered, "I want you to wear something conservative and elegant, made by a gentile tailor."

Lucania was uncertain what Rothstein meant. "What the hell are you talkin' about? My tailor's a Catholic." The only article of apparel Lucania did not buy that day were ties. "Arnold gimme a dozen French ties made by some guy by the name of Chavet; they was supposed to be the best and Arnold bought a hundred ties whenever he went to Paris. He also used to buy the silk for his shirts by the bolt at a place in France called Sulka, and he always would give me some as a present; that's how I get the rep for wearin' silk shirts and underwear and pajamas.

"So the night of the fight I had on a beautiful double-breasted dark oxford gray suit, a plain white shirt, a dark blue silk tie with little tiny horseshoes on it, which was Arnold's sense of humor. I had a charcoal gray herringbone cashmere topcoat, because it was a little cool, with a Cavanagh gray fedora, very plain. Rothstein gimme a whole new image, and it had a lotta influence on me. After that, I always wore gray suits and coats, and once in a while I'd throw in a blue serge."

All through the preliminary bouts, Lucania held court from his seat in Row A, Seat 1 at the Polo Grounds. Political leaders, high police officials, judges, stage and screen stars, sports figures came up to shake his hand, to chat, to be seen with Charlie Lucania, and they brought their wives and girl friends to meet him. It was something of a social accomplishment that night to be noticed in his company.

"For the first time in my life I had the feelin' of real power. It's what I had always dreamed about, that some day the biggest people in New York would come up to me to say hello, to say thanks for the ringside seats that their big-shot friends couldn't get for love or money. It was a pretty big thing when Dick Enright, the police commissioner of the whole city, come over to see how I was feelin'. And right with him was Bill Lahey, his police chief. Why not, they was on our payroll. There was an awful lotta people on our list — Jimmy Hines and Al Marinelli from Tammany Hall; there was an up-and-comin' politician from Brooklyn who was gonna be a big guy with our help, Kenny Sutherland [later, Democratic leader in Brooklyn] — and I even sat Flo Ziegfeld and Earl Carroll next to each other. Later on, they both told me that they never met before and they couldn't believe they actually liked each other. Bill Vare, the Republican boss of Pennsylvania, was damn glad to get tickets from me. Later on, he made the big mistake of tryin' to be a senator instead of just makin' 'em. Naturally, he got elected, and then the Senate in Washington threw him out. Boss Jim Pendergast come all the way from Kansas City in a private railroad car, and he picked up my friends in Chicago on the way.

"Of course, I invited guys on our side, too. The whole bunch from Philly was there, and a lot of guys like King Solomon from Boston, who took care of our shipments from Bronfman in Canada. We give Capone a dozen seats, but he didn't give a pair to Johnny Torrio, the selfish son of a bitch, so I had Johnny sit with me, in my row. Al was three rows behind us and he was sore as a boil. My two hundred seats mixed up everybody from whores to politicians, from society to Delancey Street. I had made up my mind I was gonna make friends from everywhere."

Just before the main bout, Salvatore Maranzano walked over from his seat across the stadium. He and Lucania greeted each other cordially, like equals, and chatted for a few moments. Then, as Dempsey was coming down the aisle to a crescendo of cheers from the crowd, Maranzano leaned close and whispered, "I have a business proposition for you."

"You mean like the last one?"

Maranzano shook his head. "No, no, it's a better deal. You'll see."

"I'll listen," Lucania said.

"Good. We meet, then?"

"Where?"

"At my club, if that is agreeable."

Two days later, Lucania, accompanied by Frank Costello, went downtown to Maranzano's headquarters in Little Italy, near the on-ramp of the Brooklyn Bridge. He had deliberately brought Costello with him to test whether there had been any change in Maranzano's attitude toward outlanders such as those from Calabria.

Maranzano greeted them jovially, put his arm around Charlie Lucania's shoulders, and led the two men into a back room. As they talked, Maranzano was effusive, declaring himself delighted that his invitation had been accepted and that Lucania had brought Costello with him, for he had long wanted to meet this associate who was gaining such a reputation as a man of excellent contacts and unusual circumspection.

After pouring glasses of wine ("not sour this time") and toasting their health and the success of this meeting, Maranzano made his offer. "As things now stand," he said, "we are interfering with each other. We are competing for the same whiskey markets, and, unfortunately, killing each other's people. This is foolish and it costs us both too much money and too many good men. This should come to a stop."

"Listen," Lucania replied, "you didn't bring me down here to recite the bible of what's right and wrong, Maranzano. What've you got on your mind?"

Still friendly, Maranzano said, "I would like you to join the great Maranzano family. You would be like my son, like a favorite son." Costello and the other Italians in Lucania's outfit would be welcomed, too, though not Lansky and Siegel, for they were Jews. If Lucania wanted to make use of them in the future, however, that would be all right. As for the terms: "I am prepared to be very generous. You will be like my own bambino."

That single word brought back to Lucania all his feelings against Maranzano, for it was the name, of course, his father had called him when he was young. "What right did that prick have to try to take the place of my old man? It was one thing to make a deal, and somethin' else to play papa with me — in Italian, 'papa' means pope. He was playin' the same goddamn game with me all over again. I could've shot him at that minute."

But Lucania hid his resentment and continued to listen as Maranzano detailed his offer: Charlie Lucania would become chief lieutenant in the Maranzano family, and Maranzano would turn over to him the family's entire liquor territory, abandoning the business himself and giving Charlie and his friends a free hand. With this one move, Maranzano said, Charlie Lucania would become the whiskey czar of New York.

Costello had said nothing up to this point; now he raised an eyebrow at Lucania. Lucania nodded, turned to Maranzano, and said, "You're talkin' like we're on top of a Sicilian mountain, Maranzano. Let's get down to the ground. What do you want?"

"The young are always in such a hurry," he sighed. What he wanted he thought quite acceptable, only that all the proceeds become part of a common treasury shared equally. To compensate Lucania for the loss that such a division of the liquor spoils would entail, he proposed that Lucania receive a reasonable — not a large, but a reasonable — percentage of all proceeds from all the other Maranzano interests — from the Italian lottery, well-planned loft and warehouse robberies, and all the rest. And, he noted, "We have considerable legitimate sources of proceeds: we own much real estate in Manhattan, including a substantial interest in the Flatiron Building, in both the land and the building. We are very large importers of foods to satisfy the tastes of our Italian brothers, and our olive oil imports, we anticipate, can be greatly increased with the elimination of an unfriendly Italian competitor in the

Bronx." That competitor was Mafia racketeer Ciro Terranova, sometimes called the Artichoke King.

"All durin' his speech, he was walkin' around the room. When he finished, he turned to us like he was expectin' us to applaud him, like he was wearin' a toga and just finished one of them big orations in the Roman Senate. That's the way he always made me feel, like he was Caesar and I was shit. Frank and I just sat there and we didn't say nothin'."

When Maranzano realized there would be no immediate response, he told Lucania to take his time, to go back and discuss the deal with his associates; such a discussion would reveal the generosity of the offer and the wisdom of a favorable answer.

"I already knew, speakin' for myself, that I'd have to turn the deal down. But I never tried to push my guys into a thing just because I said so." Back uptown at the Claridge, Lucania called a meeting of himself, Costello, Lansky, Siegel, Adonis and Genovese, explained the deal, and asked for their opinions. Adonis turned to Costello and asked, because he had been at the meeting with Maranzano, what he thought. "It's a helluva deal, and now, because of Charlie, somebody besides a Sicilian will be equal."

"I looked at all my smart friends, and I could see that everybody agreed with Frank, except Lansky. So I said, 'What's on your mind, Little Meyer?' He said, 'It stinks.'

"Everybody got all excited. Frank was sore as hell and turned on Lansky. 'Even with that adding-machine head of yours,' he says, 'you can't count the dough we can all make in this setup.' I stopped him there and I said to all of them, 'What's wrong with you guys? Don't you know the deal won't last two days? You don't have to be a big brain or an addin' machine or nothin' else to know that the minute we join up with Maranzano, that fat old son of a bitch will have us knocked off.' "

There was a silence, broken finally by Genovese. "Charlie has to be right. Maranzano can't afford to let a guy with a brain like Charlie's run around loose."

If not Lucania's brain, Maranzano was clearly worried about his ambition. It was apparent that Lucania was on the way up, was determined to reach the top, to use whatever means were necessary to get there. Anyone who even potentially stood in his way would be in very great danger one day. If Lucania's assumption was correct, Maranzano resolved to eliminate him while he was still vulnerable, and such an elimination would be a lot easier if Lucania was under his control rather than an independent surrounded and protected by strong allies.

For his friends, Lucania spelled out his own personal feelings about Maranzano and asked them to decide whether his personal sense that the offer should be rejected was based only on his revulsion or whether his reasoning was solidly based. There was a unanimous verdict that in this case the emotions and the realities coincided.

"So," he asked, "are we afraid of this guy?" It was a serious question, and one with potentially fatal consequences if the answer was wrong, for despite their success and growing power, they were still not strong enough to come to combat with Maranzano's power, influence and troops, and they knew it.

"Benny Siegel stood up then. After the Dempsey fight, he started to dress like me and I felt like he was sorta my kid brother. He said, 'If there's gonna be a war, they'll have to get over me first.' That was typical of Benny. He loved to fight and he didn't care who the hell with. He was ready to go in swingin'. Of course, I didn't want to take on Maranzano in a fight right then, but I knew that sooner or later, Maranzano would have to go. As long as he was alive, he would stand in our way, my way to the top. But when I took him on, it was gonna be on my terms."

Word was sent back to Maranzano, politely declining the offer and telling him that for the time being at least, Charlie Lucania had decided to continue on his own. Then they waited for the reaction. There was none. There was no increase in the hijackings of whiskey shipments, no increased pressure on Lucania's customers to buy their booze from Maranzano, no sudden rise in the number of arrests of Lucania's people by Maranzano's friends on the police force. There were no attempts on the lives of Lucania, Costello or the others. And when they met, as Charlie Lucania and Maranzano were bound to from time to time, Maranzano was as outwardly pleasant and cultured as he had always been, acting as though nothing had happened, never failing to call Lucania his "bambino."

"I couldn't understand why he didn't just have us bumped off, or at least try to then, when we was still small potatoes. He had the boys to do it and there was plenty of opportunities. But he never moved a muscle. I think that was what scared us bad in the beginnin', when nothin' happened, and we just sat there and waited for him to lower the boom. Then we got mad and we said, 'Screw him. We'll take our chances.' "

Lucania's rejection of this second Maranzano offer without any serious consequences spread quickly through the underworld and won Lucania increased respect from his elders and peers. He was wooed and entertained by the Mangano brothers, Philip and Vincent, and others of his age who were emerging as powers in Brooklyn. Enoch "Nucky" Johnson, boss of Atlantic City, and Moe Dalitz and Johnny Scalise, the bootleg powers in Cleveland, began cutting him in on some of their deals. Such illegal liquor suppliers as Sam Bronfman in Canada and Lewis Rosenstiel (who, a decade later, would celebrate the end of Prohibition by turning his bootleg enterprise into the Schenley Corporation) wooed him assiduously.

And perhaps most important, it resulted in some tentative feelers from Giuseppe Masseria, the self-proclaimed and generally acknowledged "Boss of Bosses" of the Italian-Sicilian underworld. Between the ascetic, intellectual Maranzano and the gross, earthy and uncouth Masseria there had long been great animosity, made greater as Maranzano hardly disguised his ambition to claim the title of "Boss of Bosses" of the Mafia and often sent his own troops in forays against Joe the Boss's enterprises. It was apparent that one day a war to the death would erupt between the two.

The first probe toward Lucania came through Dutch Schultz. He sent to the Claridge Hotel, to meet Lucania, Genovese and their associates, a major underworld leader in the Bronx and ally of Masseria's named Gaetano "Tom" Reina. The conversation was a guarded and oblique one, with Reina saying he had come only to meet a fellow Sicilian who was becoming so important, and perhaps to strike a friendship that could lead in the future to some alliances. Lucania listened, was cordial and noncommittal.

That meeting opened the door a crack, and it swung a little wider a couple of months later. "I thought at the time the way the whole thing happened was kind of an accident, but later I found out that without tellin' me a thing about it, Vito set it up on his own." Along with Siegel, several other friends and some girls, Lucania had gone to the opening of George White's Scandals as guests of the impresario ("We always gave George a few bucks as an investment in his shows; not much, but just enough to make sure we got openin' night tickets"), and then had gone on to Jack & Charlie's 21 Club. They had hardly been seated when Masseria, with some of his lieutenants and a train of pretty girls, walked in, spotted Lucania across the room, and hailed him in Sicilian. Masseria walked over and invited Charlie Lucania and his friends to join the Masseria party, insisted on it. Several large tables were put together and bottles of whiskey were brought out. Everyone was in a jovial, expansive mood, and Masseria drank heavily. At one point, Lucania leaned across the table and asked Masseria how he liked the whiskey.

Masseria smiled and nodded happily. "Best I ever tasted."

"It oughta be. It's mine."

Masseria peered at him, looked closely at the bottle and the label, sipped again. "It's real," he said.

"Damn right. It's my private stock."

If Lucania was serving straight, uncut whiskey in a speakeasy, then perhaps he was even more powerful and successful than Masseria had thought, and this would make him even more valuable as a recruit. Masseria talked expansively about how good business must be for Lucania, how it was apparent that big things were in store for him, that his future was unlimited. Perhaps, he said, it might be a good thing if they got together for a private talk, perhaps even the next day.

"It was almost the same kind of situation that took place between Maranzano and me and Costello a couple of months before, except for one big difference. Masseria didn't have the background and the education of a guy like Maranzano; he didn't have no culture. So, between bein' short, fat and havin' a round face that was first cousin to a pig, the words that come out of his kisser was rough and straight to the point: he hated Maranzano's fuckin' guts and he knew that Maranzano felt the same way about him."

The meeting took place in a small office on the second floor of

64

a little restaurant building not a half-dozen blocks from Maranzano's social club, and throughout the session, every time Masseria looked out the window, his eyes and face contorted as he looked toward the Maranzano bastion. He shook his finger at Lucania and bellowed, "You listen to me. One day, maybe tomorrow, there's gonna be war. I know what that louse is tryin' to do. He wants to keep you on ice, because that way he thinks he can beat me. And that, Charlie, is where he outsmarts himself. You come with me and we'll knock the shit out of him together, once and for all."

Lucania had little doubt that Masseria was right, but he did not wish to be hurried or pressured into a quick decision, and so his response was almost casual. "You may be right. Maybe Maranzano thinks he's still fightin' one of them Roman battles, like Julius Caesar."

"He's gonna kill himself with that crap," Masseria said. "When are you gonna wake up? Don't you know the only reason he didn't knock you off, and all them punk kids with you, is because he needs you? Get smart. Come in with me, and then you can be the first lieutenant of the real Sicilian boss of this whole fuckin' city, of the country. You want money? I'll make more money for you than you can count. Just say the word." Masseria's words were spoken almost in a guttural growl. He relished speaking English, but his accent was heavy and crude, and Lucania, as he listened, compared the suaveness of Maranzano to the boorishness of Masseria. At that moment, he was uncertain which man represented, in fact, the greater strength, which appealed to him more as a potential ally.

"Maybe it was right at that minute when I knew that eventually both of these guys hadda go. We'd already been talkin' about rubbin' out Maranzano when the time come. But this meet with Masseria made it pretty clear to me that these two guys eventually would try to carve me up. I hadda have time, and so I stalled. I told him it wasn't the right time, I had a lot of things bein' developed that involved all my guys and I hadda talk to them. He beefed a lot about it, about me not goin' in with him right then and there, but I wasn't gonna get caught in no squeeze play. I knew I could do more and go further by bein' independent and free and let the two of 'em kiss my ass for a while, until I was sure

65

that I couldn't stall 'em no longer. The best I could do was to walk a tightrope and keep the door open a little bit."

Within days of the meeting, and Lucania's rejection of Masseria's offer, several of his whiskey shipments were hijacked in the Jersey woods near Atlantic City while en route to Philadelphia, and two of his warehouses in upper Manhattan were raided by federal Prohibition agents. These were, of course, the hazards of the business and he could not expect to be totally free of some losses. But the hijackings created a shortage of his supplies for the first time. He had practically no Scotch left and his customers were demanding Scotch. He could not tell his customers that he couldn't fill their orders, that he didn't have any more Scotch and they would have to wait for the next shipment. This would seriously damage his standing as the man who could always deliver and deliver on short notice. And it would force those customers to turn to someone else, like Maranzano or Masseria, to get what they needed.

Lucania was desperate. And at that moment, he received a telephone call from Nucky Johnson in Atlantic City, perhaps Johnson's attempt to repay the favor of the tickets for the Dempsey-Firpo fight. It was suggested that Lucania drive down to Atlantic City and bring Adonis with him for a private meeting. A summons from Johnson was, in those days, like a command, for Nucky Johnson was the man who ran Atlantic City with an iron hand, controlling its politics and its very existence. Nothing happened there, or in the area around the wide-open resort, without Johnson's knowledge and permission. He imported and distributed, and dictated who sold the liquor consumed there; he had a piece of all the gambling and the newly popular slot machines that had been introduced by Frank Costello; he had an interest even in the sale of jobs at every level of the police force. And he prided himself on his neutrality; he was above the battle of the warring underworld organizations from outside who used Atlantic City, with his permission and for a price, to import their liquor, store it in warehouses he either owned or controlled in the woods up from the beach, and cut it in distilleries in the neighborhood. Nobody crossed Nucky Johnson, and nobody even tried; to do anything in Atlantic City without his permission would not only have closed off the area to the miscreant but would have meant all-out war with Johnson, and, said Luciano, "He would've come down on you from every side, includin' the whole Atlantic Ocean."

Lucania and Adonis drove the hundred and forty miles to Atlantic City, taking every back road and shortcut they knew, in three hours and met with Johnson at a mansion he maintained in Chelsea, an exclusive Atlantic City suburb, for the purpose of private meetings and accommodations for special guests. "I knew Nucky would do practically anything for a buck. For a lotta money, I figured he could be tempted to accept an offer the boys and I had decided was a good idea. So I said to him, 'Look, Nucky, I don't want to beat around the bush, and I'm not lookin' to chisel a sharp deal. I need all the Scotch I can lay my hands on, and you know everythin' that's comin' in and out. Now I want a better deal than the fair shake you've been givin' everybody. I'll make you a partner."

Perhaps it was just such a deal that Johnson himself had intended to propose when he called Lucania for the meeting. For without hesitation, the tall, urbane ruler of the Jersey coast said, "I'll give you an exclusive on my beach. Nobody else can land any stuff here. I'll give you protection all the way to the Camden Ferry across from Philly. I'll let Costello bring in all the slots he can handle. You can run gambling spots that we'll decide on, near the big hotels. Now, Charlie, what do I get?"

Before answering, Lucania had one further demand. "I need Scotch now, Nucky. So, who's makin' the next shipment?"

"Maranzano," Johnson answered. "A boatload, two trucks, of uncut stuff will come in at Ventnor two nights from now. It's going to be cut by Waxey Gordon and Bitsy Bitz in Philadelphia." He pulled out a map and marked the route the Maranzano trucks would take from Atlantic City, passing through Egg Harbor, New Jersey, by a back road.

"After gettin' information like that, I shook hands with Nucky on the deal. That day, I give him ten per cent of everythin' as long as the Volstead Act remained the law; everythin' from my outfit, that is. But the rest, includin' Costello, Lansky, Siegel and Adonis, all chipped in, so it wasn't too big a bite from any one of us.

"As Joe and me walked to the door, Nucky said somethin' that

67

made me feel pretty good. 'Charlie,' he said, 'I like the way you handle yourself. Most of all, I like the way you dress. You're starting to look like a real corporation executive.' Comin' from a guy who practically ran a whole state, I really appreciated that. As we got into the car, Joe said to me, 'That's the smartest move you ever made. It's worth millions.' And it was."

Two nights later, three cars containing ten heavily armed men, including Lucania and Siegel in the first, Adonis and Lansky in the second, set out from New York to erect a roadblock on the Egg Harbor back road. It was unfortunate, Lucania said, that it had to be a Maranzano shipment that was being hijacked, for if he and his friends were recognized, it would mean war; but he could not afford to show any hesitation to Johnson and he desperately needed the whiskey. A tree was felled across the road and at two in the morning, the Maranzano trucks appeared, with several men riding shotgun. At the sight of the tree, the trucks halted and some of the men jumped out to remove it. "Siegel started to shoot right away, and then Lansky opened up. One of the Maranzano guys was bumped off and another one was wounded, and the rest of 'em gave up right there. But that didn't do 'em no good because we took away their guns and give 'em a good beatin' before we took off with the trucks. Maybe the best thing about it was that none of 'em recognized us because we was all masked."

Lucania filled his orders from the hijacked shipment and then waited for the old Don to retaliate, certain that Maranzano would have some idea who pulled off the job and so would come down in force. But again nothing happened.

"That's when I knew that Joe Masseria had called it right. I knew then that I'd go with Masseria, no matter how much I hated him personally. Maranzano could never take on the combination of me and my guys joined together with Joe's big outfit. I decided that I'd make the deal with him as soon as possible, but I hadda work it out so he'd come to me again, instead of me goin' to him. That would give me some kind of edge when we started talkin'."

7.

By the mid-1920's, though not yet thirty years of age, Charlie Lucania had arrived at a plateau that once would have been beyond his imagination. He was rich and growing richer, the money pouring in ever-increasing amounts into his coffers. He was living in a large furnished apartment on Manhattan's East Side in Murray Hill, everything in good taste, everything expensive. His wardrobe was bursting with new clothes, all from the best stores and tailors, and as Arnold Rothstein had taught him, conservative, subdued, exuding the aroma of success and respectability. He had at his disposal a fleet of big black supercharged cars, some souped up and refined by his own hands, for he was a man who loved fine cars and was a tinkerer with motors, and some worked on by his friend Meyer Lansky, equally passionate about engines. He numbered among his friends the city's elite in politics, society, sports, entertainment; they welcomed him into their homes and they came to him seeking favors. He could choose any kind or type of woman that struck his fancy of the moment, with little fear of rejection. By watching, practicing, imitating, listening to the lessons of Rothstein, he had learned the ways of the rich, had acquired the veneer of a gentleman (though always, just beneath the surface, there was a barely concealed menace, a threat of sudden violence, and he never lost, no matter how he tried, the rasp and inflection of the Lower East Side, which was later to seem alien to the rest of him).

Charlie Lucania had become an executive, controlling an empire whose growth was ceaseless, both horizontally and vertically. It was an organization he called his "outfit," though it was only the germ of what would come. "In them days, there was no real combination. Costello had his outfit, and Siegel and Lansky had their outfit, and Adonis had his. But we all had one thing in common, and that was the whiskey and how to keep it flowin'. I never got mixed up with Costello in the slots; I didn't go on no fur jobs or jewelry heists with Adonis's guys, or things like that. Of course, I got my share, because at the top we was partners. But it got to be a thing where they all looked to me, and I'd always say to them, 'Don't ask me to make your decisions for you in your own business. All I wanna do is make the stuff that we do together pay off as big as possible.' It was a terrific arrangement and one of the reasons I think it worked so good was that I wasn't doin' a Masseria, trying to be the Big Boss."

The more his friends turned to him for advice, the more important he became, the more Lucania became concerned with "makin' our outfit into a real business, like any big corporation. Of course we couldn't advertise with a slogan or a trademark like Packard cars, 'Ask the Man Who Owns One,' but that didn't mean things couldn't be run right. So I made up a lotta rules for the guys who worked for me. Why shouldn't I? After all, don't department stores and big offices tell their people how to behave and what to wear?"

His regulations gave his men an image the antithesis of the one portrayed in the press of the day and later popularized in the scores of Warner Brothers movies of the early 1930's. Lucania's men were ordered to dress neatly and conservatively, like office workers, to avoid wide-brimmed hats, loud shirts and ties, garish suits completely. ("Let Capone and his Chicago guys do that. We won't.") When in a car, there was to be no speeding or violation of any traffic law except when absolutely necessary, for it was impossible to know who might stop a speeder and what might then be found inside the car. Anybody who was a member of the Lucania outfit was expected to be circumspect in everything, if he wanted to remain a member. But according to the unwritten code, nobody could quit, and being fired could be sudden, unpleasant and permanent.

Despite Lucania's rules, the members of his outfit had come to it, as he and the other leaders had, from a violent world of robbery, mugging, theft and other crimes, and reversion was an easy step, since there wasn't always enough work every day to keep everybody busy. Some used their spare time to return to their old callings, knocking over any place where there was loose money or marketable goods. "I tried to explain to all the boys in my outfit that there was lots of easy ways to make a buck. There was no reason to go out on their own and take chances just because they might have a couple of days or weeks on their hands with no jobs to do for me." But his words often went unheeded, for some of his boys went in over their heads in gambling or with girls and needed some extra cash. "Most of the time, they'd get caught, and then I'd have to get the mouthpieces, put up the bail and the rest, because no matter what they did, I made it a policy to back 'em to the limit. I just tried to make 'em understand the penalties of stupidity."

There was the time in the summer of 1925 when Lucania began to spread his bookmaking operation all over Manhattan. He gave Vito Genovese the job of bringing the small candy and other family-owned stores into line. "I told Vito we was gonna do somethin' none of the other outfits ever had the sense to do. We was gonna guarantee a guy in any little store a yard and a half [$150] a week to handle the bettin' slips and let us put in the phones." These were the "momma and poppa" stores, many owned by Jews, who would ordinarily have rejected any offer from a gangster. "But when we guaranteed 'em that hundred and fifty, it shut 'em up — most of 'em, anyway. And that dough sent more Jewish kids to college and made more Jewish doctors and lawyers than all the rich Hebes on Riverside Drive put together."

But where Genovese concentrated his efforts was on the Lower East Side, among the "snowball cart" peddlers, men who pushed around carts containing a huge cake of ice, quart bottles of fruit flavors and a metal scoop; for two cents, the peddler would scoop out a flavored ice into a paper cup, and the neighborhood kids were his best customers. In recruiting them, Genovese had ideas that went beyond bookmaking. "Without sayin' nothin' to me, he starts to muscle a bunch of these old geezers, mostly Italians, to pass junk for him in their neighborhoods. I almost clobbered him. I said to him, 'You stupid shithead. You had a good idea, but why screw it up with narcotics, especially when I told you — no junk. Go out and organize 'em, sure, but to take bets for us. We got all the precincts protected and no Feds to worry about.' He seen the light and in less than a month we had over two hundred pushcarts makin' book for us. That was the time, though, when I should've cut his prick off, right then and there. Believe me, I lived to regret that I didn't."

So Lucania's bookmaking empire spiraled. He and his partners owned and financed hundreds of police-protected handbooks around Manhattan, and they controlled a number of central bookmaking banks where the bets from the individual bookie could be laid off — shared — so as to avoid any great loss to them if too many bettors hit a winner. It was lucrative business, for them if not for the small bookie. They grossed perhaps $500,000 a week, or more. The individual bookie might handle $2,000 a week in bets, if his business was good. But that was his gross. Part of it went back to the winners; another part, up to half the bet, was charged for the layoff privilege with the central bank. More of the gross went for police protection, either paid directly by the bookie or, more likely, by the outfit of which he was a member out of funds he supplied. More went for rent, telephones and other expenses. If a bookie did well, he earned about 7½ per cent on the total bets placed with him, or about $150 a week. And so the supposedly generous offer of $150 a week guaranteed to the small storekeepers was anything but; it had been carefully computed by Lucania and Lansky.

But their rewards from gambling were not limited to their share of the income of the neighborhood books and the central banks. They ran, as well, a more luxurious operation in the form of horse parlors where the rich and the sporting crowd that didn't have the time or inclination to travel to the tracks to watch the horses, and yet wanted some of the excitement that was absent in betting with bookies by phone, could get what they desired. The parlors were lavishly decorated, drinks of good Scotch and other whiskey were provided free, women of polite society were welcome (which was not true at the men-only private clubhouse at Belmont), there were tables and sofas where the bettors could relax while waiting for the results, which were flashed in and announced within seconds of the end of a race, and there were betting windows that simulated those at the tracks, and the track odds or better prevailed. It was in these horse parlors that Lucania "collected a fortune in diamond bracelets and rings from some of the best ladies in Manhattan. Once in a while I took 'em home with me, the broads, I mean, so I could examine them jewels a little closer while doing a body readin' on the lady herself."

What was apparent from all this was that people wanted to bet as much as they wanted to drink, and there was no reason why the two should not be combined. The back rooms of the better speakeasies, and particularly the outlying roadhouses, were equipped as casinos, with roulette wheels and crap tables, birdcages, blackjack tables and other games of chance. House limits were generally fixed at two hundred dollars a bet, but the big players were often granted a no-limit game.

Gambling, liquor, everything they touched seemed to flourish. "I always liked to gamble, but one thing I never did — gamble in the stock market, because the stockholder on the outside don't know a thing about what's happenin' inside the company. Years later, I was down at Bradley's in Florida, and I ran into that guy Hutton who had a big brokerage firm up in New York. Hutton was a good friend of mine. He was playin' chemin de fer one night, and when he finished — I think he dropped about eighteen grand — I went over to him and I said, with an absolutely straight face, 'Hut, I wanna talk to you; I wanna help you get even for what you just dropped. It's somethin' about the market. I think it's a good idea if I could get my outfit listed on the New York Stock Exchange.'

"For a minute, he really started to think about it, and then he realized I was kiddin' him. Well, he began to laugh until I thought he was gonna choke. Then he looked at me, shook his head and said, 'Charlie, that's the greatest idea I've ever heard in my whole life — that I'll never be able to accomplish.'"

Stock in Lucania's outfit during the twenties might, indeed, have been a good investment. "Around 1925, I had a take of at least twelve million dollars from booze alone for the year. Naturally, we didn't pay no business taxes, like General Motors, but that didn't mean that our expenses wasn't pretty heavy. We — by that I mean with Costello, Lansky, Siegel and Adonis — had a payroll of about a hundred guys, lots of 'em muscle men or enforcers and guards. We had good drivers, bookkeepers, lots of messengers; and we even used to pay off a bunch of finger men who lined up jobs like a hijacking or a robbery. In them days when an honest department store clerk was drawin' down maybe twenty-five dollars a week at most, my guys was gettin' paid by us two hundred a week plus what they was makin' on their own. So we had a yearly payroll of about a million bucks.

"That meant that we had about eleven million left to cover all our expenses. By 1925, all of us guys was payin' out a 'grease' of over a hundred grand a week, which is more than five million a year, for protection. Hell, we shoveled out ten thousand a week every week like clockwork to the top brass of the Police Department, and that was only a small part of it. We hadda take care of the precincts, too, the captains, the lieutenants and the sergeants; they all had their hands out. Takers, all of 'em; and that goes for the cop on the beat."

When all the expenses of running the business had been written off, there was still about four million dollars a year that went into the individual caches of Lucania and his partners. They kept almost all of it; if they paid taxes at all, and most of them did not until years later, it was on small salaries they reported as receiving from such occupations, maintained as fronts, as chauffeurs, professional gamblers, sales managers and the like. And all this was in 1925, with the peak still in the future; in succeeding years, their business gross and their personal incomes would skyrocket.

In these years of the 1920's, illegal liquor was their main business, the major source of their revenue and their power. Gambling was still secondary, with Lucania, Costello and Siegel drawn to it at first by their passion for games of chance, and Lansky because he saw its business potential, and demonstrated it to his friends. At first, their investments were limited to the casinos, the horse parlors, the slot machines, the bookie joints and the like. Little attention was paid to the poor, to the idea that poor people might want to gamble too, would, if given the chance, do more than put a nickel or a dime in a slot machine or place a small bet on a horse with a bookie, and that such gambling, even for pennies, could yield millions.

That idea struck one night in Covington, Kentucky, at the opening of the famed Beverly Club, just across the Ohio state line.

Lansky and Lucania were there, watched the glittering array of the nation's rich who had come from all parts of the country to put their money on the tables at the inaugural. As they watched, Lansky took Lucania aside and said, "Charlie, you look around in a place like this, a real plush joint with waiters in white coats, the best booze and a fairly honest wheel, and you watch these suckers drop their dough, it makes you think of somethin'."

Lucania laughed. "What should we do? Give 'em their money back?"

"I'm tryin' to make you understand somethin'. What about the little guy who can't even bet two bucks on a horse, but would like to bet on somethin'? Ain't he entitled to some of this pleasure, even if he can only bet a couple of pennies?"

"Pennies?" Lucania stared at him.

Lucania was certain Lansky would not have brought this up unless he had already devised a plan, and so he waited. Lansky mentioned the Italian Lottery, the Irish Sweepstakes, the official lotteries of a dozen countries. All were based on numbers. All took place at regular intervals a few times a year. "Suppose," Lansky said, "a guy could bet on a number every day. If enough people bet only pennies, we could afford to make the odds high enough for the dumb bastards to buy the idea that any day of the week they could hit for a big bundle."

The two men went back to Cleveland and sat up all night, their sleeves rolled up, a bottle of their favorite Old Overholt bonded rye and plenty of ginger ale nearby, and on scratch paper tried to calculate ways to make the Lansky scheme work. "Once Meyer spelled out the idea, it all sorta fell into place. He had a way of thinkin' around a corner. When it was all put together, I knew with every bone in my body it would catch on like a grass fire." And so the policy game came into being. The daily number, of three digits from 000 to 999, would be based on a supposedly un-riggable and well-publicized total, the closing sales on a stock market or the betting totals from three races at a track, with the payoff for a winner at 600 to 1 (against the real odds of 1,000 to 1, thereby guaranteeing phenomenal returns to the operators).

Once the structure had been decided, it was agreed that the racket should get its first tryout in Frank Costello's Harlem

domain, among the blacks and the very poor. (Some fellow gangsters like Dutch Schultz initially expressed scorn; soon they would
change their minds.) The numbers racket was an instant success,
not only in Harlem (though Harlem remained the most valuable
territory, with almost every man, woman and child playing policy
every day), but all over the country. It poured millions into the
pockets of Costello, Lansky, Lucania and the others, and gained
them increased loyalty from their underlings who were granted
shares in some of the hundreds of policy banks that sprang up. "So
much money was comin' in from policy that we had to have meetings all the time to figure out what to do with the dough. That's
when I really started to respect the bankers and to be jealous of
them. They could take their depositors' money and invest it so
they could pay interest and still have a healthy profit. But we was
rakin' in hot money that we couldn't declare and couldn't bank.
Then I remembered all them poor suckers who couldn't get a loan
from a bank because they didn't have no security. That's when I
decided to organize the loan business."

Usury is an ancient business, one that through the ages has
never failed to draw those, often disreputable, with more money
than they could use for themselves. It was well known to Maranzano, who would often quote to his disciples from *The Merchant
of Venice*, though on such occasions defending Shylock despite his
Jewishness. For Maranzano had long been a moneylender in the
Italian ghetto, advancing money to new immigrants to help them
bring relatives to America, but lending it at such usurious rates
that the borrower ever afterwards remained little more than an
indentured servant, at Maranzano's bidding, forever paying out a
portion of his small weekly income. And there was no way out.
The immigrants were afraid to complain to the police, for their
image of the police was one they had brought with them from the
old country. And Maranzano had a corps of enforcers to insure
that the borrower never escaped, never complained, paid off regularly, and was always available when called upon. There were
enough examples around the neighborhood of those who had been
beaten or killed, when they resisted, to keep the others in line.

But Maranzano was not alone in practicing the trade. He was
emulated by others, including Lucania, who would later say, "I

76

think it was a rotten thing to do and, if I had it to do over again, that's one thing I never would've done, bleedin' them poor guys who was tryin' to bring their families over. Anyway, that's when I started to take another look at what Lepke was doin' in the garment district."

Lucania decided that Lepke, having some difficulty trying to follow the plan laid down for him, could use some help. "I picked out Tommy Lucchese, who they sometimes called 'Three-Finger Brown' after the old baseball pitcher, as the right guy that I could depend on. Tommy and I was friends from the old neighborhood, but for a lotta reasons we didn't play that up; we used to meet in private most of the time and it wasn't for a long time that a lotta guys knew we was close. Anyway, I tabbed Tommy, and the Lepke-Brown combination for the garment district worked like a charm."

In the garment center, style changes are one of the facts of life, occurring regularly, sometimes three or four times a year, and with each change, the manufacturers need to cut new patterns, buy new materials, and acquire new machines. The business is a high-risk one, with large amounts of short-term capital constantly needed. The banks, however, were loath to advance this money, and so garment manufacturers were forced to turn to the loan sharks, and it was in this business that Lepke and Lucchese — and Lucania — flourished. "They was gettin' anywhere from double to a thousand per cent interest for short-term loans, and, of course, if the loans wasn't repaid, no excuses was accepted."

Lucania's ideas for organizing the loansharking on a big scale turned it into a huge business, particularly when it involved working both sides of the district, with the unions and the manufacturers. Assistance was offered to the unions in their organizing drives, to get them the members and the dues; in return, the underworld was given control of a number of locals. Knowing that manufacturers were afraid of the unions, afraid that higher wages and strikes would drive them out of business, they guaranteed manufacturers who came to terms with them that there would be no strikes and that wages in union contracts would be held to a reasonable level. "And we give the companies that worked with us the money to help them with buyin' goods and all the stuff they

77

needed to operate with. Then, if one of our manufacturers got into us for dough that he couldn't pay back, and the guy had what looked like a good business, then we would become his partner.

"If it wasn't for me, them guys like Samuel Gompers and Jacob Potofsky and Sidney Hillman and David Dubinsky, and I knew 'em all, would've been bums. Me and Tommy and Lepke, we actually kept a whole bunch of them garment manufacturers alive, and we helped all them unions, the Ladies' Garment Workers and the Amalgamated, organize the places. If it wasn't for us, none of 'em, the manufacturers or the unions, would've gotten noplace. Our dough made it possible for maybe fifty manufacturers, maybe more, to cut more dresses and coats and suits than anybody else. And petticoats. We backed a guy by the name of Korn — maybe it was Cohen — and a dozen more like him. For chrissake, in the 1920's, every broad in the United States was wearin' a petticoat I was responsible for puttin' on her."

That all these goods cost the public considerably more than they would have cost if Lucania and his friends had not been involved bothered him not at all. "The public is a bunch of crumbs askin' to be taken. And as for doin' good, the garment center and the stock market was the heart of New York City; they couldn't live without each other. If my outfit helped keep the clothin' manufacturers goin', for which we got a healthy commission, then, what the hell, I was just as big a broker as my friend Hutton. So what if I used to muscle some guy because he didn't pay up? What does the stockbroker do when his customers can't meet an overcall? He just sells the guy out, and then the poor bastard goes up to the top of some buildin' and jumps off, which is what happened a couple years later."

But none of these activities of Lucania — bootlegging, gambling, loansharking, garment center invasions — could have succeeded without the protection of the city's political and police structure. The price was high, but to him and his partners, it was worth the cost. "I grew up with that whole system of money buyin' protection. I used to see it all around me. But by the mid-twenties, the payoffs wasn't just free turkeys at Christmas. This was big stuff." As they flourished, they came to realize that it was not enough merely to have the precincts in their pockets. Even if they were paying off every cop in an area, somebody higher up, at police headquarters, could always call for action without consulting the local precinct, could decide to bring them in for questioning, decide to call a quick raid on their operations. Such roustings were, at the very least, an inconvenience, and they endangered the image they were attempting to foster. "I didn't like the idea of gettin' smeared all the time when the newspapers would print our pictures. It always seemed to be the same picture; we was surrounded by a bunch of cops when we got hauled in."

"Look," Lucania told his partners at one of their high-level meetings, "what good is it if we buy one precinct or ten precincts? I don't want one or ten; I want all the precincts."

"Charlie, you're askin' the impossible," Costello objected. "You're talkin' about buyin' the real top big shots."

But Lucania was determined and he told Costello, "You're the best fixer in the whole fuckin' country; you don't realize that these 'big shots' are the same guys we got in our pockets already. They're in our speaks every night, drinkin' our best booze. It's just a matter of handlin', and how much."

"When I think about that particular meetin', it was really the turnin' point of our move to the top. None of the guys who was with me was cheap, and every one of 'em could add. We started with nothin' and when we got up into seven figures, what difference would it make if it cost us a million? We knew it'd bring in more than that."

So the decision was made to go to the very top with an unlimited Buy-Bank. "I remember Joe Adonis standin' across the room, lookin' in the mirror and combing his hair like he always did. It was his way of stallin'. Everybody else — Anastasia, Scalise, Moretti, Dutch Schultz, who came to the meet even though he had the flu and his doc told him to stay in bed; he sat over in a corner so he wouldn't spread his germs around — they all said yes. We all sat there lookin' at Joe's back while he kept runnin' the comb through his hair like a movie actor. Finally, he turned around with a big smile and said, 'The star says yes,' referrin' to himself, of course.

"Dutch ran across the room and grabbed Joe's head in a hammerlock and breathed right in his face, sayin', 'Now, you

79

fuckin' star, you have my goims.' Joe actually did catch Dutch's flu and for a solid week he was callin' me up on the phone from bed with a voice like a hoarse frog, tellin' me to warn the Dutchman to stay outa his way."

The approaches to the upper echelon of the police department by Costello and Lucania were slow, cautious and effective, and after a series of private negotiations, a payment schedule was worked out that would tie the office of the police commissioner to the Lucania organization. The first of the weekly payments began to flow from Lucania's headquarters to the police commissioner's office late in 1925. The sum agreed upon was ten thousand dollars a week; within a couple of years, during the term of police commissioners Joseph A. Warren and Grover A. Whalen, the grease, Luciano would later say, rose to twenty thousand dollars a week.

The job of carrying the money to police headquarters was entrusted to an underling in the Lucania mob named Joe Cooney, sometimes called "Joe the Coon," a nickname that never failed to enrage him since he maintained a fierce antipathy toward Negroes. Cooney was given the job both because of his loyalty and his Irishness. Carrying money into City Hall was a job that required an Irishman, like the red-haired, freckle-faced Cooney, who, dressed as a building maintenance man, could blend into the scenery.

It was one thing to hand over cash to liaison men for lower-level police and politicians at some agreed-upon site, and another thing entirely to walk into police headquarters in downtown Manhattan with ten thousand dollars in small bills, and carry them directly to the commissioner's office, as the agreement worked out by Lucania and Costello demanded.

"How the hell am I gonna deliver ten big ones in little bills right in the middle of all them cops?" Cooney asked Lucania.

"Goddammit, Cooney, just give it to him. Hand it over."

"In what? What do you want me to carry it in?"

"For chrissake, shove it into a brown paper bag, like it's your lunch, a sandwich or somethin'."

Cooney did just that, becoming the prototype of the "bagman." Dressed in his work clothes and carrying his lunch with him, he arrived at police headquarters once a week at noon, went to the commissioner's office, and handed over his cash-filled brown bag. "I told Cooney that once in a while, to make things look legit, he should change a light bulb."

The payoffs bought what they were intended to buy. The Lucania operations now ran smoothly, almost as though under the aegis of the police department. As long as innocent civilians were not harmed (and sometimes even if they were), Lucania and his men were free to do almost as they pleased. If there was need of a token raid, because "some politician couldn't fuck his wife, so he tried to have a good time fuckin' me and my guys," a police official would call or come personally to see Lucania with a warning and to work out the details to limit the damage. Charlie Lucania was even called by police when one of his cars was ticketed for illegal parking; he laughed off the tickets, but refused to have them fixed and paid them promptly, because "it was the least I could do to show I was a law-abidin' citizen."

It was about this time, at the end of 1925, that an old friend reappeared briefly in New York. Fifteen years Lucania's senior, Johnny "The Fox" Torrio was on his way for a long vacation to the town near Naples where he had been born. The underworld peace he had labored for so tirelessly in Chicago, after the murder of Big Jim Colosimo, had fallen apart amid the bullets that ripped through Cicero and in the war between Torrio's forces and those of Dion O'Banion. Torrio had dealt with O'Banion with dispatch, summoning once again his old friend Frankie Yale to murder the little florist. But in the aftermath, Torrio himself had been ambushed and nearly killed. The story has always been that the attempt was staged by George "Bugs" Moran, Hymie Weiss and other heirs of O'Banion in revenge. And, indeed, Al Capone, Torrio's chief aide, wept copious tears when news of the attack was brought to him and swore revenge on the O'Banion mob. "But I know that Al was behind the try at Torrio, even though he always said he didn't have nothin' to do with it. He tried to eliminate Johnny the same way Johnny done with Colosimo."

As soon as Torrio was sufficiently recovered, he had sought safety in an Illinois prison, surrendering to serve a nine-month sentence on a bootleg conviction. While in jail, he turned his entire Chicago empire over to Capone and in return Capone provided him with a three-car safe-conduct motorcade from the prison gates to the railroad station for his trip East. Before he boarded the train, Torrio called Lucania and arranged a meeting when he reached New York before sailing for Italy.

"Johnny was a guy who could always look around corners, just like Meyer Lansky. One time, I even told him that the barrel of his gun was curved, and he laughed at that, but he didn't deny it. When we met, he told me he was gonna take a vacation in Italy; he'd gotten his naturalization papers, so he didn't have nothin' to worry about, and he had millions stashed away. He told me he wanted to talk over a plan. He thought booze was gonna become legal again and he wanted to become my agent in Europe, to start buyin' up legal options on the best Scotch to get ready for the end of the Volstead Act. This was seven long years before Repeal, and it was almost impossible to believe. Here was a guy predictin' that my whole fuckin' bootleg business, and everybody else's for that matter, was gonna wind up in the shithouse."

The next day, Lucania and Torrio met in secret with Costello, Lansky and the other partners. When they heard Torrio's prediction, everyone was shocked, except Lansky. "He agreed, and then he said, 'The only way to get legitimate is to move in with legitimate people.' And Johnny made the biggest point; he said, 'You've gotta get into the big politics; you can buy the top politicians the same way you bought the law.' "

And then Torrio set sail. His Italian sojourn would not be as long as he thought. Mussolini's Fascists were in the middle of a bitter campaign to eliminate the Sicilian Mafia and to get rid of American gangsters of Italian descent who were returning home. Labeled an undesirable visitor, Torrio was soon back in the United States and working closely with Lucania and his other friends in New York.

But while he was gone, Charlie Lucania, Frank Costello and their top associates were making their moves into high-level politics, particularly in New York City and state. "I made it a policy from the beginnin' that we wouldn't just line up with Tammany Hall and the Democrats. To me, that would look like we was takin' sides, and the truth of it was, I couldn't've cared less. We went with the Republicans, too. In my book, it was a three-party system — them two and us."

They had plenty to offer the politicians who helped them, those candidates for the public's vote and trust. They had the money to finance any campaign, to make any tractable politician a wealthy man; they had the contacts and the knowledge to turn a willing politician on to lucrative deals in road-building, construction and more — the list is endless — and they had the strong-arm forces to terrorize any of their candidates' opponents and to incline voters to cast their ballots the "right way."

Just as they had little trouble buying the police, so they had little trouble buying the politicians they wanted, like Tammany leaders Jimmy Hines and Albert C. Marinelli. And often they did not even have to seek out the politicians, who came to them seeking assistance. "We wanted good guys — winners. Even though we played both sides of the political line, and that way we couldn't lose, still it was a good thing to have a guy elected who could do a nice job and get reelected easier. That way, the second time, the campaign didn't cost us so much. It got so I could pick political winners better than I could ever pick horses."

In the early morning hours of these years, Lucania would go home, get into bed, and read the *Daily News* and the *Mirror* ("I didn't know enough words to read the New York *Times*"), read about what his assemblymen, aldermen, congressmen and senators were doing, and the realization would grow that these were people he had made. "I'd lay there and read that stuff and it all looked so legit I couldn't even believe I done it, that it was my muscle that put them 'very respectable' guys where they was. Talk about muscle; there's muscle, and muscle. There was people on the streets with muscle to make things go the way I wanted, and I had them. Then there was the other kind of muscle, to get the laws passed the right way, to get things done smooth and legal. I had that kind of muscle, too. I personally helped elect more than eighty guys over a short time, all votin' my way, aldermen, councilmen, mayors, congressmen, even senators. They was mine. I picked 'em. I elected 'em. They belonged to me, lock, stock and barrel."

Part Two

At the Top
1927-1936

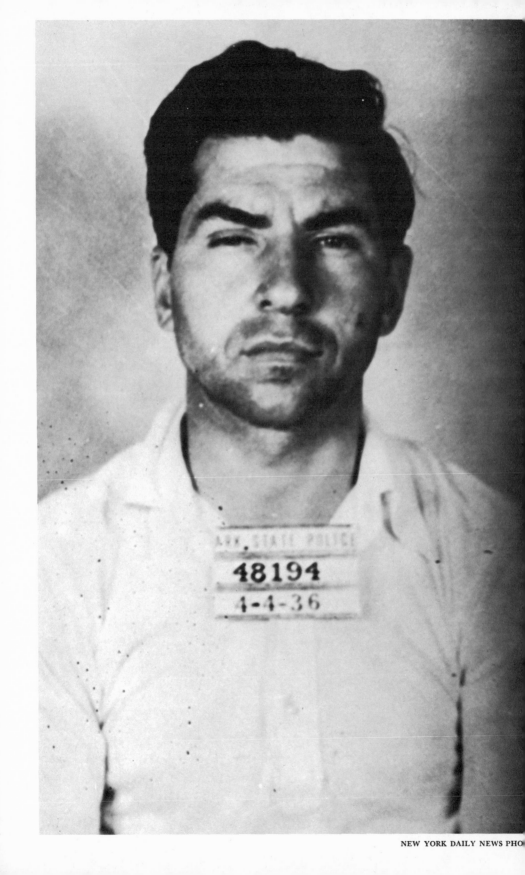

ARK STATE POLICE

48194

4-4-36

8.

There was no letup of the pressure from both Maranzano and Masseria for Lucania to make a decision and join forces with one or the other, to put an end to his hesitation and delays. The more important he became in the underworld, the more intense the wooing, though behind the soft words there began to creep in a hint of threat, a sense of ultimatum, particularly from Masseria. Whenever they met, Masseria's comments became more pointed. "Then in 1927, Red Levine — he was the best driver and hit man I had — told me that Masseria sent a message he wanted to see me and a couple of my guys right away, that we was to come to a room at the Hotel Manger on Seventh Avenue at four o'clock in the afternoon."

In the tone of the message there was more of a demand than an invitation, and Lucania quickly called a meeting of his closest friends — Lansky, Costello, Adonis, Siegel, Genovese and Frank Scalise, summoned from Brooklyn. ("That was my board of directors, you might say.") They met at the back of Moe Ducore's drugstore on Seventh Avenue; Lucania owned a piece of it, it had become a favorite hangout, and it was almost directly across the street from the Manger. "I sent Nick Gentile and Red Levine over to case the hotel while I had a session with my guys. Lansky started it off, and that kinda surprised me, because most of the time he would wait and let everybody else talk first."

Lansky was certain he knew the reason for Masseria's summons. "Let's not sit here jerkin' off," he said. "This is the showdown. It's gotta be yes or no, either Charlie goes with Joe the Boss or there's gonna be a lot of blood spilled."

Jumping to his feet and pacing the floor, Siegel, as usual, was all for violent action. "Masseria's a fat old bastard, and we don't need him. If Charlie throws in with him, he knows we'll stick with Charlie and so he'll get Meyer and me and then he'll have enough guns to steal every goddamn thing we've all been buildin'. Charlie, I say we oughta pile through that door at four o'clock and knock him right off." ("Bugsy was the only nut I ever knew who had real ice water and absolutely no fear in them days.")

The argument that followed was strident, with everyone shouting and taking differing views. Finally, Genovese took one of the pharmacist's brass mortars and threw it on the floor. Into the sudden silence, he said, "For chrissake, what the hell are you all yellin' about? You know goddamn well that Charlie has to make the decision, and that he's gonna do it. So why don't we give him a chance to hear himself think."

"That was typical of Vito. That little prick used to kiss my ass every time he had the chance. He was always tryin' to show his loyalty. Anyway, I did make the decision, and everybody went along with it. This was the day for me to join us up with Joe Masseria. I had already made up my mind that I couldn't go with Maranzano; I couldn't get over the feelin' that used to stick in my throat, that Don Salvatore was my enemy. He was always tryin' to prove that he was superior, that nobody could be his equal. I didn't wanna put myself in a position where I hadda kiss his ring at nine o'clock every mornin'. As far as Masseria was concerned, I thought he was a big fat bundle of shit. I figured I could handle him and work out a deal to join him without havin' to give up all our whiskey business, which was really fantastic by that time." And there was another logic that dictated the move to Masseria; his territory included midtown and upper Manhattan, while Maranzano operated mainly downtown and around Wall Street. In combination with Masseria, Lucania would have a lock on the wealth of midtown and above, and with Masseria to boost him, he was sure he could muscle Maranzano out of the Wall Street district.

And, too, there was another consideration. "I was sure that sooner or later, more sooner than later, Maranzano and Masseria would have a war. Them two fuckin' Sicilians would never be happy until one of 'em got rubbed out. To me, the whole thing was a matter of organizin' a business; for them, it was the pride that came first — who was gonna be the Boss of Bosses. I figured

— and this was one time I was dead wrong — that Masseria would wind up on top."

Just before four that afternoon, Lucania and Adonis left Moe Ducore's and crossed the street to the Manger. "We was both a little nervous, me especially, because I knew that if this was the wrong move, it was gonna set all of us back ten years." He knew that much would depend on the way he comported himself during the meeting. "I knew I was gonna have to feel my way, and I wasn't gonna do nothin' that would cut off the guys who had been my best friends from the beginnin'."

It was not an easy situation into which he was walking that afternoon. In recent months, Masseria had taken little trouble to disguise his growing bitterness over Lucania's continued refusal to throw in with him. There was no doubt in anyone's mind that Joe the Boss wanted a share, at the very least, of Lucania's multi-million-dollar liquor business, which continued to flourish as though nothing could stem its growth. But perhaps more, he wanted Lucania personally, for with Charlie Lucania at his side, with Lucania's political connections and protection, with all his other interests, with the guns and men he would bring to a merger, Masseria's strength would be multiplied, would so far exceed Maranzano's that there was doubt that a challenge would even be mounted, let alone have a chance to succeed.

Lucania and Adonis rode the elevator to the second floor of the Manger, where Masseria maintained a suite of offices. As they approached the door, they noticed a chambermaid's room with the door slightly ajar; Gentile and Levine were hiding there. And then they were with Masseria. "I was surprised to see he only had one guy with him, Joe [Giuseppe] Catania, who was very high up in his outfit. But there was doors to two rooms on both sides, so Adonis and me didn't know whether Masseria had anybody else listenin' in. I was pretty surprised to see Catania there, because some of my boys had been tellin' me for years, ever since Masseria started to talk to me about joinin' up with him, that Catania hated my guts."

As they came through the door, Masseria was seated at a round table, in the center of the room, that was covered with platters of Italian delicacies, hors d'oeuvres, meats, shellfish, toasted peppers, a tureen of pasta, sauces and cheeses. "There was enough on that table for a banquet and I kept figurin' that any minute half of Masseria's mob was gonna show up and sweep down on that table. But nobody showed. I think Masseria ate half of all that food himself, most of it with his fingers — and if he didn't look like a pig on two legs, I never saw one. He was one happy guy that day, talkin' and laughin', tellin' jokes, talkin' about the time he was in Sicily before I was born, and all that crap. And it really bothered me. I was expectin' to deal with a rough guy, but this old guy I was lookin' at as he was stuffin' himself was just too fuckin' happy to make me feel good."

When Masseria could eat no more, he looked up at Lucania and Adonis with a grin on his face and said, "Have you boys got a piece on you?"

"I got sore and I said, 'Cut out the crap, Joe. You said you wanted to have a meet. I don't bring *pistolas* to a meet unless it's with an enemy. Are you tryin' to tell me that you're an enemy?' "

Masseria laughed, his jowls quivering. He nodded to Catania and said, "Find out if these two boys are my enemies." Catania gave them an expert frisking and then shook his head at Masseria, who promptly rose, approached Lucania and put his hand on Charlie's arm. "Now you have a chance to be my friend or the both of you are dead men."

And so the ultimatum was in the open. "Joe, you oughta know by now that I'm not afraid of you," Lucania said. "I came here to talk business, and Joe A. is here with me as a witness. I'll give it to you straight; okay, I join up with you." Masseria smiled with pleasure, but before he could do more Lucania had something else to say. "But I've got some conditions, Joe. I have to be number two man, above everybody but you. I want a fair piece of the action, and I put into the pot everythin' that me and my guys do — everything, that is, except not one fuckin' drop of whiskey." Then Lucania waited.

Masseria's eyes bulged from his head, a mouthful of still unmasticated food spurted from his mouth all over the rug, and along with it a hoarse roar of protest and invective. He stomped around the room, grabbed dishes, a crystal table lamp, other bric-abrac, and threw them at the walls. Lucania and Adonis remained silent, watching. Catania seemed frightened, backing away.

With the same suddenness with which he had turned on his rage, Masseria turned it off. He bellowed a laugh, swung around, and put his hand on Lucania's arm again. "You dirty, skinny son of a bitch! You're the only *paisan* in this whole fuckin' town who ain't afraid of Joe the Boss. Okay, Charlie Lucania, you got a deal." He squeezed Lucania's hand in a viselike grip, pumping it up and down, then grabbed a huge handkerchief from his pocket to soak up the perspiration that was pouring down his face.

"It was really hard for Joe A. and me to believe that Masseria wanted us so bad that he was willin' to show it like that. The rest was easy and we walked out of there about fifteen minutes later, after a couple glasses of wine to close the deal, and as of that minute I was the number one lieutenant to Joe Masseria. But there was lots of good conditions, all my whiskey operations still belonged to me and my guys, and we had a clear-cut agreement there wouldn't be no hijackings of any kind and we would supply all of Masseria's joints with everything from whiskey to beer. Dutch Schultz was controllin' all the good beer in Manhattan by that time and I talked to him before the meet and got his backin'." And Masseria offered no objections to Lucania's maintaining his partnership with his old friends, who were Jews and non-Sicilian Italians.

Minutes later, when Lucania and Adonis reported back to their friends at the rear of the drugstore, they were greeted with disbelief. "Even Costello, who smiled maybe once a year, started to laugh, and he said, 'You're gonna make mincemeat outa Joe the Boss, and that's a lotta meat to chop up.'

"Then I got serious and I said to 'em, 'I wanna admit somethin'. I was wrong when I figured that Masseria could win a war with Maranzano. Not a chance. He's too fat, too old, and behind all that hard front there's nothin' left but a soft brain. It's only a matter of time, so let's use it the best way we can.'"

It took only a few hours for the word to spread that Lucania and Masseria had joined forces, with Lucania the new number two man in Joe the Boss's family. The strength implied won him new power, but it did not ease what Lucania knew was a delicate situation. He was certain that Masseria would not for long accept the holdout of the liquor business from his control. It was, then, necessary to flatter and placate Masseria constantly. "I told all my guys that the only way we could keep that fat bastard's nose out of our liquor deals was to kiss his ass in public a dozen times a day. In fact, I made up all kinds of words for us to use with him, like, 'Joe, when they made you, they broke the mold,' and 'Nobody in New York can handle this business like you can,' and 'What you forgot, Maranzano'll never know,' all that kinda crap. And that soft-brained Masseria used to lap it up like a cat lickin' cream. He'd sit there and smile and fiddle with that big gold chain he used to wear across his vest, and he'd nod his head like we was little kids payin' attention to the teacher. Shit, he really used to make me vomit."

Initially, at the end of 1927, Lucania attempted to devote much of his time to Masseria's business, working out of a two-room suite that Joe the Boss rented adjacent to his own office at the Hotel Pennsylvania. "That's where I started to organize his whole fucked-up operation. And except for not gettin' the liquor, he didn't have much to complain about. I was givin' him my time, Costello threw the slot machines into the deal, Schultz gimme about fifty speaks to toss into the pot as a show of his good faith, I combined some of the Lepke-Lucchese action with Masseria's loansharkin', and he even got Meyer and Bugsy, who was the top protection guys in the country by then. At least Masseria was smart enough to see that even though they was Jews, they could save him a fortune by protectin' the robberies the outfit was pullin' off all the time in midtown. It was a lot of business to tie up right, but in about six months, I had it all runnin' smooth as silk."

Of the more than two hundred men Lucania now had working for him, the only one he had trouble with at this moment was Joe Catania, who tried to undercut him by spreading the rumor that the merger was only a temporary thing and Lucania would not last long. About two o'clock one morning, after spending the evening at the Palais d'Or listening to Paul Whiteman's band, Lucania dropped by his Hotel Pennsylvania office. As he came in the door, he saw Catania prying open the drawer in his desk. "I don't know what this idiot thought he was gonna find, on account of we never kept no records in an open place like that. He didn't hear me come in, and I stood in the dark watchin' him. As soon as he got the drawer open, I walked over and slammed it on his right hand. While he was screamin' and moanin', I dragged him into Joe's office, dumped him on the floor, and called Masseria to tell him to send a doctor to take care of his boy. Catania used to be a pretty good bowler with the duckpins, but after that session with me, he never bowled again. And I never had no trouble with him after that, either. And all the guys in the Masseria family, they was my slaves from that night on."

For half a year, Lucania devoted himself to modernizing the Masseria empire. He brought to it the theories and techniques he had developed as an independent, emphasizing the necessity of careful planning before undertaking any kind of job — from a warehouse burglary to attempts to capture new markets for olive oil, cheese or any of the other Masseria monopolies. He instituted rigid discipline and tight controls from the top, and he fostered cooperation with noncompeting gangs. Under his executive eye, the Masseria empire flourished even more than in the past. And during this period, new power and respect poured down on Lucania, from Moe Dalitz and his Cleveland allies, in and out of the Mayfield Road gang; from Al Capone, who was having increasing troubles with Bugs Moran on Chicago's North Side and deemed it both profitable and expedient to forge strong ties with Lucania in the East; from the Purple Gang in Detroit, which needed Scotch to augment the Canadian whiskey it was ferrying across the Detroit River; from Harry Stromberg, better known as Nig Rosen, who had moved into a position of equality in Philadelphia with Waxey Gordon and Bitsy Bitz.

Then Torrio returned from Italy, one step ahead of Mussolini's Black Shirts, and decided to eschew the blood-soaked battlefields of Chicago and settle in New York. He renewed his friendship with Lucania and others and began to talk up an idea that Lucania, too, had been considering for some time both as a business practicality and as a way of strengthening his position so that the tightrope he was walking with Masseria would not turn into a noose. The idea was that the most important bootleggers in and out of New York should combine, at the very least in a loose alliance that would guarantee continued sources of supply to all and would, in the unity, protect all from powerful outsiders such as Maranzano.

In discussions with Torrio — now the underworld's elder statesman, a power not so much for what he controlled but because of his farsighted ideas, his perceptions, his criminal expertise and his organizational talents — Lucania and his friends debated, weeded, and finally selected those they considered the strongest allies. The merger was limited to seven outfits by Lucania, the perennial gambler who had implicit faith in that lucky number. The "Seven Group," as they called it, was indeed a formidable alliance in the bootlegging world: Lansky and Siegel, whose Bug and Meyer Gang covered New York, New Jersey and surrounding areas, and who functioned as prime protectors, enforcers and shippers; Joe Adonis, who operated mainly in Brooklyn; Longie Zwillman and Willie Moretti, whose territory consisted of Nassau County (in western Long Island) and northern New Jersey (including Newark, Jersey City, and Fort Lee); Bitz, Gordon and Rosen from Philadelphia; King Solomon of Boston, who ruled much of New England; Nucky Johnson from Atlantic City, the ruler of the South Jersey coast; and, of course, Lucania and Torrio.

So successful was the Seven Group in its cooperative ventures that by the end of 1928, it had struck cooperative alliances — for buying, selling, distilling, shipping and protecting — with twenty-two different mobs from Maine to Florida and west to the Mississippi River. The man who pulled it all together, who had the growing respect and trust of all his contemporaries and associates, was Charlie Lucania. As a kind of ex officio commander-in-chief of the group, he found that his New York headquarters was the clearinghouse where all the intricate problems of the Seven Group were handled. And the man Lucania assigned the task of coordinating the business, of seeing that his decisions were expedited, was Vito Genovese, whom he sometimes called "the Italian Bugsy Siegel." Genovese's main area of responsibility was in Manhattan, the center of Lucania's own empire. Italians were more and more coming to the front in that borough, and he felt it would be wiser to set another Italian — Genovese — to dealing with them than the Jews, Lansky and Siegel.

The only other Lucania interest that remained outside the cover of the Masseria canopy revolved about the joint gambling enterprises he was plying with Arnold Rothstein and Rothstein's newly acquired associate, a beefy, red-faced Scandinavian named Frank Erickson. Rothstein had taken on Erickson to handle his high-level bookmaking business, which dealt only with such big-stakes bettors as Harry Cohn, head of Columbia Pictures, and other corporate and financial executives. While Rothstein handled poker games where there was no limit on bets and, on his own, had begun to move into the narcotics business in a major way, Erickson dealt with the horseplayers, even accompanying them to the tracks around the city and personally handling their bets so that the regular track odds would not be affected. This was the beginning for Erickson; after Rothstein's death in November of 1928, his bookmaking business, on his own and in partnership with Costello, flourished so greatly that over the next twenty years he became perhaps the biggest and most important bookie in New York.

For Lucania, continued support for Rothstein was not only a repayment for earlier favors done, but was also smart business, and it paid off early in 1928. The Seven Group was then a fledgling, and responsibility for seeing the liquor supplies were adequate to the needs of the group had been given to Lucania. At first, he handled this assignment with his usual flair and efficiency, but then that winter a series of unexpected hijackings combined with the foundering and sinking of a whiskey-laden freighter off Cape Hatteras conspired to wipe out the Scotch inventory. "It was such a tough situation that I hadda call everybody together to figure somethin' out. Adonis went down to Philly to see if he could get some extra quota from Waxey or Nig Rosen, or maybe even cut some of our stuff a little thinner, to tide us over. But that would only be a drop in the bucket. We had deals with Detroit, Cleveland, Connecticut, and a lotta other places, for Scotch that we suddenly didn't have, and it didn't look like we had no place to get it. I even had a private meet with Tommy Lucchese, hopin' maybe we could work out a way to trade off some stuff with some of the guys in Maranzano's outfit, where he was still friendly. But no soap. It looked like a pretty crummy spot for me to be in."

Then from Chicago appeared a man named Samuel Bloom, who had made a fortune acquiring prescriptions for medicinal alcohol from friendly doctors and selling them to Capone. A man of education and cultivation, Bloom dressed well and traveled widely, something that had led to a friendship with Rothstein. Now he arrived in New York bearing greetings from Capone. "When I called Al to check on this guy Sam Bloom, Al was sore as hell, because Bloom went to Europe when Capone was lookin' for him in Chicago. He couldn't believe anybody would take two weeks off to go back and forth across the Atlantic Ocean. And when Al asked Bloom if he went to Italy, Al was sore as hell when Bloom told him that he never went there."

Soon after meeting Lucania, Bloom sought out his New York friend Arnold Rothstein, and then sat in on one of the gambler's poker games at the Park Central Hotel. Bloom and an Englishman who had dropped most of his cash in the game left together about dawn. As they rode down in the elevator, they began to talk, and Bloom, feeling some sympathy over the other man's losses, asked, "Do you want me to try to get it back for you?"

The reply sent Bloom scurrying to Lucania. The Englishman shrugged off the losses, explaining that he could well afford them because he was a major owner of the distillery in Scotland that made King's Ransom Scotch, perhaps the most valued of the whiskeys to the bootleggers because its heavy, smoky quality made it easy to dilute without losing its flavor. Bloom was certain he could set up a deal if Lucania wanted. There was no hesitation; Lucania didn't even bother to consult his Seven Group partners; he knew they would go along with the opportunity to corner the market in this Scotch, especially at this moment of extreme shortage. Bloom went back to his English friend, cablegrams were sent to Glasgow, and soon boatloads of King's Ransom were flowing into the Seven Group's pipelines through Nucky Johnson's Atlantic City landing zone and King Solomon's port of Boston. (When the age of Prohibition ended, Frank Costello turned up as the major legal American importer of King's Ransom.)

For some months, it was a smooth operation. Then, near the

end of 1928, about fifteen thousand cases of King's Ransom were landed in Boston, loaded on trucks, and started on their way to New York. They never arrived; somewhere along the road, they were hijacked — a loss to the Seven Group of close to $1 million in the liquor's street value.

"All us guys in the bootleggin' business knew that hijackin' was part of the business; we'd beef about it a lot and then forget it. But this time, we all had the feelin' it was somethin' a little bit different from the ordinary heist. I asked Vito to put his sharp Neapolitan nose to work and investigate." What Genovese discovered was that Bloom had dropped a hundred thousand dollars in a poker game at Rothstein's, had given the gambler his I.O.U., payable in a week, and then had paid up — the day after the hijacking. Lucania called Rothstein and the story was confirmed. "It seemed to be open and shut that Bloom had finagled the hijackin'. There wasn't no absolute proof, but with things like that, you didn't take a guy to court. You pronounced your own sentence. All the guys agreed. So, a little while later, Bugsy gave Sam Bloom a cement funeral."

Bloom's disappearance — his body, unlike others sunk in the rivers around Manhattan, never surfaced — upset nothing. He was not missed; his absence barely drew comment. He had been only the middleman, arranging the deal between the British distillers and distributors of King's Ransom and Lucania and the Seven Group. Even without him, the whiskey continued to flow without interruption into the Seven Group's pipeline.

Though the success of the Seven Group seemed assured from the beginning and its business grew steadily, "I began to feel very shaky about the whiskey business." By 1928, there were mounting signs that the Noble Experiment could not remain a permanent part of American life. It had turned a large part of the nation into lawbreakers, and many Americans, even some who hailed its original purpose, had begun to tire of it, to see it as an experiment that had failed.

Some of these opponents began to look for leadership to the governor of New York, Al Smith. Regularly, he derided the "drys" and called for repeal of the Eighteenth Amendment. In 1924, he had tried, and failed, to capture the Democratic nomination for President. By 1928, however, he seemed unstoppable.

"One day, in the early part of 1928, Costello picked me up and took me to a private house — I think it was in Westchester — and it belonged to a millionaire named John J. Raskob. He had a lot to do with puttin' up the Empire State Buildin', and he was a big backer of Governor Al Smith. I almost fell over when I walked in and saw Smith standin' there in person, in Raskob's library. I'd met a lotta big shots by then, but that was the first time I even knew that Costello had made contacts as high up as Al Smith.

"The Governor was a tall guy with a husky voice, somethin' like Costello's, and it had the streets in it, just like ours. He shook hands with me and said, 'Hello, Charlie, it's a pleasure to meetcha.'

"I looked at him and started to laugh. 'What the hell are you doin', Governor? You're tryin' to put me out of business.'

"He sort of smiled and said, 'No, I'm not. I brought you up here to do you a favor. Naturally, being a politician, I expect to get a favor in return. Whyn't you sit down and listen to what I have to tell you.'

"So we all sat down and Raskob poured some drinks; and I was too dumb to shut my mouth. I said, 'Governor, you're tryin' to repeal Prohibition, and that's gonna throw us all outa business.'

"Smith kinda brushed that aside and told me, 'My boy, in a couple of years, there won't be any Prohibition at all. I intend to get that nomination and I intend to win this election. I'm tellin' you, and I'm going to tell the American people that when I get in the White House, I'm personally going to see to it that the Volstead Act and the Eighteenth Amendment are thrown in the wastebasket, legally. That's why I brought you here. Costello has told me all about you, and I need your support right here in my own state. There are two things I want you to do: take my advice and make your plans to get into the legitimate end of the whiskey business; and, second, line up overwhelming support for me from Manhattan, Brooklyn and the Bronx, where you fellows control the delegates. I want every one of those delegates at the convention in Houston. If I get them, I'm prepared to make things good for you.'

"That's just the way he put it, and it kinda made my head swim, that maybe we'd found ourselves a President. I couldn't help but think about Hampton Farms and the Brooklyn Truancy School and I wondered whether my old man would believe me if I told him about this. We shook hands all around. Then I did somethin' real smart, and it made the Governor look at me with more respect. I told him I wanted to think about what he said before givin' him an answer. That was the truth, anyway, because I wanted to go back to the city and talk to Johnny Torrio. What Smith had been talkin' about, the end of Prohibition, was exactly what Torrio had predicted before he run out to Italy. I knew somethin' hadda be done, because now I was absolutely sure that Al Smith's figurin' was right. I kept sayin' to Frank all the way back to the city that I still couldn't figure how legit whiskey could pay off anythin' close to bootleggin'. I said, 'You know, Frank, we been in the rackets all our lives. Maybe we ain't got the imagination for a straight business.'

"'Charlie,' Costello told me, 'in our group we got enough imagination for any kind of business. It don't scare me at all to go legit as far as whiskey is concerned. That don't mean we've got to give up gamblin'; and we can do that in a big way. We can have big casinos all over the country. What the hell, more people like to gamble than drink. I think we oughta get behind Smith. At least with him, we know where we stand.' "

And, indeed, they backed Al Smith all the way. He captured the Democratic nomination, but in November he was buried in the Hoover and Republican landslide. His stand on legal liquor was only a minor factor. Smith was a Roman Catholic, the first Catholic to run for President in a Protestant nation where suspicions of Catholics as tools of the Pope in Rome were widespread; he was from the big city, New York, with the accents and manners of the metropolis basic to his nature, while the nation itself was still essentially rural and suspicious of cities; he was a Democrat while the nation was in the midst of an unparalleled prosperity many believed had been brought about by the Republican administrations; and he offered change at a time when the national mood was to keep things as they were.

What Lucania and his associates in the Seven Group read into the election returns was a sign that Prohibition would be around for some time to come. They were sure that as long as national prosperity continued — and they, along with most of the nation, could see no signs of its ending — the nation would opt for stability and against any change that would rock the boat, resulting in resistance to ending the increasingly unpopular Noble Experiment. (This they believed right up until that black week in October 1929 when the stock market crashed.)

So the bootleg business boomed along with the rest of the economy in the dizzying days of the final months of prosperity. But in that whiskey boom, there were problems: fierce competition for supplies was driving prices up wherever whiskey was made and could be bought — in Europe, Canada, the Caribbean. The chaos would end, the bitterness resulting from such competition would be halted, and everyone would profit only if some order, some logical sense of allocation could be agreed upon by the major racket bosses.

"Costello and me talked it over with Torrio and Lansky first. I asked Meyer to put out a few feelers around the country, to see if the top guys would be willin' to make a meet — you might say, like a national convention of our own."

It took months, through the end of 1928 and into 1929, before arrangements reached a conclusive stage for such a meeting. Meanwhile, Lucania was having other problems. "Masseria kept on my ass every two minutes; he was forever callin' me up to find out why I wasn't with him, or why the fuck I was sleepin' late, why I didn't go on a job the night before. That son of a bitch was always tryin' to turn me into a chambermaid."

Then there was Maranzano. The old Don's campaign for absolute control of the Italian underworld was becoming more open and intense. It was bringing him into conflict with other Mafiosi around the country — particularly with Masseria, with whom there was, anyway, extraordinary antipathy. "They come from opposite sides of Sicily and both of 'em brought the whole idea of vendetta with 'em when they came to America. I never seen nothin' like it. It was like in the hills of Kentucky, with families knockin' each other off for some fucked-up reason that maybe goes back a hundred years and nobody ever remembers why no more."

The hijackings by Masseria and Maranzano of each other's trucks increased, and so did strife in almost every area. Masseria responded by sending gunmen to kill a Maranzano ally named Gaspar Milazzo, a native of Maranzano's hometown of Castellammare, who had become the *capo* in Detroit. The move welded other natives of the Castellammare region tighter to Maranzano, and Masseria replied by declaring open season on any native of Castellammare and anyone allied to Maranzano. And so began the Castellammarese War, which dominated events in the Italian underworld until late in 1931.

"All us younger guys hated the old mustaches and what they was doin'. We was tryin' to build a business that'd move with the times and they was still livin' a hundred years ago. We knew the old guys and their ideas hadda go; we was just markin' time. The way we looked at it was that gettin' rid of a Masseria or a Maranzano was no different from some bank tearin' down an old buildin' so they could put up a new one. For us, rubbin' out a mustache was just like makin' way for a new buildin', like we was in the construction business."

But Lucania became greatly concerned when his friend Tommy "Three Finger Brown" Lucchese found himself in the middle of the approaching feud. Lucchese had become a trusted underboss to Tom Reina, head of his own outfit in the Bronx, which had given allegiance to Masseria. But as the battle was beginning to surface, Maranzano assiduously wooed Reina, offering him in exchange for support a share of the income from Masseria's rackets on the Lower East Side. "Tommy come to me and he told me the whole story. He said that Reina forced him to go with him to a secret meet with Maranzano, and Tommy was surprised that Reina seemed to like Maranzano's deal. That took a lotta guts on Reina's part, because by this time Masseria was ready to murder anybody who even looked in the direction of Maranzano.

"It's a funny thing about the Sicilians. There just ain't no secrets. There's always somebody that'll sell out one of his own. Lots of guys got fingered just for the prospect that somethin' might happen. So, naturally, Masseria got word about Reina meetin' with Maranzano. Reina was no little potato. He was a boss. And under the old-time rules, a boss don't get hit — pop, just like that. But in the case of Tommy Lucchese, that was different. It was all I could do to convince Joe that Tommy went with Reina to find out what was goin' on and report to me. If Joe hadn't bought the story, Tommy was as good as dead. But the whole situation seemed to turn Masseria into a ravin' lunatic. He used to call me from all over New York a half a dozen times a day with a new name of a guy he wanted to bump off. He was drivin' me crazy."

The demands by Masseria for demonstrations of absolute loyalty reached a climax in November of 1928. Lucania and Masseria were together in the back seat of a car, with Adonis acting as chauffeur. "That fat bastard pulls out a thirty-eight from his coat pocket and hands it to me and says, 'You're gonna carry this tonight on the payroll job. It ain't got no numbers.'

"I thought he was out of his fuckin' head, because he was talkin' about a payroll heist he wanted me to plan for some of our guys maybe four or five months before, and nothin' ever come of it. So I said, 'Listen, for chrissake, I thought I was supposed to be runnin' things; since when do I go back on the street with a *pistola?*'

"Joe grabbed the gun outa my hand and held it right against my belly. 'Listen to me, you son of a bitch, you either pull that job or I'll give it to you right here in the car. You made the plan for that job, and you gotta do it — because I say so.'

"Up front, I see Adonis noddin' his head, meanin' for me to go along; he could see the same thing I could, that the old mustache was just crazy enough to pull the trigger right in broad daylight. What the hell could I do? I took the gun back and I said to Masseria, 'Joe, take my word, this is one of your biggest mistakes.' "

Lucania was dropped off in the garment district, on Seventh Avenue, and he found waiting for him in a car Red Levine and a new recruit in the organization, Paul Mineo. The three drove to the Corn Exchange Bank at Thirty-seventh Street, parked, and left the motor running. It was nearly bank closing time, and a payroll messenger for a large textile company was just leaving with the payroll in a canvas bag. "Paulie jumped outa the car and knocked the old geezer down and grabbed the bag. One of the bank guards was lockin' the door and he sees what's happenin'." The guard fired a shot and hit Mineo, who fell to the pavement. Lucania jumped from the car, grabbed Mineo, who was bleeding heavily, picked up the canvas bag, and pulled both into the car. Levine gunned the motor and sped away. They got only a couple of blocks before police caught up with them and arrested them with an eight-thousand-dollar payroll in their possession.

"It took every bit of political muscle that Costello and me had to get the whole thing squared away. Costello managed to get the charges squashed and the record fixed up so it was listed as an error. But we hadda go to the police commissioner's office to squash things, and that error cost us a helluva lot more than eight grand. But in a way, I was almost glad the heist failed. My first thought was that it'd gimme a chance to tell Masseria off for bein' such a stubborn prick, and I swore that'd be the last time Masseria or anyone else would put me in that kind of situation."

For a short time thereafter, Masseria eased the pressure on Lucania a little. This gave Lucania a chance to turn his attention to his own business, and to the impending underworld conference. The response from around the country to the proposal had been favorable. The convention would be held in Atlantic City, where Nucky Johnson ruled supreme and the delegates could come and go as they pleased without attracting attention or suspicion, and where Johnson could insure that nothing would be lacking to cater to all their pleasures and tastes.

The only remaining question was a date, and that was easily resolved. Meyer Lansky was getting married early in May 1929, and his friends concluded that Atlantic City would be an ideal place for a honeymoon, so that pleasure could be mixed with business.

Marriage was the second major step that Lansky, with a certain calculation growing from his secure financial position and his desire for outward respectability, had decided to take in a period of just over six months. In October 1928, he became an American citizen, and, as they would at his wedding, his friends danced at his naturalization, though this time without invitation. Lansky's desire then, as through his life, was only to fade into the background unobtrusively. But his friends showed up at the Brooklyn Federal

Courthouse. "We walked into this big room and there's a whole bunch of people there. The smell of garlic could've knocked you over, on account of at least half the would-be citizens was Italian and they was dressed to kill, some of 'em even wearin' tuxedos to show they'd made a few bucks. Frank, Benny, Joe, Vito and me spotted Lansky standin' in the back, tryin' to look nonchalant and superior, wearin' a blue serge suit and tryin' to make out like he's a banker from Moscow, and he stood out like a sore thumb among all those weird costumes and fancy clothes. We sneaked up behind Meyer and Benny Siegel whispers in his ear, 'Hey, Lansky, I can fix ya up with that broad — the blonde one over there. I hear her old man owns half of Delancey Street,' and he points at this blonde girl standin' over near the window with her father and mother. She was about eighteen, but she weighed about three hundred pounds, which is about three times as much as Meyer weighed soakin' wet.

"I've seen Lansky pretty mad in my lifetime, but even when he was knockin' a guy off, he was never as sore as that minute. With just one move, he kicked Bugsy right in the balls and then grabbed his mouth so he wouldn't yell and make too much noise. A couple minutes later, Meyer walked out holdin' his naturalization papers and Benny was holdin' his balls."

Then, in May of 1929, Lansky married Anna Citron, a devout, old-fashioned Jewish girl whose father was a moderately successful produce dealer in Hoboken, New Jersey (and who, as a wedding present, put his new son-in-law on the payroll, thereby giving Lansky a respectable front and an opportunity he would later turn to his own end). In the second week of May, they journeyed for their honeymoon to Atlantic City.

They were not the only arrivals along the Boardwalk. The big black limousines carrying sinister passengers arrived from all over the country. Capone arrived from Chicago, bringing with him his close ally, Jake "Greasy Thumb" Guzik (the nickname coming from Guzik's astonishing speed in flipping through a stack of bills with a wet thumb and never losing count); King Solomon drove down from Boston; Boo-Boo Hoff, Waxey Gordon and Nig Rosen came up from Philadelphia; from Cleveland came Moe Dalitz and his allies, Lou Rothkopf and Charles Polizzi (real name, Leo Berkowitz, the adopted son of the Mafia-affiliated Polizzi family); a whole delegation of the Purple Gang came from Detroit, doing the bidding of its leader, Abe Bernstein; Boss Tom Pendergast of Kansas City sent a surrogate, John Lazia; Longie Zwillman and Willie Moretti represented New York's Nassau County and northern New Jersey. The largest delegation was from New York City. Led by Lucania, it numbered among its members Torrio, Lansky and his bride (who was unaware of the real reason for the choice of Atlantic City for a honeymoon), Costello, Lepke, Adonis, Frank Erickson (still in mourning for Arnold Rothstein) and Dutch Schultz; from Brooklyn there were Albert Anastasia, Vince Mangano and Frank Scalise.

Absent were the old Dons, Maranzano and Masseria. As Masseria's second-in-command, Lucania had debated whether to invite Joe the Boss and had finally decided against doing so not only because he regarded liquor as his private domain, despite Masseria's grumbling, but mainly because he had no intention of giving up his leadership position at Atlantic City, which Masseria's presence would have required him to do.

Originally, Johnson had reserved suites for his guests at the Breakers, then one of the most exclusive hotels along the Boardwalk. It was a mistake and caused Johnson considerable embarrassment (and the owners of the Breakers some trouble later). The hotel was restricted to white Protestants, and Johnson had made all the reservations in Anglo-Saxon aliases. But one look at Capone, Rosen and the rest was enough; they were refused rooms on the spot, and not with polite words. It was apparent that the manager did not know to whom he was refusing service.

A hurried call to Nucky Johnson, a quick call by him, and then the fleet of limousines pulled out of the Breakers's driveway and headed for the President Hotel. Before they arrived, Nucky Johnson, resplendent as usual with a red carnation in his lapel, joined the cavalcade. When Capone spotted him, he brought the parade to a halt in the middle of the street. "Nucky and Al had it out right there in the open. Johnson was about a foot taller than Capone and both of 'em had voices like foghorns. I think you could've heard 'em in Philadelphia, and there wasn't a decent word passed between 'em. Johnson had a rep for four-letter words that wasn't even invented, and Capone is screamin' at me that I made bad arrangements. So Nucky picks Al up under one arm and throws him into his car and yells out, 'All you fuckers follow me!' "

The motorcade wound up at the Ritz, behind which loomed Johnson's own mansion, and the Ambassador next door. Capone was still enraged. He stormed into the small, quiet Ritz lobby and began ripping pictures off the wall and throwing them at Johnson. "So everybody got over bein' mad and concentrated on keepin' Al quiet. That's the way our convention started."

For the first days, there was a constant round of parties, with plenty of liquor, food and girls. For those who had brought wives or girl friends, Johnson had presents of fur capes. Lansky, the bridegroom, was given the Presidential Suite at the Ritz, with a constant supply of French champagne. "I don't know where Johnson got all that bubbly, because the son of a bitch didn't get it from my outfit, on account of we never handled it. Meyer and Anna was really livin' it up, but durin' the next few days I could see that some of our friends from out of town made her a little nervous."

Each morning, the delegates would breakfast in their suites and then wander out to the Boardwalk, climb into the canopied promenade roller-chairs, each accommodating two passengers and pushed by attendants, and roll at a measured pace along the oceanfront, talking about the weather. "How the hell could we talk about anythin' else with them niggers breathin' down our necks?"

Near the end of the Boardwalk, where Atlantic City adjoined the suburb of Chelsea, the men would alight from their roller-chairs, remove their shoes and socks, roll their pants legs up to the knees, step onto the sand, and then, strolling at the water's edge, discuss their business in complete privacy.

All the decisions at the Atlantic City meeting were made out in the open, on the sand, during those daily walks toward Chelsea. Arrangements were struck to put an end to the cutthroat bidding for liquor abroad; henceforth there would be cooperation and allocations, and nobody would be disappointed, prices would drop, and all would be winners. It was the start of an organization, not with one man in control, but a group of organizations operating jointly, with decisions made by equals at the top, to develop a national monopoly in the liquor business.

There were discussions of what to do if Prohibition ended, and there was much talk of going legitimate when that day came. "After all, who knew more about the business than us?" Since liquor was basic to all their empires, they decided that some of their money should be set aside to buy breweries, distilleries and liquor import franchises as a hedge against possible repeal.

And there were discussions of moving in on gambling as a co-operative venture wherever local areas would permit. No decision was reached on this, for almost every delegate was jealous of his own sovereignty, chary of becoming totally dependent on any cartel other than bootlegging.

"But more important than all the whiskey deals and the gamblin' decisions was what happened when Capone ran into a guy by the name of Moses Annenberg on the Boardwalk. Annenberg was also from Chicago, and he controlled the mob that enforced distribution of William Randolph Hearst's newspapers in Chicago, which was no easy job because Chicago was a rough town with plenty of competition for the best corners and it took plenty of Annenberg's muscle to keep Hearst on top. When Capone and Annenberg met, that's when the talk got started about tyin' in the national wire service for horseplayers with the *Daily Racin' Form*. And it was right there, in Atlantic City, when most of the big deals was made for the system of layin' off bets throughout the United States. Frank Erickson was called in to work out the details of the organization, and that's how the Annenberg family really started to build its fortune, outa muscle in Chicago and its bettin' ties with us."

There was one more decision, and that dealt with Capone personally. The bloodletting in Chicago had brought a public outcry and pressure on the underworld all over the country. A sacrificial lamb was needed to ease the heat. Capone was to be the lamb. With Torrio taking the lead, and Lucania and others backing him, Capone was persuaded that for the good of the organization of the underworld, he had to let himself be arrested on a minor charge and sent away for a short time. Capone eventually heeded the dictate and went up to Philadelphia, where friendly cops picked him up for carrying a gun and he was sent off to a prison farm for several months.

Then the delegates packed up and went home. For Charlie

Lucania, it had been a highly successful few days. Some decisions, necessary ones, had been reached. The ideas for future develop- ment had been sowed. And, perhaps, most significant, other under- world leaders had seen him in operation, had listened to his views, had developed an increased respect for him. When the day came for him to make his final push to the top, he knew he could depend on their cooperation. Neither Masseria nor Maranzano, with their unconcealed views of non-Italians, could claim such support. Indeed, neither would have thought to seek it.

For Meyer Lansky, his honeymoon had been both successful and disturbing. He had enjoyed his marital pleasures, despite being the focus of constant ribaldry from his friends. But Anna's deep reli- gious commitment distressed him, as did her constant complaints about his "gangster friends" and her demands that he abandon them and go into her father's produce business full-time. Lansky carried his concern to Lucania, comparing Anna's complaints with what he had noticed in the wives of his Italian friends — that Italian girls devoted themselves to their homes and never intruded on their husband's business. Perhaps, he told Lucania, once Anna became pregnant, she would turn her mind to domestic matters and leave him alone.

But with Anna came a dividend — her father, Moses Citron. Lansky was certain he could use his father-in-law's position, and his own as a fifty-dollar-a-week employee of Kreig, Spector & Citron, as the lever to an independent empire. "Meyer didn't realize it, but I could read right into his head. He always thought he could wear a mask that nobody could see through. But I knew just what was goin' on. He was lookin' forward to the day when he could be his own number one guy. In my own mind, I thought down there in Atlantic City that when it came to matchin' up a Jew and a Sicil- ian, the odds would have to be six to five, take your choice. I was choosin' me."

9.

In the scope of all that he had accomplished and all that he was doing, it was only a minor problem, but it was one that constantly nettled Charlie Lucania. He had become, by the end of the Atlantic City meeting, one of the most important underworld figures in the nation — but only Italians seemed able to pronounce his name correctly. The family name was Lucania, with the accent on the penultimate syllable; but when his new, legitimate friends introduced him around at their golf clubs or at their private parties, and even when some of his new non-Italian underworld friends greeted him, they invariably called him Charlie Lucaynia.

The change to a more easily pronounced, and thus more easily remembered, name was a simple one. In the late fall of 1928, when he, Levine and Mineo were arrested for the payroll robbery, he gave his name to the desk sergeant as he was being booked as "Charles Luciano." It was just another alias, but he noticed that no one in the police station had any trouble pronouncing it and later he was hailed as Luciano by several cops on the street. The name had a nice feel and soon he was using it to the exclusion of his real name. It did not take long for his friends to follow suit, and so Charlie Lucania vanished and Charlie Luciano came into being.

Along with a new name, he changed his style of living. As his importance grew, so too did the number of people calling at his door for favors. He decided to seek the anonymity of a hotel, with its staff of buffers — room clerks, telephone operators, friendly bellboys. His first thought was of the Park Central, where Arnold Rothstein had lived. "But after Rothstein went, I didn't think that place was good luck. Besides, I wanted to have some kind of view. All through the twenties, when I started to get into the big dough, I still couldn't look out the window of any place where I lived and see a tree. If I was gonna move, that was one thing I was gonna have plenty of — trees."

So he wandered along Central Park South between Sixth and Seventh avenues, with its ranks of residential hotels, and finally settled on the Barbizon Plaza. There he rented an apartment on a high floor with the panorama of Central Park spread out beneath him. His name on the register was "Charles Lane." "When I moved in, it was winter and the Central Park Lake was frozen. Lots of times, it looked like half the city of New York was out there ice-skatin' on it. Whenever I had a tough problem, I could stand at my window and look out and watch the skaters — the little kids and their mothers — and it made me feel very peaceful; it cleared my head.

"Walter Winchell had an apartment across the street, at the St. Moritz Hotel, and somehow or other he found out I was movin' into his neighborhood and I heard he didn't like it too much. I said to myself, 'Fuck him.' Sometimes I'd take a walk down Central Park South and once in a while I'd see Winchell. I'd wave to him and say, 'Hi, neighbor.' It burnt him to a crisp."

It was about this time, too, that Luciano met Gay Orlova, a featured dancer at the Hollywood, one of Broadway's leading nightclubs. They were brought together initially by the Hollywood's master of ceremonies and one of the rising radio celebrities of the day, Nils T. Granlund, more familiarly called by his initials, NTG. The tall, slim, dark-haired and dark-eyed dancer and the slightly sinister-looking gangster soon became almost inseparable. "There was nothin' cheap about her and she understood that I was always tryin' to improve myself. I could let my hair down with her and we got along great. She was meant for good times and that's all I was lookin' for in them days. I didn't have to go with a whole bunch of other broads because she was able to keep me interested all the time. Lots of people told me I oughta marry this girl, but she wasn't always naggin' at me to get married and besides I had too many plans to think about that. And to tell the truth, I never knew too much about her, except that she'd traveled around Europe a lot and spoke French and Russian. I never even knew her real name; Gay Orlova was a nickname somebody once give her when she was about sixteen; if you pronounced it different, it could sound like Gay All Over, which she really was."

But such moments of relaxation, pleasure and contemplation were not many. Masseria, resentful from the start of Luciano's independent realm in bootlegging, was demanding more and more of his time, putting him to work masterminding and supervising the plans and proposals of other lieutenants. The ordinary soldiers in Masseria's family continued to ply their old criminal trades assiduously; Masseria demanded, and Luciano was not averse to giving, all possible assistance. When plans were brought to him, he would sit, sometimes with his eyes closed as though sleeping, and listen, then ask questions: What kind of research had been done? Had, say, the watchman's schedule been clocked? Did they know where the goods were? Did they have enough people and cars, a good route in and out? Always he would make changes, simplify, or correct obvious and sometimes subtle miscalculations.

Then he would wait for results. If everything went right, the right fence for the furs or other merchandise at the right price would be found. This was a service Luciano performed not just for Masseria's men but for his own friends, too, like Adonis. Joe A. had early established a reputation for jewel thefts, and his penchant for dealing in stolen gems would stay with him until he died in lonely exile in Italy in 1971.

Luciano was, then, an executive concerned only with overall planning, not the direct operations — which, he would claim, removed him from direct complicity. "It was like, if you're the head of a big company, you don't have every guy who works on every machine comin' up to you and askin', 'Hey, boss, what colors should I use on the cars next year?' "

But like any good executive, Luciano would not tolerate failure. When a job about which he had not been consulted, at least on the major details, failed, or when a job misfired because his planning had not been followed scrupulously, he would exact penalties. Not firing. "Some guys got their fingers broke or their knuckles cracked or maybe had their heads busted. They hadda learn how to do it the right way the next time."

But still the demands from Masseria for more and more of his time increased, until, in the late summer of 1929, a major crisis developed in their relationship. A large shipment of Scotch, worth nearly a million dollars when finally cut and retailed, was due to land one night along the Jersey coast between Atlantic City and Cape May. The successful delivery was vital to the Seven Group, which once again had overextended itself in taking orders. Wanting to make certain there would be no slipups, Luciano decided to oversee the landing personally, and to insure absolute secrecy, he did not even tell Masseria that he would be absent from Manhattan. He left the Barbizon Plaza surreptitiously about midday, driving down to the Jersey shore with Adonis and Genovese, and followed a short time later by Lansky, Siegel and Costello.

That night, they supervised the unloadings from two Scottish freighters riding at anchor just outside the three-mile limit, then accompanied a five-truck convoy of Scotch to Philadelphia, to make certain that the warehouse division under Nig Rosen's aegis was correct.

It was long after dawn before Luciano arrived back at his hotel. He had hardly gotten into bed when his private phone rang; few people had that number and no one usually dared call him at that hour.

Masseria was on the line and he was raging. He had been trying to get Luciano all night, he said, and demanded to know where the hell his lieutenant had been when he needed him.

Luciano told him he had been out, and besides, what was so urgent that he had to call at that hour of the morning?

"A couple of punks," Masseria shouted. "They got themselves picked up on West End Avenue last night and they're in the can. I want them out — loose — right now. I need them." It seemed that Abraham "Bo" Weinberg and Charley "The Bug" Workman were being held at the East Fifty-third Street Precinct and, Masseria said, "It's your district and you're the one who usin' my money to pay off the cops there. When I need your muscle, you ain't around no more. You ain't never around lately. You're always off to your own fuckin' business. That's gotta stop, and it's gotta stop right now. I wanna see ya, right now — and we're gonna get this thing settled, you unnerstan', Mister Salvatore Lucania."

"Okay, okay. Take it easy. Maybe you better come over here, Joe." Luciano was both tired and angry, else he might never have made that suggestion. It was something he had never done, telling Joe the Boss to come to him; it had always been the other way. But when Masseria agreed without argument, Luciano took a further step. "Come alone," he said. Masseria agreed.

This turn alerted Luciano, and he realized that a major showdown was at hand. Weinberg and Workman, hardly punks — though Jews, they were top gunmen in the Masseria outfit — had only provided Masseria with the excuse. Luciano immediately called Costello and asked him to get over to the Barbizon. Then he called Siegel, told him to get Torrio and Adonis and bring them to the Barbizon where they were to wait, unobserved, in the lobby until Masseria's departure, then were to come up to the apartment.

When Masseria arrived, alone, Luciano and Costello were waiting in the living room. Luciano did not even have time to greet him, offer him a drink or something to eat. Before the door had closed behind him, Masseria was bellowing. "Who the hell do you think you are?" he shouted. "I cut you in on my business, I make you my number one and when I need you, you're off runnin' your own fuckin' stuff. You know what you are, you're just a rotten punk; you ain't no better than them Jews, Weinberg and Workman. Maybe you're even worse; at least, I can trust them." Then, almost for the first time, Masseria noticed Costello. His rage magnified. "What the hell is he doin' here? You tell me, Joe the Boss, to come here alone and then you have the nerve to have that guy, Costello, waitin' for me. What do you think you're doin', tryin' to take over, to become the boss yourself? You son of a bitch, I'll show you who's the boss; when I get through with you, they'll have to get a sponge to mop up the pieces." Masseria became almost inarticulate, screaming in Italian that he would have Luciano torn apart, his eyes gouged out, his tongue ripped from his mouth. "They'll find you with your prick in your mouth, which is all you deserve."

When Masseria finally paused for a breath, Luciano tried to calm him. "You got me wrong, Joe," he said. "I know you're the boss and I wouldn't do nothin' to change that. You ain't got a thing to worry about with me; if you just think a minute, you'll see that everythin' I done since we come together has been to help you." He used all his guile to placate Masseria, and when he thought he had calmed him sufficiently, he said, "The reason I got Costello here is because he's the guy with the real connections with the cops. All he's gotta do is pick up the phone, make a couple of calls, pull a couple of strings and Workman and Weinberg'll be out on the street in ten minutes."

That was not enough for Masseria. Now he made his demand. "Stop the horseshit. I don't buy this crap from you any more. From now on you work for me twenty-four hours a day. And everythin' you get goes into my pot. You don't like it? That's too fuckin' bad."

"Joe, we got a deal. We shook hands. You're not in the whiskey. We shook hands." The repetition was to remind Masseria of the inviolate Sicilian code of the handshake.

"The whiskey belongs to me," Masseria shouted as he turned and strode to the door. "And if I want to, I drink it all myself. I break the handshake."

Within minutes after Masseria had departed, Siegel, Torrio and Adonis had joined Luciano and Costello. Lansky and Genovese were summoned, and within a half-hour, the seven sat down to a council of war.

To agree to Masseria's demand did not even merit discussion. Masseria was enraged at the moment, but given a little time, Luciano was certain, he would ease up, at least partially and at least from this open hostility. But Masseria had thrown down a challenge to Luciano and his independence, one he could not completely back away from. Luciano might be able to stall Masseria, but only for a time.

Could Luciano afford an open conflict with Joe the Boss? He was not, at that moment, strong enough, not even in combination with his partners in the Seven Group. They could count on a hundred soldiers; Masseria had perhaps five hundred.

"I noticed that Lansky was pretty quiet. We was like Mutt and Jeff by this time, and I could almost read his mind. So I said to him, 'What're ya thinkin' about, Little Man — Maranzano?' "

Lansky nodded. "That's right. We've all been so busy we've been losin' track of what's really goin' on. This thing between Masseria and Maranzano's gonna bust open any day and there'll be a real war, not the penny-ante stuff. Charlie, we have to pick the winner now, and then go with him."

"There you go again," Siegel said, "always tryin' to beat the odds. What the fuck do you think you are, some guy with a crystal ball? Between Masseria and Maranzano, it's not even six to five. Go ahead, wise guy, you pick the winner."

"I picked the winner a long time ago," Lansky said. "Charlie Luciano. All we have to do is eliminate the two roadblocks and from then on, Charlie sits on top. That's what we want, isn't it?"

10.

Luciano and his friends were convinced they had time to develop their plans, to choose the most propitious moment to put them into operation. Not so Tom Reina, who had come to a similar decision but was certain he had to move rapidly. The word of his meeting with Maranzano had gotten back to Masseria, he discovered, and knowing Joe the Boss's reaction to any dealings with the enemy, he decided to seek the protection of Maranzano immediately. A few days after the Barbizon confrontation, Luciano received a call from his friend Tommy Lucchese, requesting an urgent meeting at a Turkish bath on upper Broadway where Lucchese had arranged for them to have the privacy of the steam room. Lucchese told Luciano that the switch was imminent. "So now I knew that Maranzano was gonna call Masseria's hand and there was gonna be all-out war.

"I told Tommy to send out the word to Maranzano that I would finally agree to meet with him." To set up the arrangements, Lucchese chose a Maranzano lieutenant named Tony Bender. "He was pretty good at workin' both sides of the street and gettin' away with it." At the beginning of October 1929, Bender brought back the word that Maranzano was agreeable to a conference, to take place on Staten Island, a neutral territory controlled by Joe Profaci, another Maranzano lieutenant but an old friend of Luciano's from childhood. "I agreed to go, on the condition that Maranzano and I would come alone, and that's the way it was set up. I figured that in spite of everythin', Maranzano wanted me with him bad enough so he'd live up to his word."

Just after midnight on October 17, Genovese picked up Luciano at the Barbizon. "He tried to keep me from goin' alone; he even said he'd like to hide in the back under a blanket, but I told him to forget it." Luciano drove himself to the Staten Island Ferry, rode across, and then went to a shipping pier about a half-mile away.

"Maranzano was already there, waitin' for me. I got out of the car, we shook hands and he put his arm across my shoulder like he always did, and said, 'I'm so glad to see you again, bambino.' We walked inside this big building on the pier. It was empty and dark. We found a couple boxes and sat down. There was a couple minutes of horseshit talk and then Maranzano said, 'Charlie, I want you to come in with me.'

"I said, 'I been thinkin' about it.'"

"Good, good," Maranzano replied. "You know, I always wanted you before and now is a good time for us to shake hands."

"Yeah, I guess it is."

"But tell me, Charlie, why did you make that terrible mistake and go with Giuseppe? He's not your kind. He has no sense of values."

"Yeah, I found that out."

"Now you have thought better of that decision?"

"That's why I'm here."

"Good. We will work it out together. It is a delicate matter and we will solve it. As I always said before, you will be the only one next to me. But, Charlie" — at this point, Luciano remembered, as he reconstructed the events of that night, Maranzano's voice and manner lost their velvet and became sharp and dictatorial — "I have a condition."

"What is it?"

Maranzano stared at him, his eyes flat, his voice emotionless. "You are going to kill Masseria."

116

This, Luciano thought, was no condition at all, and he said, "Well, I've been thinkin' about that, too."

"No, no, you don't understand, Charlie. I mean you. You, personally, are going to kill Giuseppe Masseria."

That condition, Luciano immediately realized, was a trap. In the tradition-laden Sicilian underworld, one cannot kill the leader personally and then succeed to his throne; the killer cannot expect more than a secondary role in the new hierarchy and more likely he can expect to be killed himself in revenge.

"You're crazy." He had hardly gotten the words out when something smashed against his skull and he blacked out.

"When I come to, I felt somebody splashin' water in my face, and I was tied up and hangin' by my wrists from a beam over me, with my toes just reachin' the floor. There was some flashlights shinin' at me and I could make out maybe a half-dozen guys with handkerchiefs coverin' their faces, so that I couldn't tell who anybody was." Later, he said he was convinced that Tony Bender was behind one of these masks, though Lucchese told him he was wrong. "I could make out Maranzano. He was standin' near me and didn't say a word. But I could tell what he was thinkin', and I just said, 'I ain't gonna do it.' So he gave a signal and those pricks without the guts to show who they was began to work on me. They did a pretty good job, with belts and clubs and cigarette butts — until I passed out again.

"I don't know how long I was out or when I came to, but this time my hands felt like they was on fire. Because when I looked up I saw that I was practically hangin' by my thumbs." The more Luciano was beaten and tortured, the more stubborn he became, and the more determined that if he survived, which at that moment he very much doubted, he would make certain that Maranzano's days would be short. The beating continued; Maranzano watched silently, occasionally calling a pause as he stepped forward to say, "Charlie, this is so stupid. You can end this now if you will just agree. It is no big thing to kill a man, and you know he is going to die anyway. Why do you have to go through this, Charlie? Why are you so stubborn? All you have to do is kill him, kill him yourself. That you must do, kill him yourself. But, Charlie, I promise you, if you do not do it, then you are dead."

Luciano remembered later that the repetition of Maranzano's demands, the almost ritual aspect of the beating, gave him a sudden spurt of strength and he lashed out with his feet, catching Maranzano in the groin. Maranzano doubled over, fell to the ground, and began to scream with pain and rage: "Kill him! Kill him! Cut him down and kill him!" But before that could be done, Maranzano himself staggered to his feet, grabbed a knife one of his men was holding and slashed Luciano's face, severing the muscles across his right cheek to the bone. Luciano would bear the scars to his death, and would forever have a slightly drooping right eye that gave him a sinister look.

As Maranzano slashed at Luciano again, opening a long gash across his chest, one of the masked assailants took out a gun and aimed it at Luciano. Suddenly Maranzano calmed, snapped, "No! Let him live. He'll do what has to be done or we will see him again."

"Somebody cut me down and I felt like every square inch of me had a knife in it. I couldn't even move. But I never passed out completely. A few of the guys picked me up and threw me into the back of a car and about three or four minutes later they tossed me out on the road like I was a sack of potatoes. I must've laid there for a good fifteen minutes before I could crawl to a little streetlight down the block. It was about two in the mornin'. Then I passed out."

A few minutes later, a police car cruising along Hylan Boulevard in Staten Island spotted Luciano lying in the street, picked him up, and drove him to the hospital. It took fifty-five stitches to close his wounds. "I don't think there was a part of me that didn't have marks or that wasn't covered by bandages." To add to his indignity, the Staten Island police, when Luciano refused to give an explanation of what had happened, booked him on the charge of grand larceny, for the theft of a car. The charge was quickly dismissed.

Until he related this story in 1961, Luciano had never given a satisfactory explanation of that October night. He once told a story, and soon dropped it, that he had been "taken for a ride" by a gang of masked men who had beaten him and then thrown him out on the road in exchange for a promise to pay them ten thousand dollars. In his refusal to talk about that night, rumors spread; that he had been kidnapped by a rival gang at the corner of Broadway and Fiftieth Street, beaten as a warning to stop encroaching on its territory, and then dumped on Staten Island; that he had been seized at that Broadway corner by Maranzano's men and rescued at the Staten Island Ferry by Lansky and Siegel, who found him badly battered and who then left him on Staten Island to create a mystery; that he had been assaulted by federal agents who discovered him waiting for a narcotics or whiskey shipment on Staten Island; and that he had been beaten by a cop, the father of a girl he had made pregnant.

All Luciano himself would ever say was, "I'll take care of this in my own way."

Still the rumor spread and was credited by many that he had been taken for a ride and had returned, perhaps the only gangster in history to survive that experience. People began to talk about his good luck, that he was "Lucky" Luciano; the nickname stuck.

As far as Luciano himself was concerned, it was not the press or the world at large that gave him that nickname; it was Meyer Lansky. When he came back from Staten Island, still battered and forced to spend some days in bed in seclusion, Costello and Lansky visited him. To them he related the entire story of the beating. "I guess I'm just lucky to be alive."

"Yeah," Lansky replied, "lucky. That's you — 'Lucky Luciano.' "

"Lyin' in bed, I had a little time to think over what happened. For a couple days I couldn't understand why the fuckin' bastard went to all that trouble and then let me live. Finally, I figured it out. Masseria was guarded like the Philadelphia Mint; nobody could get close to him unless you was part of the outfit. Maranzano knew that because he tried a couple times and come up empty. That meant he had to have somebody close to Joe. So why should Maranzano knock me off when I'm the logical guy he needs? But it was typical of the Sicilian touch of 'Mister Julius Caesar,' that if I knocked off Masseria personally, that would be the end of my so-called career as a top man."

Looking back on the event more than thirty years later, Luciano was able to be a little philosophical. "In a way, I don't blame Maranzano, because maybe he knew — or maybe he didn't know

— what I was plannin'. But if he did, then he should've killed me. For three days, every time I even moved my pinky, it hurt so bad I could hardly stand it. That's the only time in my life I ever took narcotics. Joe A. used to come twice a day and shoot me full of morphine. Whenever I got one of them shots, I'd figure out a new way to bump off Don Salvatore Maranzano."

11.

It was late October before Luciano was ready to leave his suite at the Barbizon. On the twenty-eighth, Lansky and Costello stopped by late in the morning, and the three strolled through Central Park in the glow of Indian summer. They talked about the troubled pregnancy of Lansky's wife, Anna, which was making him distraught. They talked about the stock market, which was sliding faster than the ticker tape could keep track. "None of us guys was in the market. What the hell, we didn't have to be. But Meyer was very interested in what was goin' on and he said, 'If we're smart, we'll hold on to all our cash. When the bottom falls out of the market the whole fuckin' country's gonna need money and they'll pay through the nose for it. We'll have the garment district by the balls; they won't be able to live without us.' "

Costello pointed out that it wasn't just the garment industry that would need them. They would be indispensable to the politicians and the police: "Every one of them idiots has been playin' the market, tryin' to make the big scene. The funny thing is they're all gamblin' with our free money. Yesterday, around noon, Whalen [Police Commissioner Grover Whalen] called me. He was desperate for thirty grand to cover his margin. What could I do? I hadda give it to him. We own him."

Into this talk of national economics and its impact on them, Luciano suddenly brought up the names of Masseria and Maranzano. "Screw them," Lansky said. "Knockin' off Joe and Maranzano is the easiest thing in the world; all we've gotta do is figure it out like Charlie says: make 'em kill each other."

"It was one of the few times I ever heard Lansky really laugh, one that comes up from the belly. He really enjoyed the idea of playin' checkers with two big shots. Even Frank laughed, and for him that was almost unbelievable."

The next day, October 29, catastrophe overtook the United States. The stock market, which had been falling chaotically every day, crashed, carrying with it fortunes and hopes. Fear and despair settled like a shroud over the nation, and it would be years before they lifted. The decade-long boom of the Roaring Twenties was over; the Great Depression had begun.

The world of the bootleggers and the racketeers was not unaffected. "One day, everybody was buyin' cases of booze. And the next day they was glad to have enough dough to buy a pint. Every angle of our business was hit. Like by a tornado. The jewelry heists that Adonis loved didn't mean a thing no more. All them rich broads was out of diamonds; they had everything in hock. Costello's slots still did some business, but it was down to less than half. The only place where we didn't have a drop-off was in Harlem and wherever the numbers was runnin'. The little guy who was sellin' apples still wanted to put a few pennies on a number, prayin' he'd hit somethin', not a big bundle, just somethin'. So what happened was that pennies became the backbone of our dollars, our bread and butter. On the other stuff, we took a bath along with the other losers."

With the crash, Luciano and his friends became convinced that Prohibition would soon die, that repeal was only a matter of time. "The public won't buy it no more," he told his close allies. "When they ain't got nothin' else, they gotta have a drink or there's gonna be trouble. And they're gonna want to have that drink legal." It was necessary, they decided, to begin to plan for ways to get into the legal whiskey business when that day came. At the same time, they decided to reexamine their whole operation in light of the country's economic crisis, to see if it might be necessary to get out of some rackets and to put extra effort into others.

One thing they knew; they had some time. On the eve of the crash, Luciano had been caught in the middle. His ambitions and his very life had been threatened by both Maranzano and Masseria; both were issuing ultimatums and he could not satisfy both and still live, yet he was determined to satisfy neither. But the pressure now eased, for both the ganglords were too concerned with putting their own business into shape in the aftermath of that black week in October, and too busy with their own intensifying rivalry, to devote themselves to the Luciano problem.

In the course of the daily meetings at his apartment, Luciano and his friends realized that in a time of no hope the man who could provide some hope, no matter how ephemeral, some escape, no matter how temporary, would not lack for clients. Such hope could be found in the bottle, in games of chance and in other rackets.

Vito Genovese had another plan to provide the public with escape. Despite Luciano's admonitions, he had not ceased dealing in narcotics. Now he wanted to expand. The profits, he said, were so much greater than in anything else and once a sale was made, the customer was hooked and he had to keep coming back for more. Luciano was just as convinced that narcotics led only to trouble; he knew that from his own experience. "I kept tryin' to argue Vito out of it, but he wouldn't listen. Maybe I should've thrown him out, but you can't just throw a guy like that out cold. Especially not after all the things Vito done for me."

In Genovese, Luciano had a sure gun, and at that moment he needed all the guns he could find, guns that were trustworthy and unquestioning. So he told Genovese, "I don't wanna know nothin' about it. If you wanna do it, do it; anybody you wanna do it with, do it with. But don't tell me about it. I don't want it and I don't wanna know about it. Just remember, Vito, if you get in trouble with that stuff, you'll have to bail yourself out."

If Luciano, then, ruled out narcotics, he ruled, in a bigger way than ever, in favor of the old idea of usury. The bankers were extremely chary about lending what little money they had, and so potential borrowers had to look elsewhere. Elsewhere meant the underworld, which had amassed millions of dollars in cash during Prohibition — for it did little else than a cash business. Within a year after the crash, so fast did their shylocking business grow that millions of dollars had been put into the street in the form of usurious loans. With companies failing at a disastrous rate, it became senseless to wreak physical violence on the defaulting borrower. So more and more companies in the garment industry, meat packing, milk, trucking and other industries vital to the city's economic life began to fall under mob control, to be used as legitimate fronts for illicit activities.

Luciano himself, in these days, had his money out on the street not merely as a loan shark. As the economic panic worsened, some of his society and Wall Street friends, with no little trepidation, came to him for help, prepared to receive it at exorbitant rates. But since they were friends, Luciano was generous. "I wanted to prove to them guys that even a gangster had a heart and was willin' to help a friend out of a spot. I loaned lots of 'em whatever they needed, and I charged 'em like I was a bank — two or three per cent interest." Some never repaid, and Luciano merely shrugged off the losses.

While loansharking preyed on the need to borrow, gambling in its various forms played on the dream of a windfall. The numbers racket took a sudden upsurge beyond the expectations of Luciano, Lansky, Costello and the others; Costello's slots, after a letdown, began to regurgitate a never-ending stream of nickels, dimes and quarters. Betting on everything and anything seemed to be the passion of those who had nothing but hope that a bet would pay off.

The nationwide betting syndicate that had been seeded by Moses Annenberg in Chicago now flourished. If people wanted to bet on horses, they didn't care about going to the track; what they wanted was to place their bets and get the results as soon as possible. A national telephone wire service, which could bring the results into every bookmaking parlor, was necessary. "I always thought of Annenberg as my kind of guy," said Luciano. He had provided Annenberg with the goon squads to seize and hold prime corners in Manhattan when Annenberg, as circulation director at the time for Hearst, had led the *Daily Mirror* into New York to challenge the *Daily News*. "And I used to think of the *Mirror* as my newspaper."

When Annenberg developed the racing wire, Luciano was a prime customer and a prime backer. "The new racin' wire had been worked out with the telephone company; to this day that high-class corporation knows that it's the heart of the biggest gamblin' empire in the world. As far as Annenberg was concerned, he never could've operated without us. He needed us and we needed him. It was a good thing all around."

So, while the nation around him was falling deeper into depression, Luciano's star continued to rise. Even his family was coming at least partially to terms with his activities. "My old man never really changed. I have to be honest, sometimes he knew me better than I knew myself. But he got tired of tryin' to tell my mother that I'd always be in the rackets. To keep peace, he finally learned how to shrug it off. That Christmas of 1929 was the nicest one we had all through the years up to that time. Everybody was together and for the first time I actually sat down to dinner with my whole family and nobody talked about me bein' a truant or gettin' out of the can or nothin'. There wasn't even no mention of the marks on my face, but every once in a while when my mother would walk past where I was sittin' at the table, she'd sort of run her hand over my cheek where Maranzano knifed me and I could see that she was cryin' to herself. Outside of that, it was all very happy and for a fast few hours I almost wished I had a nine-to-five job, like the rest of the crumbs. Then I looked out the window and I seen my Cadillac parked at the curb and I knew that I'd never give that up."

But moments of calm and a time for major involvement in his own business could not last long. Soon the pressures began to mount. His friend Tommy Lucchese came to see him one day with disturbing news. The negotiations between Reina and Maranzano had reached a climax, and Reina was about to make his move and take Lucchese with him. "This was gonna put us in one lousy spot. Lepke and Lucchese was doin' great in the money-lendin' business and they had a guy with them named Abe Reles who was doin' a lot of the enforcin' for them. And Tommy said if we could put together a big enough kitty — I mean millions in cash — we could control everythin' in the district. So if Tommy's break with Masseria come too soon, it was gonna fuck up the whole combination that I put together in the garment district. Lucchese would be part of Maranzano's outfit and Lepke was still, through me, with Masseria. I told Lucchese to see if he could keep Reina from makin' the move too soon so we could have enough time to set up the garment district with a good foundation."

But there was to be little time. Soon after the new year of 1930 began, Masseria told Luciano he finally had complete proof of Reina's impending treachery; he ordered Luciano to devise a plan to stop Reina. "I have to prove to every punk who's in our outfit," Masseria said, "that there's only one boss in the city of New York and only one head of the brotherhood in America — and that's Don Giuseppe Masseria. If I close my eyes to Reina, then Maranzano will win this war without firing another shot. You must keep Reina with me and I don't care how you do it, but do it."

It was a delicate assignment; Luciano called his friends together to discuss it. They met early in January on a fishing boat off Oyster Bay, Long Island, on a cold, snowy night. Along with Luciano there were Adonis, Costello, Genovese, Siegel and Lucchese. Lansky was unable to attend. His wife, Anna, was seriously ill as a result of her pregnancy; with a premature delivery imminent, she became nearly hysterical whenever Lansky left the house. "How the hell could I ask Meyer to leave Anna? So we went on without him."

The following day, January 15, Anna Lansky gave birth to a son, who was named Bernard after a favorite Lansky uncle. The delivery was difficult and the child was born a cripple. Anna Lansky suffered a breakdown as a result, seeing the physical defect of her child a judgment from God on both her and Lansky. Distraught at his wife's outbursts at him and over the birth of a crippled child, Lansky fled from New York in the company of a good friend, Vincent "Jimmy Blue Eyes" Alo, holed up in a Boston hotel for several days drinking himself into oblivion before coming to some kind of terms with his tragedy, and then returned to pick up his life back in New York.

Even without Lansky, the decisions were made. "Tommy Lucchese showed up at last and he brought some very bad news. He'd had dinner with Reina a couple of hours before and he'd learned somethin' that Masseria didn't tell me — that Masseria was plannin' to knock off both Joe Profaci and Joe Bananas

[Joseph Bonanno] who was Castellammarese with Maranzano. If he done that and Reina could be persuaded to stay with Masseria, maybe it would keep everybody else in line. We all agreed then that there was no way to stop the war, and the only thing we should think about was how we could win it.

"That's when we suddenly realized we had to switch our old plans around — that Masseria had to go first instead of Maranzano. Now, when you're dealin' with a Sicilian, you gotta think Sicilian or you ain't got a chance. So I tried to put myself into Masseria's head and figure out why we wanted to keep Reina alive while he was plannin' behind my back to knock off Joe Profaci and Joe Bananas. That's when it got very clear. Masseria would make it look to Maranzano like I had masterminded the hits on those two big shots who was on his side and at the same time I was workin' to keep Reina from goin' over to him. The result would be that Maranzano would come after me with everythin' he had.

"The minute I explained it, Bugsy Siegel said, "We're always wastin' time. You Italian bastards are forever chewin' it over and chewin' it over until there's not a fuckin' thing to swallow. There's only one way to go — we gotta knock off Reina as soon as possible and Tommy's gotta pass the word on to Maranzano that it was a hit from Masseria. And we gotta make sure nothin' happens to Profaci and Bananas.'

"That's the way we set it up. I picked Vito for the job, with instructions that Reina hadda get it face-to-face, accordin' to the rules. I really hated to knock off Tom Reina, and none of my guys really wanted to neither. Reina was a man of his word, he had culture, and he was a very honorable Italian. He practically ran the Bronx except for what Dutch Schultz was doin' with beer and meat, and he had control of the whole ice racket, which was pretty important when you figure that seventy-five per cent of the city didn't have electric refrigerators and was usin' ice. But he hadda be eliminated so I could keep on livin' and keep on movin' up."

Luciano learned that every Wednesday night, Reina had dinner with an aunt on Sheridan Avenue in the Bronx. On February 26, 1930, Genovese was waiting outside that house about eight o'clock in the evening. When Reina emerged, Genovese called to him.

"Vito told me that when Reina saw him he started to smile and wave his hand. When he done that, Vito blew his head off with a shotgun."

The suspicion was immediate and widespread, as Luciano and his friends had hoped, that Masseria had ordered the killing and that it had been carried out by one of his assassins, Joe Catania. Masseria compounded the suspicion when he summoned Reina's top lieutenants — Gaetano "Tom" Gagliano, Tommy Lucchese and Dominic "The Gap" Petrilli — to announce that he was taking over and appointing Joseph Pinzolo as boss of the Reina family interests. "I always thought Masseria was a stupid pig, but I honestly didn't believe that he was that stupid, to expect Reina's top guys to swallow all that. As big a shit as Masseria was, he didn't hold a candle to Pinzolo. That guy was fatter, uglier and dirtier than Masseria was on the worst day when the old bastard didn't take a bath, which was most of the time."

Pinzolo immediately tried to emulate his master in dealing with Reina's lieutenants. Outwardly, they offered few objections, though their dissatisfaction was barely disguised and they carried many of their complaints to Luciano. He was, after all, a close friend to all three, particularly to Lucchese and Petrilli — he had gotten his nickname, "The Gap," when, as a child, two of his front teeth had been knocked out in a fight. "I sent him to my own dentist on Columbus Circle, and he fixed up the Gap's mouth with a bridge. Girls used to laugh at him and he had a hard time. After that, he become a real ladies' man and from that minute on, if I asked him to jump off a buildin' he would've done it." As Pinzolo became more arrogant, the three lieutenants began to plot his elimination, and in September, Lucchese asked Pinzolo to meet him at an office he maintained on Broadway near Times Square. Lucchese left Pinzolo alone to check out some receipts, and as Lucchese later told Luciano, Petrilli entered and put two shots into Pinzolo's head, right to his face, according to the rules.

"Nobody mourned, not even Masseria. He told me afterwards, 'The hit on Pinzolo was a good thing. Now maybe Lucchese and the rest of them guys will stop squawkin'.' The whole thing was dropped right then and there and Pinzolo didn't even get the regulation funeral."

While the plot against Pinzolo was maturing, Tom Gagliano picked up the negotiations Reina had started with Maranzano. Early in the summer, accompanied by Joe Adonis, he met Joe Profaci at Peter Luger's, a famous Brooklyn steak house. As Luciano was told soon afterwards, "When Adonis, Profaci and Gagliano came out of the restaurant, Maranzano was sittin' in the back of Joe A.'s car with Joe Bananas, waitin' for 'em. That's where and how the deal was made for the Reina family to make a secret switch to Maranzano.

"While this was goin' on, I talked privately to Anastasia. I knew I could count on him and I knew he would kill for me. When I told Albert what the plan was, he grabbed me in a bear hug and kissed me on both cheeks. He said, 'Charlie, I been waitin' for this day for at least eight years. You're gonna be on top if I have to kill everybody for you. With you there, that's the only way we can have any peace and make the real money. But I gotta warn you, you gotta get rid of Pete Morello before anybody else — take my word for it; you don't know him like I do — because this guy can smell a bullet before it leaves the gun. You'll never knock off Joe the Boss unless you get Morello outa the way.' "

Pietro "The Clutching Hand" Morello was a veteran gunman and Masseria's constant bodyguard and shadow. His elimination was, indeed, a necessity, and Luciano handed that assignment to Anastasia and Frank Scalise. On August 15, 1930, the two trapped Morello in his loansharking office in East Harlem and gunned him down. "There was another guy with him in the office, and he hadda get it too. Later on, I found out that his name was Pariano and he was a collector for Masseria. Albert told me that when he and Scalise walked in, Morello was countin' receipts, and they grabbed the dough after they knocked him off; it come to more than thirty grand."

Unaware of the Luciano-Anastasia involvement, Masseria was convinced that the murder of Morello had been committed at Maranzano's orders and he bought the rumors that the gunman was a hired import from Chicago. He immediately sought revenge, and it was to Chicago that he turned to exact it. There Masseria was supported by Capone, while Maranzano was receiving both moral and financial support from Capone's bitter enemy, Joseph

Aiello. "To make sure the job was done right, Masseria sent Al Mineo to Chicago to handle things." Aiello was machine-gunned to death on a Chicago street. The police blamed Capone mobsters for the killing.

On November 5, 1930, Maranzano retaliated. Three of his gunmen had been holed up in a Bronx apartment overlooking the residence of top Masseria aides in hopes of catching Joe the Boss in a crossfire if and when he paid a visit. That afternoon, Masseria, indeed, showed up, accompanied by his number two and three leaders, Steven Ferrigno and Al Mineo. Maranzano's gunmen opened up, killing both Mineo and Ferrigno. But Masseria still seemed impervious to bullets; he escaped unharmed.

The climax to the Castellammarese War was rapidly approaching. Soldiers on both sides were in hiding, gunning for each other on sight. A climate of fear had been created, diverting time and attention from the real business of the underworld, making money out of the rackets. If the war continued, public attention would focus sharply on the underworld and would lead to a severe crackdown. Once more, Luciano met with his friends at Oyster Bay. This time, Lansky was present. The time had arrived, it was decided, to put their plans into operation. Word was promptly sent to Maranzano that Luciano was now prepared, "for the good of everybody," to do what Maranzano had demanded more than a year before on Staten Island. "I knew the time for this was absolutely perfect. Masseria's luck was holdin' good, and Maranzano couldn't get within a mile of him. He'd have to have me, and nobody else but me, to settle this thing once and for all. If I was gonna negotiate, this was the time to move."

Through Tony Bender, a meeting was arranged. "Maranzano knew goddamn well, after what happened on the pier, I wasn't gonna give him the right time when it come to pickin' the place. I finally made the meet at the Bronx Zoo. I had Tommy Lucchese, Joe A. and Bugsy Siegel with me; I wanted to have a Jew so Maranzano would know he couldn't pull the 'exclusive Sicilian' crap again. He had Joe Profaci and Joe Bananas with him. It was late in the afternoon when we met in front of the lion cage. I said to him, 'I hope you appreciate that the lion is supposed to be the king of the animals.' That done it. Maranzano laughed, and his belly started to shake like jelly. He put his arm around me, but before he could open his mouth, I said, 'Maranzano, there's somethin' I been wantin' to tell you for a long time. My father's the only one who calls me bambino.' Jesus, you might think I hit him. He stopped smilin' and he really got sore.

"He said somethin' like that he couldn't understand why I should resent it, that didn't I understand that he could look on me like his own son. I said, 'After what happened between us last year, I'll never look on you as my old man, so let's stop that horseshit and get down to business. If we work everythin' out, then we'll be friends. That's it.'"

Everything was, indeed, worked out. Maranzano guaranteed the personal safety of Luciano and his friends and followers once the Masseria murder had been accomplished and peace restored. He guaranteed that he would not interfere with Luciano's business or that of Lansky and Siegel, Adonis or Costello. "And he agreed to get rid of all that exclusive Sicilian crap when I pointed out to him that it was crazy and didn't mean a fuck." When the agreement had been struck, Maranzano pointed to Luciano's face and expressed a regret that he had been provoked into doing such a thing. "Never mind. I'm ready to forget it. Let's look ahead," Luciano said.

Maranzano, reverting to his papal attitude, stretched out his hands and placed them on Luciano's shoulders. "Whether you like it or not, Salvatore Lucania, you are my bambino."

Spring had come to New York, and April 15, 1931, was a beautiful warm and sunny day. That morning at nine o'clock, Luciano and Masseria were alone at one of Joe the Boss's headquarters, on lower Second Avenue in downtown Manhattan. Masseria leaned back and listened as Luciano outlined the blueprint for the murder of a score of Maranzano's lieutenants, a bloodletting that would bring complete victory to Masseria. "I must've talked for a couple of hours and old Joe was beamin' and laughin' like he could just taste Maranzano's blood out of a gold cup. Finally, he leaps out of this leather chair about twice as big as he was and he starts to do a dance in the middle of the office. The only time I ever seen anythin' like it was in the newsreels durin' the war when they showed Hitler doin' a dance like that when he beat France. It reminded me of Masseria — two fruitcakes in search of a brain."

About noon, Luciano suggested that, the day being so pleasant, they drive out to Coney Island for a leisurely lunch to celebrate the impending victory. "I could see Masseria's eyes start to shine the minute I mentioned this great food and when I was makin' the arrangements over the phone, I swear I could see the spit droolin' out of his mouth, because I ordered enough food to stuff a horse."

Luciano and Masseria reached the Nuova Villa Tammaro in Coney Island shortly after noon, and the restaurant's owner, a friend of Luciano and many other mobsters, named Gerardo Scarpato, showed them to a table in a corner of the crowded restaurant. Never a big eater, Luciano ate slowly and sparingly, sipping a little red wine. Masseria gorged himself on antipasto, spaghetti with red clam sauce, lobster Fra Diavolo, a quart of Chianti. He was still eating when most of the other diners had departed. He still had ahead of him cream-filled pastry and strong Italian coffee. "It took him about three hours to finish that meal."

Just before three-thirty, the last customers had gone and so had most of the help. Luciano and Masseria were the last patrons. Luciano suggested that they relax for a while and play a game of Klob, a Russian-Hungarian two-handed card game that Masseria had learned from Frank Costello. Masseria hesitated for a moment, then agreed to a short game, reminding Luciano that there was still work to be done back at headquarters. Scarpato brought a deck of cards to the table and then left, saying that he was going for a walk along the beach.

They had played only a single hand, had just dealt the cards for a second, when Luciano got up from the table and told Masseria he had to go to the men's room. Masseria relaxed, enjoying a second bottle of wine.

As soon as the lavatory door closed behind Luciano, the front door of the Villa Tammaro opened. The car that Luciano had driven from Manhattan had been followed at a discreet distance by a black limousine, driven by Ciro Terranova and carrying Vito Genovese, Joe Adonis, Albert Anastasia and Bugsy Siegel. Those four burst into the restaurant, pulled out pistols, and began firing at Joe the Boss. More than twenty shots ricocheted around the room, six smashing directly into Masseria, who slumped over the table, face down, his blood staining the white tablecloth; in his right hand dangled the ace of diamonds.

Even before silence returned, Genovese, Adonis, Anastasia and Siegel were out the door and into the waiting car, its motor still running. But Terranova was so shaken that he was unable to put the car in gear. Siegel pushed him away, took the wheel himself, and sped off. The killing had taken less than a minute; there were no witnesses.

And Luciano? He emerged from the lavatory, took a look at the dead Masseria, called the police, and waited for them to arrive. "When the cops come, naturally they wanted to know whether I seen what happened. I said no, I didn't, and I didn't have no idea why somebody would want to kill Joe. They asked me where I was when it happened — and every newspaper printed that I said, 'As soon as I finished dryin' my hands, I walked out to see what it was all about.' That's an absolute lie. I said to them, 'I was in the can takin' a leak. I always take a long leak.' "

Masseria was given the funeral befitting his status. His body lay in state for some days, and then was followed to the cemetery by cars laden with flowers and limousines filled with mourners. When it was over, Luciano took Genovese aside, the first opportunity that they had to talk about the events at Coney Island. "How did it go?"

Genovese smiled. "The old man would've been proud of it."

12.

"Maranzano had it all now; he didn't waste a single day in startin' to make plans. He was gonna have the damnedest 'inauguration' that ever took place in the United States of America. In a few weeks after Masseria stopped bein' a pig and become a corpse, all Maranzano could think about was the day he was gonna be crowned king."

But Luciano was just as determined that the reign would be brief. As Maranzano was planning his coronation, Luciano called together his own cabinet to put in motion the program that would place Charlie Lucky Luciano at the top of organized crime. The decision then was to move slowly, with patience, to let Maranzano initially proceed unopposed; they were sure that Maranzano would do much to bring about his own downfall.

With an almost naïve arrogance, Maranzano assumed that no one would dare challenge him, that any threats could be eliminated with little difficulty. He sent out invitations to a formal crowning, to a ceremony of obeisance — more a command than an invitation — to hundreds of mob leaders and followers in New York and around the nation. More than five hundred jammed a large banquet hall on the Grand Concourse in the Bronx, filling every chair in a prearranged order according to rank. On the dais, facing the throng, sat Maranzano on a large thronelike chair, rented from a theatrical prop warehouse specially for the occasion. On either side of him, he placed those he was about to install as his princes and lords, the heads of the various gangs and units. Luciano sat at his right hand, the designated crown prince.

"The whole joint was practically covered with crosses, religious pictures, statues of the Virgin and saints I never heard of. Maranzano was the biggest cross nut in the world — he wore a cross around his neck, he had 'em in his pockets, wherever he was there was crosses all over the place. He was an absolute maniac on religion. In fact, he used to call guys in and bawl the shit out of 'em for not goin' to church. I remember one time — it was a little later — when Mike Miranda told me that Maranzano give it to him about the church and Mike said to him, 'How can I go to church when I just knocked off a guy?' He said Maranzano told him, 'That has nothing to do with it. Religion is only concerned with a man's soul.' "

When Maranzano rose, there was absolute silence. He spoke in Italian, lapsing into Sicilian dialect often and larding his speech with Latin quotations. He explained that a new day was dawning. There had been attempts, he said, from Chicago to thwart this meeting — there had been opposition to his endeavors to bring order, leadership and discipline to the chaos and warring of recent years. All this he regretted, but the massing of all his good friends showed that such efforts had come to nothing.

Maranzano used every trick of an accomplished orator as he spoke, intoning, lowering his voice almost to a whisper to make his audience lean forward to catch his words, stretching out his arms in the attitude of benediction. Raising a clenched fist, he proclaimed himself the Supreme Ruler, the Boss of all Bosses — *Capo di Tutti Capi*. He explained that no longer would he rule a separate organization of his own; everything would now be combined into a single organization under one rule — his. He would control a share of everything to be reaped by all the new "families" (a euphemism he ordered to replace the pejorative "gang" or "mob") and he would later tell all the sub-leaders how large a share that would be.

He outlined the details of the mergers and realignments that would create five major families in New York that would control the world of crime under his authority. They would have non-competing jurisdictions, either in territories or spheres of operations, and each member present would belong to one of those families. To head those families, to be their *capos,* he appointed (and as he cited the names, he nodded for the man to rise): Charlie Lucky Luciano, who would control what remained of the Masseria group and who would supervise the whole underworld under Maranzano; Tom Gagliano, who would take over the former Reina interests; Joe Bonanno, Joe Profaci and Vincent Mangano, who would head the other three families based on gangs they had controlled in the past.

The *capos* would be responsible only to Maranzano. Under them would be a second-in-command, an underboss, directly responsible to the *capo,* and beneath them would be several lieutenants, and then ordinary soldiers grouped in ranks of ten, like Caesar's legions. Each man in the chain would be responsible to the leader just a step above him and responsible for the actions of those below.

The key was discipline, Maranzano emphasized repeatedly, rigid discipline, with Maranzano himself the supreme arbiter of all disputes, as he would be supreme in everything. That discipline, obedience to the new rules and regulations he laid down, would be strictly enforced:

No man must ever, upon penalty of death, talk about the organization or the family of which he was a member, not even within his own home.

Every man must obey, without question, the orders of the leader above him.

No man must ever strike another member, regardless of the provocation.

All grievances to that day, imagined or real, were to be forgiven and total amnesty granted.

Total harmony was to rule both the business and the personal relationships between the families and the members; no man could ever covet another's business or another's wife.

At the banquet that followed, every invited guest — even those who had not been able to come but had sent surrogates instead — was required to demonstrate his fealty to Maranzano and the New Order. At a nod from Maranzano, the guests approached one at a time and laid cash-filled envelopes on the table. "I give the old man fifty grand cash myself, and when he added it all up it came to more than a million bucks."

What Maranzano apparently did not realize at this moment of glory was that Luciano had neither forgotten nor forgiven the past and his own desires for the future. And the *capos* and underbosses he had appointed were men who felt more empathy for Luciano than Maranzano, who felt more closely allied to the younger man's ideas and who were willing to plot with and help Luciano topple the new Boss of Bosses.

Luciano's own second-in-command was Vito Genovese, who saw his own ambitions enhanced by devotion to Luciano, not to Maranzano, and the same was true for Luciano's non-Italian allies like Lansky and Siegel. Tom Gagliano's underboss was Tommy Lucchese, Luciano's closest friend and confidant in the Maranzano organization; he had been part of every turn of the conspiracy. And the other power in the Gagliano family was also a close friend of Luciano, Dom "The Gap" Petrilli. In Mangano's family, the underboss was Albert Anastasia, who looked upon Luciano with idolatry, who would do whatever Luciano asked. Joe Bonanno had become a close friend over the years and felt he had more in common with Charlie Lucky than with his fellow Castellammarese, Maranzano. The Profaci family was riddled with allies of Luciano. And he could count, too, on outsiders, like Dutch Schultz, Lepke and Johnny Torrio.

Thus, even as Maranzano was being exalted, his throne was not founded on rock. His speech and his imperious manner may have impressed some of the soldiers, but it enraged many of the leaders. They had not fought a war, had not sacrificed lives and great amounts of money merely to fall under the supreme rule of Maranzano or anyone else. They valued their independence and were determined to maintain at least some of it.

So the plot to overthrow the self-anointed king began almost before his coronation was complete. At the Atlantic City meeting two years before, Luciano had found great favor with mob bosses around the country. Now he took steps to weld that support outside New York to his side, to probe surreptitiously whether other mob leaders would back him against Maranzano. At midyear of 1930, he and Lansky, accompanied by Mike Miranda, a trusted gunman, secretly drove to the Midwest. Their first stop was on the outskirts of Pittsburgh for a short meeting with Salvatore Calderone, the Sicilian leader of western Pennsylvania, who had been at the Maranzano banquet. Calderone was disgusted at Maranzano's attitude and promised Luciano any assistance he might need.

In Cleveland, they met with John Scalise, Moe Dalitz and Frankie Milano, the Mafia leader in Ohio and another guest at the Maranzano coronation. Santo Trafficante, long a friend of Luciano, came up from Florida by train and Capone sent a representative from Chicago. "Even though all these guys was my friends, I still knew that I had to stand up in front of 'em and make sense, otherwise they wouldn't take the chance of a really big war by backin' me if all I was gonna talk was hot air. I told 'em that the old man was nothin' better than a big tub of horse-shit who was still livin' with the *capo* crap he brought over from Sicily, and now he married it to Julius Caesar.

"Everybody started to laugh, and I knew I was tellin' 'em exactly what they felt and what they wanted to hear. I said Maran-zano's ideas made some sense but they was old-fashioned and I'd like to dump 'em in the Atlantic Ocean because they didn't fit no more. It took most of the day to explain what I had in mind and to answer their questions and lay everythin' right on the line. They hadda know we just couldn't dump Maranzano's plans, that we hadda eliminate him entirely. All the guys there was around my age and they agreed with everythin' I said."

Before the meeting was over, a coordinated joint plan had been developed and agreed to. In conjunction with Luciano's projected elimination of Maranzano, the Boss's steadfast adherents around the country would simultaneously be eliminated; when Luciano gave the word that the actual attack on Maranzano had succeeded, his allies around the country would set in motion their own plans for murder.

That night, Luciano, Lansky, Miranda and their Cleveland hosts, euphoric over the unanimity, celebrated by attending a prizefight. The preliminary bouts had hardly begun when several police officers came down the aisle, surrounded them, and, without fuss, took them to headquarters, where they were booked on suspicion and held overnight. Questioned the next morning, all Luciano would say was, "We come to see the fights, that's all." They were released and told to get out of town.

"It was a stupid thing I done in Cleveland and it could've ruined all my plans, everythin' I had been workin' for years to reach. What we should've done the minute we got to Cleveland was to go to the nearest police station and register that we was there and that we come to see the fights. I learned a lesson and never forgot it. After that, any time I would travel someplace, like I used to go to Miami a lot, before I even unpacked my suit-case I'd head for the nearest police station and check in with the big badge."

Though there was no publicity about the Cleveland arrests, Maranzano knew about them. As soon as Luciano arrived back in

New York, he was summoned to the ruler's headquarters. "Maranzano wanted to know what the hell I was doin' in Cleveland. So I said to him, 'Listen, I went to see the fights with some guys. You know I never miss a good fight. What do I have to do, check in with you every time I wanna take a crap?' "

Though Maranzano seemed to accept the explanation, some suspicion had been aroused, and he directed a subtle threat at Luciano. "By the way, I never properly expressed my admiration for the way you handled the matter of Don Giuseppe. It was a very good job, Charlie. You should have arranged for me to have pictures of you pulling the trigger."

Despite the rumors and stories about the killing, Luciano realized that Maranzano believed that he had committed the murder personally, as directed. Basking in the secret support he had just won around the country, Luciano told Maranzano the truth. "Even if you'd been there with your own camera, or sent God to do it for you, you wouldn't have gotten no pictures of me pullin' the trigger. Like the newspapers said, I was in the crapper when Joe got it. So stop jerkin' off and forget it."

Luciano later remembered that Maranzano stared at him with shock. "What I told him gave me a lot of satisfaction. But some little bell went off in my head tellin' me that I should've kept my mouth shut."

For Maranzano, this was recognition that his hold on Luciano was not so strong as he had imagined and that Luciano and some of his closest friends represented a very real peril to him. He set in motion plans of his own to rid himself of the danger without delay. He made a list of names marked for execution: Luciano, Genovese, Costello and Adonis within the Italian-Sicilian group, and such non-Italian Luciano allies as Dutch Schultz. Absent from the list, for apparently he did not consider them a major threat, were Lansky and Siegel; and absent as well, for apparently he had no idea of their closeness to Luciano, were Lucchese, Anastasia and Torrio.

Then Maranzano looked outside his immediate circle for a killer, determined that no Italian under his rule would be required to break the dictum he had laid down. He contracted with the notorious young killer Vincent "Mad Dog" Coll, a lone wolf for hire to the highest bidder.

It was almost a race to see who would be killed first — with, initially, none of the victims aware that he was marked. Maranzano, like Masseria before him, was well protected, never without bodyguards, and so nearly impossible to reach. Luciano, Genovese and the others, however, were more vulnerable; men whose business did not permit them the constant shelter of protected places.

Almost simultaneously with Maranzano's employment of Coll, Luciano devised his own scheme. It would be impossible, he knew, for anyone known to Maranzano and his bodyguards to get to the Boss; even if he could, the mission would be suicide. Only some outsiders, unknown to the Maranzano circle, would have a chance to do the job and escape, vanish without a trace. Maranzano had opened the way for just such an attempt to succeed. He spent much of his time in new offices in the Grand Central Building at Park Avenue and Forty-sixth Street, where he conducted both his legitimate fronts — a real estate business and an import-export operation — and his illegal operations. Frequent visitors to those offices were Maranzano's accountants, who prepared his tax returns.

Luciano took his plan to Lansky for discussion. "That's the way we get him. The son of a bitch is so happy to be a taxpayer that he'd even invite a Treasury agent to come in and look at his books."

Lansky followed Luciano's instructions and imported, from Baltimore, Philadelphia and Boston, three Jewish gunmen, all with stereotype Semitic features. Then Red Levine, Luciano's longtime aide, was named to head the four-man murder squad. Born in Toledo, Ohio, he was a strange man, devoted to his religion and his family and at the same time a killer. At home he always wore a yarmulke, and if he was going on a job during the Sabbath — from sundown Friday to sundown Saturday — he wore the yarmulke under his hat. And, before doing anything else on the Sabbath, he would put the tallith over his shoulders and pray.

Lansky rented a house in the far reaches of the Bronx, and there the four killers were installed in total isolation and given a crash course in the characteristic behavior of federal tax agents. They were not permitted to leave the house, or to go into the yard; everything they needed or wanted — food, women, entertainment to suit each man's particular taste — was supplied. All through the summer, Lansky worked with them, training them how to walk, talk, act so that they would appear in fact to be law enforcement officers. He showed them photographs of Maranzano in different poses, drew diagrams of Maranzano's offices. Luciano and Lansky were determined that nothing would go wrong, and they were willing to spend as much money and time as needed. Luciano estimated later that the cost of the project came to more than eighty thousand dollars.

Near the end of August, the project suddenly took on urgency. Frank Costello received a phone call from Nig Rosen in Philadelphia, who had news of great importance which he could divulge only in person. For Rosen, a close friend and ally of Waxey Gordon, to call Costello and not his fellow Jewish mobster, Lansky, was only partially a surprise. For Lansky and Gordon had become bitter enemies in the latter years of Prohibition, battling over liquor allocations, money, everything, and accusing each other of doublecrosses. By the middle of 1931, the situation had become so tense that no cooperation between them was possible. Further, Gordon was in deep trouble with the Bureau of Internal Revenue over income tax evasion. At that juncture, Luciano felt that he was being forced to make a choice, in secret at least, between Lansky and Gordon, really no choice at all. Together, he and Lansky had come to a decision on how to handle the situation. They would help the federal government do it for them. If the federal forces received information revealing a good accounting of Gordon's legendary sources of income on which he paid no taxes, his elimination could be effectively accomplished. Lansky's brother Jake, sometimes called "Jake the Hunchback," had some contacts in Philadelphia, where he often traveled on Seven Group whiskey deals. Among his friends were several Internal Revenue agents, and Jake Lansky was given the job of clandestinely feeding them the financial information that led to Gordon's indictment, arrest, and later conviction for income tax evasion.

Nig Rosen had no suspicion of the Luciano-Lansky part in the

Gordon troubles, but he was well aware of the Lansky-Gordon feud. Thus, at the end of August 1931, he placed his call to Costello rather than Lansky.

Costello made the trip, and what Rosen told him sent him rushing back to Luciano. Rosen had learned of Maranzano's murder list and of the hiring of Vincent Coll as the executioner. He had also learned some of the details — that within the next month, Maranzano would ask Luciano and one of the others on the list to his office for a business discussion. Coll would be waiting for them. Rosen had refused to tell Costello where he had gotten the information, though he did say that Angie Caruso, a trusted Maranzano underboss, had been in Philadelphia a couple of days earlier, had been drunk and very talkative.

Luciano ordered Lansky to accelerate the training of the murder team, to have the men ready to move at any moment. But Genovese complained that waiting was ridiculous; he demanded immediate steps and that he take on the Maranzano assignment personally.

"No, Vito, we got time. We'll wait for the old man to call and we'll stick to the plan," Luciano told him.

On September 9, 1931, the call came from Maranzano. He had not seen Charlie Lucky in several days, he said, and a number of pressing matters had to be discussed. He would like Luciano and Genovese to call at his office the next day at two o'clock, and they could spend the afternoon in conference.

As soon as Luciano hung up, he called Lansky with the news. That night, final preparations were made. The details were rehearsed again and again, each man running through his part of the planned assassination. When Luciano was satisfied, he left the room and returned in a moment with a muscular, fashionably dressed man of medium height in his early thirties. Without identifying him, Luciano told the killers the man would be in Maranzano's office when they arrived. If necessary, he would finger Maranzano.

Just before two in the afternoon of September 10, Maranzano was in his outer reception room waiting for Coll, and for the arrival of Luciano and Genovese. With him were his secretary, Grace Samuels, and five armed bodyguards. The door opened and

Tommy Lucchese entered, an unexpected visit that, Lucchese later told Luciano, apparently distressed Maranzano. The outer office was normally filled with hangers-on; that day, however, none were present. Lucchese was too important to be denied, particularly when he took Maranzano's arm and started to lead him toward the inner office, saying he had a vital matter to discuss at Tom Gagliano's behest.

Before Maranzano could react, the door opened again and four men entered, identified themselves as federal agents, and demanded to know who was Salvatore Maranzano. No one thought to ask what bureau they were connected with, for Maranzano was under investigation at the time for bootlegging, alien-smuggling, tax evasion and a variety of other matters. His lawyers had assured him he had no worries, but that agents might make a surprise visit, and if they did, he should be cooperative. Maranzano readily identified himself to the four "agents."

One of them noticed a quick, almost imperceptible nod from Lucchese, the man they had seen the night before. They pulled out their guns. One locked the door. Maranzano, Lucchese, Miss Samuels and the five bodyguards were lined up against the wall and frisked; the bodyguards were disarmed.

Two of the agents then shoved their guns into Maranzano's back and ordered him into his private office for questioning. Once the door was closed behind them, they pulled out knives — the weapon chosen so the murder could be committed in silence — and began to slash at Maranzano. Despite his age and girth, Maranzano fought back, crying out, striking with his arms. The battle became almost desperate and the two killers finally pulled out their guns and began to pump bullets into him. He collapsed across his desk, dead — stabbed six times in the chest and body, his throat cut, and with four bullet wounds in his head and body.

The killers dashed out, were joined by the other two in the outer office, and then all four raced out the door, down eight flights to the street where they vanished. As they disappeared, Maranzano's bodyguards followed, not to give chase but in fear of being found in the office with Maranzano's corpse.

Lucchese remained behind momentarily, looking into the inner office to make certain Maranzano was dead. As he was making a cursory examination, Girolamo Santucci, better known as Bobby Doyle, rushed in. A onetime prizefighter, he was supposedly a loyal Maranzano aide and bodyguard, but his true allegiance was to Luciano, for whom he had driven on a number of hijackings, and for whom he had committed murder. "He was a fearless guy," and he had been planted in Maranzano's midst by Charlie Lucky. On September 10 his job was to back up Lucchese, if needed. He had arrived late. Lucchese looked up from Maranzano's body and snapped at him, "Get out of here." Doyle raced out and down the stairs to the street, just as a squad of police was arriving. The cops picked up Doyle, questioned him briefly at headquarters, and then released him. Lucchese, meanwhile, calmly rode the elevator to the ground floor and faded into the crowd on Park Avenue.

Vincent "Mad Dog" Coll had been on his way up the stairs to Maranzano's office when Maranzano's bodyguards came tearing down. One of them told him what had happened. With Maranzano's twenty-five thousand dollars in his pocket and now no job to do and no one to refund the advance to, Coll turned and left. (Five months later, Coll himself fell in a Manhattan telephone booth, a victim of his own war with Dutch Schultz.)

Through the early afternoon, Luciano, Genovese and the others waited anxiously for news of their plan. That news came just before three, with a telephone call to Costello from the Fifty-third Street Precinct. More confirmation quickly arrived from Levine, Lucchese and the radio.

Then Luciano sent out the word to allies around the country that the Maranzano assassination had come off as planned. But in these hurried calls, it was agreed that the second phase of the planned attack was not necessary. "Plenty of people got eliminated before the day Maranzano got his, and it was all done as part of the plan. But all that stuff them writers always printed about what they called the 'Night of the Sicilian Vespers' was mostly pure imagination. Every time somebody else writes about that day, the list of guys who was supposed to have got bumped off gets bigger and bigger. The last count I read was somewhere around fifty. But the funny thing is, nobody could ever tell the names of the guys who got knocked off the night Maranzano got his. I, personally, don't know the name of one top guy in the Maranzano group in New York or Chicago or Detroit or Cleveland or nowhere who got rubbed out to clear the decks. It just wasn't necessary, because what we did was to tell 'em the truth — that the real and only reason Maranzano got his was so that we could stop the killin'. That it was all over."

The only known victim, in fact, of that Night of the Sicilian Vespers was Gerardo Scarpato, the owner of the Nuova Villa Tammaro at Coney Island. During that night, he was murdered.

13.

The old ways and the old leaders were finally dead and Charlie Lucky Luciano was at last a king. The fallen ruler, Salvatore Maranzano, was given a send-off befitting his status — Luciano insisted on that — with the ritual long train of black limousines, flowers, tears and eulogies. And when Maranzano had been laid to rest, Luciano announced that the old Don's autocratic ideas had been buried with him. The day of the absolute monarchy was over; henceforth there would be a constitutional government with respect for the rights of each group. Luciano was determined neither to alienate nor antagonize anyone; all should and would be treated as equals and allies.

From his experiences of the past decade, Luciano knew that he could remain at the top only if he eschewed fear and intimidation; he could not, as Masseria and Maranzano had tried to do, force into submission such men as Profaci, Bonanno, Mangano, Scalise, Gagliano, Capone and the rest of his friends who had supported him and who gave him the respect that they wanted in return. He sensed, then, that if he rejected the offered throne in name, he would soon have it in fact. This was the Sicilian-Italian paradox that he understood — the yearning for leadership but the rejection of the autocratic leader.

"I learned a long time before that Meyer Lansky understood the Italian brain almost better than I did. That's why I picked him to be my *consigliere*, to talk over the best way to handle things, how to get my ideas across to a bunch of big shots who was tired of livin' under one guy's thumb. I used to tell Lansky that he may've had a Jewish mother, but someplace he must've been wet-nursed by a Sicilian."

From all over the country, word was sent to Luciano approving his actions against Maranzano, but with the cautionary word that a fuller explanation of his future plans was much desired. "I decided not to make the same mistake that Maranzano did. Instead of callin' everybody to me, I went to them. A few weeks later, we had a meet in Chicago, and Capone acted like he was throwin' a party for me."

Despite his trial for tax evasion, Capone was a lavish host. He invited the leaders of the American underworld to the celebration, some to meet Charlie Lucky for the first time, but all, apparently, to anoint him in the old ritual. But the guest list was not restricted to Sicilians and Italians. There were Jews like Lansky, Siegel, Dalitz, Rosen, Dutch Schultz, Abe Reles; there were Irish and what would be called today Wasps. Capone took over the Congress Hotel and part of the Blackstone (he was rumored to own controlling interests in both), assigning floors to each city and group, with the best suites reserved for the chieftains. His own troops, augmented by his hirelings on the Chicago police force, ringed the hotel, keeping away the curious. Noticing the preparations and hearing stories of the perils of the city's streets, Luciano noted later, "It ain't safe to walk alone in Chicago."

The first afternoon, Luciano had a series of private meetings with the underworld leaders. "I knew they wanted to hear from me direct, face to face, not in a big auditorium. I explained to 'em that all the war horseshit was out, that every outfit in every city could be independent but there would be a kind of national organization to hold it all together. I told 'em we was in a business that hadda keep movin' without explosions every two minutes; knockin' guys off just because they come from a different part of Sicily, that kind of crap, was givin' us a bad name and we couldn't operate until it stopped. Masseria and Maranzano had been our real enemies, was the way I put it, not the Law; we could handle the Law, we was doin' it everywhere. But how can you handle crazy people?"

The basic concepts for the future of organized crime had long been maturing in Luciano's mind, and now, at these sessions, he pulled them out; each local and regional group would have considerable autonomy within its own jurisdiction; at the top there would be a national commission, like the board of directors of a legitimate corporation, to establish major policy for the underworld, and the leaders of all the larger outfits would sit on that panel, with each man an equal. Though Luciano would be the chairman — the unanimous decision of his peers — his vote and voice would be no stronger or more powerful than anyone else's.

But no matter how often in these conversations Luciano flatly disavowed any pretensions to the old title of Boss of Bosses, *Capo di Tutti Capi,* there were still many, particularly those of Sicilian origin, who seemed unable to comprehend this. It all seemed "too American" to them.

During a break late in the afternoon, Lansky took Luciano aside. He was worried. "We missed something, Charlie. Unless you straighten it out before tonight, you could blow the whole thing. There are lots of these guys who ain't able to give up all the old ways so fast. You gotta feed 'em some sugar that they'll understand. You've got to give the new setup a name; after all, what the fuck is any business or company without a name? A guy don't walk into an automobile showroom and say, 'I'll take that car over there, the one without a name.' "

The more Luciano thought about Lansky's statement, the more he agreed. "But the name has to be simple, somethin' that'll have a real meaning for these particular guys," he said.

"That's right," Lansky said. "And I'd like to suggest you call it the Unione Siciliano."

"For chrissake, that's been around for years; they been fightin' since I was a kid over who was gonna run it. If we're throwin' out all the old crap, what's so good about keepin' that one?"

"Don't you understand, Charlie, that there are too many of these guys who can't get away from the old traditions? If everybody comes into this kind of operation that's called by a Sicilian name, then the old vendettas would stop right now. It's as simple as that. Didn't you always say that to understand a Sicilian you hadda crawl into his head?"

Lansky's logic was compelling to Luciano. Immediately he began to advocate the use of Unione Siciliano as the formal name for the national organization, if anyone needed a formal name, though he himself always called it simply "the outfit."

That evening, Capone was the host at a lavish banquet, with Luciano seated next to him on the dais. It became apparent at once that despite Luciano's fine words and phrases, most of the guests had come expecting to pay obeisance to a new king in the same manner as the old. They brought envelopes stuffed with cash to Luciano as tribute. Luciano refused each offer. "I don't need the money. I got plenty, and besides, why should you be payin' anythin' to me when we're all equals?"

The would-be donors walked away, amazed. But Capone was shocked. He turned to Luciano. "Don't be a horse's ass, Charlie. Maybe it's all right to break down them old traditions, but why do you have to break that kind of tradition?"

"I told you, I got enough dough."

"That don't mean a thing. That ain't the point. All these guys are used to payin' up, so why get rid of a good thing?"

"That's exactly why. It ain't a good thing. Also, it makes them feel like I'm the boss and I don't want that. There ain't gonna be no more gifts, no more envelopes, nothin' like that."

Later, Luciano would reminisce, "I think I really made Capone sick. His face turned green, and I'm sure it wasn't from too much *vino*."

And Luciano revealed one further dictum. In the past, he said, the bosses had been too powerful, while the ordinary soldiers had been too powerless, unable to dispute a decision they were sure was ill conceived. He proposed the establishment of a layer of appeals between the bosses at the top and the soldiers at the bottom, a kind of subconsul to whom the ranks could submit their complaints. This *consigliere* would have multiple roles, not merely acting as the soldier's voice at court but as the intermediary adviser to the leaders, able to speak without fear of reprisal.

When he left Chicago to return to New York, Charlie Lucky

Luciano had realized his dreams. He had organized crime throughout the United States and, at last, he stood atop the pyramid, un-
disputed, unchallenged.

14.

Now the newspapers and the gossip columnists, when they wrote
about him, called him "The Boss," and his friends, associates and
underlings, though they still called him Charlie or Charlie Lucky,
thought of him as the boss. He continued to insist to everyone that
he was the boss of nothing other than his own outfit, of no more
importance in the Unione Siciliano than any other leader. But in
spite of his protestations, the word in the underworld after the
Chicago meeting invariably was "Charlie Lucky wants this" or
"Charlie Lucky says do that." And when Charlie Lucky wanted
something, he got it without question.

The only outward sign that things had changed for him was a
change of address. He had heard that the penthouse apartment atop
the St. Moritz Hotel was available and he decided to lease it. But
when Walter Winchell heard the rumors, he advised the hotel's
management that if it accepted Luciano as a resident, not only
would Winchell move out but he would devote his column in the
Daily Mirror to explaining why and to excoriating the hotel as a
gangster hangout. The St. Moritz turned Luciano away.

"The funny thing was that Winchell wasn't even payin' rent.
He got his apartment on the cuff for mentionin' the St. Moritz in
his column once in a while. And he talked about *me* bein' a
racketeer. Anyway, when the St. Moritz fell through, I decided to
go all the way. I moved into a beautiful apartment way up in the
Waldorf Towers. I kinda missed watchin' the people skatin' on the
park and even the ducks swimmin' on the lake. But the Towers
was the best class address in New York. And then Frank Costello
was livin' in the hotel part of the Waldorf-Astoria for a long time."

The Waldorf, indeed, had become a home away from home for Costello, where he could hold court instead of in his apartment on Central Park West. Every morning he appeared at the Waldorf barbershop for a shave, trim, massage and manicure, and for chats with those legitimate friends who always dropped in while he was being attended. "They give Costello a face like a baby's ass. How the hell can anybody get a manicure six days a week, and all the rest of that junk? In my opinion, Frank was nuts. I wouldn't let a barber get a razor that close to my face." From the barbershop, Costello would usually repair to Peacock Alley, just off the main lobby, for lunch; it became something of an office for him, a place where at his regular corner table he could hold quiet discussions with political and business friends that would attract little notice because of the apparent openness.

"The Towers was part of the Waldorf setup, and my bein' there made it easy for Frank to get to me. But the Towers was separated from the hotel and it was higher. I figured if everybody was gonna call me the boss, I was entitled to live in an apartment that was above Frank's. It was kind of a joke, but I found out later it really burned him up."

At the Waldorf Towers, Luciano was simply a gentleman named Mr. Charles Ross. In a time of economic depression when paying tenants were not all that easy to find, the Waldorf Towers accepted Mr. Ross without looking too closely. While many of the residents lived on a month-to-month basis, Luciano leased his suite — living room, dining room, kitchen, bedroom, master bath and powder room — by the year, and paid his rent — eight hundred dollars a month — in cash. He complained not at all about the service, or about anything, and left it to the management to furnish his apartment as it saw fit, just so long as it looked "classy."

"I didn't have no trouble with them until some idiot in my outfit came to see me one day. He didn't know what number my apartment was, so he asked the desk clerk. But he didn't ask for Mr. Ross — he asked for Charlie Lucky. The clerk came up to see me later in the afternoon. He said they was gettin' all kinds of complaints from other people in the buildin' about a notorious gangster livin' there. Well, I knew the Towers wasn't gonna throw me out. After all, I was payin' my rent regular, which was more than they could say about some of them bluebloods that was free-loadin' there. So I figured it was payoff time. I didn't even ask the clerk how much he wanted. I just reached into my pocket and peeled off two C-notes. And from then on I gave him two hundred every month, just for himself. I didn't have no trouble after that and a couple of years later the guy did me a helluva favor."

The Towers suited Luciano perfectly. Its small entrance and foyer off Fiftieth Street just east of Park Avenue gave it a privacy in sharp contrast to the vast entrances and lobbies of the adjacent hotel. There were attendants on duty twenty-four hours a day to screen visitors, all of whom had to be announced before riding up in the elevators. Luciano could drive his car directly into the garage and then walk a few steps to a private elevator that served only the Towers.

By this time, late in 1931, Luciano's life had fallen into an orderly pattern. One of the night people, he would rarely rise before noon. As he was finishing breakfast, his first business associates would begin to drop in. Adonis would come often and so would others of his inner circle — Genovese, Costello, Lansky, Torrio, Lucchese (now that Maranzano was dead, the Lucchese-Luciano friendship was in the open). Occasionally, Tony Bender would drop by, but unlike the others, he loved secrecy and so would ride the elevator to a different floor and then walk down several flights. Longie Zwillman would sometimes show up, for he and Luciano had much to discuss. They were partners in a growing number of businesses. They had their joint bootlegging and gambling interests and for himself and Luciano, Zwillman was heavily into the transportation of gambling equipment, slot machines, and pinball devices; he arranged the "fixing" of dice and crap tables at a warehouse in Fort Lee, and the distribution and collection from recalcitrant customers were his specialties. "We sometimes had to remind people that they were behind in their payments, or that we didn't get our take from the tables we gave 'em. That kind of thing. Longie was very good at persuadin' 'em to clear the books."

By early afternoon, business had been concluded. If the horse racing season was in swing, Luciano would dress and head for his box at one of the local tracks.

If the tracks were closed and he had not followed the horses south to Florida or elsewhere, he would usually remain at home, pick up the phone, and call Polly Adler. "She was the only madam in the whole city I could trust. If you told her or one of her girls somethin', you knew it wouldn't go no further."

It was Luciano's contention — and he maintained it strenuously through the years — that prostitution was one racket he knew about only as a customer. Any suggestion that he was the boss of that business as he was the boss of so many others filled him with an almost inarticulate rage. "I didn't have nothin' to do with that. Them broads wasn't under me and I didn't make a quarter out of 'em. Sure, I knew it was goin' on. Who didn't? But I always said that runnin' whorehouses was the lowest thing a guy could do — worse than dope. It was one of the reasons a lotta guys never trusted Capone and a lot of 'em looked down their noses at Torrio, because they was mixed up in that. Maybe some of my guys was in it, but I couldn't stop that no more than I could stop Vito or anybody else from handlin' junk. It was their business and I told 'em that. I told 'em that I didn't wanna know nothin' about it, that it was a part of the business that didn't belong to me, and I never took no part of it, not a nickel. I done a lot of things in my life, but I never had nothin' to do with makin' money outa whores."

Luciano patronized Polly Adler and her girls because, unlike most of his friends, he shunned the idea of marriage. "As things got good, all the guys around me got married and started to raise families. Joe Adonis bought a place out in Jersey and he finally wound up with a couple of kids. Willie Moretti built a place in Jersey, too, that was like a fort, and he raised a family. In fact, out of everybody in my crowd, Frank Costello was the only guy who didn't think there was some kind of Italian law that said he had to bang out a million kids. Actually, if you had all the dough Frank spent on broads — I mean in addition to his wife — and what later on he give to one particular girl friend, you could go around the world for the rest of your life on your own steamship.

"When I seen what was goin' on with all them marriages, I knew that none of the guys was really happy because they didn't have time to spend on a marriage. And that was my reason for never gettin' married in those days. I just didn't have time for a wife. Besides, I always figured that someday I was gonna wind up on a slab and I didn't want to leave a widow and kids cryin' over me. So when I wanted to get some, I used to turn to Gay Orlova or Polly Adler."

Perhaps the best-known madam of her time in New York, the short, stout Polly Adler operated from a townhouse in the West Fifties, just off Fifth Avenue, with little or no police interference. Her girls were uniformly beautiful and her clientele was the famous, the infamous and the rich. Later she would say that Charlie Lucky had been a favorite steady customer; the girls who were sent at his bidding were always what she called "straight." "I didn't go in for none of that leather and whip crap. I liked good-lookin' girls who could screw good and that's what Polly always sent me."

If the girl who arrived at the Waldorf Towers for an afternoon of fun and games with Luciano thought she was going to be paid more than Polly Adler's standard twenty-dollar fee, she was invariably disappointed. The only extra was a five-dollar tip Luciano would shove into the girl's brassiere as she dressed. "I didn't want to do nothin' different. What do you think I was gonna do — spoil it for everybody?"

When the girl had departed, Luciano would relax for a time before dressing for the long night ahead. Then he would select his clothes with care from a huge and fashionable wardrobe. He had dozens of shirts of the best cottons and silks, all made to measure with hand-embroidered initials, "C.L." in small letters on the breast pocket; he had silk underwear by the carload — "I used to get that fancy stuff from broads and I'd give away most of it to guys in my outfit, so they wound up wearin' more expensive underwear than I did." His shoes were handmade, and he bought his suits in lots of a dozen or more every couple of months. "I gave away the old ones to my guys, friends, or anybody who looked like he needed a boost and was my size. I didn't have no choice. In a hotel, you just don't have enough closets."

Dressed, Luciano looked almost like a prosperous, conservative banker, nothing of the movie gangster about him. Then he would leave for dinner, usually at a favorite Italian restaurant like the Villanova on West Forty-fifth Street, or one of the small bistros in Little Italy, on Mulberry or Minetta Street. Sometimes he would call his friend Jimmy Durante to join him, or some other entertainer whose company he enjoyed, like Lou Clayton, Durante's partner, or Phil Baker or Frank Fay, Bobby Clark, Ed Wynn, Joe Cook and others — he preferred comics.

Then he would pick up his dinner companions and drive to the restaurant, where they would often be joined by Lucchese, Costello, Anastasia, Lansky or others. And after dinner, they would drive to Little Italy, to an ice cream parlor for dessert. "I loved that stuff — spumoni, tortoni, Italian ice. But not like they made it in the fancy joints. Only the old guys in the little places knew how to make the real ice cream."

Luciano's dinner guests would be sent on their way, and then he and his associates would head uptown for the start of serious business. He still maintained his Claridge Hotel offices, but used them only for very private matters. New offices had been rented, two sparsely furnished rooms on Broadway near Moe Ducore's drugstore at Fifty-first Street. The location was ideal for one of Luciano's avocations; it was in the center of the first-run movie district. "Lots of times after dinner, somethin' would be botherin' me and I didn't know how to work it out. The best way to clear my mind was to see a movie."

When the office was first rented, there was some discussion about putting some title on the door. "Bugsy Siegel says to me, 'What name should we put on the door?' Costello says, 'Washroom.' We all got a big laugh out of that. Then I said, 'No, make it "Ladies."' " But we ended up by puttin' nothin' on the door. It was just a blank and I had the only key. Nobody went in there when I wasn't around."

There was, though, little to hide; only a few chairs, a sofa and a desk. "We couldn't keep nothin' there. We wasn't crazy. If we got raided, all they would find was a coupla guys sittin' around talkin'."

It was to this office, in the hours after midnight, that those seeking audience with Charlie Lucky came — for permission to open a policy drop, run some handbooks, operate pinballs or slot machines or juke boxes, put money on the street as loan sharks, have plans for a fur or jewelry heist checked. They would wait in the outer office until summoned inside for a brief talk with the boss, for his approval or rejection.

And to this office came those with the weekly payoff reports, checking in on schedule. They never brought money with them; everything was oral, the figures for the takes from various enterprises recited by rote. The money itself was cached in safe places — wall safes, safety deposit boxes, even tin cans — where it would be available when needed. "Every guy that come up, I knew within a dollar what he was supposed to gimme, and he knew I knew. So if some guy reported in short of what he should've some week, he hadda bring a good explanation."

The police, of course, were well aware of the new office; Luciano himself furnished them with that information, more for his own protection than to provide them with special knowledge. "After all, I was no different than any other citizen. I was entitled to police protection in case some guy wanted to have a try at me. Well, maybe I wasn't an ordinary citizen. Them guys paid taxes; I paid the cops direct."

There were times when the office was too small, and too public, for meetings of Luciano's board of directors, and so they would move nearby, to Dave Miller's Delicatessen. Luciano would say, "Davey, close up the joint, we're havin' a meet." Miller would hang a "closed" sign on the door, draw the blinds, set up a long table with Luciano's favorite corned beef, pastrami, dill pickles, potato salad, cole slaw, black Greek olives, sliced rye bread and pumpernickel, and then depart. The men would make their own sandwiches, help themselves to cold drinks and beer and, Luciano said, have "one helluva kosher ball." When they left, through the back door, Luciano would stick one or two hundred-dollar bills in Miller's cash register.

Then would come a nightly ritual. Luciano would make his rounds of the speakeasies, supper clubs and cafés to which he was providing liquor and protection. He called this his "midnight jamboree." His last stop would often be Dave's Blue Room, for a late snack with a close friend, often Tommy Lucchese, and there they would discuss quietly the progress and problems of the loan-sharking racket. Dave's Blue Room was a place where he could relax; the restaurant was open until dawn and was usually filled with show business celebrities, society, the underworld and gawking tourists.

"Around 1934, Tommy and me was sittin' having somethin' to eat in Dave's — we wasn't even talkin' because we was both tired. Then who walks past our booth but a guy named Dave Rubinoff, who was famous all over the country; he was a big orchestra leader and he played a violin on the Eddie Cantor radio show. It seems that he borrowed ten grand from Tommy to buy one of those Stradivarius violins and he still owed Lucchese half. Tommy was no guy to owe money to. The place was kinda dark, but when Rubinoff spotted Tommy I could see his face turn white. Lucchese called him over and said, 'How are ya, Ruby? Where ya been?' Rubinoff just stands there and starts to shake."

Lucchese told Rubinoff, "Ruby, you owe me some money. When are you gonna pay up?"

Rubinoff, his heavily Russian-accented voice quavering, said, "Tommy, listen to me — you don't understand, I'm a little short right now."

Lucchese reached out and took hold of Rubinoff's left hand and began to massage the knuckles gently. "You got a nice hand there, Ruby. It makes beautiful music. And it makes you a lot of money. Now, you don't want nothin' to happen to that hand, do you, Ruby?"

"I never saw a guy shake like that in my life. Maybe it was because I knew Gay Orlova and she was Russian, or somethin', but I sorta felt sorry for this guy with the accent, the way he looked at Lucchese like he was drawin' his last breath. So I said to Rubinoff, 'Do you really owe Mr. Lucchese money?' "

"Yes, Mr. Luciano, I do."

"Well, ain't you gonna pay him?"

"I will! I will! The first thing in the morning. Believe me."

Lucchese stared at Rubinoff, and gestured toward Luciano. "Never mind askin' him to believe you. I don't believe you. So I'm gonna take you outside."

"Right then and there, I saw that Tommy wasn't kiddin'. He was really gonna let Rubinoff have it. Not kill him but maybe bust his knuckles, like on his right hand, not the good left hand that he picks the notes out with. So I put a stop to it and I told Rubinoff to get the hell out and take care of his payment before noon the next day. As a matter of fact, I happened to know that he got an advance from Eddie Cantor, which was about the hardest thing in the world to do around Broadway, and he paid his bill."

His day at an end, Luciano would leave Dave's Blue Room, sometimes meeting Gay Orlova, and return either to her apartment or to the Waldorf Towers. Finally, he would get into his own bed, spread the newspapers out and read before going to sleep as the sun came up over Manhattan, the island empire he was now certain he controlled.

15.

The mood of the nation in the first months of 1932 was grim and desperate. The panic and depression set off by the Wall Street crash of 1929 had deepened and the faith of millions in the viability of the American system, and of its political leaders, had been shattered. The cry was for change. Though at midyear, a dispirited Republican party renominated Herbert Clark Hoover for a second term in the White House, it was apparent even to Hoover's supporters that defeat was virtually inevitable, that a President who seemed incapable of dealing with national crisis would be buried in a November electoral landslide.

That certainty was not lost on Luciano and his friends in the underworld. "In a way, it was kind of like a guy who shoots crap. When everything's goin' good and all his numbers are comin' up, and the stickman is payin' him on the line and in back of the line, and he's makin' all his sixes and eights the hard way, he don't let nobody touch them dice for dear life. But let him throw a couple of boxcars and snake eyes and he'll throw them dice right down the toilet. That's the way it was in politics. The crumbs didn't have a pot to piss in. To them, Hoover and the Republicans was the dice that was comin' up losers every time, and it was logical to ditch 'em."

At the Claridge Hotel, early in 1932, Luciano, Costello, Lansky and the other major underworld leaders gathered to consider the coming political campaign, their stakes in it, and how best to exert their influence on those who would take office when the votes were counted. It was apparent to them, as it was to the political experts, that the contest for the Democratic presidential nomination had narrowed to three candidates: John Nance Garner of Texas, then the speaker of the House of Representatives; Al Smith of New York, the former governor and defeated presidential candidate they had supported four years earlier; and Governor Franklin Delano Roosevelt of New York, the amiable Hyde Park patrician. Of Garner they knew little, only that he was from the Wild West of cowboys and Indians, that he wielded enormous political clout in Washington, and that he had the backing of William Randolph Hearst and the Hearst newspapers. But with the prejudices of the urban East, they discounted the chances of a Southwesterner. They were certain that when the Democratic Convention met in Chicago, in June, the choice would be between Smith and Roosevelt, the two once friendly but now bitterly antagonistic New Yorkers.

If this reading was correct, they were convinced they could become a major influence on the convention and, later, on the White House itself. Smith had deep support in the party, particularly among his fellow big-city Catholics and the machine politicians. He had risen through the ranks, had labored long and hard for the party, putting many of its leaders in his debt. He had been around so long by then that he had become something of an admired legend. On some issues, such as repeal of Prohibition, he had never equivocated, and now the majority of the country was with him.

Smith's major liability in the view of the experts was his Catholicism, which had contributed to his 1928 defeat. The hope of his supporters was that in the climate of the Depression, that could be overcome, and they worked diligently during the first half of 1932 to that end, attempting to gather support wherever it could be found. "One day, I got a call on my private number at the Waldorf from Philadelphia. This voice said, 'Is this Mr. Luciano?' And I said, 'Yeah, who's callin'?' And the voice says, 'Just a minute. The Cardinal wants to talk to you.' The next thing I know I'm on the phone havin' a conversation with Cardinal Daugherty of Philadelphia. Holy mackerel! He said to me that the Vatican wouldn't really object if the Cardinal wanted to do some campaignin' and he was callin' to remind me that I once supported Al Smith and it was very important for the public to know that Smith was a great man, not only a Catholic.

"So I said, 'Well, Cardinal Daugherty, how can I help, on account of I'm a Catholic?'

"I heard him kind of laugh and he said, 'But you're not a very good Catholic, are you, my son?'

"And I said, 'No, Cardinal. You got me. But I understand why you're callin' me, and I give you my word that I'll help Al Smith.'

"The Cardinal thanked me very much and before he hung up he said, 'My friends tell me that you live very close to St. Patrick's Cathedral. Why don't you pay a visit there sometime?'

"I said to him, 'Your Eminence, I'll make good on my promise about Smith, but please don't hold me to that walk over to St. Patrick's.'

"He sorta laughed and said, 'Try to find the way. Bless you.' And then he hung up."

Cardinal Daugherty had merely strengthened Luciano's bias toward Smith. But despite that leaning, he was not completely ready to write off Roosevelt. The New York governor was then relatively untried and unknown. He did have some public recognition — as Wilson's Assistant Secretary of the Navy during World War I, as the Democratic candidate for Vice President in the disastrous 1920 campaign, as a man stricken with polio who had recovered sufficiently to nominate Al Smith at the 1924 convention and later to win election as governor on his own — but it was more vague and amorphous than sharply focused, revolving around a seemingly enlightened if not daring philosophy, a patrician bearing, a beaming smile and great personal courage.

Through the spring of 1932, Roosevelt's agents fanned out across the country attempting to round up delegates for his run at the presidency. As the convention approached, Roosevelt had captured a clear majority. But that was not enough. Under the rules then in force, he would need two-thirds of the delegate votes at Chicago to win the nomination, and getting those last votes would not be easy. If he were to persuade the holdouts that he was indeed a viable and winning candidate, he would need the solid support of his home state, New York — not just upstate, which was already committed to him, but New York City as well, where Tammany Hall held sway and where the base of Al Smith's support appeared solid.

"There wasn't a chance for Roosevelt to get the delegates from the city without makin' a deal with Tammany, and in 1932 the guys who ran Tammany was run by me and Frank Costello. That's what we was waitin' for, because I had a funny feelin' about Roosevelt. Sure, I liked Smith and he was the guy I wanted, but he didn't talk no better than me and I sorta hated that anybody should be in the White House talkin' like a guy from the Lower East Side. I had a feelin' that maybe when it came down to it, Roosevelt would have the edge. I respected him because he came from that group of society guys I got to know real well down in Palm Beach and up in Saratoga, and they was educated people. But there was somethin' in my bones that told me not to trust Roosevelt. I told this to Costello and Lansky and they laughed at me. Costello said, 'Charlie, you don't know what the hell you're talkin' about. I live with these politicians day in and day out, a lot more than you do. And I wanna tell you right now that Mr. Roosevelt wants to be President so bad he'll do anythin', includin' kissin' your ass in Macy's window if it'd help him.' "

So they were certain that Roosevelt would eventually be forced to come to Tammany, and so to them. When he did, they knew exactly what kind of terms they would exact. The corruption that had flourished in New York City had reached the point during the administration of Mayor James J. Walker where it could no longer be ignored. Judge Samuel Seabury, a distinguished Democrat who years before had lost a bid for his party's gubernatorial nomination when Tammany turned against him, had been appointed to investigate civic corruption, and his revelations were making newspaper headlines.

"Every goddamn fuckin' move we made was gettin' into the newspapers, and that bastard Seabury was really diggin' deep. He was lookin' into our deals with the judges and he was tryin' to prove that me and Costello and Dutch Schultz, Lepke and lots of political big shots like Jimmy Walker and Jimmy Hines of Tammany — that the whole bunch of us was all tied up together. It was almost like you couldn't pick up the newspapers in '31 and the beginnin' of '32 without readin' about some new scandal Seabury dug up, about Walker or the cops or the courts. The heat was on and gettin' hotter. If somethin' wasn't done to stop Seabury from cleanin' up the town, it was gonna hurt our business bad. Besides, some of our guys, like Schultz and Vito and a few others, maybe includin' me and Frank, could take a rap.

"The first thing we did was put together a bundle of over two million in cash to buy off Seabury, to let him take a vacation and let things cool down. The bastard not only turned us down cold but he gave the story to the New York *Times* and there we was on the front page again.

"The only guy who could control Seabury was Roosevelt, and we figured that's where we had our ace. We had most of the city's delegates to the convention in our pocket, so we could stop the Governor from winnin' the state of New York; maybe that'd cost him the nomination — if a guy couldn't carry his own state, he looked like a bum. But there wasn't much we could do but wait. Then, about the middle of May, a guy stops at Frank's table in Peacock Alley for no more'n a minute, makin' it look like an accident. He was a big lawyer who lived up near Roosevelt, someplace around Tuxedo Park, and he never had nothin' to do with us before, or after. All the guy said to Frank was he would very much like to talk to him and me at my place that afternoon at three o'clock. Frank just nodded and the guy walked away.

"We had the meet and it was just like three businessmen talkin', with everybody knowin' what the other guy wants without havin' to say it out loud. This fellow's blood was so blue you could've used it in your fountain pen. He says to Frank, 'You know the Governor is running for the presidential nomination.' And Frank says, 'Yeah, I know. I read about it in the papers every day.' So I said, 'It costs a lotta money to run for President. If your guy wins the nomination — which is gonna be very tough — he's gonna need a lotta dough for advertisements, billboards and stuff like that.'

"This blueblood was no dope. He makes a remark like, 'We're sounding out some of the big contributors to see if they would be willing to make donations to support the Governor's campaign.' Frank says, 'We ain't never held back from our friends yet. If

Franklin Roosevelt gets the nomination, you come and see us. The door is always open.'

"All that beatin' around the bush was makin' me sick, so I put it right on the line. I said, 'Let's get somethin' straight. Roosevelt has a guy by the name of Seabury who's makin' things tough for some people around the city. So let's stop kiddin' around. If we deliver — and you know what I mean — then you gotta deliver, and you know what that means. But I wanna see some sign of it right away.'

"That done it. We all shook hands, smiled, slapped each other on the back and the guy leaves. I turned to Frank, and before I could say anythin' he starts to laugh. He says, 'Charlie, you're a good politician. It's too bad you went to jail or I could make you governor. I think your timin' was perfect, and we're gonna get some results from this. But no matter how you look at it, we're backin' both horses in a two-horse race. How can we lose?' "

Then Tammany Hall split. Jimmy Hines threw his support to Roosevelt and announced that he would lead a Tammany delegation to Chicago committed to that candidacy. His rival Tammany leader, Albert C. Marinelli, announced for Al Smith and claimed that the majority of the city's delegates were still solidly behind the former governor.

From Albany, Governor Roosevelt made a statement that was considerably more significant to Luciano and Costello than to the general public. In ringing, eloquent terms, he denounced civic crime, corruption and graft. Then, in carefully phrased terms, he said that while he applauded the efforts of Seabury and his investigation, he had reached the conclusion that the panel had not made a strong enough case against Mayor Walker, Tammany or its leaders like Hines to warrant any action.

"When that came out in the papers, Costello comes rushin' to my apartment all excited. He says to me, 'What did I tell you! Just like I said, Charlie, he's so anxious to be President he can taste it. I told you he'll sell anythin', buy anythin', and make any kind of deal if it'll make him President.' Costello was a lot more enthusiastic than me. 'It sounds good,' I said."

Costello was amazed at Luciano's lack of enthusiasm. "What's the matter with you?" he said. "Now we're sure we can't lose this race. No matter who wins, we come out ahead. With Seabury outa the way, everythin' goes back to normal for us. What's wrong with you, Charlie?"

"I don't know, Frank. I just got a feelin', and I don't know how to explain it. Y'see, a guy like Al Smith, he's a 'Sweet Rosie O'Grady' kind of guy — like the guys we grew up with. When you shake hands with him, you know you don't need a lawyer. But Roosevelt — lemme put it this way. All them society guys we play golf with up in Connecticut and around Westchester, whadda ya feel when you're around them, Frank? I mean, don't you always feel that behind your back they think you're no better'n shit? Tell me the truth."

Costello paused, walked about the apartment before answering. When he did, he spoke slowly. "The answer is, no, I don't feel comfortable. The answer is, yes, I hate their fuckin' guts because they were born into somethin' they didn't make themselves. It was handed to 'em. So I agree with you. But lemme tell you somethin', Charlie. The way we feel personally don't mean a fuckin' thing. So I go with Hines and you take Marinelli and we come out on top. That's what counts."

But Meyer Lansky, when Costello and Luciano discussed the decision with him, had another thought. "What happens if those two guys cancel each other out and a guy comes from nowhere and grabs the nomination as a compromise? What do we do to take care of that and see that it doesn't happen?" Lansky did not wait for his stunned associates to answer. "It's a matter of timing and strategy. We don't support anybody until the very last minute when maybe our votes'll tip the scale for the two-thirds. If we handle it that way, then we really own the odds."

Then it was on to Chicago and the convention. Luciano, Costello and Lansky traveled with the New York City delegation and kept the leaders under constant watch and control. At the Drake Hotel, Luciano took a luxurious six-room suite for himself and his old friend, Tammany leader and Smith backer Al Marinelli; they were constant companions. In the opposite wing of the hotel, Costello took an equally luxurious suite for himself and his old friend, Tammany leader and Roosevelt supporter Jimmy Hines; they were constant companions. In between, Lansky took a suite for himself, prepared to mediate and to entertain all the powers in the party, with an eye to the untapped hinterlands. And an old friend, Longie Zwillman, was splitting his time between floors and hotels, shepherding delegates under his control from New York's Nassau County and from New Jersey's northern tier.

It was like New Year's Eve, or the eve of Prohibition, that last week in June in Chicago. There was no pretense of adhering to the Eighteenth Amendment and the Democrats were ready to start celebrating victory even before they had a candidate. Liquor was for sale openly to any delegates at stands run by the heirs of Al Capone (six weeks earlier, he had begun serving a prison term for income tax evasion). In the hospitality suites run by the outfit, liquor was free to all comers, and it was poured steadily and unstintingly all hours of the day and night. The bar was never closed and the buffet tables were constantly replenished. "We had the best whiskey in the world, any kind that any guy wanted, and we poured it like it was comin' out of the sink in the kitchen. It didn't cost us nothin'. Capone's outfit — with Al away, the guys who was runnin' it were Jake Guzik and Tony Accardo and Charlie Fischetti, Al's real cousin — they supplied all the booze we needed free."

Much of the booze at Lansky's bar, and at Costello's, gurgled down the throat of a Louisiana politician, Huey "The Kingfish" Long. But he was there not just for the hospitality. Between drinks he was sober enough to explore means of bringing new enterprises to his state, and to draw cash to his own pockets. When Long had been sufficiently primed, he was brought to a meeting in Luciano's suite with Charlie Lucky, Costello, Lansky and Moe Dalitz from Cleveland. There the outlines of a deal were laid whereby Louisiana, and particularly the parishes around New Orleans, would be thrown open to the organization, to bring in gambling casinos for the high rollers and slot machines and other nickel-and-dime games for the average man and the poor. To run things for the outfit, Luciano selected Dandy Phil Kastel, a former partner of Arnold Rothstein and more recently a partner of Costello in the New York slots. "Phil was no youngster, but he had a lotta what you might call polish. After Rothstein was bumped off in 1928, he sorta went back and forth between me and Costello and Lansky and Adonis. After all, we didn't know too much about Huey Long except that he was a loudmouth who liked to drink and he seemed to control his state with an iron fist. That was good enough for me. Unless somethin' went bad with him, we figured the city of New Orleans alone could be worth millions to us. And that's the way it worked out after we made the deal in Chicago. Long opened up the state and we moved into every parish, with Phil Kastel runnin' things from the Roosevelt Hotel where we put in a gamblin' club under one of Meyer's best guys, Seymour Weiss. By the time Long got knocked off a couple of years later, his piece of the action put about three million bucks cash in his pockets. We was practically buyin' the guy solid gold underwear. But, like I told Lansky at the convention, for us it was pure platinum."

The deal with Long was one of the peripheral benefits of that convention week in Chicago. The main attention was directed at the gathering of delegates at the hall in the Stockyards. "We waited until the very last second, and we had Roosevelt and Smith guys comin' out our ears. They all knew we controlled most of the city's delegates. Without 'em, Smith didn't have a chance. Maybe Roosevelt would've won anyway, but we knew that a lot of them big boys from the important states was holdin' back their delegates, figurin' that if Roosevelt couldn't even carry his own state, maybe they oughta dump him entirely and find somebody else.

"But you could smell that the convention was leanin' toward Roosevelt and all it was gonna take was a big switch, maybe of somebody like Garner, to put him over. I'd already talked to Al Marinelli and got him to agree to go in with me whichever way was best for all of us, even if it meant switchin' the majority of the hall over to Roosevelt. With all that was goin' on, we knew we hadda make our move, either to go with Roosevelt or with some guy we never heard of. Frank, Meyer and I had a private meet, what they call a caucus in politics, with all the guys on our side of the line, like Curley in Boston, Pendergast from Kansas City, Huey Long and a few others like them. When Frank got the word that Roosevelt would live up to his promise to kill the Seabury investigation — I mean, like tapering off so he could save face — it was in the bag for him."

Once that decision had been made, Al Smith had to be told.

The question was, who would tell him? Marinelli was the logical choice, but he was reluctant to break the news to his idol. Thus, it was left to Luciano, the outward Smith backer, and the decision was to present it face-to-face. "It was like the rules in my own business. As far as I was concerned, Al Smith was a top Don and in a sense, me and Frank was about to knock him off. He was entitled to get it straight to his face."

Late that evening, Luciano made his way surreptitiously to Smith's suite at the Drake for a private conference. "I told him we figured — no, I said we was sure — that Roosevelt was gonna win and there was no way to stop him. That meant we had no choice but to throw in with Roosevelt. Naturally, Smith tried to get me to change my mind and keep the delegates in line behind him. I said the decision had been made and there wasn't no way to change it.

"Of course, Smith was nobody's fool. He asked me straight out what the deal was, and I decided to tell him. I said, 'Al, Roosevelt's promised he's gonna close his eyes to Seabury and keep 'em closed. You already saw what happened last spring when he made that statement. We gotta believe him after that.'

"What happened then really got to me. This big guy, this world-famous politician, this tough guy who grew up on the same streets of New York as me, he started to bawl. I mean, he was blubberin' all over the place. I never saw a guy cry like that. He kept walkin' around the room, holdin' his head in his hands and all he could say was, 'Charlie, you fellas are crazy. I would've murdered Seabury for you.' But what the hell, it was too late. He knew it and I knew it. As I started to leave, Al came over to me and put his hand on my shoulder. He wasn't cryin' no more. He got it out of his system and now he was the tough old 'Happy Warrior' they used to call him. Then he said somethin' that really made my blood run cold. He looked me square in the face and shook his head real sad. 'Charlie,' he said, 'Frank Roosevelt'll break his word to you. This is the biggest mistake you ever made in your entire life, by trustin' him. He'll kill you.'

"When I walked out of Smith's suite, my knees was shakin'. My bones told me that we'd walked into a trap — that Smith was right."

What Smith knew — and what Luciano, Costello and their friends had not sensed — was that Franklin Roosevelt was something more than a country squire, an aristocrat whose word, implied or explicit, could be counted on. He was a politician, and a wily one, a supreme opportunist who used people and events just so long as they were of value, and who refused to be used. With the adulation of the country beginning to pour over him as the Democratic presidential candidate, Roosevelt suddenly turned Judge Seabury loose. The smiling, affable governor, soon to be President, met with reporters in Albany and issued a new public statement about corruption in New York City. Ever since his early-spring refusal to authorize action, he had been under mounting public pressure from Seabury and New York City Congressman Fiorello H. La Guardia. He had kept his silence until, with the nomination his, he needed the Tammany machine no longer. Indeed, the Tiger had become so notorious that it was only a weight around his neck he was more than eager to shed.

Public office is a public trust, he said, echoing the words La Guardia had used to him earlier. It was the highest of public trusts and those holding it must be above suspicion. He was, then, giving Judge Seabury the power to subpoena and question fully any officeholders and politicians against whom suspicions had been raised. If their answers were not satisfactory, then as governor he was prepared to act to remove those officials from office.

"Naturally, Roosevelt had been a prick all along, but I gotta give him credit for one thing — he was really smooth. Of course, I was sorry I didn't tell Meyer and Frank about my hunch in Chicago, because now everythin' was clear. But as I look back on it, he done exactly what I would've done in the same position, and he was no different than me. I had Masseria and Maranzano knocked off to get to the top. What I did was illegal; I broke the law. Roosevelt had us and other guys like Hines and Walker sent to the can or squashed. What he did was legal. But the pattern of it was exactly the same; we was both shitass doublecrossers, no matter how you look at it. Now, I don't say we elected Roosevelt, but we gave him a pretty good push. I always knew that politicians was crooked; that you could buy 'em anytime you wanted and you couldn't trust 'em around the corner. But I didn't think it was the same with a guy who was gonna be President. I never knew that muscle could buy its way into the White House. I never knew that a guy who was gonna be President would stick a knife in your back when you wasn't lookin'. I never knew his word was no better than lots of racket guys'. But I guess nobody should become President of the United States on the back of a gangster."

With Roosevelt's blessings, Seabury hauled one Democratic city politician after another before his investigating committee and grilled them about their dealings with the underworld, about the huge caches of money that were turning up in their possession. Glad-handing Mayor Jimmy Walker spent several uncomfortable hours before Seabury, trying to evade and slide around the questions. Roosevelt, true to his promise, prepared to move against Walker. Before he could, the Mayor sent him a telegram: "I HEREBY RESIGN AS MAYOR OF NEW YORK CITY. JAMES J. WALKER." And before anybody quite knew what had happened, Walker was on a boat for Paris, accompanied by Betty Compton, his showgirl mistress; when he returned years later, the scandals were old memories and he was greeted by a wave of nostalgia for the good old days.

The shock waves from the revelations about Walker and his sudden departure reverberated through city government. Seabury questioned and castigated scores of Walker aides and Tammany bigwigs, spreading out such a portrait of municipal malfeasance that even the most jaded New Yorkers were sickened. At the top, Tammany Hall was shattered, and some of its leaders — including, a few years later, Jimmy Hines — would end up in Sing Sing. The city was ready for reform, and the good old days were over.

16.

Three weeks before Christmas 1933, the Noble Experiment, Prohibition, died. Few mourned. It had been a failure from its very inception, as attempts to legislate social attitudes and behavior often are. Its fourteen-year history had given rise to social crisis and moral breakdown, to a generation believing there was nothing wrong with breaking an unpopular law.

It had given rise, too, to a new breed of criminals who, without it, might never have been more than pariahs preying on innocent victims. But with Prohibition, Luciano, Lansky, Costello and Schultz became almost more famous than infamous and were often lionized by the "good people" to whom they provided merchandise and services available nowhere else, people who, under other circumstances, would have looked at them with opprobrium — if at all.

Though Luciano and his colleagues did not greet the end of Prohibition with joy, neither were they shattered by it; they were, in fact, fully prepared for it. For years they had been diversifying their empires, and now they stepped up the process. Increasing emphasis was placed on gambling of every kind, from nickel-and-dime policy through slot machines and candy-store punchboards to particularly luxurious high-stakes casinos. Wherever they could buy enough politicians and police to form "open" enclaves, their casinos attracted the rich and boomed — at New Orleans's Beverly Club, run by Phil Kastel, and the Blue Room at the Roosevelt Hotel, under the supervision of Seymour Weiss; at Bradley's in Palm Beach; at a score of clubs in Covington and Newport, Kentucky, Hot Springs, Arkansas, and Dade County and Broward County, Florida; at Ben Marden's Riviera and others along the Hudson in Fort Lee, New Jersey. A new agreement was struck with Nucky Johnson to open the South Jersey coast to gambling, with Johnson cut in for twenty-five per cent of the profits while the organization provided the equipment and all capital outlays.

It was a beginning, and Luciano and his friends were convinced there was a vast untapped area beyond the American borders. In the spring of 1933, Luciano convened a meeting of the Unione Siciliano at his Waldorf Towers suite to discuss a preoccupation of Lansky's. Just ninety miles from Miami, Lansky said, there was a place where the weather was good all year round, where American tourists were beginning to appear in increasing numbers, and where he could guarantee the organization would have no problems.

"Meyer and me have been workin' on this ever since the Roosevelt doublecross," Luciano said to the gathering. "We gotta expand someplace and we need a place to send our dough where it'll keep makin' money and also get them guys from Washington off our backs. Meyer's been down to Havana and he's made some good contacts. Within a couple months, by August or September, he's goin' back again and he'll probably make a deal. It could cost us a bundle in front, so everybody better get ready to put up at least half a million each."

"It was like droppin' a bomb. Five hundred thousand bucks as an ante for a kitty in 1933 wasn't peanuts. Chuck Polizzi from Cleveland started screamin', and that kinda made me laugh. I told him that we was makin' so much money out of his place in Covington that plenty of guys were gettin' rich off it, so how could he complain about takin' a piece of income that taxes could never grab, to make even more. I laid it on him pretty damn hard and from then on there was no complaints."

In September, Lansky made his trip to Havana, met with the Cuban strongman, Fulgencio Batista, a friend from earlier Prohibition days, and came away with gambling rights on the island, including control of the already established casino at the Hotel Nacional. "We hadda put up three million in cash, in front, for Batista, and Lansky did it by openin' an account in Zurich, Switzerland, for him. From then on, Batista got a guarantee of three million a year, minimum, but it always went way over that on the percentage.

"That was our first shot at the islands of the Caribbean, and eventually we opened up Nassau and places like that, because they needed us. It was my opinion that eventually our guys would be workin' in Europe, too. Nobody wanted to start a war with the Corsicans, because those guys was real cannibals compared to us when it came to muscle. But they didn't know how to run crap games and neither did the legal casinos, and the more Americans that went to Europe, the more they'd be lookin' for that kind of play."

Gambling was one aspect of the big push into diversification.

Another was into legitimate enterprises. The burgeoning of loan-sharking, one of the few sources of ready cash in a devastated economy, was often the wedge. When defaulting borrowers could not pay up to the Lepke-Lucchese collectors, they found themselves with new partners, and the garment district was soon swarming with companies controlled by the underworld.

Trucking, too, was an obvious target. "Durin' Prohibition we probably ran the biggest truckin' operation in the United States. We knew more about trucks and tight schedules than any company in the country. So we looked over the market and decided to put a little squeeze on here and there with companies that should be happy to have our experience. For example, milk spoils pretty fast and so does bread and fresh vegetables. In no time at all we had a lock on three or four of the biggest fresh-food businesses in America and we took in as much as half a cent a loaf on bread. We bought into the biggest dairies, and we're still there.

"Lepke and Schultz was doin' the same thing with meat and takin' it from both ends — from the packers to make sure the meat got where it was goin', and protectin' the restaurants to make sure they got their deliveries smooth and regular. All the top places, even Jack Dempsey's restaurant on Broadway, paid us a cut. And Socks Lanza controlled the Fulton Fish Market downtown. After all, nothin' spoils faster'n fish. That market was the biggest seafood distribution center in the world; the city owned it, but we ran it and even the Little Flower knew better than to get messed up with us down there."

Some of the inroads into legitimacy were simple. Others, however, met with resistance, and some of this resistance came from inside the underworld. "The toughest fight of all was gettin' into real estate. In a way, it was crazy that so many guys objected to it. There was no rackets, no shakedowns. It was all out in the open, clean. You had a nice buildin', which maybe didn't pay off like a slot machine, but the money come in regular. Some of the guys only knew things like rackets and the big score. When Lansky and I talked about buyin' into real estate, they looked at us like we was nuts. 'What're we gonna do with a buildin'?' We lost out on a lotta terrific deals which if we owned today would be worth a thousand million dollars. That was always my big objection to the brainpower in the Unione. Some of them guys could never see beyond a bowl of spaghetti."

Still, whiskey and beer were not forgotten in the midst of the new expansion. Until the moment of the ratification of the Twenty-first Amendment to the Constitution, repealing Prohibition, Luciano and his friends had been selling booze without pause, and selling it more openly even than during the halcyon days, for at the end there was hardly even a pretense of enforcing the dying law. "We had a whole inventory of booze socked away all over the country, in warehouses, in drops down near Atlantic City, and out in Ohio — all over. We had to get rid of it the minute whiskey became legit. Do you know what we did with it? Most of it we gave away, to churches and synagogues in New York, Chicago, Philadelphia, everywhere. We made ourselves good guys in the neighborhoods. All over the place they was havin' rummage sales. The churches and synagogues sold the stuff and kept the money. It was kinda like liquid Bingo.

"The Dutchman, who was thinkin' at the time about becomin' a Catholic, give all his booze to the Catholic churches around where he was operatin' in New York and Jersey. He became a big man with 'em, got in real good with the priests. Maybe that helped him up there later on. It didn't do him no good down here."

The underworld had already made plans to get into legitimate liquor. The outfit continued, behind the scenes, to maintain interests in the speakeasies after they had turned into legitimate nightclubs, and to supply these clubs with their whiskey. Foreign agents of Luciano and his friends arranged with distillers abroad, with whom they had been dealing for years, for the acquisition of importing and distribution franchises, though the American gangsters were barred by their criminal records and reputations from moving into control of domestic distillers (a business soon dominated by men less notorious, like Lewis Rosenstiel and Jacob Bronfman, who emerged as heads of Schenley and Seagram's respectively).

Costello and Kastel, for instance, set up Alliance Distributors as the exclusive distributor in the United States for Scotland's Whiteley Company, maker of King's Ransom and House of Lords

Scotch. The two went even further; they purchased a controlling interest in J. G. Turney & Sons, Ltd., the British holding company for Whiteley. Lansky, Luciano, Siegel, Adonis and others all had an interest in Capitol Wine and Spirits, a major importer and distributor of French wines, Scotch, Canadian and domestic whiskeys. There was hardly a bootlegger of note who didn't cut himself in for some of this new business.

Lansky, however, recognized that the bootlegging days were far from over, since untaxed bootleg booze could still be sold much cheaper than heavily taxed legal whiskey. In striking an independent course, Lansky broke his partnership with Benny Siegel in the Bug and Meyer Gang, and at the same time began drawing back from his once-total dependence on Luciano. In November of 1933, using his father-in-law, Moses Citron, as a front, Lansky formed Molaska Corporation. Its charter gave it the right to process dehydrated molasses as a sugar substitute. But the company's real aim was to use the molasses as the base for vast quantities of illegal alcohol to be turned out in stills in Ohio and New Jersey, alcohol that was for sale to distillers of bootleg whiskey and to legitimate manufacturers for bottling under their own labels as legal whiskey.

"It was a combination of things that started the Mighty Mite to look for independence. No matter how he'd try, he'd still be number two as far as I was concerned, and he knew it. So he hadda make his move. The minute Molaska was put together, I knew Lansky was settin' out on his own, not entirely, but to make a place for himself in the rackets which didn't have nothin' to do with me. But I couldn't let him get away with that without doin' somethin' about it. I called him in one mornin' about Christmastime and said, 'Meyer, it's okay with me about Molaska, I'm not askin' for a piece of it, because you earned it. But we're gonna set lots of guys up in the legal whiskey business, and I want you to make an outline of where we're gonna do it, the guys we're gonna promote, and what it's all gonna cost. That's gonna be mine, and I'll split it with everybody, like I always did, includin' you.'

"Meyer done what I asked. Of course, a couple years later, Molaska got busted by the Feds. But after that time, I knew Meyer wouldn't stop plannin' stuff of his own on the side. But when you come down to it, I always thought I could trust Meyer even if he was different from me and most of the other guys. He liked to live in the background, in the shadows. In that way, as I look back on it, he was one up on me. It was my publicity that really cost me the best ten years of my life. So I guess in that way Meyer was smarter."

If relations with Lansky, basically the relationship of equals, maintained a certain equilibrium through these years, Vito Genovese was something else. As the organization expanded its activities, Genovese was constantly at Luciano's ear, pressing the case of his favorite trade, narcotics. "The little son of a bitch would never give up. I think his mother may have been a Neapolitan but maybe his father was an English bulldog. In fact, sometimes I think he looked like one. He would never let up on the subject of junk. He just loved junk more than booze or anything — except maybe that broad Anna."

In 1932, Genovese fell in love with Anna Petillo Vernotico. Unfortunately, she was already married, but that did not stop Genovese. He hired a couple of killers, had Anna's husband, Gerard Vernotico, garrotted and thrown off the roof of a building, and then within a few weeks took the widow as his bride. For his honeymoon, Genovese took Anna to Italy. "He wanted to take her all around where he was born to let her see what kind of an American big shot he could be around Naples, where everybody knew his name. While he was there, he made some good contacts, even though I warned him against makin' any connections with narcotics guys in Italy and France. Somehow or other, he must've had an idea for the future and he planted a lotta very important seeds there.

"When he come back to New York, Joe Bananas from Brooklyn and Steve Magaddino, who ran things up around Buffalo, come to see me. They said Vito was talkin' to them private about settin' up a line of junk right from Italy, through him, that he could put out all over the United States. They was afraid of this and Magaddino even told Vito to his face that he was gonna convene the Unione council and have him knocked off. It was like talkin' to the wall. Except I didn't know at the time that Vito wasn't listenin' and was gonna keep on gettin' things set up. It served him right, the dirty little bastard, when Anna began givin' it away free a couple years later to any guy who looked at her, and especially when she started playin' house with other broads. And he really rated it later on when she blew the whistle on him."

The seeds that were being planted by Genovese in Italy eventually flourished into an industry that would become a national nightmare in the years following World War II. In the mid-thirties, however, narcotics, though extraordinarily profitable for those dealing in them, had not yet made a major impact on the nation. Genovese's plans for an immediate ripening were delayed by his own greed. He had hardly returned from his honeymoon trip when a small-time hoodlum named Ferdinand "The Shadow" Boccia brought him a sucker, a gullible and wealthy Brooklyn merchant who loved to gamble. Boccia offered to set up a poker game in return for a third of Genovese's winnings. Together with Mike Miranda, Genovese took the merchant for fifty thousand dollars, then for another hundred thousand sold him a machine they claimed would manufacture real ten-dollar bills. "When Mike told me the story, I couldn't believe it. I thought the days when you could sell the Brooklyn Bridge to anybody was over. But wouldn't you know, that son of a bitch Vito was so damn greedy he decided he wasn't gonna give Boccia his fifty-grand cut."

What Genovese did instead was hire two minor hoodlums, Willie Gallo and Ernest "The Hawk" Rupolo, to put a bullet in Boccia's head. This they did. Then Genovese went further; he paid Rupolo $175 to murder Gallo. Rupolo botched the job; on two different occasions he took a crack at Gallo, but the most he was able to do was inflict a minor wound. Gallo retaliated by going to the police and then testifying at Rupolo's trial, and he had a certain satisfaction in hearing the Hawk sentenced to nine to twenty years in the penitentiary for attempted murder.

For the next few years, Genovese, fearing that prison might turn Rupolo into a canary, walked warily, prepared to flee at the first sign of trouble. But through most of those early post-Prohibition years, the potential sources of trouble for Genovese, Luciano and the rest of the underworld were a lot more important and a lot more powerful than Rupolo. Along with Repeal had come reform, to both the nation and New York. And along with reform had come a determination to smash the racketeers and their corrupting influence.

17.

"Around Christmas of 1932, just before Hoover's term was up, Frank Costello and I got word that Dutch Schultz was gonna be the next target for the federal tax guys after they got Waxey Gordon." After Al Capone, Schultz was at the time perhaps the most infamous American racketeer, a position he blamed more on his name than anything else. He had been born Arthur Flegenheimer in Yorkville on Manhattan's Upper East Side in 1902 and had grown up in the Bronx, where he early began a career in crime (his first arrest was at seventeen, and his record would eventually list thirteen arrests, ranging from disorderly conduct to murder) and adopted the name Dutch Schultz. "It was short enough to fit the headlines," he later complained. "If I'd kept the name Flegenheimer, nobody would have heard of me."

Like his friends, Schultz flourished with Prohibition. By 1930, he was a political power in the Bronx, controlled the beer and much of the liquor that flowed there, and had organized a restaurant service that "protected" the transportation of meat and produce from wholesalers to restaurants. "Charlie," he once said to Luciano, "you're doin' the public a big favor by makin' sure they have clothes to wear. It's the same with me. I make sure the customers can walk into a restaurant and have somethin' to eat. The public oughta be grateful."

His major racket by the early thirties, though, was policy. After an initial sneer at a penny-ante game, he had seen the potential profits. With the agreement and approval of Luciano, he muscled his way into the private domains of the independent black numbers bankers — Wilfred Brunder, Big Joe Ison, Henry Miro and Alexander Pompez — and became the biggest policy operator in the country, his banks taking in more than thirty-five thousand dollars a day. Through the manipulations of his financial wizard, Otto "Abbadabba" Berman (named after a candy bar he constantly munched), Schultz's profits were boosted from the normal two-thirds after payoffs to winners to something closer to three-fourths.

"Schultz was one of the cheapest guys I ever knew, practically a miser. Here was a guy with a couple of million bucks and he dressed like a pig. He used to brag that he never spent more than thirty-five bucks for a suit, and it hadda have two pairs of pants. His big deal was buyin' a newspaper for two cents so he could read all about himself.

"But I never had no trouble with him when we needed him for somethin' important. So I hadda look on him as a dependable partner. I didn't have to love him. Besides, he done me a big favor when he knocked off Coll."

Vincent "Mad Dog" Coll, the killer hired by Maranzano to murder Luciano, was ambitious and decided to cut himself in on Schultz's empire. Schultz spurned the demand and Coll declared war. It lasted until February 1932, when Coll was trapped by Schultz gunmen in a drugstore telephone booth on West Twenty-third Street in Manhattan, near a rooming house where he was hiding out. He was riddled by a submachine gun. "The guy was really crazy, tryin' to shoot his way into Schultz's territory."

Coll was neither the only nor the most dangerous enemy of Schultz. For the federal government was now after him for income tax evasion. "That was when Johnny Torrio told every one of us that we better start fixin' up our income tax returns. A lot of us did that, startin' with 1928, to show some legitimate business. In my case, I declared an income of sixteen thousand bucks and through the next four, five years, that figure went up to about twenty-five grand a year, from 'gamblin' enterprises,' and I listed myself as a 'professional gambler.' Y' know, I always thought it was funny that the United States government would let anybody declare taxes on any illegal business and then keep the money without prosecutin' the guy for breakin' the law."

Such advice, and such filings, came too late for Schultz, however. In 1933, a federal grand jury in New York indicted him for failure to file returns for 1929, 1930 and 1931, when, it contended, his taxable income had been $481,637.35 from bootlegging alone, on which he owed the United States Treasury $92,103.34 in back taxes plus interest. If convicted, Schultz would face not merely payment of back taxes plus interest but fines of more than $100,000 and a prison term of up to forty-three years.

The case had been prepared by a young United States Attorney for the Southern District of New York named Thomas E. Dewey. He was already winning a reputation as the nemesis of the underworld, having won convictions of the notorious lone-wolf killer, John T. Nolan, better known as "Legs Diamond" and, for tax evasion, of Waxey Gordon. Dewey had amassed a mountain of evidence to support the indictment of Schultz, and a conviction seemed inevitable. Up to that moment, the government had yet to lose a tax case against a racketeer, and there was little reason to suppose it would fail this time.

But Schultz was not about to give in easily. With the overt and covert help and protection of the police he managed to avoid detection, though there were fifty thousand Wanted posters plastering the city, and he was not exactly invisible. During the first year of hiding, he lived openly at a number of apartments around the city, at addresses known to his friends and associates and to the politicians and police on his payroll. Tammany leader Jimmy Hines, a Schultz partner in the numbers racket, was a frequent visitor wherever the Dutchman was living. And Schultz turned up regularly at the better nightspots, did not even abandon his custom of dropping in at Polly Adler's a couple of times a week, where he was always welcomed as a good paying customer. With such freedom of movement, Schultz was able to continue unabated his direct supervision of his sprawling operations.

But such a situation could not last. By mid-1934, Secretary of the Treasury Henry Morgenthau decided the charade had gone on long enough, and Morgenthau found some willing allies. J. Edgar Hoover proclaimed Schultz "Public Enemy Number One" and ordered his agents to bring him in without delay. Morgenthau talked, as well, with New York's new reform mayor, Fiorello La Guardia, who had taken office on January 1, 1934, after defeating Tammany's candidate on a platform stressing war against corruption and the underworld. La Guardia ordered his police commissioner, Lewis J. Valentine, to "get your men off their butts" and start looking seriously for Schultz.

As the pressure mounted, Schultz decided to go underground for real. He turned to Luciano for assistance, and Charlie Lucky sent him to Albert Anastasia in Brooklyn, who provided a well-protected hideout.

"While I was takin' care of Schultz, the Little Flower started to throw some pretty big rocks at me and Frank Costello. The first thing he did when he got to be mayor was to give the cops orders to pick up me and Adonis and Costello and Willie Moretti and everybody else who was in New York. You know what happened? I'm walkin' down the street and this cop comes up to me and he says, 'Charlie, the Commissioner wants to see you.' This was before La Guardia had a chance to name Valentine and the commissioner was still a guy named John O'Ryan. I says, 'For chrissake, it's New Year's. Tell him I'll see him tomorrow.' I'm thinkin' he wants to talk about a deal, now that we got a new mayor and that kind of thing. But the cop tells me, no, I gotta see O'Ryan right then. He says La Guardia's down on all of 'em and they gotta bring me in to make it look good. He gives me a ride downtown and Commissioner O'Ryan's waitin' for me. He says, 'Charlie, I'm sorry about this. We hadda bring you in. If you want to go home now, we'll give you a ride.' I look at him like he's nuts and I ask him, 'Ain't you even gonna ask me one question?' He says, 'What do you want me to ask you?' So I was there about ten minutes, is all.

"And the same thing happened to the rest of the guys. They got a ride to a precinct or someplace, to make it look good, and then a ride home. Even Willie Moretti. They was waitin' for him when he came over from Jersey. They picked him up, but it wasn't no different with him. After they let him go, he comes to see me at the Towers and we had a big laugh over it. It made La Guardia look good in all the papers. But what did it mean? Nothin'. Oh, maybe we hadda throw a couple grand more in the bag every week for the neighborhood cops, but that was all.

"But that La Guardia wouldn't let up. The next thing he does is round up a few hundred of Costello's slot machines and dump 'em in the East River — makin' sure the newsreel cameras and newspapers covered every square inch of what he was doin'. And he starts throwin' my name around. Maybe Schultz was Public Enemy Number One as far as the FBI was concerned but with La Guardia I was the number one guy. Why the hell did he have to say, 'Lucky Luciano is nothin' but a cheap bum'? That little bastard knew there was nothin' cheap about me; a guy who lives in the Waldorf Towers ain't no bum.

"I just couldn't understand that guy. What the hell did he want? He was a wop like the rest of us and he wasn't goin' noplace. He'd already been a congressman and he couldn't expect to be President. If the American people didn't elect Al Smith, they sure as hell wouldn't give the right time to a half-Jewish wop like La Guardia. When we offered to make him rich, he wouldn't even listen. So I figured, what the hell, let him keep City Hall, we got all the rest — the D.A., the cops, everythin'."

But La Guardia, with his flair for publicity and his alliance with Morgenthau and other federal authorities, could make things uncomfortable, and this he did. As the search for Schultz intensified, a campaign against other underworld leaders was stepped up. But in those events of the moment, Luciano and his friends saw more than menace. They saw promise.

One day, during a meeting with Lansky at the Waldorf to discuss the Cuban gambling operations, the talk turned to the odds against Schultz if and when he surrendered. Lansky's estimation was that the odds favored conviction, and many of Luciano's friends, including Zwillman, Adonis and Genovese, were already anticipating that day, for it would mean that the Dutchman's empire would be parceled out under Luciano's direction. "I had a lotta different feelin's about that. What Meyer was sayin' was true, and it really looked like Schultz was gonna take a bath and there wasn't a damn thing anybody could do about it — no way to fix it that I could see. But I was worryin' about the heat La Guardia was puttin' on me, too. So I said to Lansky, 'It wouldn't be a bad idea if we let Dewey know that he got the goods on Waxey with my help. Then maybe he could hold back a little bit. Besides, all La Guardia talks about is how he's helpin' them guys put me in the clink.'"

The word was passed. Dewey responded: "Tell Luciano that

someday I'll show him my gratitude in court." If Luciano thought there was a promise in those words, Albert Marinelli dispelled that dream. They were, Marinelli told him, a threat.

The Schultz matter, though, was still to be handled. From his hideout now, Schultz was having difficulty attempting to run his business with the efficiency that personal attention would insure. His lawyer, J. Richard "Dixie" Davis, an attorney who divided his time between underworld clients and Broadway showgirls, had an idea that at first appalled the penurious Dutchman, who was eventually persuaded that it was his only recourse. The government was offered one hundred thousand dollars as a flat settle-ment for all back taxes if the indictments would be dismissed. Like his predecessor, Andrew Mellon, who had rejected a similar four-hundred-thousand-dollar settlement offer from Al Capone, Morgenthau flatly rejected the deal. "We don't do business with criminals," he said.

Schultz was left with few alternatives. What he feared was that the FBI men on his trail might deal with him as they had dealt with John Dillinger and other public enemies. He had no desire to face that. In November of 1934, he suddenly showed up in Albany, turned himself in, and remained in jail for several weeks while his lawyers argued with the court about the amount of bail, finally set at seventy-five thousand dollars. For more than a year thereafter, his preoccupation was entirely with his tax struggle.

The last thing Schultz wanted was to be tried in New York City, where the climate had turned frigid toward underworld leaders. Schultz's attorneys won a change of venue, and in April of 1935, he went on trial in Syracuse, New York. The government's case, developed by Dewey and his staff more than two years earlier (Dewey had resigned as United States Attorney in 1933 and gone back to private practice), was argued by John H. McEvers, a special assistant to Attorney General Homer Cummings. The defense was simple and took only three hours. There was no de-nial that Schultz's income was large, even larger than the govern-ment claimed. But, the defense argued, Schultz had not filed returns because his lawyers had told him he did not have to, since his income was from an illegal source — bootlegging (which, the defense took care to point out, was only an ancient memory since

Repeal) — and so was nontaxable and did not have to be reported. When that advice had proved wrong, Schultz had made his offer to pay the hundred thousand dollars.

The jury debated two days and then reported that it was hopelessly deadlocked, seven to five for conviction.

The government immediately moved for a second trial, this time in July in the upstate city of Malone, close to the Canadian border. Schultz, who arrived several weeks early, donned a gregarious and lavish manner as he toured the Malone taverns standing everyone to free drinks. He contributed heavily to local charities, making no secret of his gifts, and attended the major social events in company with Malone's mayor and other political and business leaders. Finally the clergy raised the alarm about this corrupting influence. Schultz's bail was revoked and he was lodged in a Malone jail cell, but not before he had made a deep impression on that economically distressed community and had, he later told Luciano and others, made a number of Malone citizens very rich.

When the new trial began, the government's case was a reprise of the Syracuse trial. The defense, too, was almost identical, with the jury informed that whether convicted or not, Schultz intended to do his duty as an American citizen and pay over to the Treasury the hundred thousand dollars he had offered. The jury deliberated two days, as had the earlier jury, but this time it found Schultz not guilty. Said the foreman, Leon Chapin, director of the New York State Dairymen's League, "We feel the government utterly failed to show that he earned so much as a nickel of tax income and we based our verdict on that belief."

Federal Judge Frederick H. Bryant was outraged. He told the jury in icy tones: "Your verdict is such that it shakes the confidence of law-abiding people in integrity and truth. It will be apparent to all who have followed the evidence in this case that you have reached a verdict based not on the evidence but on some other reason. You will have to go home with the satisfaction, if it is a satisfaction, that you have rendered a blow against law enforcement and given aid and encouragement to the people who would flout the law. In all probability, they will commend you. I cannot."

Judge Bryant was not the only one shocked by the verdict, nor

181

was Attorney General Cummings, who called it "a terrible miscarriage of justice." Back in New York, toward which Schultz promptly headed, his underworld associates were stunned and a little shaken. For more than a year they had been confident he would follow Capone and Gordon to federal prison, and they had been planning and working as though it would be years before he appeared on the streets again; they were dividing the spoils.

"We were all sure that Dutch hadda get it. We didn't think there was no way he could beat a federal tax rap that was that solid. Maybe I was the one who helped him more than anyone else. When Dixie Davis came to me to tell me about gettin' the case moved out of New York, I said to him, 'Dixie, you're representin' the biggest miser since King Midas. You gotta get Schultz to spread some loot around.' He did just that and so he bought his way out. There was a big reaction when we knew Schultz was comin' back. The guy who was most worried was Bo Weinberg."

Abraham "Bo" Weinberg was the Dutchman's senior lieutenant, the man who kept the books and who knew every facet of the Schultz empire. During his time of trouble, Schultz had been drawing off large sums from policy, protection and the other rackets to pay for his battle, and Weinberg had begun to worry that the empire might go down the drain with the ruler. "Bo went to see Longie Zwillman over in Jersey — they was in lots of deals together — and asked him to help him out. Longie listened to him and then he brought Bo over to see me for a private meet, near Grant's Tomb up on Riverside Drive." Luciano listened to Weinberg's proposal with considerable interest. Weinberg offered to reveal all of Schultz's interests and turn the empire over intact to Luciano, Zwillman and their allies, who, he knew, were already making moves in that direction. With sweat pouring off his face that cold March day in 1934, Weinberg explained to Luciano that he wanted to prevent the destruction of the empire by a war over its control. All he wanted was to continue as its overseer and receive his current fifteen per cent of the total take.

Luciano quickly called a meeting, at the Waldorf Towers, of himself, Zwillman, Adonis, Costello, Lansky, Lepke, Lucchese and Genovese. "I explained Weinberg's deal and I told them I felt like a grave-robber in a way. Here we was, talkin' about cuttin' up Schultz and he wasn't even in the can yet. Then we got down to cases. The responsibility for breakin' up Schultz's territory hadda be mine because that's the way everybody wanted it." In his division, Luciano gave policy and gambling to Costello and Lansky, liquor to Adonis, restaurant rackets to Lepke and Lucchese, as well as other enforcement operations. Zwillman received the Jersey operations, after promising to split them with Moretti.

"All the time we was whackin' up the business, I could see Vito lookin' at me like a hungry pig. So I said to him, 'Vito, what part do you think you oughta have?' Vito looked at me with his mouth open. He was expectin' me to tell him, but when I asked him, he was too fuckin' surprised to answer. So I said, 'Maybe you'd like it all?' At that minute, you could've heard a pin drop on the plush rug in my apartment at the Towers. The place turned to ice. Nobody said a word for a couple minutes. Finally, I broke it up and said to Vito, 'I want this to teach you a lesson. Someday, if you don't stop bein' greedy, it's gonna kill you. There'll be no junk, and I mean it. Don't ruin what we're doin' here today by addin' a new business to somethin' that Schultz never handled.' Then I turned to Meyer and Frank and I said, 'Vito goes in with you and he gets twenty-five per cent; you two guys split the balance.' As for me, I get a piece off the top of everythin'. And if, by some miracle, he beat the rap, everythin' would go back to him. Everybody was happy; I didn't make no enemies and I got mine. We made a solemn vow that nobody would ever know about this meet and what happened. I knew Dutch wouldn't like it, but after all, he'd have to appreciate that I didn't let his whole territory go down the drain through a war."

Then Schultz returned to pick up the pieces. He was back no more than an hour before he sensed trouble. Immediately he contacted Luciano, who told him that every effort had been made to preserve his operations and only the most capable had been supervising them so they would remain intact.

"The day Schultz come to see me at the Towers, Vito was with me. The Dutchman was so excited that we'd all been so nice to him that he almost started to cry. And then, I'll be damned if he didn't start to talk about the Catholic religion; he wanted to know what it was like to be a Catholic, whether Vito and me ever went to confession, if we knew what a guy had to do to switch into Catholicism from bein' a Jew. I almost fell over when he told us that while he was layin' low, in all his spare time, he was studyin' to be a Catholic. I swear, from that minute on, the Dutchman spent more time on his knees than he did on his feet. He told us he was sure Christ was what helped him get through the bad eighteen months, and what finally got him the acquittal.

"It's funny. When I first started hangin' around with Jewish guys like Meyer and Bugsy and Dutch, them old guys Masseria and Maranzano and lots of my friends used to beef to me about it. They always said that some day the Jews was gonna make me turn and join the synagogue. So what happens? It ain't me that gets turned, it's the Dutchman. That's some joke."

Despite his newfound concern with the spiritual, Schultz managed to spend a considerable part of his time on his feet, and what he saw as he walked around his territory he didn't like at all. Much of his time was now spent in New Jersey, in order to avoid the constant harassment directed specifically at him by Commissioner Valentine's elite unit in the police department. In New Jersey, his interests had been handled by Zwillman, but when Schultz talked to Zwillman, he came away convinced that he was being threatened with seizure. He was certain that this could not have been possible without the connivance of Bo Weinberg.

Schultz set a trap. Luciano later learned that Schultz had Zwillman's home staked out — to put a tail on Weinberg would have been a waste of time, for despite his bulk, Weinberg could have slipped one in minutes. The stakeout paid off. One warm evening in September, Weinberg's car was spotted driving through Zwillman's gate. A hurried call brought Schultz and when Weinberg left about an hour later, the Dutchman was waiting for him. Weinberg was never seen again.

"One of the boys in the stakeout seen him murder Weinberg and he told me about it. He said Dutch killed Bo with his bare hands. This fellow wanted me to know that Schultz had blood in his eye but was too smart to show it to me. It was like a warnin' that Dutch might start his own war against all of us. It was a lucky thing that Dutch never got time to go to work on us, because Tom Dewey had just been appointed special prosecutor in New York City and he had the same blood in his eye about Dutch — to put him away."

Though La Guardia had won City Hall, the situation at the New York district attorney's office had not improved. In the same election, Tammany's man, William Copeland Dodge — "stupid, respectable and my man," as Jimmy Hines described him — had squeaked through, thanks to the bankroll and the muscle of Tammany's underworld support. About Dodge's stupidity, Hines was right. In response to mounting pressure to do something about graft, corruption and the rackets, Dodge empaneled a special grand jury. Then he refused to do anything about the evidence it accumulated. The grand jury ran away. It demanded that Governor Herbert H. Lehman name a special prosecutor if he really wanted to see the city cleaned up. Lehman, a Democrat, acceded. He offered the job to several prominent Republican lawyers; all declined, until he reached the name of Thomas E. Dewey. Early in 1935, Dewey moved in and targeted Dutch Schultz.

The rumors quickly spread that Dewey was about to indict Schultz for his control of the restaurant-protection racket, that Dewey's plans went further and included a murder charge that could land Schultz in the electric chair. Luciano and his friends heard that Dewey had gathered evidence that on a snowy March night in Albany in 1935, Schultz had murdered one of his restaurant enforcers, Jules Modgilewsky, sometimes called Jules Martin or simply "Modgilewsky the Commissar." (Some years later, Dixie Davis, on trial for crimes of his own that would send him to jail, told the full story of that Albany night — how Schultz pulled a gun in a hotel room and shot Modgilewsky while Davis looked on.)

If Dewey could do the job, all well and good. But Luciano was not so sure he could. "Nobody was sure he could do it. After all, look how the Dutchman beat the federal rap. An airtight case in Dewey's office didn't mean it was gonna be an airtight case in court."

What particularly concerned Luciano and his friends was the strategy Schultz might employ to beat the charges, especially the protection one. If Schultz believed he was certain to go to prison for a long term, would he be inclined to take some of his friends with him? He knew enough about their operations, Luciano's and everyone else's, to do just that. Or would he, perhaps, to make a trade — his freedom for Luciano's and the other racketeers' — reveal all he knew? And if Schultz somehow did manage to get off without saying a word, would he then demand control of all that had been his in the past and start a war to take it?

"All of us was very worried. It seemed like Joe A. and Frank and Meyer and Torrio — the whole bunch of us — spent more time havin' meetin's than takin' care of our business, and it was all about how to handle Dutch Schultz. Finally the whole thing got settled, because Albert Anastasia came to me and said that Dutch wanted him to stake out Dewey's apartment up on Fifth Avenue. This was supposed to be a secret, but Albert never held nothin' back from me. He said that Dutch wanted to find out how easy it would be to knock off Dewey, and he offered Albert the contract at any price."

As far as Luciano was concerned, this was about the last thing anyone needed. It would violate one of his sternest precepts — "We didn't kill nobody but our own guys, if they give us too much trouble, and we never made a hit without a unanimous vote of everybody on the council. If one guy said no, then it was off. Outsiders was strictly outa bounds. I set up them rules and nobody was gonna break 'em. I just couldn't see how we'd be able to buy our way out of trouble if we let Dewey get knocked off."

Schultz had decreed his own death. But Luciano would not give the order on his own. "I called a meet of all the top guys of the council from everywhere. We took over the delicatessen early and we talked it over for almost six hours. This hadda be secret and not a word of it could get back to Dutch. You gotta remember that Schultz had made a lotta friends and this was the first time since Maranzano was rubbed out that we hadda face up to a unanimous decision of this kind. The council was either gonna work or the whole thing could fall apart right then and there. Everybody had a right to talk and everybody wanted to talk. But the vote was strictly Sicilian. Lansky made that point very clear;

186

and accordin' to the way I'd expressed it out in Chicago more than three years before, I had only one vote, period.

"Durin' the meet, Lansky took me aside and he said, 'Charlie, as your Jewish *consigliere,* I want to remind you of something. Right now, Schultz is your cover. If Dutch is eliminated, you're gonna stand out like a naked guy who just lost his clothes. The way La Guardia and the rest of them guys've been screamin' about you, it's ten to one they'll be after you next.' The way he said it to me, I really shivered. The only trouble was, things had gone too far and I realized we hadda get rid of the Dutchman, that I hadda think about everybody bein' safe and not just myself. We only took one vote and nobody disagreed."

The contract to murder Dutch Schultz was given to Charlie "The Bug" Workman, a killer who for some years had been one of Luciano's most reliable chauffeurs and bodyguards. On the night of October 23, 1935, Schultz went to his favorite hangout, the Palace Chop House and Tavern, in Newark. With him were two bodyguards, Abe Landau and Bernard "Lulu" Rosencranz, and his wizard of the numbers, Abbadabba Berman. Late in the evening, as they sat around a table in the back room, Schultz rose to go to the men's room.

A moment later, the tavern door opened and Bug Workman and a second killer, never identified, entered, walked to the rear and began shooting. Landau, Rosencranz and Berman were shot down in the fusillade; all died. Workman stood in the middle of the room, looking for the main target. He noticed the men's-room door, walked to it, and pulled it open. Schultz was standing at the toilet, urinating. Calmly and unhurriedly, Workman aimed, shot the Dutchman once, then turned and walked rapidly out of the tavern. The carnage left behind was the bloodiest since the 1929 St. Valentine's Day massacre in Chicago.

Mortally wounded, Schultz managed to stagger into the main room before collapsing. He lingered for a day, never telling who had shot him, never revealing any of his secrets. In his final hours, he accepted the last rites of the Roman Catholic Church.

More than six years later, Schultz's killer, Charlie Workman, was arrested and tried for the murder. In the middle of his trial, he suddenly changed his plea to guilty and received a life sentence.

Freed on parole in 1964, he became in his last years, through the intercession of Tommy Lucchese, a notions salesman in New York's garment district.

"Sometimes I think okayin' the killin' of the Dutchman was one of the biggest mistakes I ever made. I didn't have no choice, the way he was headin' — but look what happened. Once the Dutchman was dead — just like Lansky predicted — I was out in the open, as naked as a baby. And everybody who'd been after Dutch come lookin' for me."

18.

"Even after Prohibition was dumped, I was runnin' one of the biggest businesses in the world. We was in a hundred different things, legit and illegit. If you add it all up, we — I mean, the guys all over the country — we was doin' a business that was grossin' maybe a couple billion dollars a year. I was like the head of that big company, not as Boss of Bosses, but as a guy a lot of people came to for advice, a guy everybody expected to be in on the big decisions. But there was no way I could know what was goin' on everywhere all the time.

"Take General Motors: Does the president of the company know what every fuckin' car salesman is doin' and sayin'? Does he even know half the time what's goin' on right outside his own office? People are runnin' around doin' and sayin' things, and tellin' other people they're representin' General Motors. The president at the top, a guy like Alfred Sloan in them years, don't know a damn thing about it, and he don't even get blamed when things go wrong. But with me and my outfit, whether I knew what was goin' on or not, everybody blamed me for anythin' and everythin'.

"Durin' them years, there was a lotta different guys under their lieutenants who had their own things goin' for them. Outside of

junk, the one sideline that bothered me most of all was prostitution. But I was like the president of General Motors. I couldn't
keep tabs on what every guy was doin' on his own. There was
guys goin' around, like Little Davie Betillo and Tommy Pennochio and Ralph Liguori, who'd been with us through the years,
and they started tryin' to organize the whores. They was tellin'
the madams and the broads, 'Charlie Lucky wants you to do this,'
and 'Remember, this has Charlie Lucky's okay' — things like that.
Before you knew it, they was runnin' a whole string of cathouses
in New York and I'm supposed to be the boss.

"If I'd been the boss of General Motors, I could've fired them
guys when I heard about it. But how could I fire Betillo or Pennochio or the rest of them guys? They was valuable to me; they'd
been with me for a long time and they was always loyal. When
the booze business got killed off, they looked for a way to make
dough. What was I supposed to do, tell 'em they hadda starve?
Or kill 'em? What I did was to tell 'em to cut out all that crap.
If they wanted to run whores, that was their business, but I didn't
want no part of it. I ordered 'em to stop tellin' people that
Charlie Lucky was behind it, because I wasn't. I made it an order.

"Maybe I should've stepped on 'em hard, but I didn't have
time, and I didn't figure they'd keep goin' after I told 'em to stop.
It wasn't until later that I realized what had been goin' on right
under my nose. Believe it or not, the first real facts and figures I
ever got actually come from Tom Dewey. If anybody had ever
stopped to think about it right, they'd have realized that to a
Sicilian boss, a guy in the cathouse racket was the lowest of the
low. But nobody ever bothered to analyze it that way, and nobody
gave a damn."

Luciano had been arrested many times over the years. But after
1916, no arrest had been other than a minor or temporary inconvenience. And after his 1923 arrest by federal narcotics agents, he
had never believed that the shadow of the penitentiary could
cloud his future. His only fear, he said, if he had any at all, was
of the guns of enemies among his own kind. His business flourished and he assumed that there would be no interruptions. If
La Guardia and Valentine went on a rampage against Costello's
slot machines, well, Huey Long in Louisiana had an insatiable

desire for them and it was a simple matter to ship them to New Orleans.

During the summer of 1935, Luciano, as had become his habit, journeyed north with his society friends to watch the horses run at Saratoga and to watch these friends gamble away their money at the tables in which he had a major interest. "It was kind of a joke. There we was in Saratoga, the tables goin' full steam, the money right out in the open, and nobody doin' nothin' to stop it. Albany was only about fifty, sixty miles away. In the daytime, Governor Lehman's whole crime staff was screamin' about gamblin', the underworld, and how we all oughta be closed down. But at night, those same crime-busters was in Saratoga, gamblin' like everybody else. It was no different later on when Dewey got to be governor and was braggin' about how he broke the rackets and threw all the racketeers in jail. Saratoga kept operatin' just like before. Nobody moved a finger to stop it."

But Luciano's reign as king of the underworld was not so secure as he believed in the waning months of 1935. As Lansky had predicted, with the murder of Schultz, Luciano had become the target of Dewey. But it was no simple thing to hit that target. To know that Luciano was the boss of the rackets was one thing; to get the proof, enough proof to send him to jail, was something else again. As he had often said, Luciano had built his empire on a corporate model, and by the mid-thirties, there were layers upon layers between him and the actual perpetration of crimes. There was always someone else — never Luciano or any of his close associates — just above the man Dewey questioned. Nobody seemed able to point directly to Luciano and say, "I took my orders from Charlie Lucky," "I gave money to Charlie Lucky." Luciano was the boss; the public knew it, the law knew it, but where was the evidence that would stand up in court?

All the investigations seemed to run into that dead end — all, that is, but one. Assistant District Attorney Eunice Carter, one of the few women prosecutors on the public payroll, had been given the dubious assignment by District Attorney Dodge of presenting the city's case against prostitutes. It was a thankless job, for prostitution cases were uniformly tried in magistrate's court, and the

Seabury investigation had revealed that those courts were practically owned by the underworld.

Totally frustrated in her attempts to see justice done, Mrs. Carter became conscious of an unsettling pattern in the courts. When the prostitutes took the stand, they all told almost identical stories in almost identical words: that they were innocent working girls from out of town, say Philadelphia or Pittsburgh or Baltimore, who had been picked up while visiting old friends at houses whose purpose they were unaware of. The stories were so well rehearsed that Mrs. Carter was convinced there must be a conspiracy. She became more certain when she noticed that lawyers from the same firm almost invariably represented these girls and that hovering in the background, often in deep conversation with the girls before their appearances, was a disbarred lawyer named Abraham Karp, known to be close to the underworld. And when fines were assessed, the same people always were on hand to pay them.

Mrs. Carter became convinced that the whores had been organized, that a syndicate had taken over and was running the business in New York. At the district attorney's office, however, her suspicions were ignored or ridiculed. So she carried them to Special Prosecutor Dewey and his staff. Dewey was intrigued enough to hire Mrs. Carter away from Dodge, and to put her to work with two crack young attorneys on his staff, Sol Gelb and Murray Gurfein (now a United States district judge in New York). As they began to dig, they kept turning up the same names — Ralph "The Pimp" Liguori, a small-time punk long known to be a member of the Luciano outfit; James Frederico, Meyer Berkman, Jesse Jacobs, Benny Spiller, Abe Wahrman, Tommy "The Bull" Pennochio, Peter Harris, David Miller, Al Weiner, and, with an almost astonishing regularity, Little Davie Betillo.

As the investigation dug deeper — and Dewey kept releasing more and more attorneys to join in the digging, men such as Frank Hogan (later, for many years, Manhattan District Attorney), Harry Cole, Charles Grimes, Stanley Fuld and Charles D. Breitel (the last two later New York State Court of Appeals judges) — the aim became sharper: to tie Luciano to the vice syndicate. If they could find evidence that Luciano was giving authorization for the syndicate to operate, was getting a share of the proceeds, then they had him nailed even if he never directly dealt with a whore, a pimp or a madam. But if they could actually find a tie with the simple workers it would make Dewey's case that much neater. The key, they were sure, was Betillo, the man who was seemingly the boss of the ring. He was a known member of the Luciano organization. Would he, Dewey's investigators asked themselves, do anything without his boss's approval? They were certain the answer was no.

By the end of January 1936, enough evidence had been gathered to establish the existence of the vice ring and to identify some of its organizers — if not yet Luciano. Dewey's staff coordinated with Commissioner Valentine's special vice unit under Detective Captain Bernard Dowd, and on the evening of February 1, detectives and patrolmen fanned out across New York and simultaneously raided brothels, rounding up more than a hundred prostitutes and madams. They moved against the hangouts of the higher-ups and arrested Liguori, Pennochio and Betillo. For the moment, no other action was taken against the main objective, Luciano.

During the next weeks, working in shifts around the clock at specially rented hotel suites and offices, the Dewey staff questioned the whores and their benefactors. What quickly became evident to those under interrogation was that as far as Dewey and his people were concerned, they were unimportant. The name Luciano was mentioned repeatedly, and those being questioned soon realized that if they could talk about Charlie Lucky, somehow ring him in, all would go well with them. Not only would charges against them be dropped, not only would they be granted immunity from prosecution if they testified at a trial, but once Luciano was safely in jail, they might find living a lot easier. And the same message made its way into the prisons around the state where there might be other potential witnesses. The choice between jail for silence and freedom for testimony stirred forgotten memories.

Though Luciano was well aware that Dewey and his staff were after him, he was confident through the early months of 1936 that he had nothing to fear, that there was no way Dewey could develop a strong winning case against him for anything. He continued to move in his usual circles, kept up his usual rounds with little variation.

Then one evening, toward the end of March, "my payoff at the Waldorf Towers come through, that two hundred a month turned into a good investment." He was alone in his suite when his friend in the manager's office called excitedly saying that some men who looked like detectives were on their way up to see "Mr. Ross." It looked like trouble, he added.

"I figured it was a good time to take a vacation. Right then, I didn't know what they was after me for, but I wasn't gonna stay around and see. I just decided to go somewhere outa New York until things could cool down. I didn't even pack my clothes. I don't remember takin' nothin' with me, not even a toothbrush. I left with only the clothes I was wearin', went down the freight elevator, got in my car, and took off."

Luciano drove to Philadelphia, where he met Nig Rosen at a garage and exchanged his car for a Cadillac with Tennessee plates. He stayed in Philadelphia long enough to buy a new wardrobe at Jacob Reed & Sons, borrow twenty-five thousand dollars on his personal I.O.U. to Rosen to go with the four thousand he had in his pocket (he had left another five thousand dollars in his personal safe at the Waldorf Towers), and then head for sanctuary. En route, Luciano talked to friends in New York and discovered that a quiet search was underway for him, with nobody certain where he was. That news caused him to change his travel plans; he drove to Cleveland, left the car, and took the train to Arkansas, where, for several days, he contentedly took the waters in Little Rock. There, in the gambling enclave run by Owney "The Killer" Madden as a kind of underworld health spa, Luciano was certain he would be safe.

In New York, Luciano was now a wanted man. On April 1, Dewey proclaimed him "Public Enemy Number One in New York," to be arrested on sight. And a blue-ribbon grand jury that had been looking into prostitution, hearing the witnesses and the evidence Dewey had gathered, announced its findings. It indicted a long string of figures involved in the vice ring — Peter Belitzer, alias Peter Harris; David Marcus, alias Davis Miller; Al Weiner, and Jack Ellenstein as brokers of women into whorehouses; James

Frederico as roving field director of the ring; Jesse Jacobs and Meyer Berkman as the men charged with bailing out arrested prostitutes; Ralph Liguori as pimp and strong-arm man; Benny Spiller as the ring's loan shark; Abe Wahrman as the chief enforcer; Thomas Pennochio as the treasurer; and Little Davie Betillo, as the apparent head man.

The biggest news, though, was the naming of Luciano. The grand jury indicted him as the man who had put it all together and who ran it. He was charged with ninety counts (later reduced to sixty-two) of compulsory prostitution.

Police all over the country were enlisted in the search for him. Two days later, he was discovered almost by accident while strolling along the Bath House Promenade in Hot Springs with his friend Herbert Akers, the city's chief of detectives. A Bronx detective named John J. Brennan had arrived in Hot Springs a day earlier to investigate a murder completely unrelated to Luciano. Brennan was a little surprised to see Luciano strolling so openly when a nationwide manhunt was on for him. Maybe, Brennan thought, word had not yet reached Charlie Lucky. So he stopped Luciano, told him what was going on in New York and suggested that Luciano accompany him back to the city.

"John Brennan was a nice fellow, but that was the craziest suggestion I ever heard in my life. I was havin' a good time in Hot Springs; Gay Orlova was with me and the weather was nice. I wasn't about to take a train back to New York and fall into some kind of trap. I'd been gettin' calls a dozen times a day from New York and nobody really knew what Dewey's plan was, as far as I was concerned. We knew he'd been roustin' a bunch of pimps and madams along with their girls, but nobody could figure out what this had to do with me. I never even got a whiff that he was workin' on a frame. Anyway, I suggested to Brennan that he keep out of it. He copped a plea and said he couldn't do that because if it come out later that he seen me, it could mean his badge. He said he hadda let 'em know in New York I was spotted in Hot Springs."

New York authorities promptly requested Hot Springs and Arkansas officials to extradite Luciano to New York to face the compulsory prostitution indictment. The request was one thing;

to carry it out in what had become a wide-open protected sanctuary of organized crime was something else. "Owney Madden come up to my hotel and told me and Gay that the sheriff had got a demand from New York for my arrest and they'd have to hold me for a couple hours. Owney said not to worry about a thing; it was all set. I'd go down to the courthouse and then be released that afternoon. And as far as extradition was concerned, I could fight it in Arkansas and win. I mean, with our connections in that state, I figured there was no reason at all to worry."

Luciano was taken before Chancellor Sam W. Garrett, the local justice, who promptly released him on five thousand dollars bail, put up by two of Madden's better casinos, the Southern Club and the Belvedere Club. Then he went back to his suite and it was evident that it would take a major explosion to blast him out of it.

Dewey began to light the fuses. He fired off angry messages to Arkansas Governor J. Marion Futrell and to state Attorney General Carl E. Bailey demanding that they cooperate in efforts to bring a dangerous criminal to justice. He called in the New York press and declared coldly, "I can't understand how any judge could release this man on such bail. Luciano is regarded as the most important racketeer in New York, if not the country. And the case involves one of the largest rackets and one of the most loathsome types of crimes."

Dewey's steady barrage brought results. Governor Futrell, increasingly embarrassed at being pictured as the friend and protector of gangsters, ordered Hot Springs officials to bring Luciano in and hold him for extradition hearings. Once again, apologetically, the police came to Luciano's suite and once again took him to the courthouse, this time lodging him in a cell. "The sheriff told me there wasn't nothin' he could do, that he had orders from the governor and they hadda hold me for a while. Anythin' I wanted while I was there, he would make sure I got it. And anytime I wanted to use his office to make calls or meet people, it was okay. So I took advantage of it; I even had Gay come in to keep me company."

From that cell in Hot Springs, Luciano began to draw up plans to fight extradition. He met constantly with Madden and other underworld leaders; and Moses Polakoff, one of the most brilliant

New York lawyers, hurried down to be with him. Together, they drafted a reply to Dewey, called in reporters who had gathered to witness the drama, and with a grim, angry expression, Luciano read to them: "Back of this action is politics, the most vicious kind of politics. I may not be the most moral and upright man alive, but I have not, at any time, stooped to aiding prostitution. I have never been involved in anything so messy."

"The fact is, the newspapers and wire services didn't print everythin' I said. Especially how mad I was when it looked like Dewey's complaint against me had to do with whores. And I resented that, not because I was lookin' for publicity, but because only Dewey's side of the story was gettin' into the papers. I didn't like the idea of him startin' my trial before he had me back in New York."

The statements from Dewey and Luciano swirled back and forth, but the move to carry off extradition appeared no closer to success than it had at the start. The Hot Springs protection, which the mob had bought and paid for over the years with both money and the kind of entertainment that had turned the city into a major national resort, bringing economic prosperity to all, was wrapped around Luciano tightly. There was no hurry to hold extradition hearings and the mood of Hot Springs was such that even if they were held there, the New York request might be denied.

Well aware of this, Dewey stepped up his pressure on state officials. Finally, Attorney General Bailey ordered Luciano transferred to Little Rock for extradition hearings before the governor. But Hot Springs was not anxious to surrender its famous guest, and Luciano was not anxious to depart. The sheriff refused to honor Bailey's order. Bailey countered. He sent a troop of twenty Arkansas Rangers to Hot Springs to take Luciano into custody and move him to Little Rock. Still the sheriff refused to surrender Luciano. The Rangers massed and gave the sheriff an ultimatum: Either surrender Luciano within the hour or they would storm the jail and take him. The sheriff surrendered.

In Little Rock, Luciano was held without bail and the jail was surrounded by troops of Rangers armed with machine guns. The atmosphere was tense and ugly as Governor Futtrell prepared to hold the hearing. "If they was goin' to all this trouble just to get me back to New York, then I figured I'd be damned if I'd go." But Luciano's attempts to stay backfired. One of Owney Madden's aides approached Bailey with an offer of fifty thousand if he would make certain extradition was denied. Bailey was the wrong man to approach. At the opening of the hearings he revealed the offer and said, with scorn and anger, "It must be demonstrated that the honor of Arkansas and her officials is not for sale for blood or money. Every time a major criminal of this country wants asylum, he heads for Hot Springs. We must show that Arkansas cannot be made an asylum for them."

"When I heard that crap come outa Bailey's mouth, I couldn't believe my ears. The truth of the matter is, Bailey was always workin' with us in Arkansas and we never had a problem with him or his office before. All of us who was there thought he should've been able to handle the pressure from New York a lot better'n that. At least he could've shown some appreciation for all the things he got from us before."

Bailey's revelation killed any chance Luciano had. Futtrell upheld the warrant, and Luciano, manacled to two New York City detectives, was returned to the city he had fled. There, at a preliminary hearing, he learned officially the details of the charges, learned that if convicted on all ninety counts of the indictment he faced 1,950 years in prison, learned that his bail was an extraordinary $350,000.

Before he was led to the detention cell where he would be held until the bond was posted, he was given a few moments alone with Polakoff. "Moe, this whole thing is crazy," he said. "You gotta get me outa here. We got a lot of work to do on that son of a bitch Dewey. He's turnin' me into a whoremaster."

"But I could tell from the look on Polakoff's face that he didn't think it was all so crazy. He gave me hell, just like he done in Hot Springs when he got there, for runnin' outa New York without callin' him first and gettin' his advice. He said that just because I took it on the lam, then fought like a bastard not to be extradited, it was gonna be held against me in court. I said to him, 'Moe, that's all lawyers' horseshit. I could smell it out in Hot Springs that all Dewey wanted was to get my head in a noose, whether it was a frame or not. What did you expect me to do — hand myself over on a silver platter?'

"Polakoff talked to me like a Dutch uncle. He said he had a lotta contacts all over the place — after all, the guy used to be one of the United States attorneys — and everythin' he heard said Dewey'd built up a solid case against me. I got sore as a boil, and I said, 'So they got a lot of punks and whores to lie. You mean to say that we can't beat that? You mean to tell me Dewey expects to put me away because some crummy two-dollar whore says I was her boss, or whatever she's gonna say? Jesus, Moe, if you think that's a solid case, then maybe we better get some new lawyers to help you.' "

Luciano's bond was quickly posted and he returned to the Waldorf Towers to plan his defense. He called together his friends — Lansky, Siegel, Costello, Adonis, Lucchese, Anastasia, Torrio and a few others — and asked Polakoff to sit in. They gathered early in the afternoon, in a jovial mood celebrating Luciano's return. "Everybody was kiddin' me about all them whores I'd been screwin'. Albert gave me a whack on the back and said, 'Boy, Charlie, you must really be a lousy lay. Them broads all turned on you.' Everybody started to laugh and Benny said, 'This should make a good title for a movie — Suck and Tell.' Everybody screamed. Then Polakoff got up and his face was sour enough to turn into a lemon. The kiddin' around stopped all of a sudden, and Moe started to lay it on the line."

There was nothing to laugh about, Polakoff said. An indictment of the length and detail Dewey had obtained should not be considered something made of air, particularly not when they considered the trouble Dewey had taken to get Luciano brought back to New York. Instead of making jokes about it, they had better calm down and plan seriously how they were going to fight the charges in court. It took Polakoff, speaking slowly and deliberately, more than an hour to give his assessment, and when he finished, he was surrounded by a group of very sober and concerned men. "Okay, we gotta fight this thing. You do whatever you think is right. You get whatever you need," Luciano told him.

"It's not going to be cheap, Charlie."

"Fuck the money. Whatever it costs, whenever you need some, you'll get it." At that moment, Luciano had no conception of what the tap on his treasury would be. Later, he said that when he added it all up, the case cost him more than seven hundred thousand dollars.

Polakoff departed, to begin his preparations for the trial. A brilliant legal strategist, Polakoff himself was not a courtroom lawyer, devoting himself rather to planning and research. To argue the case before a jury, he reached out to George Morton Levy, one of New York's most respected trial counsels, and as Levy's chief courtroom aide, he selected Francis W. H. Adams, until a few months earlier Dewey's successor as United States Attorney for the Southern District of New York (and two decades later — his work for Luciano rarely mentioned — to become a highly respected and sternly moral police commissioner under New York's Mayor Robert F. Wagner, Jr.).

When Polakoff had gone, Luciano and his friends sat for a time in silence, contemplating the words that they had heard. Then Albert Anastasia broke the silence with a flat proposal. His solution, as usual, was to urge prompt action, the more violent the better. Almost from the day of his arrival as a legal immigrant into the United States in 1920, he and his brother, Anthony "Tough Tony" Anastasio, had centered their activities on the violence-ridden Brooklyn docks where they had risen to power in the longshoremen's union. Murder had become a way of life for Anastasia; he had spent eighteen months in Sing Sing's death house in the early 1920's for killing another longshoreman and had been freed, with the charges dismissed only when four of the major witnesses against him disappeared permanently. With Lepke, he had become head of the enforcement arm of the Unione Siciliano, which was later to be called by the press "Murder, Inc." and which the authorities would credit with at least sixty-three murders. Anastasia himself came to have a record listing nine more arrests (four for murder), but no convictions.

At this moment in the spring of 1935, his proposal was typical of his past, his present and his future: "The Dutchman was right. We gotta knock off Dewey. It's the only thing to do. Charlie, I'll do it myself so there won't be no slipups. And it'll be a pleasure."

The same thought had apparently been in the minds of others at the meeting, and Anastasia's plan was seconded. But Luciano was not prepared to go so far. "That ain't the way. We decided that a long time ago, out in Chicago — remember? We decided we wouldn't hit newspaper guys or cops and D.A.'s. We don't want the kind of trouble everybody'd get if we hit Dewey. That ain't the way — at least, not now."

Anastasia was forced to agree, reluctantly, and the rest of the meeting, which lasted long into the night, was taken up with logistics. The defense fund would be plentiful and all efforts would be made to discover precisely what kind of a case Dewey had erected, and what could be done, legally or, if necessary, illegally, to combat it. Despite Polakoff's warnings, most of those at the meeting were convinced the case would fail, that Dewey would never be able to convict Luciano on this charge of compulsory prostitution. "Regardless of what Polakoff said, I had a feeling that Dewey's case against me couldn't possibly be built around prostitution. Everybody in New York — the cops, the D.A.'s office, even the politicians who wasn't in our bag — knew me well enough to know I couldn't be involved in nothin' like that, not even indirectly. The reason I said to Albert when he wanted to knock off Dewey, 'at least not now,' was because somethin' in my guts told me Dewey had another angle. I didn't know what it was, and maybe I was stupid, on account of I didn't believe he could pull a prostitution frame and make it stick. I gotta admit that all through the meeting, Albert kept mumblin' that I was wrong and he kept warnin' me that I'd be sorry. So chalk that up as the number one of all the mistakes I made in my whole lifetime. I should've let Albert take care of Dewey the way he wanted."

On the eve of the trial, there was a lengthy last-minute session in Polakoff's office. Adams informed Luciano that he had learned that Dewey planned to call an endless parade of prostitutes to the stand, apparently to form the basis of his attack on Luciano. "That's when I began to feel a little better, because I was sure no jury was gonna sit there and listen to a bunch of broken-down broads claimin' I was their boss and I ran the racket. I was sure that as soon as Adams and Levy got 'em on cross-examination, they'd be cut to ribbons and the jury'd laugh the whole thing right out of court."

19.

The case of the *State of New York* v. *Charles Lucania et al.* (an unexplained blending of Luciano's real and assumed names) on charges of compulsory prostitution in violation of the New York penal codes, began on a bright sunny Wednesday morning, May 13, 1936, in New York State Supreme Court in downtown Manhattan. On the bench, presiding, was Justice Philip J. McCook, socially prominent and a stern symbol of society's moral outrage, who would stare with shock and disgust at the defendants all through the trial, and especially when lurid testimony was given, who looked with concern and dismay at the parade of bedraggled prostitutes reciting their tales.

On one side of the courtroom, facing the judge and the blue-ribbon jury of twelve upright, middle-class New Yorkers and two alternates — all chosen from a special jury list — sat the short, confident special prosecutor, Thomas E. Dewey, with his neatly trimmed black mustache, surrounded by an army of assistants. In public statements before and during the trial he would say he was society's weapon for bringing just vengeance on a group of moral lepers.

Across the well of the court sat the ten defendants and their lawyers. Three others named in the indictments — David Marcus, alias David Miller; Peter Balitzer, alias Peter Harris; and Al Weiner — had pleaded guilty and would be called as witnesses for the state.

Dewey rose to make his opening statement, to point the direction of the state's case against the defendants, and particularly against Luciano, who was, above all others, the man he most wanted to convict. Until a few years before, Dewey said, prostitution in the city had been unorganized, a business run by small independents. Then Luciano had stepped in and had told the independent operators that he was taking over and was giving the business to Betillo to run as his agent. "Such was the power of his spoken word," Dewey declared, "that they folded their tents, collected their final week's money, and left the business. Then Davie [Betillo] organized a colossal racket." The syndicate, Dewey maintained, controlled more than two hundred whorehouses in Manhattan, the Bronx, Queens and Brooklyn, employed more than three thousand prostitutes, and grossed more than twelve million dollars a year.

For the prostitutes, the labor was a dreary and deadly form of slavery. Most of the girls lived in sleazy hotels with their pimps, paying the rent from their earnings. They worked at their trade ten to fourteen hours a day, servicing all comers, yet coming away with little profit; half of what they earned went to the madam, who, Dewey said, split it all the way up the line, all the way to Luciano; ten per cent to the man who had booked them into the house; five or ten per cent into a bonding fund to make bail if they were arrested and to pay for legal services; more for board at the brothel; and five dollars a week for medical treatment.

Then, turning with disdain and righteous indignation to stare at Luciano (who stared back with a slight smile of amusement and disbelief), Dewey asserted, "The vice industry since Luciano took over is highly organized and operates with businesslike precision. It will be proved that Lucky Luciano was way up at the top in this city. Never did Lucky or any codefendant actually see or collect from the women. Luciano, though, was always in touch with the general details of the business. We will show you his function as the man whose word, whose suggestion, whose very statement, 'Do this,' was sufficient. And all the others in this case are his servants."

Dewey then began his parade of sixty-eight witnesses to the stand, a procession that would last three weeks. Most — forty — were simple laborers in the ring or madams who had come up through the ranks, girls with names like Rose Cohen, alias Renne Gallo; Muriel Ryan; Dorothy Arnold, alias Dorothy Sherman, alias Dixie; Betty Winters; Sally Osborne; Mary Thomas; Helen

Kelly, alias Nancy Miller; Kathleen O'Connor. None had ever seen or heard of Luciano. Their dealings had been at the lowest levels, though most could point to Ralph Liguori as the man who had put them into the brothels; and they could point to Betillo as someone they had seen around, to Berkman, Pennochio and Spiller and a few others as frequent visitors more interested in giving orders than availing themselves of the services of the girls.

They talked about the houses and the madams, women with names like Jenny the Factory, Gussy, Little Jenny, Cokey Flo, Nigger Ruth and Jean Bradley. They talked about the bonding service and how Abe Karp, the disbarred lawyer, had advised them, coached them on the stories they were to tell before the magistrate's court.

Luciano's name was never even mentioned in these first days. From the testimony of the witnesses, he seemed a man who did not exist. "It was like I was someplace else. They wasn't talkin' about me and I never ever seen none of them broads. I kept turnin' to Polakoff and sayin', 'See, Moe. I told you. They ain't got a thing on me.' But Polakoff kept telling me, 'Wait, Charlie. He's just building this case. He must have a few surprises ready.' Moe was right."

What Luciano did not sense was that Dewey was using the witnesses for more than just building a solid case against the co-defendants. The prostitutes came to the stand looking indeed like fallen women who had been ill-treated, not just by society but by those they declared responsible for their fall, who kept them prisoners in a profession from which there was no escape. Most were narcotics addicts, but all said they had kicked the habit since their arrest, thanks to treatment provided by Dewey and his staff. They claimed that the defendants had kept them constantly supplied with drugs, giving and withholding them as reward and punishment, and so chaining them to the ring. The repetition had its effect. More and more, McCook and the jurors began to look at the witnesses with growing pity and compassion. McCook's voice and manner grew harder and sterner as he repeatedly overruled defense objections, and the glances the jurors directed at the defense table were increasingly contemptuous. Thus, when the name Luciano was mentioned even in passing for the first

203

time, the allusion was enough. It appeared to courtroom observers that both judge and jury at that moment had only been waiting for the mention, were prepared to believe whatever was said.

When Al Weiner, a codefendant who had pleaded guilty, was sworn, to testify for the prosecution, tension filled the courtroom. "I told my lawyers that I had never seen this guy, except for his pictures in the newspapers." As Weiner told his story, Luciano and his legal staff visibly relaxed. He had been an independent operator whose thirty-five houses had been taken over by Davie Betillo after threats to his life if he didn't join up. His contact was always Betillo and as far as he knew, it was Betillo's business.

But a couple of days later, another of the codefendants, turned witness, was called: David Marcus, alias David Miller. He said he had objected to Betillo taking over his business. His objection had been met by six shots fired at him from a moving car, and the next day Betillo had told him to join promptly or "Charlie would take care of me."

"Did you ask who Charlie was?" Dewey asked.

"No," Marcus replied.

"Who do you think Charlie was?"

The question had hardly been spoken and Marcus had not even opened his mouth to reply when George Morton Levy was on his feet in rage, voicing a loud objection, which McCook sustained. But the name Charlie hung in the courtroom. Dewey turned away with a satisfied smile; he had made his point.

A couple of days later he strengthened it, when the third co-defendant who had pleaded guilty, Peter Balitzer, alias Peter Harris, was called. He had been turned from one of the biggest independent operators in the city into a manager and booker for the syndicate. When he had expressed some reservations, Betillo had told him, "Don't worry, Charlie Lucky is behind it." But, Balitzer added, Betillo had ordered him on pain of serious injury never to mention Charlie Lucky's name to anyone, particularly not to his madams. As for himself, he had not seen or dealt directly with Charlie Lucky, though he had gotten further confirmation of his feeling that Luciano was indeed at the top. One of his houses had been held up and the stickup men, young punks well known in the underworld, had been taken out in the country for a beating by Abe Wahrman, the syndicate's enforcer. During the beating, Balitzer testified, Wahrman said, "Didn't I tell you to keep away from those houses because they belong to Charlie Lucky?"

"When this guy Balitzer come up with this cockeyed story, I grabbed Moe Polakoff's arm and I said, 'How can Dewey get away with this? For chrissake, Moe, I'm not a lawyer, but ain't that what they call hearsay? Ain't you gonna object?' " Levy did, indeed, object, but McCook overruled him. And several members of the jury stared at Luciano with growing distaste.

Then came Joe Bendix. "I knew the punk. I knew him from way back and he was nothin' but a cheap thief, a guy who was always tryin' to butter me up. If I wanted a sandwich, he was the first guy out the door on his way to the deli. But I couldn't figure what he was doin' at my trial. I heard he was up in Sing Sing for life."

Indeed, that was where Bendix was, serving a life term as an incorrigible thief under New York laws mandating such a sentence for multiple convictions. He had answered the call from Dewey's office that had gone out to the prisons offering leniency to those with information about Luciano that might help the prosecution.

He had known Luciano since 1929, Bendix told the court, when he used to see him on Seventh Avenue in front of Moe Ducore's drugstore. Then, after a couple of prison terms, he had seen Luciano again in 1935 and talked to him at least three times about working in the prostitution syndicate.

How had this come about? Dewey asked.

Jimmy Frederico was a good friend, Bendix said, and he knew that Frederico was in the business and was in with Charlie Lucky. He had talked to Frederico and a couple of weeks later Frederico had taken him to the Villanova Restaurant on West Forty-sixth Street to meet the boss. According to Bendix, Luciano said, "Frederico talked to me about you. I understand you want a job as a collector for the houses of prostitution. I understand you're a little too high-hat for the job. What's the idea of wanting a job that pays only thirty or thirty-five dollars a week?"

As Bendix related his tale, Polakoff gripped Luciano's arm tightly — he would continue to do so from then to the end of the trial.

"My arm was black and blue from where Moe was holdin' me."
Luciano turned to Polakoff and whispered, "The bastard's lyin'.
There ain't a word of truth in it."

Bendix said that he was willing to take the collector's job because "that's better than going back to stealing." If he were caught
stealing again it would mean life in prison under the multiple-
felony statute.

Luciano answered, Bendix said, "If you're willing to work for
forty dollars a week, it's okay with me. I'll tell Little Davie to put
you on. You can always meet me here." They had met at the
Villanova twice more, with Luciano pressing him to take the job.
"Lucky," he said, "definitely promised me the job."

When Dewey finished, Levy took Bendix on. Had Bendix
accepted this so-called job offer?

No.

Why not?

Bendix didn't know. He had been planning to, when he went
back to stealing, got caught, and was sent up to Sing Sing for life.

How had he come to be here in court, testifying?

He had read about the case in the newspapers and felt he ought
to do his duty. He had written Dewey offering his services.

Had he been promised anything in return for his testimony?

Yes, Bendix said. He had been promised a reduction in sentence if he testified and helped convict Luciano.

Levy sat down. Some in the court thought he had cast considerable doubt on Bendix's testimony, but those who looked at the
jury and the judge were not so certain. It was as though both had
been waiting for someone, no matter what his reputation, to come
forward with an eyewitness account of Luciano's involvement.
Bendix had done just that and it was apparent to observers, including both Polakoff and Levy (if not to Luciano, who was convinced at that moment that no one could believe Bendix after
Levy's cross-examination), that the tide was running strongly
against Luciano.

Dewey's most devastating witness appeared the next day, May 22.
Into the silent, tense courtroom, the name Florence Brown echoed.
"The door opened, and we all turned around to look. This beat-up
broad comes down the aisle to the stand. She looked like she'd

really been through the mill, like the gutter would've been a step up for her. Polakoff hits me in the arm hard, and he says, 'Who's she?' I looked at her real close and I says to him, 'How the fuck should I know? I ain't never seen her before.' Then Polakoff says to me, 'Hold on, Charlie. I've got a feeling she's real bad news.' He didn't say it strong enough, believe me."

Florence Brown was known in the trade as Cokey Flo Brown, and sometimes as Flo Marten and Flo Marsten and at least a dozen other names. Since her mid-teens she had been a prostitute and, for almost as long, a drug addict. Until the February raid, she had been madam of one of the syndicate's houses. Since then, thanks to Prosecutor Dewey and the Women's House of Detention, she had finally managed to escape both prostitution and narcotics, and for the first time in her memory she could look to the future with some hope.

Dressed in a shabby, ill-fitting blue dress, worn shoes, her dark hair disheveled, Cokey Flo was in her mid-twenties, though her age would have been hard to guess. She looked like a waif, a girl defenseless against life's cruelties and vicissitudes, who had been ill-used by the world and by its men. There was about her an aura of innocence destroyed and almost everyone in the courtroom seemed to feel an immediate sympathy for her. Dewey treated her gently; so did McCook, and the jury stared at her with pity and at the defense table, as she related her story, with obvious rage.

She had been, she said, Frederico's girl, and he had enticed her into prostitution. Through him, she had met Luciano many times, had attended meetings of the rulers of the vice ring at which he presided and gave orders. At one of those meetings, she testified, Luciano had turned to her and said, "I'm gonna organize the cathouses like the A&P."

At another meeting of the top leaders, at which she had sat in, Luciano had expressed some fear of official investigations. He had said, Cokey Flo asserted, "Dewey's investigating and we may get in trouble. It may get tough. I think we better fold up for a while."

Betillo had argued against that move. "Betillo said, 'Well, there's been a lot of pinches and that took money out of the combination. But when we get them all in line, it'll be okay.'

"Lucky said, 'I'd like to quit awhile. Maybe then we could reopen and we could even syndicate like they did in Chicago. We could have one combination instead of three or four.'

"Betillo said, 'I don't think it'll be so tough. The Dewey investigation won't get us. They'll just pick up a few bondsmen and let it go at that.'

"Luciano said, 'We could syndicate the places on a large scale same as a chain store system. We could even put the madams on salary or commission. It would take a little time, but we could do it.' "

That, Cokey Flo said, was Luciano's goal, the constant theme of the meetings she so often attended. He gave the orders for the beating, torturing, threatening and drugging of the girls to force them to work steadily and without complaint, for the use of strong-arm methods to bring madams and bookers into line. "First you got to step on them. Talking won't do no good. You got to put the screws on," she quoted him as saying.

When Cokey Flo had finished, Dewey sat down contentedly. Her story had shocked the court and horrified her listeners, and it had tied Luciano directly into the racket. There was about Dewey at that moment, those in the courtroom would later say, the air of a man who knew his case was won.

The depression at the defense table did not lift during Levy's cross-examination. No matter how hard he pressed, Cokey Flo could not be shaken. She stuck by her story, repeating it almost by rote as Levy attacked, tried to shatter her confidence, destroy her credibility. She maintained that she had told only the truth. Much of Levy's power was blunted by Dewey's constant objections, many sustained by McCook, who began to appear to some observers as her self-appointed protector.

Eventually, Levy turned away in frustration and disgust. "I could see he was really worried. They started tellin' me that things didn't look good. So I began to get worried, too, even though I couldn't understand how anyone could believe Flo Brown's testimony. She sounded like Dewey'd rehearsed her for the leadin' part in 'Bertha, the Sewin'-Machine Girl.' "

Four days later, Dewey had another shock for Luciano and the defense. He called twenty-six-year-old Nancy Presser, a hard, sharp-faced, buxom, faded woman who had practiced her profession since the age of thirteen and had degenerated from high-priced call girl into common laborer in a two-dollar Harlem whorehouse, a whore who was not even acceptable to the male "madam" of the house, James Russo, but was foisted on him at the orders of her pimp, Ralph Liguori. While still a teenager, she testified, she had been at various times the mistress and playmate of Waxey Gordon, Dutch Schultz, Ciro Terranova, Joe Adonis, even of Joe the Boss Masseria. It was Joe the Boss, she said, who had introduced her to Charlie Lucky; it had been a casual meeting but she had been much taken with him, though he seemed immune to her charms.

Three years later, at Kean's Tavern near Madison Square Garden, she had renewed old acquaintances and had given Luciano her telephone number. But he didn't call, and in the meantime she met Ralph Liguori and became first his girl and then his whore. Until that moment, she had been high class, charging her customers fifty or a hundred dollars. Liguori put a stop to that. He booked her into Russo's brothel and told her, "Low prices but big volume." And Liguori did something else. He switched her from the opium pipe she had been smoking for some time to the needle and morphine, and it was downhill all the way from there. (Like those who had preceded her to the stand, Nancy Presser said that thanks to Dewey, she had given up the habit after February 1.)

Under Liguori's constant harassment, she said, she felt as if she was working on an assembly line. Every ten minutes he would beat on her door and order her to finish the customer she had and get ready for the next. Then, she testified, at the lowest moment of her life, the phone rang and it was Luciano.

"I couldn't believe it when she started that story. It was like somebody hit me on the head with a baseball bat. Can you imagine me callin' a beat-up broad like that, who was workin' in a two-dollar cathouse? But when I looked around, I could see that the goddamn judge and jury really believed her."

Luciano, Nancy Presser said, asked her to come to his Waldorf Towers apartment, suite 39-C. She went, then and often thereafter, and nobody ever questioned her or stopped her; she would just walk through the entrance, get on the elevator, ride up, and go to his door. With Dewey prodding, she gave a detailed description of the suite, the couches, chairs, colors, arrangement, a description that seemed to impress judge and jury, who watched her closely. That first time, Nancy Presser testified, Luciano listened to her troubles and told her he would fix things up with Liguori. Then, she said, she got into his bed while he slept on the couch. And that was the pattern that was invariably repeated on all her many visits.

Didn't anything at all happen between them? Dewey asked.

"When Charlie called me over, he'd give me a hundred dollars, but we'd just talk. That's all. We never went to bed together. Charlie couldn't. You know what I mean?"

Luciano started at her aghast and enraged, and even a quarter of a century later the memory filled him with fury. "Here was an ugly broad who probably'd been throwin' her fanny around fifty thousand times with different guys, and she's layin' in my bed like a queen while I'm layin' on the couch because I can't get it up. I looked at Judge McCook when she was tellin' that bullshit and that little prick was starin' at this broad like she's the Queen of England and I'm worse than dirt. It was bad enough for that louse Dewey to try to become a big shot on my back, railroadin' me in the worst way; but then right in the middle of it, to throw a zinger that Charlie Lucky Luciano can't get a hard-on! I started to get up from the defense table. All I knew was that I hadda hit somebody and at that minute I didn't give a shit who it was or what it cost me. Moe Polakoff saw me start to move, so he grabbed me by the arm and ground his foot right on top of mine. My right foot was so sore I couldn't've moved if I wanted to, and I let out a yell because he hurt me so bad. The whole courtroom turned around and looked at me and it took a couple minutes before it was quiet again. I noticed that George Levy was makin' notes like mad; I was seated between him and Moe, and he whispered to me, 'Take it easy, Charlie. This girl's helpin' us.' I made a silent prayer that he knew what he was talkin' about."

But Nancy Presser had more to say than just a description of Luciano's lack of sexual prowess. She said she had listened on the telephone and through partially open doors as he discussed the prostitution ring with Betillo and others, had once heard him assert, "The take ain't so good. Looks like we'll have to raise the two-dollar houses to three and boost the five- and ten-buck joints too."

When Levy began his cross-examination, however, it was apparent that Nancy Presser had not done her homework as well as she could have, or should have. Her description of Luciano's apartment proved faulty; she was not sure about the couches or chairs or colors. ("She's not an interior decorator," Dewey later explained.)

Had she been shown pictures of the suite? Levy asked.

No — well, perhaps. She couldn't remember.

Then Levy attacked her on her description of the Waldorf Towers itself. She said that she had come and gone late at night, undisturbed and unstopped. Weren't there any regulations in the place about visitors?

Not that she knew of, she said, and nobody ever interfered with her. After all, she had usually come at night when nobody was around (J. David Hardy, the Towers's assistant manager, would testify for the defense that the Towers had strict security regulations and that late at night, no visitors could enter without being checked and announced to the host.)

When Levy asked her to describe the hotel itself, she was unable to do so, unable to say where the entrances were, unable to describe the location of the elevators or what they were like and, it turned out, she wasn't even sure where the Waldorf Towers was, other than somewhere on the East Side around Park Avenue.

If Dewey was at all concerned about this witness's memory, he did not show it and he quickly began to recoup. In open court, he announced that the lives of many of his witnesses, especially those of prostitutes and madams, had been threatened. With great indignation, Judge McCook at once issued bench warrants for the arrests of several minor hoodlums who until that moment had not figured in the case and were never really linked to it, and he sternly warned that he would hold the defendants responsible for any harm to the witnesses or any repetition of the threats. The effect of this revelation on the jury, and the judge's response, was apparent.

Step by step, Dewey continued to build his case. He summoned personnel from the Waldorf Towers and the Barbizon to show that Luciano had been meeting with the other defendants for years, and thus the prostitution ring was of long standing. But Frank Brown, the Barbizon Plaza's assistant manager, shocked the prosecutor. It had been anticipated that he would testify to having seen Betillo, Pennochio, Liguori and the other members of the syndicate at the hotel, visiting Luciano, often. Instead, Brown said that of course he knew Luciano; after all the man had lived at the Barbizon for years; but he had never seen the others and didn't know who they were.

Dewey was stunned and enraged. He demanded that the court declare Brown a hostile witness so that he could cross-examine him. Brown would not be shaken. Dewey's staff, he said, had shown him photographs of the other defendants and told him, "You must have seen that one and that one." When Brown said he had not, one of the Dewey staffers "persisted in telling me so. He warned me about jail if I didn't tell the truth. There were three or four in the room. They were very insistent about my identifying the pictures. When I said I couldn't do it honestly, they threatened me. They hinted that Mr. Dewey was very powerful and could do as he liked."

Brown's testimony, with its various implications, set Dewey back for only a moment; and the judge and jury appeared to discount it almost entirely. From their attitudes, it seemed that they were now prepared to believe almost entirely anyone who supported Dewey's case, and disbelieve anyone who countered it.

Dewey moved quickly to repair the damage. He called Mildred Balitzer, wife of Peter Balitzer, partner of her husband in his string of whorehouses. She was another admitted narcotics addict, or, rather, a former one; she, too, had overcome the habit thanks to Dewey.

Did she know Luciano? She did indeed, she testified. When Betillo moved in on her and her husband, he had told them he was working for Charlie Lucky. And later, in Betillo's company, she had met Luciano in a restaurant and been introduced to him with the words, "I want you to meet the boss." She had turned to Betillo and asked, "Is Lucky really behind this?" Betillo had assured her he was.

All during her involvement with the syndicate, she said, there had been trouble with Betillo and other defendants; they were constantly shaking the Balitzers down so that they were on the verge of financial disaster even though the business was booming. She decided to go to the top for help, and at a racetrack in Miami she had approached Luciano and told him that Betillo was bleeding her husband and forcing him out of business. She testified that Luciano told her, "I can't do anything for him. You know how the racket is."

"Yeah, I remembered that. I was only tellin' her I couldn't do nothin' for them because I didn't have no part of it. How the hell was I supposed to know what Betillo had been tellin' 'em? And then she got up there on the stand and made it sound like I was runnin' the whole damn thing. All Dewey did was take the truth and just twist it around to make it come out like he wanted it to, not like it really was."

On May 29, 1936, at 6:40 in the evening, after three weeks of testimony and about sixty witnesses, Thomas E. Dewey rested the state's case against Luciano and his codefendants.

Outside the courtroom, Luciano was all smiles. He told reporters, "I certainly expect to be acquitted. I don't know any of the people who took the stand and said they knew me or talked to me or overheard me in conversations. I never met any of them. I never was engaged in this racket at all. I never in my life met any of the codefendants, except Betillo, before this trial."

The outward calm was sham. Inwardly, Luciano was very worried indeed, because his lawyers were worried. "Polakoff was tellin' me that we hadda start thinkin' about an appeal, and that it was gonna cost a fortune and would take a lot of time. I told him if we couldn't lick the case right there in court, I didn't give a damn how much it cost, he should do whatever was necessary to beat it."

Luciano's defense was simple. His witnesses were professional gamblers and bookmakers who testified that, as far as they knew, his sole business was professional gambling, that he bet hundreds of dollars a day with them on the races. All said that they had often been to his apartment at the Towers and had never seen any of his codefendants.

Would Luciano himself take the stand? On the evening of June 2, with all the other witnesses gone, that was the major unanswered question in the courtroom. "We had a meet that night and both Polakoff and Levy started warnin' me not to go on the stand. I didn't have to do it, they said, and it probably wouldn't help because by that time the case was stacked against me. But I told both of them that I was goin' up there. I said it was crazy; them broads was lyin' in their teeth and the only way to show it was for me to go up there and tell the truth. Levy and Polakoff, and especially Adams, warned me about Dewey. I told 'em I could handle that little prick. They told me I hadn't seen him really operate, that he was only waitin' for a crack at me. I said I was sure I could handle myself. What a mistake that was."

Luciano was the final witness for the defense, taking the stand on the morning of June 3. Under the gentle questioning of George Levy, his testimony did not take long. He denied knowing any of his codefendants, except Betillo, before the trial opened; he denied knowing any of the prosecution's witnesses; and he categorically denied all the charges against him.

Briefly, guided by Levy, he went through his life. With almost his first statement, he lied, claiming that he had been born on East Thirteenth Street in Manhattan. ("I was a wise guy, and Levy and Polakoff wasn't fast enough to stop it.") He quickly brushed over his arrest for narcotics at eighteen, said that within a few years of his release, he had gone to work for the operator of a dice game, had soon graduated to running his own game, and then branched out to become a leading racetrack handicapper. He talked about his arrest in Hot Springs, declaring the only reason he had fought extradition was because he had heard that Dewey intended to put him on trial within forty-eight hours after his return to New York and he wanted to give his lawyers enough time to prepare an adequate defense.

At the end of direct examination, Levy asked him whether there was any truth to the charges against him. In a loud and belligerent voice, Luciano said, "I've never had anything to do with prostitution, I've never gotten a single dollar from a prostitute or from the prostitution racket."

"Your witness," Levy said to Dewey and turned back to the defense table.

"Sure, I lied up there on the stand. I lied when I said I never met some of the other guys who was on trial or any of them girls who testified against me. What else could I do? I knew it was their word against mine, and if I ever admitted that I knew any of 'em, nobody would even hear nothin' else I said. The truth of the matter is in them days, and even in all the years after, people come up to me all day long to ask for somethin', to get a handout, things like that. Sure maybe I'd be standin' in front of Ducore's drugstore and a couple of them broads might come by and wave at me and say, 'Hello, Lucky,' or 'Hi, Charlie,' and I'd wave back. I wouldn't let none of them come within ten feet of me as far as goin' to bed was concerned. My girls come from Polly Adler or they was girls I knew from shows or from society. Period.

"After George Levy questioned me, I had the feelin' that I done pretty well. Then I looked over and watched that little bastard Dewey get out of his chair and walk towards me. At that second I was more scared than I ever had been in my whole life. I had a hunch that he was about to skin me alive. He walked over real slow, and he had a look on his face like I was a piece of raw meat and he'd been goin' hungry for a month. He kept comin' at me, takin' his time — and that's when I began to regret not listenin' to my lawyers about not takin' the stand. But it was too late."

In the stillness of the expectant courtroom, Dewey played the silence to the point of torture. Finally, he asked his first questions. They were mild and seemingly innocuous. Was Lucania the only name the defendant was known by? Wasn't he also known as Charles Luciano, and Lucky Luciano, as Charles Ross, as Charles Lane, and other names? How many others? The defendant didn't remember? Well, let's go on.

The prosecutor thumbed through some papers. Had Luciano recently been convicted of carrying a gun, a concealed weapon, while in Miami, Florida, say within the last five or six years?

Sure, Luciano said, he had been picked up for that. But there wasn't any law in Miami against carrying a gun.

Well, Dewey asked, holding out a Florida newspaper clipping, what about this article that quoted him as saying he was carrying the gun because he was going out hunting in the Everglades.

"There's a lot of things in the newspapers that ain't true."

Even Dewey smiled briefly at that. But he quickly turned to the attack, thrust by thrust, destroying any semblance of respectability that Luciano had attempted to present. Year by year, Dewey went through Luciano's life since 1920, drawing from him the not-so-startling information that he had been a bootlegger during Prohibition as well as a professional gambler. At any time during those sixteen or seventeen years, Dewey asked, did Luciano have any legitimate occupation? Luciano said no, not that he could remember. Then, some minutes later, as Dewey was taking another line, Luciano interrupted. He had just remembered that around 1929 he had owned "a piece of a restaurant" at Broadway and Fifty-second Street.

Dewey stared at him for a moment and then shot out sarcastically, "Oh, the only legitimate business you've had in eighteen years you forgot?" Luciano shrugged.

"Well, let's go on," Dewey said. Had Luciano ever been married? No, Luciano said. Had Luciano ever been arrested? Yes, he admitted reluctantly. Had Luciano ever told an arresting officer that he was married? "I might've said so. I don't remember."

On the stand that day, Luciano had declared he was born in New York. Did he ever tell arresting officers that he had been born in Italy? "I might've said so. I don't remember."

Had Luciano ever told officers arresting him that he was employed as a chauffeur? As a salesman? As a fruit dealer? "I might've said so. I don't remember."

Had he ever lied to the police then, Dewey demanded. Luciano tried to hedge. Dewey pounced, forcing him to stumble, then to admit that he had, indeed, lied, and lied frequently to arresting officers. But, he insisted, those lies were unimportant.

What, Dewey snapped, would he call his response to an arrest for traffic violations in July 1928? He had told the police when they found two pistols, shotguns and forty-five rounds of ammunition in his car that he had been up in the country shooting pheasants. Dewey was incredulous: "Shooting pheasants in July?"

That was exactly what he had been doing, Luciano maintained, and the answer was the truth. (Even twenty-five years later, Luciano insisted that answer, at least, had been no lie. "Some guys and I had been invited up to Connecticut to what they called a 'shoot' and that's what the shotguns was for. They wasn't sawed off; they was regular ones for huntin' and they cost over three hundred bucks apiece. The funny part of it was, when it come to shootin' them birds, I missed by a mile. What made the whole thing look so bad when it come out in court was that the cops found two revolvers in the car. That was standard equipment in them days. I never went nowhere without some hardware. Things was very dangerous in 1928.")

Suddenly, Dewey switched his line. "How many times in your life have you been taken for a ride?"

Spectators leaned forward in anticipation. Luciano appeared to be unmoved. ("I knew he'd get to that, so it didn't surprise me.") "Just once," Luciano replied, then added he couldn't remember exactly when, but he thought it was six or seven years before.

"Do you remember," Dewey asked, "that you were found on Staten Island by a police officer, that you had been badly beaten and cut up, and had tape over your eyes and mouth, and that you told him you wouldn't give him any information, that you would take care of this in your own way?"

"I gave him all the information I could."

Did he, Dewey pressed further, tell the grand jury, as he had told this court in direct examination, that he had been taken for a ride by men who had demanded ten thousand dollars ransom and who had released him when he promised to pay it, though he had never paid it?

No, Luciano said, he had not told that story to the grand jury.

"So you lied about that, too."

"Yes."

Dewey paused, letting that answer hang in the silent courtroom, then turned to another area. Had Luciano ever been arrested for selling narcotics? Yes, when he was eighteen. Had he been picked up again, in 1923? Had he given federal agents at that time information that led to the seizure of a trunkful of narcotics? Yes. "Didn't this make you a stool pigeon?" Dewey asked.

"No. I was picked up myself, so I told them what I knew."

Then Dewey read off a list of names: "Do you know personally Louis Buchalter, who is known as Lepke?"

"Yes."

"Do you know Jacob Shapiro, who is known as Jake 'Gurrah' Shapiro?"

"Yes."

"Do you know personally Benjamin 'Bugsy' Siegel?"

"Yes."

"Did you know Joe Masseria, who was known as 'Joe the Boss,' before he was killed in Coney Island?"

"Yes."

"Do you know Owney Madden?"

"Yes."

"Do you know Al Capone?"

"No." Dewey let that pass for the moment.

"Do you know Ciro Terranova?"

"No."

Dewey turned back to the prosecution table and picked up some papers, returned to Luciano and read them to him. They were Luciano's telephone records from the Waldorf Towers and the Barbizon Plaza, showing repeated calls to the unlisted number of Terranova in Pelham, New York, and to Capone in Chicago.

And then, in moments that caused the sweat to flow from Luciano, that made him wriggle uncomfortably on the witness stand, Luciano began to hear Dewey read off the record of repeated calls at all hours of the day and night from his apartment to Celano's Restaurant on the Lower East Side, the headquarters, Dewey charged, of the vice ring's sub-leaders. How did Luciano explain them, Dewey demanded.

The spaghetti was good, Luciano said, and he went there a couple of times a month to eat, often calling ahead. Friends hung out there, and he used to call them for a talk. But he had not made all the calls Dewey was reciting; he couldn't possibly have done so, for during much of the time he was out on his usual rounds of the city. Somebody else must have gotten in and used his phone. Dewey and the court stared at him with disbelief.

For four hours Dewey hammered away. By that evening, when Luciano finally stepped down, "I felt like I'd been through a washing machine, and I really looked like it. I went to the washroom, and my shirt was all wrinkled and I seemed to be perspirin' from head to foot. That night, when I read the *News* and *Mirror,* they said it was a bad day for Charlie Lucky. Them writers didn't have no idea how bad it really was. I never felt so tired, like I could sleep for a week. I couldn't wait to get outa the courthouse. I practically ran.

"We all met at my apartment a little later, for dinner that I had sent up from Jack and Charlie's. I knew I was gonna get convicted, that I didn't have a chance. The only thing was, I figured that maybe Polakoff and Levy could work out somethin' on an appeal, so that if I got a year or so, the appeal maybe could wash it out and I wouldn't have to go to the can at all. It's a funny thing how when you hope for somethin' very hard, you sorta talk yourself into believin' it's gonna happen. Then I looked at George Levy's face and I got the same shivers inside that I had in court.

"Everybody left early and Gay Orlova come up about eleven. She'd been in the courtroom, and the minute she walked in, she started to cry. Well, that did it. I figured if Gay already had me convicted, there was no point in hopin'. Durin' all the weeks of the trial, she spent a lot of time with me, but we never did nothing — y'know what I mean. Either I'd get home too tired, too upset — anyway, who the hell could get in the mood. But that night, she made love to me. She was so kind and understandin', I almost asked her to marry me. Of course, the minute that idea occurred to me, I forgot it. How can you ask anybody to marry you if you don't know whether the next day you're gonna be in jail? Anyway, that was probably the best night I ever had with a girl to that minute, and I'll never forget it."

When court reconvened, George Levy made his final attempt to win freedom for Luciano, though even Luciano sensed he had no chance to prevail. "I'm not accusing Tom Dewey of suborning perjury," Levy began his closing argument, "but I say his assistants, anxious for a pat on the back and a bit of glory, have collected a group of actors who had constructed a drama which Mr. Dewey accepted as true.

"There is no evidence on which Tom Dewey can hope to convict Lucania. He hopes to do it with prejudice, hysteria, through what you have read and by what the public has been taught to believe by this master showman. He hopes to do it by crimes Lucania committed years ago; because he was taken for a ride; because he lied to get a pistol permit. He hopes to railroad him because Lucania lied when he said he was a chauffeur in obtaining an automobile license, when he was nothing but a bootlegger and a gambler."

Levy went through Dewey's witnesses. Joe Bendix he categorized as a convicted felon and a liar who had come to court hoping to perjure his way out of a life sentence. As for Cokey Flo Brown, "If anybody told you such a cock-and-bull story in your own business, you would tell him to get out of the place because the story was so ridiculous." There was no doubt in his mind, Levy closed, that when the jurors examined all the evidence they would return a verdict of not guilty.

Then it was time for Dewey to have the final say. Admitting that many of his key witnesses were simple prostitutes, he told the jury it "could not hold that a prostitute is unworthy of belief. You must give her story the same weight as you would to that of a respectable person. If you believe what she says, then the story stands and the fact that she is a prostitute is of no moment."

Staring intently at the jury, he asserted, "We did not offer a witness we didn't believe." There were some who might discredit his witnesses because they had been granted immunity. But, he said, how else could the state have gotten them on the stand to talk about crimes they had committed? Justice had been served by the testimony of Cokey Flo Brown, Mildred Balitzer and the others.

Then there was Nancy Presser. "For two hours I sat with her, trying to persuade her to testify, and that she would not be murdered. If you want to know what responsibility is, try to persuade a witness trembling with terror to go up on the stand. The defense did everything to blast her. They resorted to every device known to corruption to break down her story. Why did they try to destroy her by all their evil means, except that they didn't dare face the truth?"

Coming to the end, he turned to stare directly at Luciano. With rage coloring his words, he pointed at Luciano, who, he said, had committed "a shocking, disgusting display of sanctimonious perjury — at the end of which I am sure not one of you had a doubt that before you stood not a gambler, not a bookmaker, but the greatest gangster in America." For seven hours Dewey transfixed the jury.

"I knew I was done for when that little son of a bitch finally sat down. I took one look at the jury and there was no question about it — the twelve people looked like they all wanted to stand up and applaud."

If anyone at that moment had any doubts about the outcome, Judge McCook quickly dispelled them. In a charge lasting two hours and forty-one minutes, he made little attempt to hide his own predisposition. He dwelt at length on Luciano's use of aliases as an indication of his lack of character and believability. He explained to the jury that it did not need to find that Luciano directly received money or had direct contact with prostitutes. "If anyone received money which was the proceeds of prostitution, even though not directly received from the women, if it was in furtherance of a scheme to carry on prostitution, that person is guilty of an unlawful act."

In his final words, he voiced his own personal view: "The crimes of which these men are accused are vicious and low, and those who would aid and abet such crimes are not to be met in polite society."

At 10:53 on Saturday evening, June 6, 1936, the jury retired. Later, some of the jurors would say that after listening to George Morton Levy's summation, there were doubts and some were leaning toward acquittal. But those doubts had been dispelled by Dewey's stinging, stirring rebuttal. After only ten minutes in the jury room a vote was taken; the count stood at eleven to one — for conviction. Then the jurors went over exhibits and documents before taking a second vote in the predawn hours of Sunday. At 4:30 in the morning, they sent word to Justice McCook, who was waiting for the news in his chambers, that they were ready.

Nearly an hour later, at 5:25 on Sunday morning, June 7, the courtroom was called to order. McCook ordered the defendants to rise and face the jury. Foreman Edwin Aderer read the verdicts. The first name was Luciano's. In a strained voice, Aderer read: "Guilty on all counts."

Luciano's expression did not change from unemotional stoicism. But, he said later, "Inside, my stomach was turnin' over. But I wasn't gonna give those bastards a chance to see it."

The rest was anticlimax. Guilty verdicts were read for all the other defendants, McCook scheduled sentencing for June 18, the defendants, manacled, were quickly led to a waiting security van and driven to the Tombs, the first stop on the way to prison.

They were back in court eleven days later. Justice McCook peremptorily denied a series of defense motions to set aside the verdicts for lack of evidence, to delay sentencing until the appeals process had been concluded, to release the defendants on bond while they made appeals. Sentencing, he said, would take place immediately and the defendants would begin serving those sentences as soon as they were announced.

Then into the record was read a parole report on Luciano, prepared by Irving W. Halpern, chief probation officer of the Court of General Sessions, a report drawn largely from information supplied by Dewey's aide Sol Gelb. "The defendant has a controlling interest in almost every racket to which this city is subjected. . . . His freedom from conscience springs from his admitted philosophy: 'I never was a "crumb," and if I have to be a "crumb," I'd rather be dead.' He explains this by stating that a 'crumb' is a person who works and saves and lays his money aside, who indulges in no extravagances. His description of a 'crumb' would fit the average man. . . . As he achieved a measure of success, his attitude toward his antisocial activities became one of an entrepreneur. His ideals of life resolved themselves into money to spend, beautiful women to enjoy, silk underclothes and places to go in style."

Then McCook began the ritual of sentencing:

David Betillo: twenty-five to forty years in the penitentiary.

Thomas Pennochio: twenty-five years as a third offender.

James Frederico: twenty-five years as a third offender.

Abe Wahrman: fifteen to thirty years.

Ralph Liguori: seven and one half to fifteen years.

Jesse Jacobs, Benny Spiller, Meyer Berkman: sentencing postponed at the request of Dewey, who hoped to persuade them to testify at future trials in exchange for light sentences. (They were eventually given minor terms.)

The defendants who pleaded guilty: Jack Ellenstein: four to eight years; Peter Balitzer and Al Weiner: two to four years; David Marcus: three to six years.

Then it was Luciano's turn. McCook asked whether he had anything to say before sentence was pronounced. Luciano leaned over and talked briefly with George Morton Levy. "I asked him if I should say anythin', and he said it was up to me. So I got up and looked right straight at McCook. I said, 'Your Honor, I have nothin' to say outside the fact that I need to say again, I am innocent.' "

McCook shook his head, stared at Luciano, and then began: "The evidence upon the trial and reliable information since received have convinced the court that these defendants will be responsible for any injury which the people's witnesses might hereafter, by reason of their testimony, suffer. Let the record show that should any witness for the people be injured or harassed, the court will request the parole authorities to retain in prison the defendants against whom such witness testified for the maximum terms of the sentences imposed."

Looking down at Luciano, Judge McCook declared: "An intelligent, courageous and discriminating jury has found you guilty of heading a conspiracy or combination to commit these crimes, which operated widely in New York and extended into neighboring counties. This makes you responsible, in law and morals, for every foul and cruel deed, with accompanying elements of extortion, performed by the band of codefendants. . . . I am not here to reproach you but, since there appears no excuse for your conduct or hope for your rehabilitation, to extend adequate punishment."

The court, McCook then declared in a solemn voice, sentenced Luciano to "a total of from thirty to fifty years in state's prison." It was the longest sentence ever meted out for compulsory prostitution.

Luciano trembled slightly, then regained control of himself. "They told me I'd get a stiff sentence, but I didn't think they'd throw the book at me. I figured there was plenty of grounds for appeal and that Polakoff would get me off pretty soon. Still, it ain't easy to stand there and hear that. It was like gettin' a life sentence. Even with good behavior I'd be an old man before I got out — or maybe I'd be dead."

The court adjourned for the last time and Luciano was led away quickly, with no ceremony, handcuffed for the ride to Sing Sing, the first stop on the road to Dannemora in far upstate New York. It was there that it appeared that he would spend the next thirty to fifty years.

Afterwards, Dewey stood on the courtroom steps and talked to newsmen about his victory. "This, of course," he said, "was not a vice trial. It was a racket prosecution. The control of all organized prostitution in New York by the convicted defendants was one of their lesser rackets. The prostitution racket was merely the vehicle by which these men were convicted. It is my understanding that certain of the top-ranking defendants in this case, together with other criminals under Lucania, have gradually absorbed control of the narcotics, policy, loan-shark and Italian lottery syndicates, the receipt of stolen goods and certain industrial rackets." Unable to trap or convict Luciano for his control of these major rackets, Dewey admitted that he had nailed him for a minor one.

"Naturally, I read Dewey's whole statement. After sittin' in court and listenin' to myself bein' plastered to the wall and tarred and feathered by a bunch of whores who sold themselves for a quarter, and hearin' that no-good McCook hand me what added up to a life term, I still got madder at Dewey's crap than anythin' else. That little shit with the mustache comes right out in the open and admits he got me for everythin' else but what he charged me with. I knew he knew I didn't have a fuckin' thing to do with prostitution, not with none of them broads. But Dewey was such a goddamn racketeer himself, in a legal way, that he crawled up my back with a frame and stabbed me. If he'd hauled me into court to stand trial for anythin' I done, includin' conspiracy to commit murder, I'd've taken it like a man. But this was somethin' that was like a boil startin' to grow inside me from the minute I heard what Dewey said outside the court. Someday that boil was gonna break open and somehow, in some way, I was gonna get even."

So, on June 18, 1936, Luciano's prison years began. The next day, as he was being processed through the system as a convicted long-term felon, forty-five thousand people, including many of his old friends, gathered in New York's Yankee Stadium to watch a long-awaited heavyweight prizefight. The young and supposedly invincible Brown Bomber from Detroit, Joe Louis, was meeting the former champion, Germany's Max Schmeling, in what was supposed to be Louis's final hurdle on the way to the title. He tripped over that hurdle. Schmeling found a weakness and knocked him out in the twelfth round.

"I thought I'd be there. It was a fight I really wanted to see. I even bought a whole block of tickets right down in front. Instead, I was sittin' in a cell that night, half listenin' to the radio, wonderin' what the hell was next for me — and not even givin' a shit who was gonna win the fight."

Part Three

Prison Years
1936-1946

20.

Dannemora sits on a barren plain in a nearly inaccessible corner of New York State. A grim, forbidding place surrounded by thick gray stone walls, it is a maximum-security prison, and only the most incorrigible prisoners are sent there. In summer, it endures the broiling sun; even the walls glisten with sweat. In winter, the gales howl down out of Canada, coating the walls with thick layers of ice. To the American underworld, it is known as Siberia.

"When they told me I was goin' to Dannemora, I wasn't sure I'd be able to take it. It meant movin' outa the Waldorf Towers into a sewer. The worst part of it was, we didn't have no connections up there and that meant I was gonna be in for a real rough time, no matter how quick Polakoff could work the appeals and get me sprung. I was willin' to put up a million-dollar bond — and I told 'em that, as soon as I heard about Dannemora. But once they had me, they wasn't gonna let me go."

Before he had departed for his years in prison, Luciano tied off the loose ends of his life in New York. "I felt like I was practically actin' out my own will, and there's no feelin' a person can ever have in his whole life as bad as that. My clothes and all my fancy stuff — I put everythin' in charge of my brother, Bart, so he could put it all in storage and take care of my jewelry. I took care of Gay; she'd been really good to me them last few months and she rated somethin'. My family hadda be protected and I hadda protect my own situation when it came to lookin' out for my dough and what would be comin' in while I was away — and if I was gonna get it. I worked it all out with Lansky, and that's the point where Meyer became the real treasurer of the outfit. I put him in charge of my money and later on he started to take care of the finances of quite a few guys."

As he was driven, shackled to other prisoners, through the gates of his new home, Luciano made a resolve. "I remembered what Goodman told me twenty years before, the other time I was in the can. He said, 'Do what they tell you. Don't make no trouble.' He was right, because they got you by the balls when you're in jail and the way to get along is to follow orders. Otherwise, the only trouble you can make is for yourself. On my way up there, I made up my mind that I was gonna be the best fuckin' prisoner in the place."

But Luciano's thoughts were not just of the endless years stretching out ahead. "I couldn't get it out of my mind that I was bein' sent up the river on an out-and-out frame. It was there, twenty-four hours of every day — me, Charlie Lucky, the big shot, caught in a net that was big enough to see comin' a mile away, and I walked right into it with my eyes wide open. It was like a knife in my belly. Sometimes in those first nights at Dannemora, I'd dream about that knife, and I'd wake up screamin' because I could feel Dewey twistin' it inside me and cuttin' me open."

At Dannemora, Luciano was not, of course, the usual prisoner; he was, after all, the king of the underworld, and his peers inside accorded him that status, as it had been accorded him on the outside. "Wherever I went in that place, practically from the first day I got there, there was always other cons after me, askin' me to do 'em favors, to put in a good word with the guards or the warden. They all thought I was gonna beat the rap and I guess they wanted to make sure when I got out and they got out, that they could come to see me back in New York and I'd give 'em a hand."

In the yard at exercise time, as though he were back in his New York headquarters, Luciano would hold court, surrounded by sycophants and courtiers and available to anyone seeking to enlist his favor. "But I was no king or any bullshit like that. I talked to anybody who wanted to talk to me and I did what I could to help out the guys who needed help. I wasn't lookin' to be the leader of Dannemora; it just happened. When a con was about to get out, he'd come over to see me and maybe ask for some names to see on the outside. As a matter of fact, we got quite a few fellows for the outfit back in New York durin' the time I spent in jail that way."

For prison officials, at first anyway, there was an attempt to deal with Luciano, their most notorious convict, as though he were just another inmate. He was given no special treatment and, as soon as he had been processed, was assigned to work in the laundry. "Even though I made up my mind to be a guy who wouldn't cause no trouble, that was goin' too far. Back in thirty-six, a prison laundry wasn't like a big laundromat. We didn't have no electric machines, no air conditionin'. There I am, in a place that's like a sweatbox, a boiler room, and I'm supposed to wash and iron the shit all the other guys was wearin', like I was some kind of washerwoman. So after a few weeks I found out where to spread the dough around — a few bucks here and there, because what prison guard has more than a pot to piss in? — and pretty soon I was up in the library, where it was clean, quiet and I could do some real thinkin' and plannin'."

In the library, in his cell, everywhere, Luciano's obsession was no different from that of other inmates — how to get out. "I really felt like I was in Siberia when it came to the strategy that Levy and Polakoff was workin' on in Manhattan. It was the first time in all my years that I had no control and nothin' to say about what was goin' on in my life. It was like I had — claustrophobia. I felt closed in, not just because I was in prison, but because I was like in solitary with no connection with the outside world, my world in Manhattan."

After a few months, the raging frustration at his position, the constant nightmares began to subside and Luciano came to accept as inevitable the fact that release would not come soon, that the appeals process would be a long one. He began to come somewhat to terms with his situation, particularly in the library. "There I was, surrounded by all them books and I started to think about Lansky — how Meyer was always walkin' around with a book stuck in his back pocket and his nose buried in another one. The son of a bitch was always readin', always learnin' somethin', mostly havin' to do with numbers. That's when I started reading."

Unlike other convicts, who, if they read at all, devoted themselves to lawbooks looking for legal loopholes to win freedom, Luciano turned elsewhere. "I figured I was payin' my lawyers plenty, so why the hell should I spend my time doin' what I was payin' them to do? So I started to read books on history and geography that had to do with America. No matter what anybody says, I was a good American and I always think of myself as a good American. But I didn't know shit about my country. I didn't know where anyplace was. Sure, I knew Chicago and Miami and Hot Springs and Saratoga and all the towns in between, but I didn't know much else. Before I went to work in the Dannemora library, if you asked me where the hell Des Moines was, I couldn't've told you. And I read a lot about Sicily and Italy. I was born in Sicily and I had a lotta relatives still livin' there, but I knew less about that place than I did about America. By the time I got out of the can, though, I knew more about the history of Sicily and Italy than a lotta college professors in the United States.

"I was reading so much that one day, when Frank Costello came up to see me and I started tellin' him about all the books I'm reading, Frank says to me, 'Charlie, you're becoming a god-damn Sicilian Meyer Lansky.' Whadda you think of that?"

In his cell at night, Luciano read, and he practiced penmanship. Hour after hour, he sat at his desk with yellow lined paper and a pencil and wrote carefully, again and again, forming each letter painstakingly, copying the forms in the penmanship books he took from the library. In later years, his handwriting would have a round, studied look, without distinctive style, merely an imitation of clear and well-formed school penmanship.

But, in prison, Luciano did not abandon the empire he had constructed back in New York, and he was determined to maintain a close and continuing control over it. He had left behind Joe Adonis as his liaison with the Unione Siciliano, Meyer Lansky in charge of finances and Frank Costello as caretaker of his personal holdings and as immediate superior to Vito Genovese. They made regular trips upstate to see him, to discuss important decisions, and to carry back a steady stream of messages and orders. It was not the same as when he had been in charge in person on the scene, but still his orders were obeyed and his suggestions rarely, if ever, questioned. Though he continued to share in the profits, he was unable to see, to savor, to relish the results; he could only hear about them in letters or from his visitors.

"It was lousy. I was sittin' up there in the library while down

232

in New York and all over the country everybody was scorin' big and I could only hear about it and dream about it. I could taste it but I couldn't swallow it.

"And I was pretty upset after a while when Lansky hadn't been up to see me for a couple of months. So I sent word, about Easter-time in 1937, for him to come up right away. Instead of Lansky, Adonis came up, and he wasn't so full of smiles."

Adonis told Luciano that Lansky had been unable to make the trip and when Luciano asked why, Adonis hedged. "Well, he had some business out of town and I knew you'd want me to come up here and tell you about it."

Luciano sensed trouble. "Stop shittin' around, Joe. What's goin' on?"

Adonis hesitated, then said, "Lansky's down in Havana. I got word yesterday that he made a deal with Batista and he's got control of the casino at the Hotel Nacional. So far, nobody knows who gets cut in for what."

"When Joe A. told me that, I was pretty pissed off. It was hard for me to believe, after Molaska and all that stuff, that Meyer could still do anythin' so stupid as to go out on his own like a sittin' duck. So I told Joe not to jump to no conclusions and to pass the word around for everybody to hold their water, and to get in touch with Lansky and tell him to get his ass up to Dannemora right away."

Within a week, Lansky was in the visitors' room at the prison, accompanied by Polakoff — who was present at most meetings to give them a semblance of legitimacy; prison officials were always told that Luciano's visitors were working on his appeals. As was his habit, Polakoff sat off to one side of the room, far enough away so that he could not hear the discussion.

"What's it all about, Little Man?" Luciano asked Lansky quietly.

"Joe A. told me you wouldn't yell," Lansky said, "and I should've known better than to think you would. The Cuba deal is for everybody, just the way we talked about it four years ago. The only thing that's mine is a deal I made in Havana for sugar, and that goes into Molaska. You have a piece of mine, Charlie; I never wanted it any other way. About Batista — it's the best thing that ever happened to us. I've got him in my pocket, whether he's president or whether he puts somebody else in, no matter what happens. He belongs to us. I handle all his money — every dollar, every peso he takes, I'm handling the transfer to his account in Switzerland."

Luciano was assured. Then he and Lansky turned to other matters of moment. Bugsy Siegel was particularly in Lansky's mind. Siegel had moved to Los Angeles, where he was handling the outfit's West Coast activities. "I know Benny's a good-looking boy," Lansky said about their old friend, with a hardness and a dispassion that distressed Luciano, "but he's no movie star and he's beginning to act like one out there. If he was just using his new friends, all these movie people, as a front, I could understand. But he ain't. He's really playing the part of a Hollywood big shot and that's no good for a guy who should be handling our private business. I'm saying this now because I've got a feeling that someday Bugsy's gonna be a serious problem."

The conversation then turned to Vito Genovese, who had sent a message through Lansky asking permission to leave the country. Genovese had become convinced it was that or go to prison, perhaps even the electric chair, for his activities as one of Luciano's regents had fallen under Dewey's scrutiny, and authorities, too, were beginning to dig into his role in the murder of Ferdinand Boccia. "Lansky knew I hated the little bastard's guts, and I hated the way he kept playin' around with junk in spite of every warnin' I give him, and maybe we'd all be better off if we let the cops get rid of him for us. But I told Meyer I still couldn't bring myself to give the order, to let him go to the chair; I still couldn't forget that he helped to make a lot of it possible for everybody, with what he done for all of us with Masseria and Maranzano and other important jobs like that. Meyer started to argue with me, but I stopped him cold. I said, 'No, he can go to Europe and take anythin' with him that he wants to, but I don't want him floatin' around noplace but Italy. Tell him to stay there and keep his nose clean.'

"Meyer took the message back and Vito left New York with two million in cash. He worked out a deal with contacts in Naples that he'd made a few years before to bring the money to Italy in a big suitcase that would never be opened when he went through customs. He also bought a house in the Jersey Highlands for his wife, Anna, on account of she had to stay behind until he could see what was doin' in Italy, and he left two hundred and fifty grand in a vault in the Manufacturers Trust Company bank on Fifth Avenue, with two keys — one of 'em for Anna and the other he gave to Steve Franse, one of the few guys in the world Vito trusted.

"When Vito left, I'm positive up to that minute, the only thing he ever read in the papers was about what maybe was goin' on in our outfit. I don't think he knew a thing about Hitler or the problems in Europe. He just knew that Mussolini was a big shot in Italy and little Vito had already made his good connections so that everything could be nice and easy for him until things cooled off in New York and he could come back."

Before Lansky left Dannemora that afternoon, Polakoff was called into the discussion, to hear the matter uppermost in Luciano's mind — his appeals and the possibility of freedom. Levy and Adams had left the case soon after the trial, and Polakoff had been joined by another outstanding trial lawyer, George Wolf, who managed to combine courtroom pyrotechnics with the kind of behind-the-scenes planning and strategy that complemented Polakoff's abilities. "I thought Levy done a lousy job. I paid him a fortune to top Dewey and he gave me as much showmanship as an Oyster Bay flounder. So we switched to the best, Georgie Wolf; he cost me over ninety grand plus expenses, just to handle an appeal. But I can't argue, because he eventually dug up the one piece of ammunition I'd need to get out of Dannemora and get free."

As the appeals process began, Luciano had given Polakoff and Wolf an open checkbook to develop the evidence that would overturn his conviction. The initial appeals, based on several obvious errors of the prosecution and the court during the original trial, were rejected peremptorily by higher courts (this was a day when the rights and protections of defendants, particularly notorious gangsters, were of less than overwhelming concern to appeals justices).

Once this avenue had been closed, the defense took another

235

direction, and, of necessity, was forced to move slowly and with extraordinary circumspection. Because of Judge McCook's warning during the sentencing, holding Luciano and the other defendants hostages for the safety of the prosecution witnesses, only the most subtle and oblique approaches could be used to persuade those witnesses to recant their testimony; if a single witness was intimidated or threatened, Wolf and Polakoff warned Luciano, then any appeal would surely fail even if every other witness admitted perjury.

"I'd been yellin' at Polakoff that he and Georgie hadda find a way to get them lyin' broads to tell the truth, that they was the key to any chance we had. Then one day Polakoff comes up and tells me that they can't find them girls, that they seemed to have disappeared into thin air. I said to him, 'What the hell am I payin' you guys for? Use whatever dough you need; get detectives, a hundred detectives — I don't give a shit. But find them broads.'"

At Dannemora that afternoon, Luciano directed Lansky to join Polakoff and Wolf in the hunt for Cokey Flo Brown and Nancy Presser. "For chrissake, Meyer, we got enough guys around on the street to be able to locate anybody. I want you to drop everythin' you're doin', don't bother about nothin' else, but find them broads."

But every trail was cold, every lead a dead one. Then, late in 1938, the first break came. A photostatic copy of a letter addressed to Sol Gelb, of Dewey's office, found its way into the hands of Wolf and Polakoff. Written by Cokey Flo Brown and postmarked from Paris, France, it was bitter and complaining. It seemed that Cokey Flo, Nancy Presser, Mildred Balitzer and several others had been secretly given all-expenses-paid vacations in Europe, with the stay hopefully to be, it appeared, permanent. But Cokey Flo's letter revealed an increasing unhappiness over the constant surveillance under which they were kept, which hampered their movements and their enjoyment of the gay life, and over a diminishing flow of expense money. The letter ended with a threat: If more money and more freedom were not forthcoming, the girls would consider doing something Dewey "wouldn't like."

The discovery of the whereabouts of these witnesses sent defense investigators and lawyers hurrying to Paris. Cables back to Polakoff revealed that no pressure, only a sympathetic ear, would be necessary to win from the girls what was desired. Cokey Flo, Nancy Presser and the others signed affidavits recanting their testimony at the Luciano trial and asserting that not only had that testimony been fabricated but that it had been fabricated by Dewey's office and fed to the girls. They had agreed to lie, they said, because they felt they had no choice; they had been threatened with strenuous prosecution and long prison sentences as prostitutes, madams, drug addicts, unless they testified. But if they talked, they had been promised protection, immunity and a long vacation in Europe.

Almost simultaneously, a letter arrived at Polakoff's office from Sing Sing, from the equally unhappy Joe Bendix. His promised deal for reduction of sentence, parole and freedom had been forgotten by the prosecutor. Convinced he had been double-crossed, Bendix decided to turn on his ungrateful benefactors. He wrote that he, too, had lied at the Luciano trial, that he had been sought out by Dewey's aides, who had concocted the story he told, briefed him, and fed him the lines he had recited on the witness stand.

When Luciano heard the details from Polakoff he was elated, convinced the gates of Dannemora were about to open wide for him. "Moe came up and told me about the affidavits and said he was gonna reorganize our appeal. I felt I could start packin' my stuff and be back home in New York in no time."

Against the sworn statements of Flo Brown, Nancy Presser, Mildred Balitzer, Joe Bendix and others that they had perjured themselves, and that the perjury had been suborned by Dewey and his staff, Dewey used ridicule, scorn and righteous indignation. The reputation of Luciano, he said, was a prime concern for the court of appeals, and Luciano's background alone was enough to show that this recanting of testimony must have been gained, despite Judge McCook's warning, by threats, intimidation, bribery and every other weapon at a hoodlum's command. A reading of the documents, the prosecutor asserted, demonstrated that they were "reeking with perjury" and were "a fraud upon the court."

With but a single justice dissenting (and this on grounds that the sentence had been excessive), the court of appeals rejected

Luciano's plea. And it ended there. The United States Supreme Court refused to entertain arguments. For the moment, at least, the legal avenues had been closed and the sentence was to be served.

"Polakoff came up to Dannemora to tell me the news. We met in the visitors' room and Moe didn't look so good. He was kind of white and shaking. He said to me, 'Charlie, I've got bad news for you.'

"I said to him, 'What happened, Moe?'

"He said, 'They turned down your appeal, Charlie.'

"I looked at him for a minute. I wasn't sure right then just what he meant, so I said, 'What does it mean, Moe?'

"He said, 'That's it for now, Charlie.'

"I still didn't get just what he was talkin' about and I asked him again what it meant. He told me that it was the end of the line, at least for a while, that the court had turned down the appeal because they just didn't believe the affidavits. I almost screamed at him. I yelled, 'Moe! Them broads, they signed them statements. They admitted they lied. Whadda you mean, the court don't believe them?'

"He said, 'I don't know what to say, Charlie. I have to tell it to you the way it happened.'

"I was knocked over. I just wished the whole floor would open up and swallow me. I couldn't see no hope. It was all black, like not even a tiny little light anyplace. That must be the way a guy feels if all of a sudden he goes blind. Naturally, Moe tried to make me feel better. He told me they wouldn't stop workin', but he warned me that it wasn't gonna be easy, that the whole thing was never easy from the beginnin' — just like he said up in my apartment when we had the meetin' with all the guys. It was right then and there that I had the most respect for Polakoff. He never shitted me, he always leveled, and he'd been smarter than anybody else from the start. At least, when I saw Moe walk out, I knew that I had somebody on the outside I could trust, and if there was any possible way to manipulate some legal loophole, Moses Polakoff would find it.

"Back in my cell, I looked at the bars and I wondered if I'd ever see them from the outside instead of the inside."

21.

In the years before he had gone to Dannemora, Luciano had exercised a restraining influence over some of his more volatile associates. He, Costello and Lansky, particularly, had long since reached the conclusion that violence was in most cases unnecessary, was to be shunned unless unavoidable and then used most judiciously. He and his fellow leaders of the Unione Siciliano had tried to keep a tight reign on the two major proponents of indiscriminate violence, Lepke and Anastasia, with the dictum that no killing could be carried out without the unanimous consent of the council. When he was on the scene, in control, his influence had been pervasive and few ignored his orders and disobeyed his dictates.

But now he was in Dannemora, hundreds of miles from the seat of his empire, and the surrogates he had left behind were often absent from New York, as well, unable then to exert a restraining influence on Lepke and Anastasia. Costello was often in New Orleans or elsewhere, working with Dandy Phil Kastel and others on his burgeoning gambling interests; Lansky was spending more and more time in Broward County, attempting to establish a network of casinos in the Miami area, and in the Caribbean, cementing his profitable friendship and partnership with Cuba's Batista.

"Up in Dannemora I had enough things to bother me, like my own plans for the appeals and different ideas to help me get out. Then I began to get a lot of reports about what Lep and Albert was doin', just because Costello and Lansky wasn't around every day to stop 'em. Then I heard that Lepke was goin' around tellin' some of our guys that he wasn't gonna use his muscle for the benefit of nobody but himself. In other words, the garment district and the bakery business, for example, was gonna be his without cuttin' nobody else in."

By the middle of 1937, Lepke was in deep trouble. He lived lavishly and loudly, was often in the newspapers and so became an obvious target for prosecutor Dewey. "And then the shit hit the fan when word got around the narcotics guys was buildin' a case against Lep for somethin' that even surprised me. The stupid jerk got himself mixed up with a shipment of junk from Hong Kong to the United States that was supposed to be worth ten million bucks — I heard later it was a helluva lot less than that. It was bad enough that I always had to worry about Vito with that hard stuff — now this muscle-headed son of a bitch Lepke gets himself involved up to his belly button in somethin' he don't know a fuckin' thing about.

"So, of course, he needs help and he sends Joe A. up to see me. My first reaction was to tell Joe to let him take the rap. For years, I'd been tryin' to help him, and it was always like talkin' to a stone wall. But you can't throw a guy to the wolves, so I sent Joe back to New York with an okay for Anastasia to hide Lepke. I knew he and Lep was close and he'd give it extra special attention."

At the end of 1937, Louis "Lepke" Buchalter disappeared, and for two years he was the subject of a nationwide manhunt. Dewey, calling him "the worst industrial racketeer in America," offered a twenty-five-thousand-dollar reward for his arrest. A little later, J. Edgar Hoover, apparently alarmed that so many others — Dewey, Narcotics Bureau chief Harry Anslinger, New York Police Commissioner Lewis Valentine — were encroaching on his province as the chief nemesis and scourge of the underworld, chimed in with a statement that Lepke was "the most dangerous criminal in the United States" and so was worth five thousand dollars to the man who turned him over to the FBI. Circulars flooded the country, but did not flush Lepke. There were rumors that he was hiding out in Florida, Arkansas, California, Chicago; not in the United States at all, but in Cuba, Poland, the Far East.

"But the real laugh for me come sometime in 1939. The FBI was sendin' guys all over the place. One guy got a free vacation down in Havana, where he went to see Lansky, and another guy went to New Orleans to talk to Costello to see if he knew where Lep was. And then it happened. Hoover sent an agent up to see me at Dannemora. He wanted me to help them find Lepke. Can you imagine the gall of that guy Hoover? I told the agent I wanted to send a message back to J. Edgar — if he would arrange to commute my sentence, I could let him have Lepke in twenty-four hours. No commutation, no Lepke, and as far as I was concerned, Hoover could go fuck himself — and maybe that was a good idea.''

To Luciano and the others in the underworld hierarchy, Lepke's whereabouts was no secret. He was under the rigid protection of Anastasia, much of the time at 101 Third Street in Brooklyn. But he was doing more than hiding out. He was attempting to govern his rackets as usual. He was dispatching his and Anastasia's killers from Murder, Inc., to eliminate every potential witness against him and so force the collapse of the cases prepared by the authorities. And he was meeting often with the upper strata of the underworld and becoming more and more belligerent with his associates.

Lepke's attitude finally sent Tommy Lucchese — accompanied as usual by Moses Polakoff — hurrying to Dannemora to see Luciano. Two nights earlier, Lucchese related, Anastasia had brought Lepke to a meeting with Lucchese, Willie Moretti, Gerardo Rullo (who, some years later, would be better known as Jerry Catena, one of the major caretakers of the Vito Genovese interests), Longie Zwillman and several others. Lucchese had called the meeting to broach to Lepke his increasing dissatisfaction with Lepke's attempts to tighten his own personal control over the garment industry at the expense of Lucchese and his other partners. Lepke's response was to claim that the garment district belonged to him exclusively and he would fight any incursions by others. Then Lepke stormed out of the meeting and ordered his aide, Abe "Kid Twist" Reles, to drive him back to his sanctuary.

"Ever since you've been gone," Lucchese told Luciano, "things ain't the same. I've got the feeling that Frank Costello is doing too much on his own and that little genius, Lansky, disappears down in Havana someplace and we don't see him but maybe once a month. Charlie, you've gotta do something about this Lepke thing, because Dewey and Hoover would give their left arms to grab him and until they do, they're putting plenty of pressure on everybody. They ain't gonna let up on none of us until they grab Lepke."

"I felt like we was pushin' the calendar back again to Dutch Schultz. I thought it over for a few minutes and then I finally made the decision. We couldn't knock off Lep the way it happened with Schultz. That would just mean more trouble. Hoover would be sore as a boil at anybody stealin' his glory and Dewey would go through the ceilin'. We had to get Lep out of our hair once and for all, but we had to do it some way that'd still give Dewey and Hoover their piece of the cake. So I told Tommy to get hold of Meyer and Frank and Joe A. right away, and to make sure Anastasia got my message — I ordered him to stop protectin' Lepke and I didn't want no arguments about that.

"The way I figured it, the most important thing was to make it look to Lepke like we'd worked out a deal with Hoover. If he'd give himself up to the FBI and take the narcotics rap, he'd have Hoover's guarantee that he wouldn't be turned over to Dewey, and by the time he finished the federal stretch, the Dewey case would probably've caved in. I knew that Lep was scared to death of Tom Dewey, especially after what that prick done to me. Of course, we didn't make no deal at all with Hoover, but it had to look damn sure to Lepke like we did. I also told Tommy that the plan hadda be put across to Lep by somebody he'd trust; he wasn't gonna come outa hidin' and run up to Dannemora to see me, and I knew he'd never trust Joe A. or Frank or Meyer. They had to get a messenger who was close enough to Lep so he'd buy the plan without question.

"Then I wrote a note to Lansky, sealed it up, and gave it to Polakoff to take to Meyer in New York. I laid the whole thing out for Meyer and told him that after all the arrangements had been made for Lep to surrender to the FBI, he and Costello should make sure that Dewey got the word that I had masterminded the whole thing — Hoover gets Lep first and then turns him over to Dewey. I also wrote that I wanted Frank to contact his best man on Dewey's staff and say I was willin' for the whole outfit to back Dewey in a run for governor of New York. I told him I couldn't say no more about that part of it until I had all the details worked out in my mind."

Lansky, indeed, knew exactly the man for the job of persuading Lepke — Moe "Dimples" Wolensky, who had worked in gambling operations for both Lansky and Lepke and was known to have Lepke's confidence. Wolensky was dispatched as the intermediary, unaware he was leading Lepke into a trap. Two years underground, with the mounting pressures and tensions of hiding out, had turned Lepke pliant enough to be willing to accept what seemed reasonable terms.

At the beginning of August 1939, word reached Luciano of Lepke's compliance, on condition that he surrender to J. Edgar Hoover personally and that Albert Anastasia drive him to that meeting. The only question remaining was who would now set up the details with the FBI chief, unaware until that moment. A number of names were suggested, and the choice narrowed down to three — William O'Dwyer, a Kings County (Brooklyn) judge who owed his political success to the outfit's muscle and money; Morris Novik, a special assistant to Mayor La Guardia and an impartial and incorruptible public servant; and the noted New York *Daily Mirror* gossip columnist and longtime friend of Hoover, Walter Winchell.

"When Frank came up with this information and mentioned Winchell, I was ready to hit him. After all, he knew how Winchell had acted when I was still at the Barbizon. But then Frank explained it, and I figured he was right. Winchell was buddy-buddy with Hoover and usin' Winchell would convince Lepke for sure that it was all on the up-and-up. Besides, it wouldn't do no harm to give Winchell the biggest scoop of the century. That kind of favor he knew he hadda repay, and with what I had in mind, I could use every bit of muscle I could get.

"I gave Frank the okay on Winchell, and then we started to talk about Dewey. We knew the son of a bitch wasn't gonna be satisfied bein' D.A. for the rest of his life. He'd already made one crack at tryin' to be governor [losing in 1938 as the Republican candidate against Herbert Lehman] and he was beginnin' to make a lot of noise about runnin' for President in 1940. We figured he was too goddamn young for that, and besides, I wanted him in Albany, because that's where he could do me some good. So Frank went back to New York with a guarantee from me to Dewey that not only would he get all our backin' to run for governor next time, but also that Lepke was gonna be turned over to him on a silver platter, with my compliments, plus evidence."

Just before ten o'clock on August 24, 1939, a sweltering Manhattan summer night more than two years after Lepke had first vanished, a four-door sedan driven by Albert Anastasia stopped at 101 Third Street in Brooklyn, picked up a passenger, his coat collar turned up, his face masked by large sunglasses, and drove rapidly over the Brooklyn Bridge into Manhattan. At Fifth Avenue and Twenty-eighth Street, Anastasia spotted a black, curtained limousine at the curb, and pulled up a short distance behind it. The rear door of the sedan opened, its passenger got out, paused for a moment for a last word, and then walked quickly to his rendezvous. Winchell, behind the steering wheel of the limousine, opened the right front door, leaned over, and stared intently at the partially disguised figure, then looked behind at the stocky occupant of the back seat. "Mr. Hoover," he said, "this is Lepke."

Hoover nodded, reached across, and opened the rear door, motioning Lepke to enter. "How do you do?" he said brusquely.

"Glad to meet you," Lepke responded. He entered the car and settled into the seat next to the FBI director. But any pleasure he might have felt at that meeting quickly evaporated. With Hoover's first words, he discovered there was no fix, no deal, at least as far as he was concerned. Either Hoover wasn't admitting that a deal had been made or he didn't know about one. Bluntly, Hoover informed Lepke he would be quickly tried on the narcotics charges by federal authorities — which Lepke expected — and then, to Lepke's horror, would be turned over to Dewey for trial on charges Dewey had publicly proclaimed would send Lepke to prison for five hundred years. "I wanted to get out of that car as soon as I heard that," Lepke said later. But that was impossible. As soon as Winchell turned on his car lights and pulled away from the curb, a fleet of other cars, filled with FBI men, surrounded the limousine and escorted it to FBI headquarters in Manhattan.

Within a month, Lepke was in a federal courtroom, on trial for narcotics conspiracy. He was sentenced to fourteen years. Hardly had sentence been pronounced before the stunned racketeer was turned over to Manhattan District Attorney Tom Dewey, who saw him as another and major stepping-stone on the path to Albany at the very least and possibly to the White House. In state court, Dewey won a conviction of Lepke on charges of extortion and other crimes in the bakery racket and had the satisfaction of hearing Lepke sentenced to a term that just about matched Luciano's — thirty years to life.

With the scalps of two of the nation's major racketeers — Luciano and Lepke — dangling from his belt, the political fortunes of Thomas E. Dewey, the racket-buster, were clearly on the ascendant. "It was a matter of life and death for me to make sure that Dewey got to Albany first, before he tried for the White House. I needed him in the state capital, because, as governor, he'd have the power to grant me a parole. So there was two questions that hadda be solved. One, to make sure Dewey beat the shit out of Lehman or whoever the Democrats put up; and, two, to put aside enough money for Dewey's personal campaign that would make him really obligated. Except, this time there would be none of that crap like happened with Roosevelt, where we put it up first and then got screwed. I had somethin' else in mind for Mr. Tom Dewey that would give me the edge."

22.

Early in 1940, Frank Costello appeared at Dannemora with some disturbing news. "Listen, Charlie," he whispered through the visitors' screen, "our friend Bill O. has Reles stuck away in the Tombs for some old rubout. What are we gonna do about it?"

"We do nothin' unless the Kid opens his mouth. That we can't afford. But what's more important, will O'Dwyer protect us? I thought you told me you had him in your pocket?"

"Sure we do," Costello said, "but he's got big dreams. We put the money up that made him D.A. in Brooklyn, but as sure as we're talkin', he wants La Guardia's job." Then Costello added something that made Luciano see his plan for gaining quick release from Dannemora begin to fade. "I don't know whether we can hold him in line. This guy Turkis [O'Dwyer's Assistant District

Attorney Burton Turkis] has a lot of ambitions, too, and he's been talkin' to Reles, squeezin' him. We can't buy Turkis; he's an honest bastard. So Bill O. may have no choice but to give him a free hand."

"I couldn't sleep at all that night. That's how strong the feelin' was that Reles was gonna blow every hope I had at that time of gettin' sprung by Dewey, if and when he became governor. I could hardly believe what was happenin' to me, because, among other things, I learned from Costello that afternoon that he'd made a good contact with Dewey through one of the guys on Dewey's staff, and the word had been passed to Dewey that he was gonna get plenty of money for a run at Albany. Costello said Dewey didn't turn down the offer, and in my book that was as good as acceptin' it. And now along comes this stuff from left field and maybe it can upset the whole fuckin' apple cart. I knew if I was in New York I could do somethin' myself to handle a situation like this. But stuck away in Siberia, I hadda leave my chances a hundred per cent in the hands of other people and my bones told me it was gonna be bad news."

The small, squat, hard-eyed "Kid Twist" Reles had been one of the prime executioners in the Lepke-Anastasia enforcement group, a merciless man who had never been out of trouble with the law since his first arrest at sixteen in 1924 — his rap sheet listed forty-two arrests, including six for murder, and he had been in prison six times. But Reles's serious problems — and those of others in major positions in the underworld — began early in 1940 when a minor hoodlum named Harry "The Mock" Rudolph, serving a short term on Riker's Island, decided to talk about a murder he had witnessed six years earlier. His friend Alex "Red" Alpert, he told Brooklyn police, had been killed by Abe Reles, Martin "Buggsy" Goldstein and Anthony "Dukey" Maffetore. On the basis of Rudolph's statement, Brooklyn District Attorney William O'Dwyer won murder indictments against the three; they were arrested, lodged in separate jails, and grilled relentlessly.

On March 31, more than forty days after his arrest, Abe Reles's wife appeared at O'Dwyer's office and declared, "My husband wants an interview with the law."

Luciano's fears were about to become fact. Reles was rushed from the Tombs in Manhattan to O'Dwyer's office in Brooklyn, where he demanded a private interview with the district attorney. "I can make you the biggest man in the country," he told O'Dwyer, and then, alone, proposed a nonnegotiable exchange: if all charges against him were dropped, if he were granted immunity from any further charges growing out of what he or anyone else might say, and if his future freedom were guaranteed, he would tell all that he knew about organized crime and would testify in court as a witness for the state.

It was the break O'Dwyer had been praying for, but at that moment neither O'Dwyer nor anyone else realized just how big a break this was.

Reles was placed under constant police guard at the Hotel Bossert in Brooklyn, only a few steps from the district attorney's office. Then he began his grisly confessions. The first gush lasted twelve days and filled twenty-five stenographic notebooks with tales of wholesale slaughter, of murders he knew about personally. He provided the names of accomplices and of corroborating non-accomplices — a necessity under the law if convictions were to be won — and where to find them. Kid Twist's memory for details was staggering, and he led Turkis and other interrogators in O'Dwyer's office down a tangled path of an underworld enforcement-murder operation that was almost impossible to credit.

Initially, Reles recited a list of minor hoodlums and their crimes — "Happy" Maione and "Dasher" Abbandando, who murdered a loan shark named George "Whitey" Rudnick by stabbing him sixty-three times with knives and ice picks, shattering his skull and strangling him; "Pittsburgh Phil" Strauss and Buggsy Goldstein, who garrotted and cremated a small-time gambler named Irving "Puggy" Feinstein on orders of Albert Anastasia, who was acting at the behest of fellow ganglord Vince Mangano (inexplicably, neither O'Dwyer nor anyone else ever questioned Anastasia or Mangano about the Feinstein murder), and a host of others.

Reles's testimony would eventually send Maione, Abbandando, Strauss, Goldstein and others to the electric chair. But that would come later. At first, the fascinated Brooklyn prosecutors merely listened, copied down his words, and ordered arrests. That he was singing was supposed to be a total secret. It did not remain so long, at least not from the underworld. A few weeks after his meeting with Luciano about Reles, Costello was back at Dannemora, talking in whispers through the screen.

"Reles is singin'," he told Luciano. "O'Dwyer told me he's got no way to hold it back."

"How much is he singin'?"

"Plenty. The cocksucker's got a memory like an elephant and a voice like a canary. He just keeps vomitin' stuff up like he can't stop pukin'. If he keeps on goin', they're gonna get everybody for murder, and that includes that shithead Lepke. But it'll also include Benny Siegel and Albert, take my word for it. Reles tied in Allie Tick-Tock and I hear that Allie's made a deal with Turkis."

"I don't give a crap about Lep. Whatever he gets, he's got comin'. But we've got to work somethin' out to get Bugsy and Albert out of this."

Lepke was, indeed, about to get what was coming to him. On the basis of evidence supplied by Reles and Allie "Tick-Tock" Tannenbaum, a key assassin on the Murder, Inc., payroll, O'Dwyer, in May of 1940, demanded that federal authorities return Lepke to Brooklyn to stand trial for the 1936 murder of a candy-store owner named Joseph Rosen. A former garment trucker, Rosen had been forced out of business by Lepke and had threatened to make complaints to authorities. Lepke had ordered his murder and had given the contract to three killers — Mendy Weiss, Louis Capone and Pittsburgh Phil Strauss, who fired seventeen bullets into their victim.

It took nearly a year and a half before that trial was finally held. Then, in November of 1941, with Turkis guiding the prosecution and Tannenbaum as the star witness, Lepke, Capone and Weiss were convicted of first-degree murder (Strauss was already on his way to the electric chair for the Feinstein killing, so he was not tried for this crime), and two and a half years later, on March 4, 1944, all three were executed at Sing Sing.

The murder that had the potential of sending Bugsy Siegel along the same route was that of a Lepke enforcer named Harry "Big Greenie" Greenberg. During Lepke's time of trouble in the late thirties, Greenberg had fled to Canada for safety, had soon run short of funds, and had written back asking for five thousand dollars and implying that if his friends didn't send it quickly, he might decide to return for a long talk with Tom Dewey. That threat earned him an underworld death sentence and Tannenbaum was given the contract. Greenberg, however, succeeded in eluding him until late in 1939, when he surfaced in Los Angeles.

The West Coast was the province of Siegel, who decided to take a personal hand. He imported another killer, Frankie Carbo (later to come to prominence as a prizefight manager), once Greenberg had been tracked to his hideout. Then, shortly after dark on November 22, 1939, Tannenbaum, Siegel and Carbo drove to 1804 Vista Del Mar in Los Angeles and waited in their parked car for Greenberg to return from his only daily outdoor excursion — a short drive to pick up the newspapers. When Greenberg's car pulled up in front of the house, Carbo and Siegel stepped out to meet him. With guns supplied by Longie Zwillman and brought to California by Tannenbaum, they completed the long-delayed contract and then sped away with Tannenbaum at the wheel.

Less than a year later, during his own recital for Brooklyn authorities, in exchange for immunity and eventual freedom, Tannenbaum told Turkis the story of that murder. Though convincing, his evidence could not convict anyone without the corroboration of a nonparticipant. Reles, who had not been part of the plot, provided that corroboration; he had been advised, he said, of all the details since the inception.

Armed with the statements and other evidence, Turkis flew off to California for discussions with Los Angeles authorities, then took Reles and Tannenbaum out to testify before the grand jury. Siegel, Carbo and Champ Segal, who had been present in a backup car, were indicted for murder, and Lepke and Mendy Weiss were indicted for having ordered the killing.

Before the warrants could be served, Benny Siegel and Carbo were alerted and both vanished — Siegel into the attic of his two-hundred-thousand-dollar mansion on North Linden Drive in Beverly Hills, from which he eventually emerged to surrender. In his cell, Siegel, visited often by his Hollywood friends who professed utter disbelief that he could have been involved, was supremely confident. With the approval of the outfit in the East, he had donated thirty thousand dollars to the campaign of John Dockweiler as Los Angeles County district attorney, and when Dockweiler was elected, Siegel had boasted to Costello and others, "He's my man." That claim was given some substance when Dockweiler asked the court to dismiss the indictments in early December 1940, on grounds that his staff had discovered that a witness — not Reles or Tannenbaum — had lied to the grand jury. The indictment was dismissed and Siegel walked out of jail.

But Los Angeles authorities decided to seek a second indictment. O'Dwyer was asked to send Tannenbaum and Reles back to California for another grand jury appearance. He refused at first and then reluctantly permitted only Tannenbaum to make the trip. Another indictment was forthcoming, this time naming only Siegel and Carbo for the murder of Greenberg. Once again, Siegel disappeared, part of the time relaxing in his mansion, part journeying to New York for meetings with his friends.

With Siegel loose, the object of a massive manhunt, and with the Lepke trial in progress, Charlie Lucky Luciano, viewing all this as a major derailment of his plans for release from prison, summoned Costello to Dannemora in the fall of 1941. By then, some of the restrictions on Luciano had been relaxed; Dr. Walter Martin had replaced William Snyder as warden of the prison and had expressed the view that Luciano's sentence was both harsh and unusual, and so he was willing to grant some small privileges, including privacy with his visitors.

When Costello arrived, Luciano wasted no time. "Frank, I'm gettin' sick and tired of all the shit that's happenin' between Benny and Albert. No matter what kinda heat they got on 'em they're still outside, walkin' around. I'm locked up and I want out. We gave O'Dwyer a pisspot full of money, now what the hell are we gettin' back for it?"

"Charlie," Costello said, "we can't put a blanket on what's goin' on. O'Dwyer is worse than Dewey when it comes to ambition. I've told him he's a fuckin' idiot to dream about goin' to Washington. I've tried to convince him to be patient and we'll get him the mayor's job, get La Guardia the fuck outa there. But the son of a bitch has stars in his eyes. It's almost like you can't talk to him no more."

"But what the hell is he doin' for us?"

"I hate to tell you," Costello said, "but the answer is, nothin'."

Luciano was disgusted. He demanded, "Then what the hell are you doin' about Reles? Now he's tied Albert in for the killin' of Moish Diamond a couple of years ago. That dumb bastard, Albert — I warned him not to go around hittin' guys unless it's somebody in the outfit. You hit guys on the outside, it's like askin' for trouble. He was crazy to knock off Diamond. He didn't have to do it. I sent him the word that if he did it he was off his head."

(Teamster official Morris Diamond had been murdered in May of 1939 after he had resisted increasing encroachment by racketeers and threatened to go to Dewey. With Anastasia looking on and giving the orders, Diamond was cornered on a Brooklyn street and shot six times in the head. Allie Tannenbaum, one of the killers, had told the story to Turkis and O'Dwyer, and Reles had corroborated it.)

"Frank," Luciano said, "Reles has gotta go. That's the only way we can save Benny and Albert. Without him, all the O'Dwyers and Turkises and Deweys in the world can't convict them two guys, and we owe 'em enough so we gotta save 'em. You gotta make a move and get the little bastard."

"That's one of the things I wanted to see you about," Costello said. "We got a deal just about set up and I came up here to get your okay. They got Reles stashed away like he was gold in Fort Knox. He's surrounded by cops day and night, even when he's sleepin'."

"We been payin' off them Brooklyn cops for years. What's so hard about this job?"

"There's just no way we can get to Reles. The cops'll have to do it for us."

"So what. Let 'em do it. Christ, let 'em do somethin' to earn their dough."

"Okay. But remember, it's gonna cost like hell."

"I don't give a fuck what it costs — pay it."

Costello nodded. "That's what I thought you'd say. But I came up here to get the word straight from you."

"All right, you got it. And when you're a hundred and ten per cent sure, tell Benny to give himself up — beforehand."

In October, Siegel walked out of hiding and surrendered once again to Los Angeles authorities. When Luciano heard the news, he knew that Costello had worked out all the arrangements. "There was a big-shot cop on the New York Police Department, name of Captain Frank Bals. He was in charge of all the investigations for O'Dwyer, and them two was together like two fingers. And so Bals did us the big favor of arranging for Reles to get lost, like out of the window of his hotel room. I'll never forget the date, because it was one of the turnin' points of my life — November 12, 1941."

That morning, Abe "Kid Twist" Reles was, as usual, in his room, 623, at the Half Moon Hotel in Coney Island. As usual, his door was open. His protectors that morning were three plain-clothes detectives, James Boyle, Victor Robbins and John E. Moran and two patrolmen, Francesco Tempone and Harvey F. X. McLaughlin, all under command of Frank Bals and his chief aide, Sergeant Elwood Divvers. (A sixth guard was normally assigned to the shift, but who he was and whether he was there that morning have been a continuing source of controversy and mystery; some police officials have insisted there were only five men there, others that there were six, but they have never identified the sixth.)

Sometime before seven in the morning, the assistant manager of the hotel heard a thud on an extension roof beneath Reles's room, but he ignored it. About the same time, Detective Robbins said he checked Reles's room and the Kid was in bed as usual. At ten after seven Robbins checked again; Reles was gone. Robbins said he rushed to an open window and looked down, and forty-two feet below lay the remains of Abe Reles, fully dressed, with two knotted bedsheets nearby. The body was sprawled more than twenty feet out from the wall.

O'Dwyer placed the investigation of the sudden death of his star witness in the hands of Captain Bals. Within hours, Bals had reached his conclusion: there was nothing unusual in the fact that Reles had been alone in his room, checked regularly by guards, for this was the normal practice. (Later, Tannenbaum would assert that he and Reles were never left alone, that a guard was always present in their rooms, even when they were asleep.) Bals said that Reles's death was an unfortunate accident, but only an accident. The captain theorized that it could have happened in one of two ways: Reles had attempted to escape by means of the knotted bedsheets and had fallen to his death when the sheets gave way; or Reles — a notorious practical joker, according to Bals — had been attempting to play one of his pranks by sliding down to the fifth floor and then walking up the stairs to surprise his protectors, and had fallen to his death in the process. (Other police officials, not including Bals, later offered a third theory: Reles had suddenly become conscience-stricken over his past and fearful of his future and so had committed suicide.)

"The truth of the whole thing was," Luciano said twenty years later, "that the whole bunch of cops was on the take and Bals handled the whole thing. We paid him fifty grand and set aside some more money for the other guys in case they hadda take a rap. The way I heard it was that Bals stood there in the room and supervised the whole thing. Reles was sleepin' and one of the cops give him a tap with a billy and knocked him out. Then they picked him up and heaved him out the window. For chrissake, he landed so far from the wall he couldn't've done that even if he jumped."

For some of those assigned to guard Reles from the underworld's vengeance, there was comparatively minor punishment — the five policemen were put back in uniform and assigned to walk the beat. No blame fell on either Bals or Divvers — or on O'Dwyer. And, in fact, when O'Dwyer was elected mayor of New York in 1945, he appointed Frank Bals a deputy police commissioner. "Bals became our bagman for the whole department. He got ten grand in small bills in the same goddamn fuckin' paper bag that was always goin' someplace down around City Hall every week, just like clockwork. And let's get this straight — the dough went to Bals and the split was his responsibility."

So Abe Reles was dead and the "perfect murder case" against Albert Anastasia for the killing of Morris Diamond, about which O'Dwyer had boasted repeatedly, had gone out the window too. What emerged in the aftermath, though, was equally shocking to many. During the nineteen months between the time Reles and Tannenbaum had first talked about the murder and Reles's death, a period when Anastasia had gone underground and O'Dwyer was supposedly scouring the country in search of him, the Brooklyn district attorney did not bother to obtain an indictment of Anastasia for the Diamond murder. Not only that, but he never directed anyone on his staff to obtain such an indictment and, in fact, actually forbade anyone to do so — even though, Turkis would later say, "He was fully aware that Anastasia had to approve every murder done within organized crime in Brooklyn." O'Dwyer's explanation? Anastasia was a fugitive and it would have been a waste of time to indict him before he was found.

A few months after Reles's sudden fall, O'Dwyer took a leave of absence from his job as district attorney to enter the Army, from which he would emerge at the end of World War II a brigadier general, something of a hero, and a major political power among New York Democrats. But before he left office, he placed the disposition of the Anastasia case in the hands of Captain Bals, who filed a confidential memorandum on its status: "In the case of Anastasio [Anastasia's real family name], legal corroboration is missing. . . . On November 12, 1941, Abe Reles who was under police guard in the Half Moon Hotel, Brooklyn, attempted to escape and fell five [sic] stories, being instantly killed. This not only seriously hampered the investigation, but deprived the state of his testimony and information. At the present time the only testimony adducible against Anastasio is that of accomplices."

(A Brooklyn grand jury in 1945 had what may have been the last legal observation on the affair; it charged that there had been "negligence, incompetence and flagrant irresponsibility" in O'Dwyer's handling of the Anastasia case, for the district attorney was "in possession of competent legal evidence that Anastasia was guilty of first degree murder and other vicious crimes. The proof admittedly was sufficient to warrant Anastasia's indictment and conviction, but Anastasia was neither prosecuted, indicted nor convicted. . . . The consistent and complete failure to prosecute the overlord of organized crime . . . is so revolting that we cannot permit these disclosures to be filed away in the same manner the evidence against Anastasia was heretofore 'put in the files.' " That grand jury report and knowledge that the underworld was making huge contributions to O'Dwyer's political fortunes did not stop Tammany Hall from backing him in his successful mayoralty campaign in 1945 and in his successful re-election effort four years later.)

With the collapse of O'Dwyer's "perfect murder case" against him, Albert Anastasia once again was omnipresent in Brooklyn, strutting with new confidence in his invincibility along the water-front. He did not, however, remain there long. Within weeks, Pearl Harbor was bombed and the United States was at war. Anastasia's criminal record might ordinarily have made him a very unlikely candidate for service in the American war effort, but times were perilous and able-bodied men were needed. So Anastasia, proclaiming his devotion to his country and his willing-ness to serve (and, too, envisioning life as a soldier as protection against any unpleasantness that might arise from civilian authori-ties), offered no objection when he was drafted, particularly when he was awarded a technical sergeant's stripes and put to work at a camp in Pennsylvania for two years instructing G.I.'s in the art of being longshoremen. In return for this valuable service, Anasta-sia was not only granted an honorable discharge in 1944, but was awarded United States citizenship as well.

The war brought rewards to others, too. Herbert Lehman left Albany to enter the service of his country, and New York District Attorney Thomas E. Dewey was elected to succeed him as gover-nor of New York.

And up in Dannemora, Luciano finally unveiled his master plan to win freedom. "You could say," he laughed years later, "that Albert was the spark that sprung me, and my new best friend, Tom Dewey, was the ignition."

23.

"I've read a million stories about me and Dewey and how I got paroled, and all of 'em are so much horseshit. The idea started in 1940, when I gave Moe Polakoff the note for Lansky about backin'

Dewey for governor. And it kinda grew from there, with some things comin' in from left field, like the time McCook come to see me, until everythin' finally fell into place."

The first big leap forward toward success came at the end of 1940 when an unexpected visitor arrived at Dannemora. "I wasn't expectin' nobody and it kinda made me nervous, what with all that was goin' on in New York with Reles. I could only think it hadda be some bad news. Then to make me even more jittery, instead of takin' me to the visitors' room, the guard walks me to Dr. Martin's office. When I walk in, the warden tells me to sit down and then he clears out, leavin' me alone. A half a minute later, the door opens and that son of a bitch Judge McCook walks in. Jesus, I hardly recognized him. In four years, this guy had aged a million years, I mean he looked like he was ninety. He comes over and shakes my hand and he asks me how I'm gettin' along, are they treatin' me all right, that kind of thing. I say, yeah, sure. Then he sits down and just looks at me. So I sit down and look back at him, just waitin'. Pretty soon, he starts talkin' and the words pour out of him like he can't shut off the faucet. He tells me he's a good Christian; he says he goes to church every Sunday and he always tries to do the right thing. I can't understand none of this, so I just sit there and don't say nothin', just listenin' and wonderin' what the hell he's gettin' at.

"Then McCook starts to shake like he was made out of jelly. Then the next thing, he starts to bawl, real tears. Can you imagine a big important guy like him, a society guy, breakin' down that way? A fuckin' judge who sends people up to the pen, who puts guys in the hot seat, sittin' there and shakin' and cryin'? He asks me what he done to deserve what's happenin' to him. Well, I figure it must be pretty bad if he's actin' like that and comes all the way up to Dannemora to tell me about it, to cop a plea with me, of all people, that he never done nothin' wrong to nobody.

"The whole thing sounded so crazy that I thought the guy blew his top. Then he gets to it. He tells me that after he sent me up, his house burned down to the ground and everything he owned was destroyed. But that was only the beginning. He says his wife and one of his kids died and he was gettin' hit by all kinds of disasters, one right after the other. He says that from the time he sentenced me, everythin' in his life went sour.

"When he tells me all this, you know how I felt? I didn't feel no pity for that dirty bastard. Why should I? What did he feel when he sent me up on that phony rap, which he knew goddamn well was a phony? So why the hell should I feel anything for him when he starts havin' troubles? At that minute, I had all the troubles of my own that I could handle. But I didn't say a word to him. I just let him talk, because now he was no different than some shitheel in my outfit who'd come up to my office to make a confession about what he done that was wrong and hope to Christ I wouldn't break his head. They would always beat around the bush as long as they could and then they'd have to come to the point.

"That's the way it happened with McCook. When he gets all finished, he turns to me and says why did I put a Sicilian curse on him? I didn't know what the fuck to say. I just looked at him like he was loony. Then he gets down on his knees, crawls over to me cryin' like a baby; he grabs hold of my hand and starts slobberin' over it — he even starts callin' me, 'Mister Luciano,' and beggin' me to take the curse off him, pleadin' with me to help him. He swears he didn't mean to do me no wrong, that what he done in court was what he thought was right. But now, after thinkin' about it and searchin' his soul, as he said, he thinks maybe he made a mistake and he has to make up for it. Right then and there, I knew McCook was my pigeon.

"It was all I could do to keep from laughin'. I tried to calm him down and that wasn't easy. Here's a guy who sent me to the can for fifty years and now he's down on the floor kissin' my hand and beggin' me to take off the Sicilian curse. If it was in a movie, nobody'd believe it, but that's the way it happened. Finally, I told him he shouldn't worry about the curse no more because I'd arrange to have it taken off. I told him to go home, just not to worry no more, and one of my guys would be around to see him later on to discuss what he could do for me. When I said that, I could see that McCook got scared. But I told him he wouldn't be asked to do nothin' dishonest or illegal; only that one of these days it might

257

be that he could help me get out of jail, and then the curse would be off permanent.

"So out of a clear blue sky, this guy fell right into my pocket. I didn't have to pay him off or nothin' like that. When I went back to my cell, all I could think of was that I finally got justice out of McCook, only it came four years late." (In 1943, when Luciano made his first bid for parole, it was Judge McCook, in his role as a justice of the New York State Supreme Court, who heard the arguments. Though Luciano then had served only seven years of his sentence, McCook said, "If Luciano continues to cooperate and remains a model prisoner, it may be appropriate at some future time to apply for executive clemency.")

McCook's mellowed and more benevolent view of Luciano was the first step, but it would be some time before any use could be made of it, for the continuing disclosures of Reles and Tannenbaum in New York were creating a climate hardly conducive to granting freedom to Luciano. What was needed, for the moment, was patience to wait for the pressures to subside. "When the Japs bombed Pearl Harbor and Roosevelt declared war, I got my second break. With a thing like that goin' on, who cared about gangsters and all that crap that was on the front pages practically from when my trial was on five years before? So I knew the time had come to make my move.

"I sent word to Polakoff that I wanted him to bring Costello and Lansky up to Dannemora right away. We met in the visitors' room and this time I told Moe to sit in with us; I wanted him to know the details of my plan and to try to punch holes in it if he could. I told them it had more twists and turns than a pretzel but that I'd been thinkin' about it and I knew it would work if we played it right. I told them the only way I'd ever have a chance to get free was if we had a strong and direct line to the governor of New York. Who was the governor that would spring me? I figured it hadda be nobody else but Tom Dewey. He got the headlines that made him a big shot in New York on my back and now he was a natural to run for governor in 1942, and that was why I had sent word earlier that we would back him. With all the time I had to think it over, I come to the conclusion that Dewey was no better'n me, except he was a legal gangster and I wasn't. Anybody who'd make up that kind of frame that he did to put me away hadda be a crook at heart. Inside of me, I just knew that Dewey could be bought, if it was handled by the right middleman, and if it was for somethin' big enough to make his mouth water. Costello had already set up a go-between if and when we needed him, so that part of the plan was already set.

"I didn't know how long that fuckin' war was gonna last, but it handed me a lot of favors; one of 'em was that them goddamn whores who was stashed away in Europe hadda come back to New York and they was on their own — Dewey had a lot of other things on his mind and the last thing he wanted to bother about was them lyin' broads. I told Moe that I wanted 'em again. But this time he hadda tie 'em up with tighter affidavits, that they hadda be worked on stronger, and that included all the witnesses against me. What I wanted most of all was a confession from all of 'em that it was Dewey himself that made 'em lie; that it was Dewey that coached 'em; that it was Dewey that paid 'em off, and so forth. The blame on Dewey hadda be open-and-shut, that he master-minded every fuckin' detail of the frame against me. I told Moe to handle it just like he was getting ready with another plea for a new trial.

"While I was layin' it out, Lansky popped in and said we'd already done that, paid a lot of dough for it, and it hadn't worked because McCook wouldn't buy it. That's when I started to laugh. I told them the story about McCook comin' up to see me; I think that was the only time I ever saw Costello's mouth open so wide he couldn't get it shut. Meyer just stared at me. But Polakoff was sore. He wanted to know why I hadn't told him about it before; he said if I had, it could have saved a lot of waitin'. But I told him it wouldn't've worked, that the time wasn't right back in 1940. In fact, I said I wasn't even sure that I wanted to use the new testimony until after Dewey was elected.

"Then Costello stuck his nose in. He said, 'What happens to this whole fuckin' plan if Dewey don't make it to Albany?'

"It was a good question, so I turned to my little addin' machine and I said to Meyer, 'What are the odds that Dewey runs and wins?'

"It didn't take him more than a minute. He said, 'I make it a good five-to-one or better. If he don't break a leg and he has our help, he'll walk in. He's a good fifty-to-one to run because the Republicans haven't got nobody else. But without our support, he's only sure of carrying upstate and that's not good enough. With us, he can do good enough in the city to walk in.' The way Lansky come on, I could see he'd been studyin' the situation and was sure of himself, which made me feel good.

"Then Polakoff come up with the key question. He said, 'If you expect to get a parole after Dewey becomes governor, just like that, you're making a big mistake, Charlie. He'd be impeached, that's how serious a mistake it would be. It would kill his chances to be President, and he's not going to jeopardize himself whether you give him political support or not. Did you think about that?'

"I'd already thought about it and I told him I wasn't stupid enough to think Dewey could spring me without the best possible excuse that would keep his face clean all the way through. That was the third big point. I told 'em that about six months before the war started I got a letter from Vito from Rome, where the little prick was livin' it up pretty good — he had big contacts, includin' Mussolini himself. I knew Vito inside out, and the one thing I was sure of was that he never bragged; he liked to pull fancy tricks, but he never boasted to me. In his letter, Vito told me how great he was doin'. He made a lot of contacts down in Sicily with guys whose names I give him before he left. The most important thing he said was that in Sicily my name was like a king. Vito said that Mussolini was really pourin' out the shit on Americans, but as far as I was concerned, down in Sicily they thought of me as a real number one guy. And that set me to thinkin' how I could give Dewey the legitimate excuse he'd need to let me out.

"I had a newspaper with me and I showed them how the Navy Department was givin' out a lot of stories about sabotage and fifth column and that kind of thing. There was even a story on the front page about a campaign they called 'Zip Your Lip,' which shows how worried they was about German subs sinkin' our ships or some spies blowin' up ships in the harbor. It looked like the whole Eastern waterfront, especially in New York, was a mess of sabotage.

"I could see Lansky start to smile while I was layin' it out, because he was the first one to see what I was gettin' at. He said, 'Charlie, I get it, I get it. It's terrific. How can Dewey turn down a patriotic hero? I gotta hand it to you.' Then he looked at Costello, and Frank said, 'Charlie, I think we can handle all the angles. We got a lot of people with the Navy guys down on Church Street and we can pass the word about anything. I think you're as good as out.'

"So I said to them that they had two things to work on without delay. First, there hadda be somethin' that would deal with sabotage and it hadda be front-page stuff that would make it necessary for the Navy or someone to come to us for help. And they hadda line up all them witnesses and get 'em signed, sealed and delivered, strong enough to make sure we could get a new trial if we needed to. They all thought it would be dynamite. But I said no, I had somethin' else in mind and I wanted to hold it. I just needed to be absolutely sure we had it under lock and key."

For a month after that meeting, Luciano waited anxiously, nervously, for some news. All he heard was that his friends had yet to come up with an idea that would start things moving. "I lost all my patience. I got into fights with guys in the yard; fellows would come up to see me and I'd turn away from 'em. I knew I was actin' like a shitheel but I couldn't help it; my nerves were ready to give up."

Then in late January of 1942, Luciano's future brightened. Learning of Luciano's need for a front-page event that would bring the potential peril of sabotage to the front, Albert Anastasia brought an idea to Frank Costello. "Costello got in touch with me right away. Albert had worked this idea out with his brother, Tough Tony [a major power in the International Longshoremen's Association]. Albert said that the guys from Navy intelligence had been all over the docks talkin' to 'em about security; they was scared to death that all the stuff along the Hudson, the docks and boats and the rest, was in very great danger. It took a guy like Albert to figure out somethin' really crazy; his idea was to give the Navy a real big hunk of sabotage, somethin' so big that it would scare the shit out of the whole fuckin' Navy. This big French luxury ship, the *Normandie,* was sittin' at a pier on the

West Side of Manhattan, and accordin' to what Tony and Albert was told, the government was workin' out a deal with that guy de Gaulle to take it over and turn it into a troopship. Albert figures that if somethin' could happen to the *Normandie,* that would really make everybody crap in their pants.

"It was a great idea and I didn't figure it was really gonna hurt the war effort because the ship was nowhere near ready and, besides, no American soldiers or sailors would be involved because they wasn't sendin' 'em noplace yet. So I sent back word to Albert to handle it.

"A couple days later, I heard on the radio where the *Normandie* was on fire and it didn't look like they could save her. That goddamn Anastasia — he really done a job. Later on, Albert told me not to feel too bad about what happened to the ship. He said that as a sergeant in the Army he hated the fuckin' Navy anyway."

Within twenty-four hours, the *Normandie,* once the pride of the French luxury fleet, was a gutted wreck listing at the dock, finally turning over on its side. The cause of the disaster was debated, investigated and speculated on in the newspapers, with no satisfactory explanation ever emerging, only theories that the conflagration had been started by a welder's torch, by spontaneous combustion, by saboteurs. But the headline-making blaze did have an immediate consequence. There were cries that help was desperately needed to prevent further disasters on the New York waterfront, to prevent possible shipping bottlenecks or the leakage of information about sailings.

The Navy heeded those calls. It was deeply concerned at that moment about the New York waterfront. Many of the businessmen there and many of the dock workers were Italians and Sicilians, a majority immigrants or sons of immigrants. Thus their loyalty to the United States came under question and there was fear that they might incite strikes or commit acts that would seriously affect the war effort, that they might even use their fishing boats to carry information and supplies to German submarine packs lying offshore.

And so the next phase of Luciano's plan was put into effect. Italian political leaders around the country — sparked by the influence of Costello's friends — came to the defense of the loyalty of Italian immigrants. Even the Italian and Sicilian gangsters, they said, though criminals, were above anything else patriotic Americans who would gladly help their country in time of crisis. The Italian-dominated underworld was deeply entrenched along the waterfront, even controlled it; if the Navy turned in that direction for help, it would be forthcoming.

Thus was born the idea for what became known as "Operation Underworld."

Approved in Washington and centered at naval headquarters at 90 Church Street in Manhattan, Operation Underworld was put in the hands of a young reserve officer, Lieutenant Commander Charles R. Haffenden. His job: to investigate the feasibility of utilizing underworld leaders and the underworld itself to help the war effort. But Haffenden knew little about either the waterfront or the underworld, and so he turned for assistance to the office of Manhattan District Attorney Thomas E. Dewey. Dewey himself was too busy with his campaign for governor to become directly involved. He steered Haffenden to his anointed successor as Manhattan district attorney, Frank S. Hogan, and to Murray Gurfein, one of the key men in the original investigation and trial of Luciano. Dewey ordered them to extend every assistance, and they turned Haffenden to Joseph "Socks" Lanza, the notorious semi-literate czar of the Fulton Fish Market.

For years, "Joe Zox," as his friends called him, had wielded absolute power over the city-owned fish market, subject only to the jurisdiction of the Luciano outfit to which he owed allegiance. No seafood came in or went out without tribute to Lanza — one hundred dollars from every boat bringing in fish and fifty dollars from every truck hauling it away. No stall operated without Lanza's approval. He was a man of such uncontested power that he was able to run his province even from a prison cell in Flint, Michigan, during the mid-thirties when he was serving a federal sentence for conspiracy to monopolize and regulate the freshwater fish industry in New York. He was also a man of considerable ruthlessness; he had been in and out of prison since boyhood and had beaten murder and gun indictments growing out of his seizure of control over the fish market. And he was a man with wide contacts and influence — he was a close friend of Luciano's friend,

Tammany leader Albert Marinelli; he was a brother-in-law of Tammany leader Prospero Vincent Viggiano; he was an associate and ally of Adonis, Luciano and Costello, who had been best man at his wedding in 1941.

At the start of the war, Lanza was beset by troubles — from labor unions and from Dewey's office, which had indicted him for extortion. But these troubles did not affect his absolute suzerainty over the market and over the fishing fleets that daily sailed from New York into the open seas. He was the logical man for Haffenden to see.

"All my guys, especially Costello, had worked things out perfectly, right down to crossin' every T and dottin' every I. They even worked it out so that a typical Navy kid with pink cheeks and still wet behind the ears was assigned to the job. And Socks was rehearsed by Costello and Lansky right to the last syllable."

Lanza agreed to a meeting, but only if it was held in private — a public meeting could make trouble for him, he said, if word got around that he was seen talking to someone in uniform. So a rendezvous was set for midnight on a park bench at Grant's Tomb on upper Riverside Drive. Haffenden asked for Lanza's help in combating sabotage and fifth columnists. Specifically, he wanted Lanza to permit naval intelligence to install sophisticated communications equipment and place agents in the fish market and aboard fishing boats. Lanza said he would help all he could in the market, but he told Haffenden, as he had been rehearsed, that he had no power over the docks or over the other areas the government might want to monitor. If the government really wanted to get the entire Italian-Sicilian population cooperating fully, and especially if it wanted the help of the underworld, there was only one man to see. Haffenden asked for the name. Lanza told him — Charlie Lucky Luciano, currently an inmate at Dannemora prison.

Haffenden went back to Gurfein for advice. Could Luciano, he asked, really be persuaded to put aside what must certainly be considerable bitterness at authorities and agree to help his country? Gurfein thought so and telephoned Moses Polakoff to arrange a meeting with Luciano. It was a call Polakoff knew was coming. He suggested that instead of an immediate conference with Luciano, a preliminary meeting be held to explore the possibilities, a meeting to which he would bring one or two close friends of Luciano who might have greater persuasive powers over the imprisoned gang leader. That session was held over breakfast in a hotel dining room overlooking Central Park. Meyer Lansky was Polakoff's companion.

(Years later, while seeking a haven in Israel from United States tax-evasion indictments, Lansky offered his version of that breakfast: "Gurfein," he said, "explained the situation to me. I went immediately to see Frank Costello, telling him the story and asking what does he feel about it. Frank was patriotic and felt that help should be given. So . . . we decided that we will tell Charlie Lucky that if he will be helpful in this case, it might help him to get out of prison.")

The next day at Dannemora, Luciano was called to the warden's office to take an important call from New York. "Dr. Martin tells me that this is a confidential call and he hands me the phone. It's Costello on the other end. He hits me with the news that the government wants me to do 'em a favor. He asked if it's okay to bring up some guys from the Navy Department who would like to talk to me. I said, 'Listen, Frank, I'm not talkin' to anybody to do favors. If they're so anxious to see me, let 'em bring me down to New York. I don't feel like doin' favors while I'm up in this dump.' And while I'm sayin' this, I kinda smiled at the warden, because I don't want him to think it's nothin' personal. Frank asks me to hold on for a minute, then he gets back on the phone; he tells me that he's with guys from Dewey's office and they said, okay, they'll bring me down to Sing Sing for the meet. But they have to get an okay from Judge McCook because accordin' to the law, he's in charge of me."

McCook signed the transfer order within days. "It was like goin' from Siberia to civilization. It was really great. I got a very nice cell all to myself, a clean one with hot and cold running water; I even had decent toilet paper for the first time in six years. A little thing like that can mean a helluva lot when you're shut up in jail.

"That afternoon, they took me to the lawyers' room. I walked in and one of Dewey's top guys is there with Polakoff and George Wolf, also Costello and Lansky. Before I even had a chance to say

265

hello to anybody, I spot a table in the middle of the room loaded down with all kinds of cold cuts — just like the table we used to have in the back room of Dave Miller's Delicatessen. So I said, 'Fellas, before we talk, you'll have to excuse me,' and I made a dive for that table. It was Lansky's idea to load it up with all the stuff he knew I liked, and he even had them kosher green pickles and the Dr. Brown's Celery Tonic I loved. I said, 'Hey-y, Little Man. Where the hell did you get these pickles?' And Meyer laughed and he said, 'For you, Charlie, I stopped down at the pickle factory on Delancey Street before we drove up here. I told 'em it was for you and they sent their regards. Those pickles are from the top of the barrel.' And they was, the little tiny ones, crunchy ones that I used to get by the bagful and bring to my apartment at the Waldorf Towers. I couldn't get the smell of garlic out of the place for a week. But that minute, the taste of them pickles was almost as good as freedom."

Everyone waited until Luciano had eaten his fill, and then the urgency of the situation was pressed upon him: the government needed assistance with its security program among the unions, specifically the longshoremen, along the New York docks. Haffenden asked whether he would be willing to use his influence to help.

"I put on a very serious face and I kinda thought it over. Then I said, 'Why are you fellas so sure that I can handle what you need while I'm locked up in the can?' After all, I didn't want to make it look like I was gonna jump at this. But Haffenden came right back and said that he had it on 'very reliable authority' that any word I sent out from anywhere would be listened to and followed through.

"When it was all set, that's when I just sat there and listened while the deal was bein' put to Dewey's guy. Now I wanna make it clear that he knew just what was goin' on, that this whole thing was rigged just the way they rigged me six years before. As far as Haffenden was concerned, he didn't know nothin' that was goin' on except that he was sittin' there with his mouth open, prayin' I would say yes and help his whole department down at 90 Church Street. Finally I said, yes, and I could see him let out a big sigh of relief. He was a very happy guy. Then Dewey's guy suggested that Haffenden go into another office and call his people at naval intelligence, so that we would have a chance to confer on the details of how this would be worked out.

"When the kid left the room, that's when we got down to cases. We put it right on the table. I said that the way we figured it, after Willkie beat Dewey for the Republican presidential nomination in 1940, Dewey hadda win the governorship of New York in order to get in line for another shot at the nomination. Costello chimed in and said he'd already gotten word that the Republican big shots had agreed to push Dewey for President in 1944 even though he was runnin' for governor on the promise not to try for President in two years.

"I repeated my promise that Dewey would get all our support and we would deliver Manhattan, or come damn close, in November, which would mean he'd be a shoo-in. Then, as soon as he got into office, he hadda make me a hero. The only difference would be, a hero gets a medal, but I'd get a parole. That was it. I made it very strong that if Dewey didn't buy the proposition immediately, I'd pull out all our support and throw it against him. And even if he won as governor, next year, in 1943, when they would start buildin' him up for President, I'd be ready to start my campaign for a new trial, and I'd make an appeal that would be based on every rotten thing he done at my trial. I told Dewey's guy I wouldn't level my heavy guns at him or Sol Gelb or any of the other guys on the staff, just at Dewey; all I wanted to do was to let the newspapers know how Dewey got them witnesses to commit perjury, how he put words in their mouths, how he bribed them broads for phony testimony — the whole works. I said that sure, I knew we'd tried for an appeal with that kind of thing before and it hadn't worked, but it wasn't as loaded as we had it now. Besides, we'd make sure it was in the newspapers — maybe they wouldn't buy it before, but with Dewey tryin' to be President, a lot of the big papers would print any kind of dirt they could get on him, and he wouldn't be able to stand that. I said it was one thing to become governor on the back of a gangster but I'd be a son of a bitch if I'd want the President of my country to get there on my back with no favors to me. That was it.

"Dewey's guy left the meetin' to carry the message. I told Levy and Polakoff to take a walk around, and then Frank and Meyer and me sat down and talked our own business — about how we was doin' with ration stamps and if this deal with Dewey could help us maybe get a bigger corner on the market, especially with gasoline and meat. Tommy Lucchese had taken over a lot of the restaurants that Schultz used to control and the outfit was not only supplyin' meat but we was sellin' 'em the stamps so they could buy it. Frank told me we had a good lock on about four hundred gas stations where we bought a piece in each one all the way from New York to Louisiana — that was some business until the war was over.

"But as far as my helpin' the government was concerned, then or even the following year when they said I helped 'em open up Sicily for the invasion by gettin' the cooperation of the Mafia guys to help the American troops, that was all horseshit. It would be easy for me to say there was somethin' to all that, like people have been sayin' for years and I've been lettin' 'em think, but there wasn't. As far as me helpin' the army land in Sicily, you gotta remember I left there when I was, what — nine? The only guy I knew real well over there, and he wasn't even a Sicilian, was that little prick Vito Genovese. In fact, at that time the dirty little bastard was livin' like a king in Rome, kissin' Mussolini's ass."

Luciano waited at Sing Sing for Dewey's answer, refusing to talk any further to anyone. Soon, Polakoff was back with the reply. It was an agreement in principle on all but one point. Luciano had demanded immediate and unrestricted parole that would permit his return to New York to pick up the reins of empire. Dewey would have none of it. He agreed to work out a process for parole and freedom when he won the governorship, but it would be granted only on condition that Luciano agree to his deportation to Italy and permanent exile from the United States.

"I knew right away what that little mustached prick was gettin' at. In order for me to help him, and what's even more important, not to go against him and hurt his chances to be President, the bastard was willin' to let me out — but he wanted me far, far away. That meant I'd have to agree to leave my own country, because I was a legal citizen ever since my old man took out papers when I was a kid. They couldn't deport me if I didn't agree to it. And I realized another thing he figured: it would make him look good that he was gettin' rid of that terrible gangster Lucky Luciano for the benefit of the United States of America.

"But it meant somethin' else, too. It meant I'd have to stay in jail until the war was over. They couldn't send me to Italy while we was still at war and it was an enemy country. So, you see what happened? It's like guys tryin' to commit a perfect crime. I had worked up the perfect plan, I thought — and every goddamn point of it worked like a breeze, until Dewey come up with his condition. We argued like crazy, tryin' to get Dewey to change his mind, but it was no use. Dewey was standin' pat. Finally, I thought, what the hell — it was better than nothin'. At that point, it was a helluva lot better than rottin' in stir for years and tryin' to fight a losin' battle. Also, it occurred to me that maybe somethin' might happen later and I could find a way to get back after the war was over and everythin' cooled off. One thing, though; Dewey promised not to put the heat on the outfit like they did from 1939 to 1941. In other words, they would act sensible. And that's when I said okay, and all the fellas could sit down and work out the details.

"Then we got to the price. Dewey got ninety grand from me. It was supposed to be a contribution to his governor's campaign. As a matter of fact, the way I remember it, he wanted a lot more. But the way I looked at it, that phony conviction of mine cost me so much money that Dewey oughta pay me to get out of the country. Besides, Costello didn't exactly forget that lovely doublecross we got from the gentleman from Hyde Park and we wasn't about to shell out a big bundle in front, like before. We finally settled for twenty-five grand as a down payment. It was supposed to go into a secret Dewey campaign fund, and we agreed to put up the rest, the sixty-five thousand, when I got out. And we did pay it, in cash, in small bills, the minute I set foot on the boat that was gonna take me to Italy. You might say the cash was put in an escrow bag that was earmarked personally for Dewey's fund. Later on, I made a check about that ninety grand. It never showed on none of our books for tax returns, naturally; but it never showed up on none of Dewey's campaign returns either."

Once the deal had been confirmed, Luciano suggested to Haffenden that it would be a lot easier for him to make his contributions to national defense if he were not confined in Dannemora, so far from everyone he knew and would have to confer with. He would need to have constant contact with his friends in New York and around the country, he told Haffenden, would need to talk personally with couriers who would pass on his orders to the hierarchy of his nationwide organization. Among those he would need to see constantly, he said, were Lansky, Costello, Lanza, Albert Anastasia and Tony Anastasio, Adonis and several others. For them to journey regularly to Dannemora would be a great hardship.

With the concurrence of Dewey and Judge McCook, Luciano was immediately transferred to the "country club" of the New York penal system, Great Meadow Prison in Comstock, just north of Albany. There he settled in comfortably, waiting for the end of the war and his freedom. It was an easy life; he had the run of the prison, food of his choosing was brought in at his expense from the outside, he was allowed to install personal furnishings in his cell. At the request of naval intelligence, a private office was set aside for his conferences with Haffenden and with the steady stream of underworld visitors who poured in several times a week, supposedly involved with the top-secret "Operation Underworld." Those conferences, however, dealt not with the war effort but with the mob's own business, in gambling and black markets, and particularly with plans for the postwar years.

"The warden was a guy named Vernon Morhous, a really very sweet guy. Naturally, we had him in our pocket, but there wasn't nothin' unusual about that; there ain't a jail in the world where money can't buy a little bit or a lotta favors. Morhous made no trouble for me; he gave me anythin' I wanted that was reasonable; in fact, a couple of times he even let me go to Albany with a guard for a little relaxation, just to walk around the streets without handcuffs. I gave him my word I wouldn't pull nothin' and I never did. He trusted me, and I could've ruined him if I broke my word.

"But it was no tea party, the time I spent in Great Meadow. The war didn't end until 1945 and by the time they got through with all the shitty paperwork and red tape, I never really got free until the beginnin' of 1946. That condition of Dewey's cost me almost three and a half long years in jail, just because he didn't have the guts to let me out sooner. Also, we hadda get things movin' long before the war was over; I mean, to start the wheels in motion."

The course of the war fascinated Luciano now, for his personal freedom was deeply involved. He covered one wall of his cell with a huge map of the European war zone and marked on it the course of battles and the progress of campaigns. He was elated with news of Allied victories, deeply depressed at word of setbacks. He became a fervent admirer of General George S. Patton and complained frequently that General Dwight Eisenhower was not giving Patton the free hand he needed. Soon Luciano began to see himself as a master military strategist, and to his visitors he talked often of tactical errors and stupidities committed by the military and political leaders.

"I was goin' nuts. The war was drivin' me crazy. Around the end of 1943, there was all that talk about openin' a second front in Europe to get the war over in a hurry, but it was nothin' but talk, and all the time I was wastin' away in Great Meadow wonderin' why the hell those masterminds in Washington couldn't get the lead out of their asses. Finally, I couldn't take it no more and I sent word that I had to see Tommy Lucchese and Joe Adonis right away.

"They came up the next day and I told 'em somethin' hadda be done with this guy Hitler. I said that if somebody could knock off this son of a bitch, the war would be over in five minutes. They started to laugh at me and I got mad. I said, 'What the hell are you laughin' at? We've got the best hit man in the world over there — Vito Genovese. That dirty little pig owes his life to me and now it's time for him to make good on it. He's so fuckin' friendly with Mussolini and that punk son-in-law of his, that Count Ciano, he oughta be able to get close enough to Hitler to do it.' I got so wound up and I was yellin' so loud that one of the guards comes runnin' in to see what the hell was goin' on. They're all lookin' at me like I'm crazy. And then I suddenly realized what the hell I'd been sayin'. It was funny. But it was no joke to me, really. It shows what it means when they say a guy can go stir-crazy.

"When you're stuck away in places like Dannemora, or even in Great Meadow, you begin to do one of two things. Either you get sore at the world and you wanna hit back as soon as you can, or you begin to think about your mistakes; not the mistakes you made in general. You got plenty of time to think behind bars and if you're workin' in a quiet place like a library, like I was at Dannemora, you got more than plenty of time to size up your life. I can't say I was ever sorry or that I should've gone straight; that was too late a long time back. But when somebody from my family come up, especially to Dannemora, I couldn't talk to nobody for a week. I'd see my brother walk out and then I'd go back to my cell and hit my head against the wall. One time it started to bleed and they hadda sew it up. I never really knew for sure in those days just what bothered me, whether I was blind mad because I was stupid and got caught or whether I'd been an idiot for gettin' mixed up in the rackets and breakin' the law. I never really understood, myself, about the whole thing until long afterwards.

"Of course, when I got down to Great Meadow I had a lot more visitors; it was easier to get people in. One night, Warden Morhous let me out with a couple of guards. We went to a little place, a kind of roadhouse near Albany. Gay Orlova met me there and she brought along a dozen thick sirloin steaks from a frozen meat locker Costello had in New York. The four of us had a great dinner and then Gay and me went to a nice room upstairs and we spent most of the night together. It was beautiful. And I kept thinkin', so what, Dewey owes me this."

As he waited impatiently in Great Meadow for the war to end, Luciàno was suddenly faced with a major new problem. Vito Genovese was back, in jail in Brooklyn, facing a trial for the old murder of Ferdinand Boccia. The question that had to be decided was whether Genovese should be helped, and if so, how much help should be given.

Luciano's initial feeling was to turn his back on his old lieutenant; for years, bitterness against Genovese had been festering and growing within him. "Vito went over there with a bundle big enough to choke a horse. When the war started, he didn't have to live in a country that was an enemy of the United States; there was plenty of safe places for a guy with money. But he was just rotten greedy. We heard everythin' he was doin' — word got back to us through Lisbon and other places because we had plenty of pipelines in and out of Europe. We heard Vito had gone big into junk.

Anythin' that easy for him was hard to pass up, even if it meant betrayin' his own country.

"He found out that Mussolini's son-in-law took cocaine, and that was all Vito hadda know. From then on, he was Ciano's personal supplier. He had Ciano hooked so bad the bastard couldn't live without him. One time, Ciano flew him to Istanbul in his own plane, right in the middle of the fuckin' war, for chrissake, so he could set up a big connection in Turkey, and he arranged to bring the stuff back to a couple of refiners in Milan. And, believe it or not, Italian pilots actually ferried the junk over to Africa, even to Tangier, all the time that Rommel had control of North Africa. That prick, Vito — junk was his whole life. Once, in 1944, Joe A. brought Steve Maggadino from Buffalo to see me at Great Meadow, and Maggadino showed me a letter he got from Vito sayin' that he hadda work out a new way to transport the stuff because the Americans took over North Africa and screwed up his route. And he was mad about it, that his own country was beginnin' to beat the shit out of the Nazis.

"But what Maggadino didn't know, because Vito couldn't write it in a letter so open, was that he was beginnin' to feel the pinch between the Americans makin' their way up into Italy and his friend Mussolini and all of his crowd runnin' like hell out of Rome. Vito never had the brains to figure that might happen and he didn't have no connections with the new guys who took over. So he was up shit's creek without a paddle and as usual he was screamin' to me for help. I'm locked up at Great Meadow, four thousand miles away, and he turns to me to fix up his stupid situation.

"I told Maggadino that I'd already sent word to Costello to make sure Vito wound up on his feet in Italy. I was thinkin' of myself when I did that, because all the plans I was makin' would mean that I'd have to go to Italy, at least for a while, and I might need Vito over there with me. As it happened, the Army appointed Charlie Poletti, who was one of our good friends, as the military governor in Italy and Poletti kept that job for quite a long time. His headquarters was in a place called Nola and Vito wound up as the official Italian-American interpreter. Maybe if I had it to do

273

over again, I would've arranged for Poletti's troops to line Vito up against a wall and shoot him."

In mid-1944, Italy surrendered to the Allies and the American forces promptly established a military government under the direction of Colonel Charles Poletti, a former New York lieutenant governor, and, for a short period after the departure of Herbert Lehman for wartime service, acting governor. The bilingual Genovese appeared at the headquarters one day and was immediately hired as official civilian interpreter. Within weeks, he established himself at the head of a vast black market operation throughout Allied-occupied Italy; on his payroll were a number of American military and civilian officials, and a small army of Allied soldiers who opened the doors of Army warehouses for him, who drove military trucks in his employ, and who sold merchandise at his direction. His position in the inner circles of the American military government gave him freedom of movement and, for a time, freedom from suspicion.

Captain Charles L. Dunn, the provisional officer at the huge supply base at Nola, employed Genovese as his personal interpreter in January of 1944, and wrote that he "has been invaluable to me . . . is absolutely honest and, as a matter of fact, exposed several cases of bribery and black market operations among so-called civilian personnel. He . . . is devoted to his adopted home, the United States of America." Major E. N. Holmgren, civil affairs officer at Nola, used Genovese as an interpreter for more than a month and said that he "would accept no pay; paid his own expenses, worked day and night, and rendered most valuable assistance to the Allied Military Government." Major Stephen Young, for whom Genovese also worked, said: "I regard him as trustworthy, loyal, and dependable."

But, then, Genovese could well afford to offer his services for free to the authorities. "He made more than a million dollars in untraceable cash in almost no time. That connivin' louse was sellin' American goods to his own Italian people, things that'd save their lives or keep 'em from starving. He made a fortune outa penicillin, cigarettes, sugar, olive oil, flour, you name it. He even used U.S. Army trucks to ship this black market stuff all over Italy, right behind the army."

But there was one man on the military government staff who was not so credulous. His name was Orange C. Dickey, a sergeant in the Army's Criminal Investigation Division. He began to investigate the losses of vast quantities of vital supplies from Nola and other bases, and soon came upon the name Genovese — signed to papers diverting shipments, assigning trucks, allocating supplies. Dickey looked further and came upon two Canadian soldiers involved in the black market. They told him the password for the operation was "Genovese sent us." More confirmation followed, and Dickey discovered other interesting facets — that counterintelligence, for one, had suspicions that Genovese, because of his long history of close ties with Italian Fascist leaders, might actually be a German spy.

In the summer of 1944, Dickey reported his findings to Captain Dunn and others in positions of authority. They ordered him to drop the matter. Dickey refused and in August 1944, on his own authority, arrested Genovese on charges of black market activities and possible espionage. But it was one thing to make an arrest and another to make it stick. Dickey could find no one to back him up. In frustration, Dickey sent a message to the FBI in Washington about his apprehension of Genovese, asking whether anybody in the United States wanted him.

Somebody did — the authorities in Brooklyn. During his years in prison, Ernest "The Hawk" Rupolo had grown increasingly bitter and had finally, as Genovese feared, talked about the Boccia murder, had even provided a corroborating witness, a cigar-store salesman and underworld hanger-on named Peter La Tempa. With La Tempa's testimony that he had overheard the details of the killing, Brooklyn authorities obtained a murder indictment against Genovese and Mike Miranda, and then took La Tempa into protective custody.

Genovese was ordered returned to the United States, to New York, and Orange Dickey was assigned to take him there. Genovese tried to buy Dickey off. "I was offered many things," Dickey later said. "At one point, I was offered a quarter of a million dollars to let this fellow out of jail." Genovese also offered jobs, anything that Dickey wanted. All were refused. Genovese then began to threaten Dickey's life and the lives of his family, but still Dickey would not be deterred. He brought Genovese back in irons and turned him over to his superiors. Though a civilian employee of the Army, Genovese was technically under custody of and liable to trial by the Judge Advocate General's office. But the Army relinquished its claim to him.

"You gotta realize that the muscle we had with the Army was pretty good, but I knew there wasn't a prayer we could get Vito off, because we couldn't buy a court-martial. Besides, I was up in Great Meadow workin' on all them complicated things of my own. So, I thought, screw the bastard. It's time he took care of himself.

"Then Willie Moretti and Frank come up and they said everybody in New York, includin' Anastasia, was talkin' about how we couldn't let Vito take a long rap; they was coppin' a big plea for him. It was Frank's idea that we should use muscle to get Vito transferred out of Army jurisdiction over to the Brooklyn D.A., and we worked this out. Vito's case was gonna be handled by the assistant D.A. of Brooklyn, a guy by the name of Julius Helfand, and we didn't have a good contact with him. But there was somethin' we did have — a way to get into the jail where La Tempa was bein' held in protective custody. Anastasia fixed it up, spreadin' around quite a bundle of money — which Vito later paid him back — and one mornin', I think it was in January of 1945, Pete La Tempa woke up with a pain in his stomach. His whole insides was bad, he had ulcers, he needed an operation for gallstones, but he was afraid to let anybody do it. Anyway, he took what he thought was his regular pain pills and went back to sleep. He never got up again."

With the death of La Tempa, the case against Genovese collapsed; he was held in jail for nearly a year longer and then released.

And then the war in Europe was over. On the very day it ended, May 7, 1945, a petition for executive clemency and freedom for Charles Lucania was sent to Governor Thomas E. Dewey. He quickly turned the matter over to the state parole board, whose members were all his appointees. Luciano's attorneys told the board he "has cooperated with high military authorities. He is rendering a definite service to the war effort." And so he should be freed. Haffenden wrote a personal letter lauding Luciano for his efforts, which, Haffenden said, had helped shorten the war in Sicily and Italy. Precisely what those efforts had been, the board was not told; Haffenden did not say and the Navy refused to reveal any details.

But the parole board knew what the governor wanted. Though it could develop no evidence of any war assistance by Luciano, it nevertheless sent Dewey a unanimous recommendation for his parole.

On January 3, 1946, Governor Dewey announced that Lucky Luciano would be freed — not to remain in the United States but to be paroled to his birthplace in Sicily. "Upon the entry of the United States into the war," Dewey said, "Luciano's aid was sought by the armed services in inducing others to provide information concerning possible enemy attack. It appears that he cooperated in such efforts, though the actual value of the information provided is not clear. His record in prison is reported as wholly satisfactory."

Some years later, in an interview with the New York *Post,* Dewey went a little further: "An exhaustive investigation . . . established that Luciano's aid to the Navy in the war was extensive and valuable. Ten years is probably as long as anybody ever served for compulsory prostitution. And these factors led the parole board to recommend the commutation, combined with the fact that Luciano would be exiled for life, under law."

On February 2, 1946, Luciano walked through the gates of Great Meadow Prison for the last time. He was taken to Ellis Island in New York harbor and held there while the final preparations for his exile were completed. En route through Manhattan to the harbor ferry, he had a fleeting glimpse, his first in a decade, of the city whose underworld he had ruled, a city he, in his way, loved. For a week, from Ellis Island, he could see the skyline, so near yet so unapproachable.

"When they drove me through the city I asked the detectives to stop, just for a couple minutes. I only wanted to get out and put my feet down on the street in Manhattan. I wanted to feel it under me. I wanted to know that I actually walked in New York without bars hemmin' me in. But them guys said they couldn't allow it. So we went right on through the ferry and across the bay. All the time, for the next week, I'd stand outside on Ellis Island and stare over at the buildin's. I'd look at the Chrysler Buildin' and think back a few years to when Walter Chrysler used to come up to Saratoga and gamble at my clubs and sometimes I'd okay his markers. Once I was good enough to okay Chrysler's markers and now I couldn't even walk into his buildin'. And there was the Empire State. Once the guy behind that fantastic buildin', John Raskob, needed my okay so his best friend, Al Smith, could run for President. From Ellis Island, I couldn't even take a ride in one of his elevators.

"That week of waitin' was real rough for me. I kept sayin' to myself, 'Fuck 'em all. I'll be back.' I swore I'd figure out some way to change the deal."

Part Four

Exile
1946-1959

24.

Thrown together in the chaotic frenzy of wartime, without thought to grace or beauty or comfort or speed or permanency, with concern only for utility, destined to live for a few years and then to rust on the scrap heap of the useless remnants of battle, the S.S. *Laura Keene*, like so many of her sister Liberty ships, had tossed and churned her way across the treacherous North Atlantic for a season or two, loaded with vital cargo and miserable crew.

Early in 1946, a battered, barnacled hulk, she was granted a few years of extra grace, was refitted and assigned the task of bringing home some of the troops who had helped defeat the Axis, and carrying away, along with cargo necessary for the troops that remained and for the starving populations of Europe, men no longer welcome on American shores.

On the morning of February 9, 1946, the *Laura Keene* was docked at Pier 7 off the Bush Terminal in Brooklyn. At noon, she would sail for Genoa, Italy, carrying with her America's most notorious criminal. Brought ashore from Ellis Island and hustled aboard, Charlie "Lucky" Luciano was about to begin his years of exile.

It was a cold February morning in New York, the icy wind whipping off the harbor. Reporters had gone to the dock to witness the departure and to attend a shipboard press conference promised them by the United States Immigration and Naturalization Service — the agency in charge of Luciano's deportation. But when they arrived, there was no press conference and they were told there would be no statement and no interviews. Luciano wanted to talk to no reporters, and as a federal prisoner until he had passed the three-mile limit, his wishes had to be respected.

When the reporters tried to get to the ship, they were met by a solid mass of longshoremen, armed with sharpened baling hooks.

They had been sent to guard the pier and insure privacy by Albert Anastasia and his brother, "Tough Tony" Anastasio. The reporters appealed to officials from District Attorney Frank Hogan's office, who were on the scene. The appeal for access to the ship was denied. The reporters could only stand, freeze, and watch in frustration as the longshoremen threatened and barred them, and then opened ranks to permit the passage of one long black limousine after another, the passengers hidden behind curtained windows. At precisely noon, the *Laura Keene* began her slow passage through the channel and out toward the open sea. What had happened through the morning on board was unknown to those who had stood outside in the cold, a hundred yards distant.

"A couple days before the sailin', Polakoff brought Lansky and Costello over to see me at Ellis Island. They said they was gonna throw a big farewell party for me on board the ship and that friends of mine was comin' from all over the country. They asked me if I needed anythin', and I said my brother Bart had been over a few days before with a trunk full of my clothes he had stored away. Believe it or not, a lotta the suits still fit, though they was a little tight because I put on some weight from all that good food that was bein' sent in to me at Great Meadow. We arranged that all that stuff he had been savin' for me from the Waldorf Towers would be put on board. But I said it might be a good idea if Frank and Joe A. stocked me up with a bunch of clothes in the new styles from Cye's store, maybe one size larger. I figured I'd be able to take off the extra weight durin' the two weeks it took to get to Italy.

"Then I told 'em to make sure there was some dough because I was gonna need plenty of that when I got to Italy." The fortune Luciano had amassed during his years in power had been, to a great extent, dissipated during his years in prison. The cost of his trial, his appeals and his various legal and extralegal maneuvers during that decade had come to more than a million dollars. More had gone as his share of the expenditures necessary to insure the success of his organization and his position even in absentia. "The story went around in 1946 when I shipped out that I was carryin' from a million to forty million dollars in a trunk. That was all horseshit, but I never did nothin' to deny the reports. I knew my

282

Italians pretty good and I figured that I would get more respect as a millionaire than just as Charlie Lucky, the American big shot. When I told Meyer to make sure there was some dough, I meant it, because I needed it. He told me not to worry about that neither, because everybody was gonna bring somethin' to the party and I'd have more than enough to see me through until we all got together again. I already had plans for that reunion.

"Then Meyer asked me if there was anythin' else I needed for the trip. I said, 'Yeah, it wouldn't be a bad idea to have a few broads to keep me company out on the ocean.' At first, I thought Gay Orlova was gonna come with me, but she had a lotta trouble with all that red tape about passports and where she was born and that kind of crap, so she had to cancel out. When I mentioned girls, Meyer started to laugh and he said, 'I took care of that, too, Charlie. Three very nice ones are gonna go along with you. We worked that out with Dewey's guys. We're givin' the girls some extra dough so they can take a vacation in Paris on the way home.'

"I didn't feel too happy about what Meyer said. His taste in women was nothin' to write books about; I always thought he didn't know a pig from a filly and if he was the one pickin' the dames, then I was sure my worst enemy wouldn't wanna screw 'em in the dark. Frank and Meyer could tell what I was thinkin' and they laughed like hell. Finally Frank explained that they had given the assignment to Joe A., on account of he was in charge of the Copacabana, where they had the most beautiful broads in the world. So I figured if Joe couldn't make an A-number-one selection, then I'd have to depend on Meyer to get me a pinochle partner. Actually, it turned out that they was three really beautiful and swell girls and I was worried for nothin'."

What was also arranged that day was the division of Luciano's interests, the supervision of them in his name and behalf while he was gone. Costello was assigned all the American gambling, except for that in Miami and Havana and the new casinos being planned for the Bahamas, which would fall under Lansky's regency. Lucchese, Torrio, Scalise, Adonis and several others handled other business in which Luciano had an interest. "One thing, though, bothered the hell outa me, and it festered for a long time after I got to Italy. I was bein' cut out of almost all the legit business that my 'good friends' was goin' into durin' and after the war. That's why I didn't talk about the next part of my plan to nobody but Lansky. I needed him in order to set it up, and it would be a sort of test to see whether he was still on my side.

"The last day on Ellis Island, Lansky and me had a meet, just the two of us. I told him somethin' that none of the other guys knew up to that point — that I had already made connections in Italy to get visas under my real name, Salvatore Lucanía, that would be good for Cuba and Mexico and a whole lotta countries in South America. I told Meyer I figured it would take me about six months of layin' low, gettin' adjusted in Italy, and makin' personal contacts instead of havin' guys front for me. I said that if there was gonna be any problem for me to get back into the United States, I'd even be willin' to become a Cuban citizen, and then take back control from there. I also told Lansky that I wanted him to make a meet for some time around the end of 1946 that would be attended by every top guy — I mean the head of every family and all the people on the Unione council. I said I'd try to arrange things so that the meet could take place in Havana around Christmas. At that time it would be easier for a lotta guys to make the trip, like it was sort of a holiday vacation and it wouldn't draw no spotlight.

"Of course, I had another reason for pickin' Havana. The war bein' over, people was beginnin' to flock there, what with the place bein' wide open, the gamblin' good and the broads beautiful. With a combination like that, Lansky and his friend Batista was rakin' the dough in and I had no intention of bein' left out of that. Batista wasn't president no more, but he had his own guy in there, a doctor named Ramón Grau San Martín; Lansky and Batista had him strictly in their pockets.

"By lettin' Lansky know all the details of my plan for Havana, that was really a test of his loyalty. It meant I was gonna be able to cut the four thousand miles Dewey was puttin' between me and New York to just ninety miles between Miami and me in Havana. Lansky knew I was countin' on his muscle with Batista to work out all the things I wanted to do."

There was one more detail for Luciano to arrange in his meetings on Ellis Island with underworld allies. That was the matter

284

of Vito Genovese, still in jail awaiting the official dismissal of the Boccia murder charges. Luciano summoned Costello, Adonis, Lucchese and Anastasia. "Naturally, I was pretty upset. Here I was, bein' thrown out of the States for somethin' I didn't do, while at the same time I had been helpin' that little bastard get free to walk around the streets of New York without no problems. So I reminded Tommy and Albert of somethin' they knew about and that I didn't want 'em to forget, which happened in 1943.

"When the war was still goin' pretty good for Mussolini, Vito was always tryin' to prove what a good friend he was to that Fascist son of a bitch. There was a newspaper publisher in New York by the name of Carlo Tresca. He was strictly anti-Mussolini and he was knockin' the shit out of him in every edition of his paper, which was called *Il Martello* [*The Hammer*]. It drove Mussolini nuts. So what does that prick Genovese do? He tells Mussolini not to worry about it, that he, Don Vitone, would take care of it. And, goddammit if Vito don't put out a contract from Italy on Tresca, with Tony Bender to do the job. Tresca gets knocked off in broad daylight as he's gettin' outa his car on lower Fifth Avenue; it was an old-fashioned hit with a shotgun in the back. When I heard about it up at Great Meadow, I made up my mind that someday I was gonna have a little talk with either or both of them guys — Vito and Bender. They knew the Unione rule that nobody on the outside gets hit under no circumstances without a vote of the council.

"I had a feelin' in my bones that someday Vito was gonna be bad news for everybody. So I told the guys I had somethin' special in mind for the little bastard and I warned all of 'em that I'd hold 'em responsible to see that Genovese kept his nose clean. When he got out of the can, he was to go back to work like before on all my things, and the minute he got out of line, I wanted to hear from somebody about it without no delay." (Genovese was released from detention in July 1946, when the Brooklyn district attorney's office reluctantly admitted in court that its case against him had collapsed.)

All the necessary business for Luciano before his departure was conducted on Ellis Island. On the boat there would be only festivities. There his underworld friends would take leave of him. With his family, though, the farewells were reserved for the final hours on Ellis Island. "My mother and father was gone by then and not able to see me set free. I didn't wanna do nothin' to make my brothers and sisters uncomfortable or bring bad publicity on 'em, so that's why I wouldn't let 'em come to that madhouse on the boat. It wasn't easy to say goodbye to 'em, because they was my family and I loved 'em. Besides, with Sicilians, no matter what you do with your own personal life, it don't never change the feelin' you have in your guts where your family is concerned. We all said goodbye and everybody cried, even me. I wanted to tell 'em not to worry, to tell 'em about my plans for comin' back home, because I knew that would make 'em feel better. But until that was worked out, it was best they didn't have no idea of it."

By the time Luciano boarded the *Laura Keene* on the morning of February 9, everything was ready for him. His new wardrobe had been delivered to his cabin; the three girls selected by Joe Adonis, with the assistance of his former girl friend, Virginia Hill (now the mistress of Bugsy Siegel), were in adjoining cabins; hampers of delicatessen foods, turkeys, roast beefs, pastas and other Italian delicacies, magnums of the finest French champagne, wines and the best liquors were spread out on tables. Luciano's closest friends, of course, were there — Lansky, Costello, Bugsy Siegel from California, Willie Moretti, Longie Zwillman, Tommy Lucchese, Joe Adonis, Joe Bonanno, Albert Anastasia, Steve Magaddino from Buffalo, and the rest. With Anastasia came a newly prosperous Carlo Gambino, whose fortunes had waxed in the black market in food and gasoline ration stamps, and who had become an important underboss in Brooklyn.

There was hardly an important underworld leader in the country absent from the *Laura Keene*. For some, it was a time for reunion after years apart. Phil Kastel embraced Owney Madden, and Moe Dalitz from Cleveland smiled broadly at the sight of the boys from Philadelphia.

But the underworld was not the only world to send its representatives. "We had some of the country's top political leaders there, too, and a few who couldn't come at least sent a representative. I helped elect over eighty important politicians in my time, so the least they could do was to drink a glass of champagne and wish me a good sailin'. Anastasia's boys kept the newspaper guys far enough away so that none of 'em could get any good pictures, which was my way of doin' them a good turn for showin' up."

The party was a gay one, for there seemed little doubt in anyone's mind that there was nothing permanent in this voyage; Luciano was just going to take a short vacation and soon he would be back in New York where he belonged.

Then, abruptly, the farewells were over and the *Laura Keene* was on her way. "I felt like all of a sudden I was alone. Well, I don't mean exactly alone, because there was these three beautiful girls who was half crocked down below somewhere, havin' their own party, and there was about fifteen other deportees on board — I only knew a couple of 'em. But I really felt like I was in the middle of nowhere. I began to get this real sour feeling in my stomach, and when the pilot horn started to blow, the sound of it seemed to fill the inside of my belly. The only other time in my whole life that I had this kind of experience was when the gates closed behind me up at Dannemora.

"It was real cold the day we sailed and I stood up there on deck, watchin' the skyscrapers of Manhattan goin' by. I looked at the Statue of Liberty and I made myself only think of one thing — that I was takin' a vacation trip and pretty soon that Lady would be sayin' hello instead of goodbye. Then I realized that I wasn't alone. Two guys was leanin' on the rail, watchin' me. One guy was from the U.S. Immigration Department, to make sure I didn't jump off the boat until we was in the middle of the Atlantic. I didn't find out who the other guy was until about a half an hour later.

"The *Laura Keene* suddenly stopped movin' because a fireboat pulled up alongside. I see some guy in a fancy overcoat with a velvet collar scramble up the boardin' ladder. It was the honorable mayor himself, Bill O'Dwyer. He grabbed me around the shoulder and the other fellow, who didn't give his name, starts walkin' ahead of us and we followed him to my cabin.

"O'Dwyer said to me, 'Charlie, this is Murray Weinstein, one of my personal men. He's on Captain Bals's staff downtown, and he'll see that nobody bothers you. I made a personal guarantee that you wouldn't pull anything, so the Immigration man is getting off with me. Please don't let me down, Charlie.'

"I said, 'Don't worry about nothin', Bill. I want you to know I appreciate the fact you come out to do this personally.' He said, 'Charlie, I owe you everything I have, along with lots of apologies we don't have to talk about any more. You know I couldn't go to Bush Terminal, but I couldn't let you leave without personally shaking your hand and wishing you well.' I almost blubbered; I wished there was some way to answer him, but I just couldn't get the words out. He gimme a whack on the back and said, 'Arrivederci,' and I started to laugh at the way he said it with his half-assed Irish brogue.

"That was the last goodbye inside the three-mile limit, and the next thing I knew, I was surrounded by nothin' but water. The skyline was gone and the only thing you could see from any part of the ship was a big ocean. I guess that's when I really knew I was on my way back to Italy, and I didn't like it one bit."

25.

"The *Laura Keene* wasn't exactly the *Queen Mary*. One little wave, and we was ready to launch the lifeboats. Personally, I'm not a very good sailor. I remember when we used to go deep-sea fishin' off Miami, I was always the first guy to hit the rail. So, the first night out, I was green from my head to my toes. All I wanted to do was lay on my bunk and groan.

"But, in the morning the sun was out and we was sailin' on a sea that was as smooth as glass. When I woke up and seen the sunshine comin' through the porthole, it was like a real shot in the arm. I took a quick shower, and then I stood in the middle of my cabin, surrounded by four wardrobe trunks full of clothes. That's when I realized that I was scared shitless; there was three gorgeous girls waitin' for Charlie Lucky to throw one of 'em a nod. I was so

288

nervous, that all I could think of was that time I went to Jenny's place to get the clap — the time I couldn't get it up. So, I'm standin' there, stallin' with myself, and wonderin' what to do. Then I got the idea that I should open up the trunks, the biggest one first, that had all the new stuff from Cye's that Costello and Adonis picked out for me. And the others that my brother Bart had been holdin' for me in storage was next. I spent the next three hours tryin' on every single suit, and pants, and shirts, and underwear in all them four fuckin' trunks.

"Finally, there's a knock on the door, and in comes this guy Murray Weinstein. When he gets a look at what must've seemed like five hundred garments spread out all over the floor, and the bunk, and the chairs, he busts out laughin'; he says, 'Charlie, what the hell are you doin'?' I says, 'Murray, what the fuck does it look like? I'm tryin' on my clothes.'

"Weinstein shakes his head and says, 'If I ever tell this story when I get back, nobody would believe me. You're not in here trying on clothes; you're just afraid to come out and face those beautiful babes who've been waiting for you since nine o'clock this morning.'

"Of course, he was right, and he broke the ice for me. I was really worried how I was goin' to make a choice. The only thing I didn't know was that they had me figured right down to the last nail; they knew I was gonna be chicken, so they had already tossed a coin to see who would get first whack. It turned out to be this girl Billie. She was a blonde, very tall, and with a build that couldn't be believed. The minute I walked out on deck, there she was, waitin' for me.

"I followed her to her cabin. On the table in the middle of the cabin there was a whole layout of Nova Scotia salmon and warm bagels, cream cheese and scrambled eggs. She sat me down and started to serve me from the buffet.

"She must've seen that I had a funny look on my face, so now she smiles and says, 'If you're gonna be with a Jewish girl, Charlie, then learn how to eat a real Jewish breakfast.' Then she says, 'My name really isn't Billie — it's Rebekah; so from here to Genoa, forget the Billie and call me Becky. I only let my friends call me that.' I didn't leave her cabin until three o'clock the next mornin'. I wasn't green no more — just tired.

"I don't wanna sound like I was some kind of a lover, a Rudolph Valentino. But a funny thing happened — after a few days, them three girls started to fight over me. Now, it don't make no difference whether I spent nine and a half years in jail or not; at that point I was pushin' fifty and I was no rabbit. I hadda use Murray to keep 'em off me once in a while so I could get a rest. But the first time I heard them three girls screechin' at each other in their cabin about who was gonna get the next shot, that's when I knew I was free, free, free."

Luciano had other reasons to feel a sense of security in his rediscovered freedom. Once out to sea, he opened the bon voyage envelopes left for him by his business associates, and counted up more than $165,000 in cash. The amount itself made little impression on him, just that a quick calculation showed it would be enough for his purpose when he arrived in Italy, especially since he had been assured of a continuing flow through Costello, Lansky and Adonis from the interests he had left in their care back in the United States.

The two weeks at sea provided Luciano, for the first time in a decade, with plenty of time to relax and contemplate the future without restrictions or constant pressures. He paid little mind to the other deportees sailing with him. "They was under guard on the deck below mine. A couple of 'em was from my outfit and one time I seen 'em. The first thing they said was that they expected me to take 'em under my wing when we got to Italy. I let 'em know right away not to expect no favors. After all, who knew what one of them crazy guys might pull and then screw me up in Italy, from one end of the country to the other. I couldn't afford to take that chance."

So Luciano spent his time with the three girls and with Weinstein and embarked on a rigorous program of gymnastics, weight lifting and calisthenics to take off the fifteen pounds he had gained at Great Meadow and get himself back into solid physical condition. "When I arrived in Italy, every one of my suits fit like a glove, the old ones and the new ones. I was probably the best-dressed guy that ever come over from America; I had a different suit for every day of the month and my underwear, shirts and pajamas all had the same little initials on 'em — real class. I found out later that Gay had it done; she was nuts about initials, the same as Arnold Rothstein."

In moments of solitude, Luciano thought much about a serious problem that had been discussed with him just before his departure — Bugsy Siegel's new venture in Las Vegas, the Flamingo Hotel and casino. "Siegel's original estimates on how much the joint was gonna cost was way outa line. It looked like he was gonna run over by millions just to build a plush hotel and casino in the middle of a fuckin' desert. On top of that, Joe A. had told me Siegel was absolutely crazy about Virginia Hill and there was kind of a feelin' among the guys that Benny might be stashin' away some of the buildin' money without tellin' nobody about it. And I knew Lansky was burned to a crisp at Siegel, but it was my opinion the Flamingo didn't have nothin' to do with it, that it went back to the time the Bug and Meyer mob broke up and Bugsy went to California. There was bad blood between 'em that never came to the surface up to that time. So I had a lot to think about. It was a touchy situation that the Unione council couldn't settle because of Lansky and Siegel bein' Jews and havin' no vote. I thought about it all the way over to Italy, but I just didn't get no idea how to take care of it."

Then Genoa was in sight. On the eve of the docking, Luciano threw his first party in more than ten years. At his request, before sailing, Costello and Lansky had stocked the liquor and food lockers with provisions for the event. "I told 'em that I wanted to arrive in Italy in style, like I was the captain of the boat, and that the party was on me. We was lucky to arrive in one piece, because after that party there wasn't nobody on that whole fuckin' boat that was sober, from the guy who was steerin' it to the fellows workin' down in the hold. We docked at Genoa in the mornin' with one complete hangover from stem to stern.

"The next thing I knew, the deck was swarmin' with Italian policemen and all kinds of officials. You could hardly tell anybody without a scorecard; there was the *carabinieri* guys with their fancy uniforms and them shiny patent leather hats, lookin' like a bunch of Napoleons, and there was the plainclothes detectives and customs officials in uniforms. Then I spotted a half a dozen guys from what they call the Mobile Squadrone and other guys from the Guardia di Finanza [the Italian military treasury department] — and to me that meant narcotics. So the nice trip was over and I could smell in a minute that my troubles was all startin' up again."

26.

In early 1946, scarcely eight months after the cease-fire in Europe, the huge harbor of Genoa, Italy, teemed with boats of every description, from Allied warships to tiny fishing craft. The arrival of the S.S. *Laura Keene* would normally have gone unnoticed; but not when it carried Charles Lucky Luciano, even though he appeared on the passenger list by the name he would officially carry henceforth — Salvatore Lucanía. The officials who swarmed over the ship at first studiously ignored him as they processed the other passengers — the fifteen Italian-American deportees, the three American girls.

Then it was Luciano's turn. "The whole goddamn rigamarole took over two hours before they got to me. I'm standin' there on the deck watchin' them Italians yellin' at everybody, spittin' on the deck, and fightin' over nothin'. There must've been twenty-five guys in and out of uniform, each one tryin' to prove he had more authority than the other one.

"Murray Weinstein come over and took me aside. He said, 'I hate to tell you this, Charlie, but I think we've got trouble.' I noticed he said 'we' and I really appreciated that. He told me, 'It seems that the Italians have orders from the Ministry of the Interior in Rome to ship you back to your hometown in Sicily.'

"I couldn't believe it. I started to yell, 'Do you mean to say I gotta live in Lercara Friddi for the rest of my life? What the hell's goin' on here? I served my time; I'm supposed to be free. Who the hell is doin' this to me?' Murray just shook his head and I realized I was puttin' him on a spot. He didn't owe me nothin', but to prove what a nice guy he was, he opened up with me. He told me that orders had come from the head of the Narcotics Bureau of the U.S. Treasury in Washington, from that dirty son of a bitch Asslinger [Luciano's constant corruption of the name of Harry Anslinger] to keep me under twenty-four-hour-a-day surveillance.

"Then Weinstein told me, 'Charlie, this is out of my hands. I'm only a New York cop. All these people are getting their orders from America and they say Washington has the crazy idea that you had yourself paroled to Italy so you could supervise the drug traffic from this side of the Atlantic.' I was ready to explode, but Murray stopped me. He said, 'Hold your water, Charlie. You have some friends here. But you have to realize that all the Italian officials are under the thumb of the American Army in Italy. They lost the war, and so what America wants, America gets. You have to face it and wait it out. They're going to go through a lot of red tape with you; the best thing you can do is just be patient and don't blow your top.'

"There wasn't nothin' I could do except to follow what he told me, practically to the letter. I was really sorry I'd hadda shake hands with Murray and say goodbye the night before because I knew we couldn't do it in front of people. I wanted to give him five grand for doin' nothin', just for bein' a nice guy. But he wouldn't take a quarter — the same as the three girls; they wouldn't take a penny and they couldn't thank me enough for a wonderful trip.

"The next thing I know, they take me down to the big main cabin of the *Laura Keene,* where we had our party and which still looked like a hurricane hit it. Some guy with a whole bunch of ribbons tells me that he's sorry about what he's gotta do. As far as this guy was concerned — and he said he was speakin' for everybody — he would just as soon let me go anyplace in Italy I wanted to. He tried to make me understand that it was the *Americani* who asked 'em to send me back to Lercara Friddi and it was gonna take some time to work out all the details. Then he gives it to me; if I wouldn't mind, they'd like to take me to the pokey until everythin' is worked out, but I shouldn't think of it as bein' in jail; I should think of it more as a hotel, only he was sorry I would have bars on my windows."

If Luciano was given the impression his stay in a Genoese jail would be a matter of hours, that was soon corrected. After a day, as his patience and his temper wore to breaking, a guard told him casually that he could not expect to be released for at least five or six weeks. "It was like an absolute stranger walked into my cell and hit me over the head with a baseball bat. All some guy hadda do was sign one simple paper to transfer me over to the police in Palermo. That's all that hadda be done. So I said to this monkey, 'What the hell are you talkin' about, five or six weeks? I can walk halfway around the world in that time and all we gotta do is go down to Palermo.'

"Well, this guy looks at me and he spreads his hands out and says, 'Signor Lucanía, welcome to Italy.'

"I learned a big lesson from that guy. I realized I would always be a fish outa water as long as I thought of myself as an American in a foreign country. I hadda make myself understand that livin' in Italy meant you couldn't snap your fingers and get things done right away. Time didn't mean a fuckin' thing, at least not the way it does in New York."

The following morning, however, Luciano's problems suddenly disappeared — with no explanation to him. He was removed from his cell and, with two *carabinieri* in full regalia on either side, installed in a first-class compartment aboard one of the large, fast ferryboats to Palermo. Once in the Sicilian capital, he was turned over to the Sicilian *questura* (police headquarters), whose officials took a decidedly different view of the American demands than did those on the mainland.

"Signor Lucanía," the *questura* captain told him, "here in Sicily we are more remote from Rome than our colleagues in Genoa. This gives us a feeling of independence from unnecessary political influence. To us, you are a man who is about to return to the place of his birth after an absence of many years. You are entitled to some peace. Perhaps, after a short time, we might also arrange some freedom of movement for you. In return, I pray you will give us no cause for concern. May we have an agreement on that?" The captain extended his hand; Luciano shook it and nodded.

"I don't know how to describe that particular moment except that there was one thing I recognized immediately — the captain and I was Sicilians first and that was the foundation of everythin'. There was nothin' shady about this guy, because it turned out later he was as solid as the Rock of Gibraltar. But he thought all that red-tape crap that went on in Genoa was a joke."

The next morning, accompanied by a Mobile lieutenant and a military police driver, Luciano was on his way to Lercara Friddi, eighty kilometers inland. As they drove through Palermo, a city he had seen briefly forty years before on his way to America, he had his first view of the ravages of war. Though the war had moved out of Sicily to the mainland over two years earlier, the city still appeared a mass of rubble, here and there a single wall of what had once been a large building loomed starkly in the emptiness, and over everything, like an acrid cloud, was the odor of charred wood and debris. Beggars were everywhere and when the car stopped at intersections they surrounded it. Luciano handed out coins from the window and then was horrified to see small boys and men fighting desperately for the almost worthless lire.

"It almost made me sick," he said, and when the car finally left the city, he sat back with relief. But the war had come to the countryside, too. On the mountain slopes along which the car sped, there was no green; the trees were gone and the land was cratered by bombs and shells, unable yet to be cultivated. The lieutenant told Luciano that much of the population was homeless and hungry: there were few jobs and little money, and the country seemed constantly on the brink of chaos, the government in danger of collapse, besieged by a huge and militant Communist Party. The only prop was from the Americans, who provided not merely assistance but advice, orders and influence the Italians felt they had to heed. If the Americans departed, Italy would surely fall apart.

"If I live to be a thousand years old I'll never forget that ride to Lercara Friddi. From the minute I woke up that mornin', I saw nothin' but horrible things — people starvin', really starvin'; maybe more than a million people who didn't know if they could make it from one day to the next. And then, as we started to climb up through the hills along this narrow, bumpy road full of shell holes, I got so nervous we had to stop so I could get out and take a leak. I was scared. I don't mean about goin' from the Waldorf Towers to Lercara Friddi. I mean, I was scared shitless there wouldn't be no Lercara Friddi there at all. Can you imagine? Twenty-four hours before, I hated the idea of bein' sent back to Lercara Friddi. And now, I'm prayin' that the town'll still be there, with some people still alive in it."

Even before the signpost told him he was about to arrive, Luciano seemed to know by instinct that around the next bend he would see Lercara Friddi. The driver came to a stop and pointed off to the left. The town was intact, with no sign of war damage, less than a half-mile away. The roofs of the small houses were still the same slate gray he remembered and the same gray haze covered the village just as it did in his memory of the day he left it. Then it had been his entire world. Now it seemed so small he could not imagine how it had managed to survive the war. As he stared out at it, he said, he began to feel a sense of pride and told himself, "That's the town the Lucanías come from. No Nazi kraut could ever take over your hometown."

"I could really hear them words inside of me and all of a sudden I just couldn't wait to get there. I told the driver to step on it. I didn't care if the whole goddamn place had a total population of eighteen or nobody never heard of me. I just wanted to get home."

As the police car made an abrupt turn into the main piazza of Lercara Friddi, Luciano was stunned. Several hundred people were massed and the square was festooned with banners, flags and streamers. On one side was a small decorated platform, and on it were four serious, mustachioed musicians who immediately and enthusiastically broke into a discordant version of "The Stars and Stripes Forever." When the car stopped, the people, dressed in their best clothes, began waving miniature American flags and shouting cheers of welcome.

Giovanni Tinorello, now perhaps the town's oldest citizen, remembers clearly the day in 1946 when the man he still calls "Meester Sharlie" came home. It was, he said, perhaps the most important day in the town's history. "We were told in advance when to expect the arrival of this most famous son of Lercara Friddi, this Looky Luciano. It was like a holiday. All of the stores and the school and everything closed up so that we could gather in the piazza to give him a proper reception. Of course, we knew that he was a man who had done maybe some bad things, but for us he was not a gangster, like the men from that place they call Chicago where people kill on the streets. No, when Signor Looky left here, he had nothing; but he came back as a rich and famous personage — *Il Milionario*.

"I remember it like it was yesterday. When the Fiat of the *questura* turned into the piazza, the band began to play the wonderful American music. Then our mayor came to the car and opened the door and he shook hands with Meester Sharlie. Our mayor — he was Aurelio D'Accurso, a farmer of wheat — we used to call him *Il Stupido,* that fool was wearing a red sash across his chest. Now, I ask you, does one wear a red sash to welcome a famous *milionario* from America? Everyone knows the red sash is reserved for occasions of state. This was a time for prosperity to begin, for was not a *milionario* from America to become once more a part of Lercara Friddi?"

The old man may have been incensed at the red sash, but Luciano was moved by it, by the honor done to him. Then he noticed a long table in front of the fountain where he had played as a child. Mayor D'Accurso ceremoniously led him to it, to an open book that rested on it, and asked him to sign his name in the Official Register, signifying that he was once more a legal resident of Lercara Friddi. From his pocket the mayor drew a treasured American fountain pen and handed it to Luciano. The crowd surged forward to watch the signing. The name Luciano inscribed was the one he had been given at birth — Salvatore Lucanía. The cheers were even louder than at first. The famous American was home at last.

Then Luciano was shown where he would live — the town hotel, on one side of the square. "I can't understand to this day why a little village like Lercara Friddi ever needed a hotel. I don't remember as a kid that we had one, or that anybody came through who stayed long enough to use one. This two-story, broken-down, weatherbeaten joint was gonna be my Sicilian version of the Waldorf Towers. While I was lookin' at it, a guy steps outa the crowd and comes over to shake hands with me. He introduces himself as my cousin, Paolo Rotolo. He was the son of the uncle on my mother's side who helped my father with the money when we went to America. His father had died and left him the properties, which included a half interest in that fleabag. He was such a nice guy that we became friends right away. He seemed to understand that I was a little disappointed in where I was gonna live, but I told him not to apologize for it, that in many respects I was god-damn glad to be there.

"So he took me inside, and they had fixed up half of the second floor as an apartment for me. It would've fit into a corner of my place at the Waldorf Towers. But I tried not to show how I felt, and I smiled and thanked him. And then he brought in a few other relatives who was still livin' in Lercara Friddi, on my father's side, all Lucanías. One of 'em was a cousin who was younger than me, Calcedonia Lucanía, and as soon as he met me he called me Uncle, as a mark of respect, because I was older. We became very close almost from the beginnin'.

"They finally left me alone to take a little rest. I unpacked my suitcases and put some things away. Then I noticed somethin' really cute: the bathroom had an old-fashioned iron tub, and there was a note on the wall in Italian which said 'American Shower' — there was a rubber tube with a flower sprinkler as a head, and it was hangin' on the wall above the faucets. Well, how can you feel blue when you see a thing like that? You realize how hard these people are tryin' to make you feel like an American who didn't come to a country of barbarians.

"I took a nap for about an hour, and then a lotta noise from outside woke me up. I went over to the window. It was about eight o'clock, dark, and they was shootin' firecrackers down below in the piazza. They had the whole place lit up with coal-oil lamps, and them tables that was empty when I arrived was now loaded with food and bottles of wine. The whole town was there, and it seemed like everybody was lookin' up at my window like they was waitin' for me. As soon as they saw me, they started to yell, 'Sharlie! Sharlie!' and they was all motionin' for me to hurry down."

For days, the women of the town had been hoarding their

meager rations and cooking sauces, grinding grain and making pastas of all shapes and sizes. Tables and chairs were set up all around the square and the people of Lercara Friddi sat down to eat, drink homemade red wine, and honor their distinguished native son. Giovanni Tinorello remembered, "I had the best dinner of my life that night. Not all the women in Lercara Friddi were such good cooks, but I had an opportunity to go from one table to another to taste the best things from each. I remember that Meester Sharlie had mostly spaghetti with the sauce marinara that was made by la Signora Rotola; she made the finest pasta anywhere on the island of Sicily."

In the days that followed, Luciano became the town's bountiful patron. He distributed money and sent off to Palermo for clothing, food and other supplies to meet the needs of the people. When his wardrobe trunks finally arrived, he gave his relatives a dozen suits, whether the men were his size or not, for their wives assured him it would be no trouble for them to do any necessary alterations.

Luciano's cousin, Paolo Rotolo, lived around the corner from the hotel in a three-story building. He and his wife lived on the top floor, another family leased the second, and the ground floor was empty. Luciano discovered that he and Rotolo shared the same passion for movies, with Rotolo invariably throwing thousands of questions about Hollywood at him, assuming that since he came from America, he must know every star. It was then that Luciano made a gesture that insured him a permanent place in his cousin's — and the town's — heart.

"I got an idea I knew the whole fuckin' town would love. I give 'em a movie theater. It cost me a fishcake, because everybody in the town pitched in to make over the bottom floor of Paolo's house into one big room that would seat a couple hundred people. Calcedonia and Paolo got a truck and went into Palermo with the money I give 'em and bought a whole bunch of secondhand chairs. Then I made a connection with a guy up there to buy a thirty-five millimeter projection machine from one of the movie theaters that had been hit during the war. And in about three weeks, the town of Lercara Friddi seen its first movies in about ten years.

These was pictures we found in a fireproof warehouse where they used to keep films in the old days and all these cans was saved from the bombings.

"The funniest thing, most of the pictures was them gangster movies that Warner Brothers made, with Edward G. Robinson and Jimmy Cagney. As a matter of fact, the first picture we showed, *Little Caesar,* made me such a big man like you'd never believe. The people was comin' up to me and practically kissin' my hand — not only because I brought them the pictures but because they wanted to show me that I was a bigger shot than Little Caesar. They made me feel like Salvatore Maranzano."

But Lercara Friddi was not where Luciano intended to spend his life. It was out of the current of his world, and besides, he was continually embarrassed by the constant adulation heaped upon him. He persuaded the chief of the local *questura* to drive him to Palermo for a talk with the captain in charge there. The captain was sympathetic and agreeable to a proposed change of residence. "It is ridiculous to assume that you can be watched any more closely in Lercara Friddi than in Palermo," he told Luciano. "I, for one, will place no surveillance on you, but I would suggest that from time to time we might take coffee together and you can report to me informally the nature of your daily activities."

So Luciano moved to Palermo, into the Grande Albergo Sole, one of the best hotels. Though not New York, Palermo was still the capital city of Sicily, where contacts could be made and plans for the future expedited. But Palermo, too, was a city decimated by war. Survival was the only law, and any means to achieve it seemed permissible, if not with the overt assistance of authorities, at least with their knowledge.

"All day long, I was approached by dozens of guys with deals phonier than Vito Genovese's money machine. Them guys in Palermo was workin' petty larceny worse than anything we ever done in New York in the twenties. And here I am, twenty-five years later, and these Italian bastards're tryin' to do it to me — tryin' to con me out of a hundred here, two hundred there. And lemme tell you, in 1946 a single American dollar in Italy was unbelievable what it could buy."

Luciano sought from his friend, the captain of the Mobile,

relief from the unceasing horde of con men and petitioners who seemed to line up waiting for him at his hotel. "I asked the captain what to do to get rid of all them jokers. We was sittin' in the bar of the Sole, facin' the street, and the captain starts to laugh. He says, 'The first thing a man like you has to do is move out of this hotel.' Then he points across the street — there's this very elegant municipal building with a lotta wide steps leadin' up to it, and behind an iron railin' there was a plaza in front of the building filled with statues. The captain asks me if I notice anything unusual about the statues. I looked and looked and finally I said, 'Yeah, them statues are naked.' He smiled and told me that was the whole point. It seemed that for years they called the place the 'Plaza of Shame' because of them naked statues. A lotta religious women in Palermo thought there was somethin' wrong about that kind of art and they wouldn't even let their daughters walk noplace near it. So the plaza turned into a hangout for pickpockets, bandits, whores and pimps. By livin' in a hotel overlookin' that place, I was just drawin' all the people that'd been badgerin' me.

"That's when I decided I had enough of Palermo, and I put the wheels in motion to get to Rome. I knew I couldn't do nothin' too soon about the move to Havana; I hadda stick it out in Italy for a while to make things look good. Rome was where the action was, where the big politicians hung out and where I hadda get my contacts established. But I decided, while I was waitin', not to waste the time and maybe do a little business.

"The first thing I done was get in touch with a cousin of mine, a guy they called *Il Barone*. His real name was Riccardo Barone, and he was related to me somewhere on my mother's side. He was a real hotshot in the black market and I had word that he was reliable. He went to work for me right away, settin' things up, carryin' dough and all that stuff. Also, he was in the Mafia.

"There wasn't nothin' strange about that, and it wasn't nothin' like what J. Edgar Hoover and all them guys was always screamin' about in the States. Half the people I met in Sicily was in the Mafia, and by half the people, I mean half the cops, too. Because in Sicily, it goes like this: the Mafia is first, then your own family, then your business, and then the Mafia again. In a way, you might say it's like a private club that a lotta people belong to, all over Sicily. So Riccardo was very helpful to me and I didn't have to made no open moves that would get me in trouble with the police. Besides, before I left America I was supplied with a lotta the right names, not only in Sicily but in Naples and Rome. Riccardo started to make my contacts for me."

The opportunities were nearly limitless in postwar Italy, a nation beleaguered by shortages of almost everything. "That's when I remembered Lansky's Law — the law of supply and demand. It was kinda like the good old days when bootleggin' was the name of the game, when we could supply somethin' that everybody was demandin'. In 1946, Italy was the same thing all over again, except now it was whiskey, medicine, cigarettes — you name it, and that's what was goin' on in the black market all over the country. Everybody was in it, the legit guys, the ex-Fascists, the Communists, every fuckin' son of a bitch was tryin' to make some money and he didn't give a goddamn how he got it. It was just a question of survival. And that goes for the priests in the churches, too. There was plenty of them padres who learned to look the other way in order to keep the people in their parishes alive.

"From the time I got to Italy I went heavy into the black market. That means I had just gotten out of the can and I was mixed up in crime again. But that was entirely different. A big part of the black market involved gettin' the real necessities of life for the people in Italy outa the American PX's and commissaries. Then, pretty soon, I had a fleet of old fishin' boats comin' and goin' from Tangier, which was a free port. A dozen nylons could buy a half-interest in a bank in them days, and the same thing went for a carton of American cigarettes. When I finally got to Rome, I found out that for a carton a girl would live with you for a week, do your laundry, sleep with you, and then go out and sell that carton — one cigarette at a time — and come up with a bundle that would keep her alive for a couple weeks more.

"But I wasn't only buyin' and sellin'; I actually became a fuckin' banker, and I don't mean a shylock but a real banker like the guys on Wall Street. I had a lotta cash dollars and I used 'em to buy lire cheap because the lira was worth practically nothin'.

Then I'd send Riccardo over to Tangier to change the lire back into dollars at a better price. It was kind of a merry-go-round and it paid off like nothin' you ever seen; in less than six months, I almost doubled my bankroll."

By June of 1946, Luciano had pulled enough strings to ease his way out of Sicily across the bay to Naples, where he moved into the luxurious Excelsior Hotel. During the war it had been expropriated by the Germans, who turned it into a rest and relaxation center for high Nazi officials; now it was back in Italian hands and providing, once more, de luxe service to travelers. "I had the most beautiful apartment you ever seen, overlookin' the Bay of Naples."

With hardly a moment's pause, he took over the black market network that had been established by Genovese, picking up the contacts at the huge American naval base and the American colony and opening a pipeline through which passed American foods, canned goods and staples, and American home appliances available nowhere else. "Our men and their families was gettin' everythin', from Virginia hams to the finest refrigerators, electric toasters, irons, everythin' under the sun. All the Americans, from the civilians workin' at the consulate to the military, was up to their necks in things an Italian would give his eyeteeth for and couldn't get legit. Of course, the Americans bought them goods for less than wholesale at the PX and the commissary; a bottle of booze, for example, was only two bucks and a pack of cigarettes was about twelve cents because it was sold without no U.S. tax.

"If you think we made big profits from bootleggin' in the States in the twenties, it didn't compare to the Italian black market. It was the old story that everybody's got larceny in 'em, and practically the whole naval base in Naples was in the dry goods business, the appliance business, the food business on the black market. Now, a sergeant, for example, could buy an unlimited amount of stuff, but he wasn't gonna peddle it himself on a Naples street corner. There hadda be a middleman, and I arranged to be the guy behind the guys in the middle. I never showed up in front of none of this."

But there was one operation that Genovese had set up that Luciano rigorously shunned. "It didn't take me long to discover

303

that regardless of my orders, that little bastard was dealin' in junk all the time he was in Italy, practically to the day the U.S. Army sent him back to New York. But I never — and I mean never — had nothin' to do with junk. I took over the rest of his operation, but not that."

Luciano stayed in Naples only long enough to solidify his control over the black market. Then, his political contacts giving the okay, he moved to Rome, to the famous Excelsior Hotel on the Via Veneto, to an apartment even more luxurious than the one at the Excelsior in Naples. In Rome, he assiduously cultivated government officials, and, too, he began to cull the ranks of American deportees for experienced and reliable lieutenants to help in his black market operations.

"But it was like a temporary thing, like I was playin' a game, because none of this was really serious to me. I didn't figure I was gonna stay in Italy very long. All that black market crap was just somethin' to keep my mind occupied. I was only waitin' for the first word from Lansky, that's all."

Early in the fall, the message arrived, brought in a sealed envelope by a newly arrived deportee. The message was only three words: "December — Hotel Nacional."

"This was very important to me, not just because it meant the arrangements was made, and it meant that everybody down the line was expectin' me, but also because the messenger also brought me some very disturbin' news. He said that Vito was beginnin' to act like I wasn't never comin' back. He was outa jail and walkin' around my territory in New York like he owned it. And then, right on top of that, I heard from Costello that the 'California matter' was bad. I knew right away what he meant, that Bugsy was probably tappin' the till for even more dough than I knew about before I left Ellis Island. So I sent a message to Lansky that I would make my arrangements."

In late September, Luciano obtained not one but two Italian passports made out in the name of Salvatore Lucanía, with visas for Mexico, Cuba and several South American nations. "The passports didn't have to cost me a nickel. I went to the right people and I talked to 'em in the right way and they said, okay, that they didn't have nothin' against me, that I hadn't broken no

Italian laws, so why shouldn't I have a passport. While I was at it, I arranged to get a second one, just for insurance, and so I spread around a little dough."

Then he suddenly vanished from the Italian scene.

27.

The new guest checking into the Hotel Nacional in Havana in late October of 1946 attracted little attention among all the other tourists flocking to the island that fall. He signed the register with the name on his Italian passport — Salvatore Lucanía — and was shown to a suite that had been reserved for him by a prominent American businessman with wide Cuban holdings — Meyer Lansky.

"When I got to the room the bellhop opened up the curtains on them big windows and I looked out. I could see almost the whole city. I think it was the palm trees that got me. Everyplace you looked there was palm trees and it made me feel like I was back in Miami. All of a sudden, I realized for the first time in over ten years that there was no handcuffs on me and nobody was breathin' over my shoulder, which was the way I used to feel even while I was wanderin' around Italy. When I looked down over the Caribbean from my window, I realized somethin' else; the water was just as pretty as the Bay of Naples, but it was only ninety miles from the United States. That meant I was practically back in America."

It had been a long and circuitous voyage. Luciano had left Italy in early October, on a freighter bound for South America. He landed in Caracas, Venezuela, the ship's first port, remained there a few days, and then flew to Mexico City, where he stayed a few days more. Then he chartered a private plane for the last leg, to Havana. He had gone this long way for definite reasons. "I wanted to establish a beachhead in a few cities besides Havana under the

305

name of Salvatore Lucanía, and besides I wanted to make sure I wasn't tailed. I spread enough dough around Naples, too, before I got on the ship so there wouldn't be no publicity about my leavin', and there wasn't. And when I got to Havana, it was on the far side of the airport in the private plane, and Lansky was there to pick me up in a car. We breezed right through customs and nobody looked at me twice. I was sure I managed to get to Cuba without Asslinger or Dewey or none of the American officials knowin' about it. I knew they'd find out sooner or later, but I wanted to stall it."

As soon as Luciano was settled at the Nacional, Lansky returned to the United States, leaving him with the word that the scheduled underworld conference would begin on December 22 and everyone summoned would be there. Within a week, Luciano, luxuriating in his new freedom, moved out of the hotel and into a spacious house in the exclusive Miramar suburb, among the estates and yacht clubs of wealthy Cubans and resident Americans. In his Spanish-style mansion on Quinta Avenida, Luciano had everything he desired; a crew of gardeners daily manicured the lavishly planted grounds and a staff of servants, selected with the assistance of Lansky's aides, provided for his every need. In these peaceful surroundings Luciano made a decision, to take what had once been offered and refused.

"I thought about this for a long time. I remembered back to the time in Chicago, when they wanted me to become the Boss of Bosses, and I turned it down, like a stupid jerk, because I thought it was all a lotta shit. But I had plenty of chances to think back over that mistake, and I had no intention of lettin' the title slip away this time. The guys was comin' to Havana, not because I asked them to; I ordered it. So I was gonna plow right into 'em and take the top spot because I knew what them guys really respected was a leader with a title. In fact, I started to laugh at myself when I was makin' plans for what I was gonna say and I thought maybe I oughta have a crown made. I'll bet that would've made 'em sit up.

"Anyway, I took it easy for the next few weeks. I had breakfast in bed and then I'd put on a pair of slacks and walk around my estate and supervise the four gardeners and we would discuss the kind of flowers I wanted 'em to plant. The house was furnished with fantastic antiques and there must've been a thousand yards of all kinds of silk, from curtains to sheets. It was one helluva change from Dannemora and Great Meadow. The place was owned by a rich sugar planter, but it was the time when things was very low and I only paid eight hundred bucks a month for the whole joint, includin' all the servants and the gardeners."

Meanwhile, preparations were under way for the first full-scale meeting of American underworld leaders since the Chicago conclave of 1932. Lansky made several trips from his home in the Miami area to fill Luciano in on events within the outfit throughout the country, and together they made plans for Luciano's extended stay in Cuba. A legitimate front would be necessary to insure this, and so Lansky proposed that Luciano purchase an interest in the casino at the Hotel Nacional. Since the casino was controlled jointly by Lansky and Batista (then living in Florida while preparing to make a Cuban comeback, but still the power behind the government of President Ramón Grau San Martín), that interest could not be a gift but would have to be paid for at a realistic price. The figure of $150,000 was set for a small percentage.

"The only question was how I could avoid shellin' out the dough myself. I had plenty of money with me and I could've bought the stock outright. But Meyer suggested another way to handle it. He said that if all our guys was happy to bring envelopes to my bon voyage party on the *Laura Keene,* they'd be more'n happy to bring envelopes to welcome me back again across the Atlantic. So that's the way we worked it. All the fellas brought me 'Christmas presents' and the envelopes come to over two hundred grand; that's how I bought the interest in the casino."

Staying in Havana, of course, was to be only temporary. Luciano still hoped to return legally to the United States, but he thought it would take two years before that could happen. He and his friends were certain that Thomas E. Dewey would be the Republican candidate for President in 1948, and that Dewey would win the election. They were also certain that Dewey would welcome secret financial support for his campaign from the underworld and as reciprocity, once in the White House, would arrange for an end to

Luciano's exile. The first necessity, though, was to make certain that Luciano remained close at hand in Cuba. Lansky initiated negotiations with his friend, Cuban Minister of the Interior Alfredo Pequeno, for automatic six-month extensions of Luciano's visa as long as necessary, and as a further courtesy, a permit for Luciano to bring an American automobile to Cuba for his personal use without the customary import tax that often trebled the original price of the car.

The first of the American underworld leaders to arrive for the convention was Vito Genovese. He was installed in a penthouse suite at the Hotel Nacional, the conference center for the week, where all the guests would stay and where the meetings would be held.

"It was a couple days before I was expectin' anybody, around the twentieth of December, when Vito called me at my house. It was a private number and he got it from Lansky. He tells me he come down a little beforehand to get a couple days' rest on the beach. Now, I knew that little prick well enough to know he didn't come to Havana to get a suntan. That wasn't the way he operated. I knew he had somethin' in mind, because I had been hearin' from Lansky that he was makin' moves into Anastasia's territory in Brooklyn. I guessed that was what he wanted to talk about in private, so I told him to come over to my house for lunch.

"I hadn't seen Vito for almost ten years, but when he walked in, I could see he hadn't changed at all — he was still the same short, pudgy son of a bitch that I always remembered. And he was wearin' the same kind of wrinkled-up suit that he always wore, with the same cigar ashes all over the front of it. We greeted each other like brothers — y'know, the old Italian crap. We threw our arms around each other and said how much we missed each other, and that the last ten years felt like a thousand.

"Then, we have a lunch in the formal dinin' room, and he don't even have the courtesy to say how fancy my joint is. He didn't notice nothin'; he's the kind of a guy who could walk through John Jacob Astor's mansion in Newport like it was a Brooklyn subway station. Then we go out to the patio, all alone, and sit in the sun, in our shorts. That's when Vito decides it's time to get down to business. He says to me, 'Charlie, I'm worried about Albert.' And I say to myself, 'Sure you're worried about Albert, because if you keep tryin' to move in on him he'll blow your head off.' I pretend I don't know nothin' and I ask him, 'What's about Albert?' "

Genovese looked surprised. He said, "You know as well as me that Albert's goin' off his rocker. All he talks about is hittin' people. Before I came down here, Albert and some of the guys had dinner with me, and all he talked about was hittin' that guy Anslinger in Washington, because he's makin' so much trouble about junk. Remember, Charlie? — that was just what he was sayin' about Dewey ten years ago when you was havin' all the trouble."

"Yeah, I remember, but I wasn't the only one who was havin' trouble with Dewey. He was after your ass, too, Vito, for the Boccia thing — which was about the dumbest caper you ever pulled in your whole fuckin' life. That's why you hadda take it on the lam to Italy."

"But back then," Genovese said, "remember what you said? — that it would only make more trouble if he hit Dewey? So wouldn't things be even worse now if he hit Anslinger?"

Luciano nodded. "Sure it would. So, I stop him."

"You'll have to, sooner than you think," Genovese said. "He's gonna bring up a hit on Anslinger at the meet and that's why I thought I oughta talk to you about it ahead of time."

"All right, so you talked to me about it. When he brings it up, I'll just tell him no, and that'll be the end of it."

Genovese shook his head. "Maybe. But how do you know you can trust Albert any more? I tell you, he's off his rocker. He could go out on his own and do it."

"Vito, cut out all that shit; Albert don't have no big interest in narcotics, the way you have. Whatever he does with junk is small-time, and only because you pushed him into it, on account of tryin' to move in on Brooklyn. What is it with you, Vito? Do you think I don't know what's goin' on?"

Genovese persisted, "I'm tellin' you, Charlie, he's becomin' a danger to the outfit — I mean, the outfit that I'm helpin' to run for you. One of these days we're gonna have to take care of him, or he'll wreck the whole thing."

309

"The first thing that come to me," Luciano said years later, "was that the real danger from Albert was for Vito personally, and he wants the council to okay puttin' him away. But I figure as long as Anastasia is alive, he's one friend that I can count on, and his just bein' alive will hold Vito back. So I said, 'I don't see it that way, Vito. I want to let it ride for a while. If Albert really starts makin' trouble, I'll always know about it in advance and be able to cut it off. Besides, you know goddamn fuckin' well that Albert is gonna be here in a couple days. Since when does the Unione council have a 'table' on a guy in front of his face? To talk to him, yes — but not to make no decisions on a hit. Vito, when I made them rules back in 1932, everybody accepted 'em. Are you tryin' to change 'em?' "

Genovese stood up, paced the lawn for a moment before returning to his chair. "That's another thing I wanna talk to you about, Charlie, private, before the other guys get down here. Y'know, you been away for a long time. You don't realize how much things are changin'."

"You been away a long time too, Vito. What are you gettin' at?"

"Well," Genovese said, "I'm back now, right in the middle of it, in New York. But you're still outa the country, Charlie. Things is changin' every day, and you ain't really in touch."

"He didn't really know how much I was in touch," Luciano said later. "I knew everythin'. I could figure what Vito was comin' to, but I wasn't gonna help him get it out. I wanted him to do it all by himself. So I just sat there and waited. Finally, he springs it."

"Let me tell you what I think, Charlie — it's a good proposition. I think you oughta quit — I mean, retire. You'll have all the dough you can ever need, and I give you my personal word on that. You won't have to worry about what's goin' on. You won't have to think up ideas how to get back to New York — which is gonna be tough. And you'll still be the boss, the *capo di capi re*. Everybody'll think of you as the guy who put it all together back in the old days, and they'll still come to you when they need advice. It's like you'll be the head, but I'll be runnin' things on the spot. That's all there is to it."

"That guinea son of a bitch! But, I always knew he was a gutsy bastard, so I should've known that he'd have the nerve to stand up to me, to my face — just as long as nobody else was around. All he really wanted was to take over and cut me out. His whole life he wanted to be boss. He was the same as Joe Masseria; he learned from Joe; he envied Maranzano; and he hated it that he wasn't born in Sicily. I looked at Vito very calm, like talkin' to a schoolboy, and I said, 'You forgot what happened in Chicago when I set this thing up. There is no Boss of Bosses. I turned it down in front of everybody. If I ever change my mind, then I will take the title. But it won't be up to you. Right now you work for me and I ain't in the mood to retire. Don't you ever let me hear this again, or I'll lose my temper. Now — let's talk about some pleasant things.'

"I only said that just to see whether Vito would have that last ounce of guts to keep on goin'. But he didn't. He shut up like a clam. In a few minutes he said he wanted to go back to the hotel; I had a car with a driver and I sent him back. Naturally, I realized that he went away plenty unhappy, but I didn't give a fuck. I knew there was enough guys on my side to keep him in line, so all that fat little bastard could do was to dream. I'll tell you one thing, though — it wasn't easy to keep my hands off his fat throat. He'll never know how close he come to it."

The next day the delegates began arriving. The upper four floors of the Hotel Nacional had been set aside exclusively for their use. Unlike the Atlantic City convention, which many had attended accompanied by wives and girl friends, this event was, for the first days, strictly male. From New York and New Jersey came Joe Adonis, Albert Anastasia, "Joe Bananas" Bonanno, Frank Costello, Tommy Lucchese, Joe Profaci and his heir apparent, Giuseppe Magliocco, Willie Moretti, Augie Pisano and Mike Miranda. From Buffalo there was Steve Magaddino. Chicago sent its council chief, Tony Accardo, and the brothers Fischetti, Charlie and Rocco, cousins and heirs of Al Capone (who was then out of prison and dying of syphilis of the brain in his mansion on Palm Island off Miami Beach). Carlos Marcello arrived from New Orleans and Santo Trafficante from Florida. ("This is a guy who always managed to hug the background, but he was tough and reliable. In fact, he's one of the few guys in the whole country that Meyer would never tangle with.") And there were two high-ranking delegates who had no vote, because they were Jewish: Meyer Lansky and the New Orleans partner of the outfit, "Dandy Phil" Kastel.

If anyone had asked, there was an outward reason for such a gathering. It was to honor an Italian boy from New Jersey named Frank Sinatra, the crooner who had become the idol of the nation's bobby-sox set. He had flown to Havana with his friends the Fischettis to meet his friend Charlie Luciano, and during the holiday week a gala party would be given in his honor.

"Frank was a good kid and we was all proud of him, the way he made it to the top. When I was in Dannemora, the fellas who come to see me told me about him. They said he was a skinny kid from around Hoboken with a terrific voice and one hundred per cent Italian. He used to sing around the joints there and all the guys liked him. When the time come when some dough was needed to put Frank across with the public, they put it up. He had a job workin' for Tommy Dorsey's band and he was gettin' about a hundred and fifty bucks a week, but he needed publicity, clothes, different kinds of special music things, and they all cost quite a bit of money — I think it was about fifty or sixty grand. I okayed the money and it come out of the fund, even though some guys put up a little extra on a personal basis. It all helped him become a big star and he was just showin' his appreciation by comin' down to Havana to say hello to me.

"I don't wanna give the idea that he was ever asked to do somethin' illegal — by me or anybody else that I know about. He give out a few presents to different guys, like a gold cigarette case, a watch, that kind of thing, but that was it. As for me, the guy was always Number One Okay."

The mezzanine was strictly out of bounds for other guests at the Hotel Nacional that week; it was reserved for the meetings, banquets and parties of the underworld organization. As each delegate arrived in Havana, his first call after checking into the hotel was to the Miramar villa of Luciano, to greet the leader, reaffirm loyalty, and acknowledge him as the chairman of the board, still ruler of his own organization and the man from whom overall guidance and final judgments could be expected. A dinner that night, hosted by Lansky, Costello and Adonis, was a public show of the private affirmations, and everyone came forward with envelopes stuffed with cash.

"I was a little embarrassed about takin' the money so soon after the *Laura Keene* farewell party, but Meyer put out the word that it was for a legit business, and I figured what the hell, they owe me a lot more, so why not let 'em do it? I took a hundred and fifty grand and let Meyer have it for my points in the Casino, and he handed me stock in the business."

The next morning, in a sealed-off and tightly guarded conference room on the mezzanine floor, the first general meeting of the council of the Unione Siciliano in more than a decade was called to order. Luciano sat at the head of the huge rectangular table, flanked by Lansky, Costello, Genovese and Adonis. There was no protocol beyond that. The other leaders made their own selections of seating places.

"I opened the meeting by expressin' my thanks that everybody I asked for accepted the invitations. And I thanked 'em for the envelopes, too. That's when I explained that I was now back on the American side of the Atlantic — legitimate — and that I had used the envelopes to buy points in the Casino at the Nacional, and that arrangements had been fixed up with the government for me to stay in Cuba for as long as would be necessary. I told 'em I would be runnin' things from Havana under my right name of Salvatore Lucanía. I asked 'em to please remember to call me that, and not use the name Luciano, or Charlie Lucky — because it was important that we have as little noise as possible about my bein' out of Italy, until everythin' cooled off in New York and Washington.

"Even though I told Vito that I didn't want the title of Boss of Bosses — I really didn't, except I knew it was necessary — I sort of mentioned it casually. The minute I used that expression, Anastasia got up and said, 'Charlie, pardon me if I interrupt. I want to say this in front, before this here meeting goes any further. For me, you are the Big Boss, whether you like it or not. That's the way I look at it, and I would like to hear from anybody who don't feel the same way.'

"Albert was sittin' right across from Vito, and he looked him square in the eye as he stood up. Everybody noticed it, and everybody knew what it meant. There was a big silence. Nobody said a word, and that was all I was after — first, to teach Vito a lesson in public without him losin' face, and also to get the title without havin' to fight for it. So I won my first point, and frankly, I didn't give a shit what happened after that.

"Actually, that's not really true. Somethin' did happen that bothered me, because I didn't exactly win the next order of business. I figured I might as well beat Vito to the punch. I told the meetin' that when I was in Italy, I heard about the trouble between Vito and Albert. I said I also heard some news about other guys who was tryin' to move in on brothers, and I explained that every one of 'em was good friends of mine, and that they hadda make an effort to get along better with each other.

"I laughed when I said I didn't expect 'em to love each other, because I knew that was impossible. I reminded 'em of things that they liked to forget about — about the old Mustache Petes, about Masseria and Maranzano, and so forth. I told 'em that jealousy was our biggest enemy, jealousy of what some other guy in another outfit had. I told 'em about their own figures, their own takes, and their own profits, and I said unless any one of us was a greedy pig — I didn't look at Vito when I said it — that in our kind of business there was so much money to be made that nobody had the right to be jealous of nobody else.

"I must've talked for an hour, maybe more. When I felt that I had 'em goin' along with me complete, I got around to the subject of narcotics. That sorta made everybody sit up. I could see that they was all lookin' back and forth, from me to Vito, and it was very clear that he was gettin' real upset, because he knew what I was gonna say. I told 'em I wanted 'em to get the hell outa that business, to stop it right then and there, and to forget it. I said that they knew when I was a young punk, only nineteen, I had trouble with the stuff and it sent me to stir. And I reminded 'em about the other time in 1923, when it cost me a fortune.

"I told 'em it had become clear to me that there was so much dough to be made in everythin' else we had, why ruin it with the dangers of playin' around with junk that would only bring the federal guys down on us and the Interpol people that was startin' up in Paris. I tried to make 'em understand that everythin' was different now that the war was over; we was businessmen runnin' businesses and givin' people what they wanted in a way that didn't hurt nobody. People wanted to gamble, we helped 'em gamble;

they needed booze, cigarettes and meat durin' the war, we took care of that. Sure, here and there we would squeeze some guys, but on the other hand, look at all the money we was puttin' in circulation just from other good businessmen buyin' our protection. I said there wasn't a politician or a cop who could hold on to none of the money we paid him off with, that they spent it as soon as they got it, and that was very good for the American economy — to put money in circulation.

"When I said that, I looked right at Meyer Lansky and we both couldn't hold back laughin'. Then everybody else chimed in and it sorta eased up the tension.

"But it didn't mean a fuckin' thing. On the subject of narcotics, I could see I wasn't gettin' through. All the time I was talkin', most of 'em had stone in their faces. Then Steve Magaddino got up on my side. He told the story about Vito writin' him from Italy and what I said when he come to see me in stir. He made a very strong point by sayin' that jealousy was our number two enemy; junk was number one.

"That kinda opened up the discussion and I was a little shocked to see that almost all the guys didn't wanna go along with me. Frank Costello had the same feelin' and he leaned over and whispered to me, 'Charlie, don't hit your head against the wall. Vito rigged it before the meet started. Try to get out of it as soon as you can. Someday, they'll all be sorry.'

"I took his advice and I told the meetin' I would never go against the majority. But it was goddamn obvious to me that the majority wanted to play with fire and that's why I wanted to make one thing very clear; there was a son of a bitch by the name of Asslinger who couldn't think about nothin' else except that Charlie Lucky was king of junk. So I said, 'For chrissake, keep me out of it or else I'm gonna take an ad in the New York *Mirror* and declare myself.' That got another laugh. But Frank was right. Vito won that round. And it would cause more trouble in our outfit than anythin' we ever done up to that day."

Then a sober Meyer Lansky rose to discuss what he called "The Siegel Situation." (Siegel had not been informed of the meeting, since he would be the subject of major discussions and decisions; that he would learn of it no one doubted, but it was important that he learn only later.) Lansky focused on Siegel's current activities in the small, sleazy Nevada oasis called Las Vegas, in 1946 little more than a stopping-off place for east- and westbound travelers in need of food, water, gasoline and dry ice to cool their cars on the trips across the desert. Reno was then the state's thriving metropolis, thanks to quick divorce laws and legalized gambling in Nevada. But Siegel envisioned Las Vegas not merely as a rival. He was sure he could create an organized gambling Eldorado there that would turn the city into the promised land for the underworld, an oasis of glittering hotels with all the services and entertainment the high-rollers demanded. He had communicated his enthusiasm to his partners in the underworld and persuaded them to go along, with Luciano, then at Great Meadow, giving the final authorization in 1943.

So Benny Siegel started to work on his initial venture, a hotel and casino he named the Flamingo. Once he had owned an interest in Florida's Hialeah racetrack, where large flocks of pink flamingos nested in a lagoon in the infield and soon became the track's trademark. Siegel saw the bird as a good-luck omen and he adopted it. Its color, pink, would be the motif of the hotel; and to decorate the Flamingo in the most grandiose and lavish manner, he gave a free hand to his mistress, Virginia Hill. From that moment on, the Flamingo was Siegel's preoccupation, to the exclusion of almost everything else. Though he saw huge profits flowing from the legal gambling games, despite Nevada's taxes, he was realist enough to understand that he would have to provide more than the tables to woo customers from Reno. He planned to lure them with the finest food and best wines, the most luxurious accommodations and the biggest Hollywood stars — all at such low prices that no one would be able to pass Las Vegas by.

As the Flamingo rose, anything Siegel wanted, he got, through the influence and muscle of his underworld partners. In these first postwar years, construction materials were difficult to find, but pressures were put on suppliers and on the underworld-dominated Teamsters Union for the trucks to haul those supplies to the desert. And when Siegel needed more money, as his ideas far outran his budget, Lansky and others reached into the underworld treasury to provide it. When he had begun, Siegel had said that the Flamingo would cost one million dollars. By December 1946, Lansky told the delegates in Havana, the costs had skyrocketed to nearly six million. And with the hotel still unfinished a year after ground had been broken, Lansky said, Siegel had even turned to outsiders for more money, soliciting his friends in Beverly Hills and throughout the movie colony, telling them, "You're in on the ground floor of the biggest gold mine in the world."

Some of those outside investors, disgruntled at the long delays in the Flamingo's opening, had begun to complain. Led by an executive of American Distillers named Samuel Rothberg and his brother, C. Harry Rothberg, who between them had put up more than $250,000, a number of the private investors started to make motions about taking an active role in the operations to protect their money. To forestall such a move, Siegel realized that some visible evidence of his success was necessary, and so he announced that the hotel and casino would open on December 26, 1946, even before it was completed.

Much of this was known to the Havana delegates; for some time their anger at Siegel had been growing as they watched their own multimillion-dollar investment in his hotel seemingly going down the drain. If Siegel could, indeed, make a success, they would smile on him again. But Siegel's old partner, Lansky, had news that deepened the frowns. He had learned, he said, from sources in the private banks he dealt with in Zurich that Virginia Hill had been making regular trips abroad, accumulating an unusually large wardrobe, that she had taken a long lease on an apartment in Switzerland, and, most disturbing, that she had deposited more than three hundred thousand dollars in a numbered account in a Zurich bank.

"There was no doubt in Meyer's mind that Bugsy had skimmed this dough from his buildin' budget, and he was sure that Siegel was preparin' to skip as well as skim, in case the roof was gonna fall in on him. Everybody listened very close while Lansky explained it. When he got through, somebody asked, 'What do you think we oughta do, Meyer?' Lansky said, 'There's only one thing to do with a thief who steals from his friends. Benny's got to be hit.'

"So it was put to a vote. Naturally, Meyer and Phil Kastel didn't have no votes, but that didn't make no difference; the result was unanimous, and Bugsy was as good as dead. Then it was decided the contract should be handled by Charlie Fischetti, and he said he would be in touch with Jack Dragna on the Coast. Jack was the outfit's number two guy in Los Angeles under Bugsy, but that wouldn't cut no ice because he would do what he was ordered.

"Then Meyer got up again and said he recommended that the hit shouldn't be made until after the Flamingo opened. If the place was a success, there was ways to take care of Benny for stealin' without bumpin' him off, and he could be made to pay back the money. Benny had been a valuable guy for a long time, almost from the beginnin' with me and Lansky and Costello, so none of us really wanted to see him get it. But if the Flamingo was a flop, well, that'd be it for him."

By Christmas eve, the pressure of that day-long meeting and a number of smaller discussions that followed had brought the delegates to a point where a break was necessary. Wives and girl friends arrived and that night a gala holiday party was held at the Nacional, ostensibly in honor of Frank Sinatra, but in reality for Luciano. The food was good and plentiful and so were the wines, the liquors and the entertainment. The celebration lasted until early in the morning. But the Havana papers the next day, and throughout the week, failed to mention any of the activities at the hotel. "In them days, the word was around that what was goin' on at the Hotel Nacional was off limits. There was maybe twenty papers in Havana, but that was a place where the politician was boss and it was easy to lose a license to publish a paper if you ran somethin' you wasn't supposed to."

Once again, on the night of December 26, the delegates gathered in the conference room, this time to wait for news from Las Vegas. The time difference was three hours and so it was long after midnight, on the twenty-seventh, when telephone reports about the long-awaited opening of the Flamingo began to arrive. The first news was not good. The weather in Las Vegas was cold and raining.

Lansky took Luciano aside and told him, "Charlie, with that kind of weather, only a miracle can save the Flamingo. And there's somethin' else I have to tell you. Before I left New York I asked some questions about opening a hotel the day after Christmas, and some people in show business up there laughed at me. They said the week between Christmas and New Year's is like Death Row as far as entertainment is concerned."

"I knew Meyer was right. Benny was so desperate to make a showin' he took the big chance to beat the odds on show business. Of course, he did have one thing goin' for him, a terrific show. I hoped against hope that maybe all of this talent would attract business and bail Benny out."

Siegel had, indeed, rounded up talent that normally might have insured success. He had enticed George Jessel as master of ceremonies, Xavier Cugat and his band to provide the music, and Jimmy Durante and George Raft to star in the show and greet the customers. But at three A.M. in Havana, a telephone call to Lansky revealed that almost no one had come to see, listen and gamble, and the opening of the Flamingo had been a flop.

When Lansky passed around the news, rage boiled over, and there were loud voices demanding that the contract on Siegel be fulfilled with dispatch. Lansky, however, advised caution, suggested a short delay. In the meantime, he said, the Los Angeles lawyers for the Flamingo should explore the advisability of throwing the hotel corporation into receivership. This, he said, would put a stop to the losses. Then, the outfit could form a new syndicate to buy out the original corporation and its creditors at pennies on the dollar. To those who thought such a move might mean just pouring more money down the rathole, Lansky was blunt. He still had complete faith in Siegel's vision that Las Vegas could be turned into a gambling gold mine; it was just a matter of going about it the right way. Lansky was persuasive. With the approval of Luciano and the council, he immediately set to work on his plan. By the middle of January, the Flamingo was closed, and then new money was poured in from the underworld to put it into shape before a second opening. As for Benny Siegel, he had been reprieved — for the moment.

"Naturally, we was pretty damn depressed about what happened in Vegas, and nobody felt like talkin' much to nobody else that night. By this time it was four o'clock in the mornin'. I started to leave, but Vito stopped me and asked could I come up to his suite on the top floor. He said he had some things he wanted to talk to me about, private. So I said, okay, figurin' now he was gonna finish what he wanted to say when he come out to my house when he first arrived in Havana. We went upstairs, not sayin' a word. Then he closes the door, turns to me and says, 'Charlie, I want half of Italy.' I looked at him like he was crazy. I said, 'Vito, what are you talkin' about?' "

Genovese said, "Charlie, after all, I set up that whole thing in Europe — the black market, the truck routes to Germany, everything. It's all yours and you were operating it before you got here, and it's waitin' for you when you get back."

Luciano was puzzled. "You're nuts, Vito. I ain't goin' back. I'm stayin' in Cuba."

Genovese shrugged. "I understand different. I heard that Washington knows you're in Havana and they're gettin' ready to put the screws on these jerks in Cuba to get you thrown out. There's gonna be so much heat that nobody can do nothin' to help you. Charlie, you're gonna have to get outa here and go back to Italy. By rights, everything that's over there is half mine — and I want it."

"So that fat little son of a bitch finally coughed it up. But he wasn't kiddin' me. He never had that edge on me, because I could read him like a book. The dirty cock was tryin' to take me. It was like an obsession with him, and it come to me that minute that there was no difference between Vito Genovese and that prick Asslinger; they had the same idea in common — get Charlie Lucky Luciano. Maybe Asslinger figured he'd be a big man if he could nail me, like Vito figured if he could muscle me out he would finally get up that last step of the ladder and be the Boss of Bosses.

"Just as sure as I was alive it meant that Vito had tipped off Washington about my bein' in Havana and probably made it sound like I was handlin' junk. So what could I do? I called him a greedy fuckin' pig to his face and he starts callin' me a few things. I lose my temper maybe once in five years and that was the day. As we was yellin' at each other, it suddenly come back into my head what that shitheel had done during the war, how he managed to set up all them pipelines that he's braggin' about when he was workin' hand-in-glove in Italy with our enemies and with the Nazis, all durin' the time they was tryin' to beat his own country in the war. So I done somethin' that I never done before, and it was against all the rules that I myself set up. I pushed him up against the wall and I beat the livin' daylights out of him.

"He was a tough little prick, but I was bigger and a helluva lot tougher. Besides, I was damn mad. I started to knock him around the room like he was a rubber ball. I didn't hit him in the face — I didn't want to mark him up. I just belted him in the guts and in the kidneys, and when he fell down I just started to kick him in the belly, and every shot I took with my fists and my foot I told him he was only a shit and a son of a bitch and a dirty rotten Neapolitan louse — even worse, he was a fink American who turned on his own country like a fuckin' traitor.

"I beat him up so bad he couldn't get out of his room for three days. The only guy who knew about it was Anastasia, because when Vito was layin' on the floor, out like a light and not movin', I suddenly thought maybe I broke somethin' inside him. So I went over to Albert's room and brought him back to Vito's suite with me. Then I got a doctor to patch him up. The doc knew Lansky and he also knew how to keep his mouth shut."

Luciano had broken three of Genovese's ribs and fractured his left arm, in addition to afflicting countless bruises all over his body. The next morning, Luciano told Lansky of the fight and asked him to make certain the doctor permitted no visitors to Genovese. Then they circulated the story that Genovese was in bed with a sudden attack of a virulent and contagious form of the flu, and that while he could have no visitors, he would welcome fruit, flowers and personal get-well messages — and they poured in through the next days.

"What I done to Vito was very serious. It could've meant that he could have me over a barrel; he could even have called for a 'table' and asked to have me knocked off. But I wasn't worried. For one thing, who the hell'd believe Vito over me? There wasn't a mark on him, except around his body, and we had already fixed up the doc to say that he'd slipped in the bathtub. Then, just before me and Albert put him on the plane, while we was ridin' to the airport in the car, I said to him, 'Don Vitone, if by any chance you should make the mistake of mentionin' what happened between us to anybody else, then I — Charlie Luciano — will get back into New York, if only long enough to do a final job on you.

I'll walk right up to you and I'll put a gun between your eyes and I'll blow your fuckin' brains out. You won't get it in the back, the way you like to do it, you Neapolitan prick.'

"I don't believe Genovese ever told nobody, because it never come back to me. But when I saw that bastard get on the plane, I turned to Albert and I said, 'As long as that round tub of shit is alive, we can never rest easy, none of us. I figure he's got some angle with Washington and all we can do is wait until it develops — if it does.' "

It did not take long for Luciano's fears to bear fruit. By early in January, word that the mysterious resident of Quinta Avenida was none other than Lucky Luciano had spread among the other Americans living in Miramar. "I was really surprised how many invitations I got to cocktail parties and dinners and things like that. It reminded me of the good old days in the late twenties and early thirties when all the society people around New York used to want me to come to their home, like I was some kinda celebrity. I guess I was a little nutty for acceptin' them invites, but I just couldn't help it. I was dyin' to be with American people who was straight and legit and had nothin' to do with the rackets. Some of the guys belonged to good golf clubs and it made me feel I was back in Westchester and Connecticut, like in the days before I went to the can. The way things turned out, it all led to a lotta trouble."

An American freelance journalist named Henry Wallace, a stringer for a number of papers in the United States and gossip columnist for the English-language Havana *Post,* spotted a familiar face one night during his rounds. He was told the man was a recent arrival named Salvatore Lucanía. It did not take Wallace long to discover that Lucanía was, in fact, Lucky Luciano.

"This guy Wallace comes up to me in a club and says he knows who I am. He tells me he's a reporter and he's gonna write about me bein' in Havana instead of Italy where they shipped me. Then he stood and kinda waited. Well, I knew what he was after, but I played it straight. Finally he says he could protect me, not let it out who I was and so forth. The creep was just tryin' to shake me down. I got a couple guys to throw him out of the joint and I guess they done it a little rough. That was a big mistake on my part, because I found out that Wallace was a very close friend of two important officials in Havana. One was no less than the chief of the Cuban secret police, named Benito Herrera; and the other guy was the Minister of the Interior, Alfredo Pequeno.

"Then I met this beautiful girl at one of them American parties. Her name was Beverly Paterno and she was high up in New York café society. Well, I'm only human and pretty soon we was goin' everywhere together, to the racetrack, the clubs and restaurants. But how in hell did I know this broad was crazy for publicity? It's one thing to go around with a good-lookin' girl who's also good in the hay, but why the fuck did she have to hire a press agent to advertise every place we was goin' before we got there? It got so we could never make a move without a million flashbulbs poppin' in our puss, and our pictures was all over the papers in Havana. Then all of a sudden, the New York papers was blazin' with headlines that Charlie Lucky Luciano, the king of vice and narcotics, was runnin' crime practically on the doorstep of the United States. I guess that guy Wallace had a hand in that."

When the story broke, Lansky immediately went to see his friend Batista at his Miami home. He was assured that while Luciano had been unwise in his social life, nothing would be done to force him out of Cuba so long as he held a legal Italian passport and Cuban visa and could prove a legitimate business reason for being in the country — his interest in the Hotel Nacional's casino.

Lansky brought that news to Luciano. "I guess Meyer thought this'd make me feel better, but it didn't cheer me up too much. I had one of them hunches of mine that trouble hadn't even started."

He was right. In February, Harry Anslinger declared that as long as Luciano remained in the western hemisphere he was a danger to the safety of the United States; he sent a formal demand to Cuba for Luciano's expulsion. Cuban authorities at first refused to do more than politely acknowledge the Narcotics Bureau chief's note. "I made a real good friend, a guy by the name of Indalicio Pertiere, who was a Cuban congressman and also the head of the Jockey Club that ran the racetrack I liked to go to. He was always broke from losin' at his own track and I used to help him out. Because he was a nice fella, he tried to help me. He arranged that some other congressmen should join him in havin' Cuba tell Washington that I wasn't breakin' no Cuban laws and so why the hell should they throw me out."

A similar response came from Police Chief Herrera and Interior Minister Pequeno. They advised the American Embassy in Havana that while they were aware of Luciano's presence, they had no evidence that he was doing anything illegal. Said Pequeno, Luciano "is a dangerous character and a perjurer, to be sure. But his papers are in perfect order."

"As much as I appreciated what them guys was tryin' to do, I knew their help wouldn't hold up if Asslinger decided to get tough. And I couldn't shake the feelin' I had about Vito blowin' the whistle on me in Washington. I called Meyer and Frank Costello over to Havana and we talked about the situation. I knew that the American system where you're supposed to be innocent until they prove you guilty didn't hold up for me. Look what happened to me with Dewey. So, if somebody said that Charlie Lucky is runnin' junk out of Havana, well, them guys in Washington was sure I hadda be doin' it. Things didn't look good."

Cuba's refusal to act sent Anslinger to President Truman. He told the President that in recent months the narcotics traffic from Havana to the United States had increased sharply. The reason: Luciano's presence in Havana, for, Anslinger said, Luciano was directing the business. It was vital for American security that the Cubans be forced to send him back to Italy. Anslinger was persuasive and Truman gave him the power to take whatever steps were necessary to accomplish his end. Anslinger promptly announced publicly that until Cuba sent Luciano back to Italy, and no place but Italy, the United States would embargo all shipments of ethical drugs and other vital medical supplies to Cuba.

Cuban President Ramón Grau San Martín was outraged at the "injustice" of the American threat. Dr. Jose Andreu, the country's director of public health and a signatory to the International Convention covering the use of drugs by all nations, not only disputed Anslinger's claim that Luciano was behind an upsurge in illegal narcotics traffic but also asserted that there was "no legal force able to choke off Cuba's supply of legitimate drugs while it complies with the provisions of the agreement." The American actions, he said, were "arbitrary and unjust." But these were only words. For the Cubans, in reality, had little choice but to accede to the threats and demands; the country had no capacity to manufacture the much-needed medicines and was totally dependent on the United States for them.

"They say you can't fight City Hall, but that never bothered me, because I used to buy City Hall. But I couldn't figure how I was gonna buy the whole Treasury Department in Washington. I figured that my plans to stay in Cuba was pretty well fucked up."

As the pressure from Anslinger mounted, Batista and Lansky met again. Batista held that President Grau San Martín would not be able to resist the American pressure for long. Thus, Luciano should make the first move and voluntarily leave Cuba. Batista would arrange for him to maintain his interest in the casino at the Hotel Nacional, and when times changed — with Dewey's election as President in 1948, which seemed a sure bet, or Batista's return to the Cuban presidency about the same time — Luciano would be able to return.

Luciano, however, was still not prepared to surrender. He felt that his position at the top of the American underworld would be jeopardized if he left Havana to return to Italy. "I had a pretty good lawyer in Havana, a guy by the name of Gonzalez, who was friendly with President Grau San Martín. So, he and some Cuban senators cooked up an idea to help me fight back. They would ask Grau San Martín to cut off the shipment of sugar to the United States if Asslinger's embargo was allowed to stick. I thought it was a terrific idea except for one thing: Gonzalez told me that in the end we would lose.

"Then, one day I'm havin' lunch in a restaurant; it was a Saturday afternoon, I think it was February 23, and the assistant police chief, Hernandez, come up to my table and arrested me. His boss, Benito Herrera, didn't have the heart to do this to me personally." Luciano was placed under house arrest and given a few days to settle his affairs. Then he was thrown into the Tiscoria Immigration Camp until his ultimate fate was decided. "It's the Cuban version of Ellis Island, but what a difference. It was surrounded by a big swamp, hot as a son of a bitch and so humid that your clothes just stuck to your body. I knew I couldn't take that very long. It was the same old story of what happened to me in Italy. When the big United States started to put the squeeze on a little country like Cuba, what choice did they have?"

While Luciano sweltered and waited, the Cubans tried to strike some kind of compromise that would somehow satisfy everyone. They would grant Anslinger his demand that Luciano be expelled, but they proposed that instead of sending him to Italy, he should be permitted to seek sanctuary elsewhere — say in Caracas, for the Venezuelan government had agreed to grant him a residency permit. But Anslinger was adamant. If the Cubans wanted the embargo lifted, they would send Luciano to Italy and nowhere else.

"So I told my Cuban friends to forget it, that I would agree to go back to Italy and not take the matter to court. In other words, I volunteered to go just so Asslinger couldn't put the last nail in my coffin. The only thing I asked for was that I could buy first-class transportation on a boat. But Asslinger put so much pressure on the Cuban government that I hadda leave almost instantly, and the only boat goin' out to Italy that week was a cargo steamer called the S.S. *Bakir*. When I heard that tub was a Turkish boat, I just threw my hands up and said, well, that clinches it. Turkey and narcotics are one and the same; now, for sure, Charlie Luciano has to be tabbed as the king of junk."

28.

It took the S.S. *Bakir* more than a month to make the trip from Havana to Genoa. "The weather was so lousy the goddamn ship felt like it was gonna go under at least four or five times a day. And it wasn't like when I went back on the *Laura Keene;* I knew then that somehow I was gonna get back to America or some place close to it. But this trip looked like it might be for good, unless I could come up with somethin' that would get me outa the spot

Asslinger had put me into. You'd think more than four weeks on the ocean would give you time to plan anythin'. But all the angles I could think of or invent just come back to one thing. My only hope was that Tom Dewey would beat Harry Truman in 1948. I'm not much of a guy for prayin'. But much as I hated Dewey for what he done to me, I used to pray every night that he would make it to the White House in '48. With Truman, I didn't stand a chance. With Dewey, I bought him once, so there hadda be a way to buy him again."

The freighter docked at Genoa on April 11, 1947, and Luciano was promptly taken into custody by police. He expected that this was a mere formality, that he would be sent immediately back to Lercara Friddi and that once again he would quickly be able to arrange the same kind of unrestricted status as before. But now there were those determined that this would not occur. Premier Alcide de Gasperi was greatly concerned about the publicity surrounding Luciano — about his activities in Italy, his departure, his Cuban adventures, his return to Italy, and speculation about what he would do now. De Gasperi was about to meet with a dozen top leaders of his Christian Democratic Party in Sicily to discuss strategy for the forthcoming national election, and he wanted nothing, like Luciano's presence on the island, to interfere. It was the premier's wish that Luciano be sequestered, in Genoa's Marassi Prison, until after the party caucus and then be returned to Lercara Friddi and held there.

De Gasperi was not the only one holding a jaundiced view of Luciano. The new inspector general of police in Palermo, Dr. Giuseppe Massara, did not look upon him kindly. He asked Genoa police to arrest Luciano on his arrival and hold him in prison until a determination of his status could be made by a special high commission sitting in Palermo, a commission composed of the chief of police, the prefect of Palermo, a *carabinieri* officer, a judge and a private citizen, with Luciano represented by a lawyer of his own choosing. At the conclusion of its hearings, the commission was given power to hand down one of three decisions: that Luciano was a menace to the country and should be confined to Lercara Friddi for not more than five years, after which his case would come up for review; that he be strongly admonished to behave himself and then be permitted to live anywhere he wanted in Sicily, with the condition that his movements be restricted by a nightly curfew and that he report daily to the police; or that he be given unrestricted freedom with the warning not to get into trouble and notice that a single infraction of any law would bring him immediately before the commission for stern punishment.

For some weeks, the commission heard testimony and arguments. Authorities demanded the most extreme decision, for Luciano was a peril to the state. His lawyers, Cesare D'Angel-Antonio and Antonio Calasudo, maintained that Luciano was the victim of an unremitting vendetta by the American police and that he had been released from prison in the United States "because authorities realized the injustice of the sentence." Luciano testified in his own behalf, and told the commission that he had returned to Italy of his own free will, and had not been deported from Cuba. "I never intended to abandon my Italian citizenship," he declared.

On May 14, 1947 — the feast day of San Fortunato, or, in a free translation, Saint Lucky, as some Italian reporters noted whimsically — the commission reached its decision. Luciano was to be released from jail in Genoa and given full freedom. He was not "socially dangerous," the commission held, and added, "In this moment, you, Salvatore Lucanía, are a free citizen who has the right not to be molested and to live his own life, but who at the same time has the duty to behave himself like a gentleman. . . . You must abstain from any illicit activity."

For the next several weeks, Luciano remained in Palermo, but by the end of June he had persuaded friendly authorities to permit him to move once more to Rome. He stopped off in Naples for a week or so, to pick up his contacts and reestablish himself at the head of the still-thriving black market, still a necessity and a basic way of life for most Italians.

He took the time, too, while in Naples to travel across the bay to the slopes of Mount Vesuvius to see Father Francesco "Ciccio" Scarpato. They had met a year earlier, in 1946, when Don Cheech, as the priest was familiarly called, was ministering to the spiritual needs of unreleased Italian prisoners of war at the Palermo detention camp and waiting for permission from American authorities to return to his own mainland parish, from which he had been absent while serving as an Italian army chaplain during the war. That parish at Massa di Soma, one of scores of small villages dotting the slopes of Vesuvius, had been buried under molten lava from the volcano's eruption in 1944. Excavation was proceeding slowly and Don Cheech had sought out the famous American *milionario* for financial help so that when he returned he could speed up the work. Luciano had given it.

At their new meeting at Massa di Soma, Luciano found the returned priest beset by additional troubles. He was in the midst of a bitter struggle with a militant Communist Party, led by Russian-trained Ivan Montoni, that had taken control of the village administration. He asked Luciano for more help and more money. Such assistance, he said, could be vital in his battle with the Communists for the people's loyalty, for it would demonstrate to the villagers that he, a simple priest, had direct and personal access to the limitless funds of the famous American from New York.

"Don Cheech was a little, roly-poly guy and he had a smile that was terrific. How can you turn down a guy like that who's dedicated to nothin' but the best things in life for everybody else but who don't ask nothin' for himself? So I give him some dough. He needed an altar for the church, too, and he wanted to replace the religious pictures the volcano had destroyed and things like that, so I helped him with them things, too. Most of all, he told me he needed to be able to say that Lucky Luciano was his friend and would help him. From what I could see later, it helped, and I was proud that he was knockin' the shit outa the Communists up there."

In the third week of June 1947, Luciano was still in Naples, preparing to move at last to Rome, when events in California sent Italian police descending upon him.

On the afternoon of June 20, Bugsy Siegel was having his weekly manicure at Harry Drucker's barbershop in Beverly Hills and talking to a friend, Carl Laemmle, Jr., the film producer. Siegel was in a relaxed mood. His two daughters, he said, were on their way from New York to spend the summer with him, and he was expecting his girl friend, Virginia Hill, to return from a European trip any day. And, too, his business was beginning to improve. The Flamingo had finally been completed and reopened in March, and though at first its luck was bad and the hotel and casino both lost money, things had turned around by May and the enterprise was at last climbing into the black. When Siegel left the barbershop, he was smiling.

That night, at ten-thirty, he was relaxing in the living room of his Beverly Hills mansion on North Linden Drive with a friend, Allen Smiley. Upstairs, Virginia's brother, Charles "Chick" Hill, was with his girl friend, Jerry Mason. Suddenly, a fusillade from a .30-30 carbine crashed through the living room window. One bullet tore through Siegel's head, ripping out his eye. Four other bullets smashed into his body, cracking ribs and tearing his lungs, and three more missed. Smiley was unharmed, but Benny Siegel's career had come to a sudden and dramatic end. The last item on the agenda of the Christmas meeting in Havana had been disposed of.

Hardly had the echoes of the gunfire in Beverly Hills faded when, two hundred miles away in Las Vegas, a trio of Meyer Lansky's men walked into the Flamingo and advised the staff that they were taking over, "on orders." Gus Greenbaum and Morris Rosen, long employed by Lansky in his gambling empire in Miami, Havana and elsewhere, would henceforth manage the hotel and casino, while Morris Sidwirtz, better known as Moe Sedway, would be in charge of relations between the hotel staff and guests.

While those events were taking place in America, it was already the morning of June 21 in Italy. When the news reached Naples, the Guardia di Finanza, acting on orders of American officials in Washington, took Luciano into custody to question him about the Siegel murder. But to all questions, he had the same answer: "Beverly Hills is seven thousand miles away from here. How in the world could I have anything to do with a murder of an old friend?"

"I never knew who actually done the job on Bugsy. But I remember that Jack Dragna had a rep for bein' a pretty sharp shot.

But I really didn't know and I didn't care who done it. All they hadda tell me was the results."

The Siegel murder, however, left some loose ends — most important, Virginia Hill. "I didn't know this Virginia. She was apparently a good-lookin' girl from the South somewhere, and Adonis was the first one to latch on to her when she come to New York. He give her a job workin' our numbers bank and I heard that she was a real crackpot, slept around a lot and so forth. Naturally, after Bugsy went, she was a big danger because she knew too much. There was one thing everybody was sure of — on them nights that Bugsy spent on the pillow with her, he spilled enough into her pink ear about the outfit and the top guys that could cause plenty of trouble. The logical thing was to get rid of her. But we had a big bookmaker in Chicago, Joe Epstein, who handled our layoffs and he was nuts about her; he kept protectin' her, sendin' her money, even durin' the time she was with Bugsy. In fact, practically all the guys in the outfit who ever laid her — and that just about included everybody — stood up for her to make sure she didn't get hit. Besides, Lansky wanted to get his hands on that dough in Switzerland.

"But Virginia was scared to use the money, even though we heard that lots of times she was pretty bad off. When the Kefauver hearin's started in the States a couple years later, Virginia was subpoenaed to testify. She got in touch with me in Naples and wanted to come to see me. I knew that meant a shakedown. So the boys arranged that if she would keep her mouth shut, we would let her dig into the Swiss account, keep some of the money, and return the rest to the treasury in New York. She never spent none of it until after the Kefauver hearin's was over and we could be sure she done the right thing as far as we was concerned when she testified. She got a lotta laughs on the witness stand but she never really said nothin'."

In March 1966, Virginia Hill committed suicide.

The questioning of Luciano about the Siegel murder was brief and futile. He was soon released and quickly departed Naples for Rome, where he took a suite at the Savoia Hotel just off the Via Veneto. He remained there only briefly before moving back to the Excelsior, where he could look out directly over the fashion-able boulevard. There he registered as "Sig. Salvatore Lucanía — Palermo, Sicily."

In Rome, he soon became a target for the cameras of the Italian *paparazzi,* the freelance photographers who descend with an en-raging unconcern for privacy on the famous and infamous. On the advice of his lawyers, Luciano refused all requests for inter-views and photographs. "But it didn't make no difference whether I talked to them bastards or not; they made up stories anyway, just to print somethin'. There was hardly a day when some news-paper didn't publish a story that Lucky Luciano was the biggest tourist attraction in Italy next to the Isle of Capri.

"From the time I got back to Rome in June of '47, I never did nothin' really bad. I mean, only black marketing and the changin' of money, like before. Even though everybody in the country was doin' it, I hadda be especially careful, 'cause I was the 'gang boss' and everywhere I went, guys with cameras was followin' me. And that Asslinger wasn't gonna give up on me just because the com-mission in Sicily said I could walk around like a human bein'. I got tipped off the American Embassy in Rome had orders to force the Italian police to keep me under surveillance. I couldn't hardly turn around without fallin' over them guys."

But still, despite the surveillance and the pressures of American authorities in Italy, Luciano maintained his power over the under-world in the United States. His deportation did not change this. No important decision that might affect the future of organized crime in the United States, he said, was made without his consul-tation and advice during the next decade.

There were personal contacts and couriers arriving and depart-ing with his messages regularly. And he set up a secondary channel for written communications. Two friendly American Army offi-cers, one in Naples and the other in Rome, let him use their APO addresses in Italy. Incoming letters were usually in pink envelopes and postmarked from Brooklyn or one of several cities in New Jersey, with no return addresses.

The couriers who arrived with messages often went away with oral replies from Luciano. But they brought not merely word from the United States; they brought, too, packages of American currency, averaging, he said, twenty-five thousand dollars a month; this was his allotment to himself from the profits of the enterprises his partners were running for him back home. There were also profits from the casino in Havana and other underworld investments he held jointly with Lansky and others, and this money was allowed to accumulate, to be used for any unforeseen emergency or as a fund for future investments.

Always, in whatever he did, Luciano was forced to be wary, for he knew that the American narcotics authorities in Italy were constantly attempting to trap him. "Almost every day, guys would come up to me with some kind of deal, a way to make a quick buck. I'll bet about half of them promotions had to do with narcotics. It was just what I was scared about in Havana, when I had the fight with Vito. No matter what I would say or do, or try to do, Asslinger and his whole organization was set on trippin' me up for pushin' junk, one way or another. So I took steps to make sure as possible that it didn't happen."

What Luciano did was to arrange with his hotel managers wherever he lived in Italy that the same domestics cleaned his suite or apartment daily, and only when he or a friend was present. He had the only key to his apartment, and no one was to enter when he was not there. No mail or packages could be delivered to the apartment; they were handed to him in the lobby and opened in the presence of the desk clerk or the manager. "A couple years later, I put guys on my payroll in order to protect myself from every son of a bitch who wanted 'Charlie Lucky's help.' I used John Raimundo — he was called 'Cockeye' because that's what he was, cockeyed — and a fella by the name of Joe Di Giorgio to find out what guys wanted before they could see me. It sounded like I was actin' like a big shot, but I hadda worry all the time about police guys and dope agents in Italy and America who wanted to make a big name by nailin' Lucky Luciano. Joe and John done all the checkin' on things for me, and I trusted 'em all through the years."

In the late fall of 1947, despite American help advanced through the newly conceived Marshall Plan to aid European recovery, Italy was still destitute. Much of the money for reconstruction, employment and more failed to reach the workers as Italian industrialists and politicians siphoned off dollars. American charities, especially the Salvation Army, stepped in to aid the poor. Large shipments of clothing were sent to Italy for free distribution. Again, this help was blocked — this time by petty Italian gangsters. They knew that freezing people would spend whatever they had for clothes to keep themselves and their children warm. The racketeers hijacked the clothing and began selling it at huge prices on the black market, and the police seemed powerless to intervene.

"One day a priest come to see me at the Hotel Excelsior. At first he was a little embarrassed to get the words out, but I told him just to say it out loud. So he explained about the clothes bein' hijacked. He figured that because I was the big American gangster, I could help fight fire with fire. I think this priest's name was Father Moldato and he had his parish near my hotel. The day he come to see me it was so cold in Rome that you could freeze your balls off. And right down below my window on the corner of the Via Veneto, them thieves was sellin' Salvation Army clothes at Fifth Avenue prices. I thought it was a real rotten racket and I told the Father that I would look into it. After all, thief or no thief, there has to be a limit to how far a crook can go."

Luciano made contact with the Italian gangsters. "I don't even remember their names no more; I think one guy was called Vittorio and he seemed to be one of the leaders of the whole setup all over the country. I got this clothes hijacker and his pals together for a meet. It was in a garden restaurant around the corner from the Excelsior; it was closed because of the cold weather. I knew the owner and he let me use the joint. These guys knew who I was, and I told 'em, 'Cut out the fuckin' hijackin' of American clothes — or else.' They started to argue with me, but I said to them, 'If I walk outa here, ten minutes later you'll all be dead. So gimme your answer right now and don't shit around.' So the hijackin' of the Salvation Army shipments stopped right away, and from then on them clothes reached where they was supposed to be goin'. The only compromise I made with them pricks was that they could sell the stuff they already socked away, and that would be it.

"A couple days later, the priest comes to me again. His parish had just received a whole bunch of clothes for kids and older people, diapers for babies, Christ knows what. He thanks me all over the place and says to me that people should know what I done, to understand I'm not the big American monster Washington wanted everybody in Italy to believe. Not more'n two days later, some newspaper guys was told about it by the Father and they started to write stories that I was the one behind the used rags racket and was makin' a fuckin' killin' on it. That's the way it always was for me.

"Then, as I started to think about it, I realized that the Father was right when he come to me with the idea of fightin' fire with fire, on account of I was an expert. Nobody never thought to use me like that before, and I told the priest about it. I'll never forget what he done. He reached out and put his arms around me and said, 'There's fire in all of us, my son. Now you are beginning to learn for the first time how to control it. I give you a blessing for what you have done.'

"The next night I got the first results of that blessin'. I met Igea."

29.

"I first set eyes on Igea Lissoni before the Christmas holidays in 1947. There was a lotta days in my whole lifetime that was especially important and they stayed with me clear as crystal. But that was the most important one."

Igea Lissoni was then twenty-six; Luciano was fifty. One of several children of a bourgeois family from Milan, where culture and the arts are a way of life, she early revealed a talent for dancing and was encouraged by her family, who enrolled her in the ballet school of La Scala Opera Company. Though she later danced in the company's corps de ballet, it soon became apparent to her that she did not have the talent to become a prima ballerina and so the slender, blonde Igea turned from ballet to nightclubs, becoming a featured performer in some of the better clubs in Italy immediately after the war.

"She was dancin' in a club in Rome. It was like some instant thing happened. I was acquainted with the guy that ran the club and I told him I wanted to meet the dame that was dancin'. After the show, he brought her over to my table. He called me Signor Lucanía, but she must've recognized me from my pictures in the papers and she froze up. Without sayin' a word, she got up and walked away. Now, I never had no trouble meetin' broads before that; in fact, it seemed like they all wanted to meet me, so I didn't have no idea I was gonna have any trouble with her."

Luciano returned to the club again and again, but with no success. "It happens that I knew a girl by the name of Loretta Masiero who was a big singin' star in those days and she was married to a guy named Johnny Dorelli, who was like the Bing Crosby of Italy. Loretta knew Igea real well, so I tried to have her fix things up for me. A couple of nights later, she brought Igea over to the table where we all was and even though she talked a little bit, she was still givin' me the cold shoulder. Igea was a girl from a good family and the idea of bein' seen with a gangster like me just went against everythin' she was ever taught. And I guess more important, she was from Milan and I was a Sicilian. As far as Italians was concerned, that meant like she was on top of the skyscraper and I was in the cellar."

But Luciano persisted. He began to court Igea in an old-fashioned, gallant way, sending her flowers and presents, waited for her every night at the café, calling on every lesson in charm and polish he had learned. "All my life until then, I never needed nobody. It was always easy come, easy go, and there was always another broad another night. After a few weeks of Igea playin' hard to get, which is somethin' that never happened to me before, I found I was thinkin' about her all the time. None of the other broads meant nothin' to me. In the beginnin', I thought she was just playin' a cute game, but when it went on I realized she wasn't foolin'. Now, I don't claim to know what love is. But when I began thinkin' about her all day long, about bein' with her and doin'

336

little things with her, one thing I became sure of — Igea Lissoni was no one-night stand."

Luciano's persistence finally succeeded. In the spring of 1948, a few months after they had met, Igea Lissoni went to live with him as his mistress. "I wanted to marry her. She was the only girl I ever loved in my whole life; in fact, she was my whole life, and she was the only girl I ever wanted to marry. But as it worked out, we couldn't get married. She was willin' to live with me, just like we was man and wife. She even wore a gold weddin' band. When she first took up with me, I used to wonder what made a nice girl like her hook up with a hoodlum like me. It was months before I had guts enough to ask her. It was so simple when she explained it to me I should've realized it. She said, 'That you were an American gangster or perhaps that you were in trouble with the police had nothing to do with it. It is merely that I discovered what every woman must have — you love me and you need me.'

"Before we started to live together in my apartment at the Excelsior Hotel, it seemed like all we did was talk. Sometimes I felt like this was my first girl and I never knew nobody before her. But I leveled with Igea like with nobody else in my life; I told her everythin' she wanted to know and a lot of things she didn't. One night, we was havin' dinner alone in a little garden restaurant outside Rome. I was tellin' her about the way things was in America, all about New York, and then I started to tell her about my trial. She stopped me all of a sudden and she said, 'Sharlie, no more. No more, now or ever. I know only one thing; you love me.' That night she come back to my place at the Excelsior and it was the first time we ever made love. No girl I ever knew could compare with Igea. That night was the last time we talked about marriage. She asked me if I wanted children and I told her I'd like to have ten but we couldn't even afford to have none. What kind of a life could it be for a kid of Lucky Luciano? That'd be sentencin' the kid to a life of misery before he was born, and I couldn't do that. I thought that might bust us up, but Igea understood what I was gettin' at, without a million words of explanation. And there was another thing. I told her with my kind of life, maybe she could be a widow any minute, because somebody would put a slug in me. So, if she married me, she could have all my dough, everythin'.

337

But she didn't want that. All she said was, 'Sharlie, I don't want your money, any of it. I want you.' What the hell could you say to that?"

Igea made only a single demand when she moved in with Luciano: that they leave the Excelsior, where he was too accessible to the constant parade of "business" offers that could put him in danger with the Italian police and with Anslinger. They moved to the more residential Hotel di Savoia, but even there those with propositions for Luciano to enter the narcotics traffic managed to evade the hotel security and camp outside his third-floor suite. Finally, Igea proposed that they abandon the nomadic life of hotel dwellers and find a permanent home.

"If that was what she wanted, I figured what the hell, why not. We started to look for an apartment and about a week later we found one in the Parioli." In that exclusive, parklike residential section of Rome, they took over the lease of an American Army officer who was returning home after a tour in Italy. "It was a big break for us," Luciano said. "It was almost like bein' back in the States. That apartment had beautiful American furniture, a new Westinghouse refrigerator with a freezer, an electric stove with an oven, and we even got one of them little infrared broilers that was just comin' out at the PX. With my connections, we had no trouble gettin' stuff at the PX and the American commissary had plenty of good food, just about anythin' we wanted. Outside, Rome was a mess, where people had nothin'. Inside that apartment, for me it was the happiest time of my life."

He was happy, too, because he was meeting people from a world outside the rackets, people who seemed to like him and want to help and asked for nothing in return. "There was this guy in 1947 who had just finished a tour in the Army in Italy where he'd been in charge of public relations for General J. C. Lee, who was the United States commander in the Mediterranean. I met this fella in the Excelsior restaurant when he come over to my table and introduced himself. He told me his background and said that he knew all the Italian newspaper guys and he suggested that maybe he could help me get a better break from them and change my image in public. I told him that was a good idea and I'd put him on the payroll and try him out. He started to laugh and told me he didn't want no dough; he said he figured I'd served my time and I oughta have some peace and he'd like to help me, for free. He knew I was in the black market and we used to joke about that. He'd say to me, 'Charlie, you've got a lot of good company in the black market — the whole U.S. Army in Italy.' After about two years he went back to the States and I sure was sorry to see him go."

Those who saw Luciano in these days remember him as being more relaxed, more outgoing than ever in his life. He appeared to have few concerns, and the money was pouring in torrents to him, from the black market and from his interests across the Atlantic. With Igea, he toured Italy, taking her to all his favorite places — the Quisiana Hotel on Capri, the Sicilian resort of Taormina, the Villa Igea in Palermo, a modern hotel designed to look like an ancient castle; the name alone intrigued Igea and when she saw it she was captivated, wanting to return often.

They went, too, to Milan. Soon after they began living together, Igea decided she would rather have her family learn of her relationship with him from her than from the newspapers. So she took Luciano north and there told her outraged parents that she was abandoning her career to become the mistress, the wife in all but law and church, to Luciano. When they left after two days, it was to harsh demands from her father that she leave "this American killer." Her parents would eventually relent, Igea told Luciano. She was right. Within a few years, the Lissonis had begun to look upon him almost as a proper son-in-law.

But there were shadows over this world, and suspicion was never far from Luciano. He was constantly under surveillance, constantly accused of involvement in the rackets, constantly harassed and brought in for questioning. He realized that he needed a front, some legitimate business that would at least partially get the police off his back. The word was spread and each afternoon scores of promoters would approach him at one of the outdoor cafés along the Via Veneto with propositions; all seemed to assume that he had an unlimited bankroll and wanted only to invest without asking questions and without playing any role in the operation. All were turned away.

"And then big shot Charlie Lucky got taken by his own *paisanos* worse than anybody ever took me in my life. I've been bugs about ice cream and candy since I was a kid; it was almost like a trademark. Well, these two bastards knew it and they played me like a fuckin' fiddle. I was sittin' outside at Donay's on the Via Veneto with a couple of guys when who should come walkin' by but Momo Salemi, a cousin of mine from Lercara Friddi, and a friend of his named Pasquale Enea. They looked surprised to see me and they come over to my table. I asked 'em what they was doin' in Rome, and they tell me they're in business together and they come up to make a deal. Then they sit down at the next table and start talkin', and of course, I hear what they're talkin' about. They was plannin' to start a candy factory in Palermo. My ears go up and I'm like a lamb waitin' to be slaughtered. I hear Enea talkin' about this great formula he's got for makin' fantastic candy and how they've got customers all lined up in Rome who're gonna help 'em sell the stuff all over, especially in the States. The guy they're supposed to see is gonna lend 'em the money to get their factory goin'.

"I was what Lansky used to call a schmuck. Here was these guys, one of 'em a cousin of mine and the other from my home town, so who would ever think they'd try to pull the old con game on me? I turned around and I told 'em I heard what they was talkin' about. I asked 'em how much dough they need. Enea said about a million lire, which in my market would cost me only a little more than a thousand bucks. So I thought, this is just what I've been lookin' for, a legit business I'm really interested in and it'll be operated by guys I know and can trust. I took 'em up to my apartment and I hand 'em a million lire and tell 'em to get their asses back to Palermo right away and get the business started."

The fish had swallowed the bait. It was not long before Salemi and Enea were back in Rome asking for more money; costs were rising far beyond their anticipations. Luciano gave it. Soon they were back again. "Every time they come up, they'd bring along a few boxes of candy and it was goddamn delicious, chocolates and nougats with fruit in it, the best I ever tasted. So I got hooked tighter each time, especially since Igea thought it was a good thing for me to be involved with a nice business like that and a business where I could help with gettin' the American distribution since I knew a lotta guys over there who could help make it a big success.

"After about a year, Igea tells me I've shelled out about sixty grand. All I had to show for it was a couple of boxes of candy. I'd never even asked 'em a question, I just took their word that they was pilin' up stock and buyin' machinery and stuff like that. So I got in touch with my cousin in Lercara Friddi, Calcedonia Lucanía, who was runnin' a little paint store. I asked him to go up to Palermo and take a damn good look at the candy business. He was to walk in and tell Momo and Enea that I sent him to see what was goin' on, and he was to look at everything."

It was only a few weeks later that Calcedonia Lucanía arrived in Rome with the news that the boxes of candy he had received were about all he was going to get out of his investment. Calcedonia had carefully examined the books, had discovered that indeed the business was prospering, with production and sales moving steadily upward. But he had discovered, as well, that Luciano's partners had been putting the profits in their own pockets.

"Calcedonia was a straight guy and I knew what he told me was the truth. I was practically on the next train south with him and Igea. When I showed up at the factory, Momo wasn't there, which was lucky for him. But Enea was there, in the office. I could see around the place and I seen the factory part had extra machinery for dippin' chocolates and mixin' and so forth, so I was sure they didn't steal all the money, just all the profits. I stood in the doorway and just looked at this bastard without sayin' nothin'. He started to get red and I could tell he knew why I was there. I said to him, 'You son of a bitch. You're a fuckin' thief. You been stealin' from me and you think because you're from my hometown I ain't gonna do nothin'. Well, you got a big surprise comin'.'

"The little bastard looks at me and turns green. Then he falls down on his knees and grabs my hand and starts kissin' it like I'm some kind of priest, and he's beggin' me not to kill him. He says he knows I'm in the Mafia and I can kill him any time, only please don't do it and he'll make it up to me. I was so mad I could've killed him on the spot, because there was no doubt about it, I'd been taken for the first time in my life and it hadda be by a

341

crummy rotten Sicilian I'd trusted. I told that jerk I was thinkin' maybe of cuttin' off his fingers or cuttin' out his tongue or loppin' off his ears. The more I threatened him, it was almost funny, the crazy way he was actin'; he was down on the floor, cryin', kissin' my shoes, screamin'. I practically scared him to death. Then it occurs to me that maybe the bastard'll have a heart attack and drop dead on me, so I tell him the only reason I ain't gonna do none of that shit is because the cops are watchin' me and I can't make a goddamn move without their knowin' about it, and in my book, he ain't worth goin' to jail for. Then I said to him, if I ever see him again, that'd be his last minute on earth. He run out of there like a rabbit and I never did see the bastard again."

Salemi, too, disappeared for a time, taking to the Sicilian mountains for sanctuary and sending inquiries from time to time to his family in Lercara Friddi asking whether it was safe to return.

"I put Calcedonia in charge of the candy business and the first thing he done was grab all the money Enea had socked away. It wasn't much, only about five grand. Enea and Momo had blown the rest livin' it up. Then Calcedonia went to work to put the business into shape. He turned his paint store over to another cousin and after that he spent all his time in Palermo. It took him a couple years, but he managed to build the candy business up pretty good. Then, as soon as he got it into the black, I run into another problem that killed off the whole thing. The American narcotics agents began to spread the story that the real reason I was in the candy business was to smuggle junk into the States in boxes of candy. When that story got around, I knew I had too much stacked against me. I told Calcedonia to get the business solid so we'd be able to sell it, which we did. We finally figured that I got taken for forty grand, which is a helluva lot of dough to pay for a couple boxes of candy."

Luciano's carefree, almost idyllic life with Igea lasted for about a year. But a web of narcotics involvement was being spun around him, and it began to tighten at the beginning of 1949, at first at long distance. On January 8, Charles E. Wyatt, the customs agent in New York, announced the arrest of several wealthy importers and some others in connection with a three-hundred-thousand-dollar cache of opium and heroin discovered aboard the French freighter *Bastia* when it docked in New York. But, said Wyatt, he had evidence that Lucky Luciano was "positively involved." What the evidence was, Wyatt never revealed, and no charges were ever brought against the exiled gangster. But the words were enough, and soon stories about Luciano and narcotics were breaking regularly in America, though always rumors, always claims that he was involved, was the brains behind the traffic, never any solid facts.

Then, on June 25, 1949, the stories came right to his door. In cooperation with American narcotics authorities, Italian police had been trying desperately to track down and stop the growing narcotics traffic from Italy to the United States. Early in June, they received a tip that sometime late in the month a major shipment would be passing through Rome airport. In the third week in June, that tip paid off. A minor American hoodlum named Vincent Trupia was hauled out of the transit lounge on his way from Germany to New York via Rome; in the lining of his suitcase was found six kilograms — a little over thirteen pounds — of pure cocaine. Trupia was hustled off to prison for interrogation. He talked, and among the names he mentioned as Italian contacts was that of Ralph Liguori, a deportee once called "The Pimp," and a codefendant at Luciano's vice trial.

That was enough for the Italian police. Immediately they arrested Liguori, a friend named Antonio Lo Manto and Liguori's suspected narcotics contact in Genoa, another American deportee named Mazzarino Discianni.

They arrested Luciano, too, for he and Liguori had been seen together on several recent occasions in Rome. "Sure, I seen Liguori from time to time, just like a lot of other deportees who was in Rome or Naples or everyplace I went," Luciano said years later, and told police then. "I knew a lot of 'em back in the States, so why shouldn't I see 'em when they're in Italy? Especially in 1949, when most of 'em was down on their luck. Even though they was Italian, most of 'em couldn't even speak the language and that gave 'em no chance to get into any rackets. Some of 'em was even starvin', so I'd slip 'em a few bucks, a ten or a twenty, sometimes a little more, and I even give a couple of 'em some work runnin' errands for me. I don't mean carryin' junk; it was just that they'd go to the store and pick up some shirts or ties, shoes, things like that. I didn't want to give 'em money for doin' nothin'; after all, they wasn't my family. But, hell, after a while there was over four hundred American deportees in Italy and most of 'em was just moochers.

"But all of that crap some of the papers was printin' about me and Liguori bein' partners, or him workin' for me, was crazy. There was even one story that Liguori and I set up a business to take American tourists to the cleaners by sellin' 'em phony antiques or hot money. And there was another story that we was runnin' a string of clip joints for the tourists in Rome. It was all a lot of horseshit. After all, in 1949, there wasn't many Americans in Italy anyway because things was tough, like there wasn't no heat in the hotels, and Americans don't like that kind of inconvenience. The only thing I ever did, and the police knew about it and never did a fuckin' thing to stop it, was to arrange for foreigners to buy lire at a black market price. For chrissake, everybody was doin' that until American Express put the squeeze on the American Embassy because the black market was ruinin' their business of changing lire and dollars at the legal rate.

"As far as this Trupia was concerned, I never seen him and I didn't even find out until a lot later that the kid was workin' as a courier for Vito. Joe Biondo, who was in my outfit in New York, had a lotta contact with Liguori and he's the one who finally told me about the Vito connection."

Arrested, Luciano was taken to Rome's largest prison, the Regina Coeli (Queen of Heaven) and jailed for nine days on suspicion of complicity in narcotics smuggling. He was questioned constantly, and fruitlessly, denied that he knew Trupia or anything about his work. Luciano's apartment was torn apart, but in a five-hour search the police found only the usual household furnishings and a few letters from his brother Bartolo and some postcards from others. "No evidence of anything unusual was found," one of the investigators reported.

All the time he was held, Igea camped outside the prison gates, besieged the offices of public officials, demanded his release, and so won a degree of admiration for acting like a proper Italian wife whose husband was in trouble.

Finally, Luciano was freed, but not before he was accused of having started a fire in the prison in an attempt to escape. American officials were forced, reluctantly, to agree with their Italian counterparts that there was no evidence against Luciano despite their suspicions and convictions. Trupia had named only Liguori and did not know Luciano. Liguori had named no one. In fact, the whole case eventually collapsed against everyone and Trupia was freed and shipped back to the United States. There he was gunned down on a Harlem street. "Trupia was murdered on order from Vito Genovese," Luciano claimed years later. "Tony Bender had the contract, but I don't know who pulled the trigger. But when I found out about it, it proved to me that Vito intended to use Trupia to scare me and prove to me how easy it was for him to set me up."

When Luciano was released from jail, to greet the waiting Igea and a crowd of reporters and photographers (that afternoon, Italian papers were filled with pictures of the two embracing), he discovered that his troubles were not over. Under pressure of American authorities, the Italian Minister of the Interior and the Guardia di Finanza declared that he was a danger to the state. He was given a few hours to pack his belongings at the Parioli apartment and then shipped back to Lercara Friddi once more, there to live under constant watch and with a strict eight P.M. curfew.

Though Luciano wanted Igea, at the very least, to take a suite at the Villa Igea in Palermo while he tried to extricate himself from Lercara Friddi, she refused to be separated and so accompanied him to his hometown, back to the hotel where he had lived when he first arrived three years before. If Luciano was not happy to be back, the citizens of Lercara Friddi were almost overjoyed at his return. Mayor D'Accurso went so far as to suggest that he might retire as the town's chief official in favor of Luciano. "Why not?" he said. "Signor Lucanía is a big businessman. The sulfur mine is reopening, more workers are returning to Lercara Friddi, and the population is increasing. We could use someone with his American ideas. Everyone in Lercara Friddi would vote for him."

The offer was rejected. Luciano had other ideas. He pulled every wire he could and soon won a reprieve. He and Igea left the village and settled into the Villa Igea in Palermo; from there, he could try more influence to win his way back to the mainland.

"You know what was one of the worst things about that whole time? It wasn't the prison. The worst thing was that I had to miss the baptism of my godson. I was about to become a godfather just at the time when I was picked up by the police in that Trupia case. Calcedonia's wife had just given birth to a son. They was gonna name him Francesco and they wanted me to be his godfather. In fact, Calcedonia made a special trip up to Rome to ask me in person. He wanted to assure me that he and his wife would consider it an honor. For the Sicilians, to be a godfather of the whole family or even of a gang was pretty important stuff, but when you become the godfather of a Sicilian kid, well, that's when you really hit the big time. It carries a lotta responsibility, like you gotta make sure the kid is goin' in the right direction and if anything happens to him, you gotta agree to step in and help out. In the States, all the guys in my outfit was forever knockin' out kids and always wantin' me to be godfather. But I never did. But when Calcedonia come all the way up to Rome, and because he was also part of the good things that happened to me, Igea was the one who urged me to do it. So I agreed that I would go down to Palermo to the church and sign the baptismal certificate and make it all official. It would be the first and only time I would ever be a godfather.

"Then them bastards picked me up on that phony junk thing and I'm sittin' in jail. I was ready to explode because it was somethin' I promised Calcedonia I'd do and it was somethin' I really wanted to do. I got the police to let me send a wire down to Palermo givin' my power of attorney to a notary there, which is legal, and he acted as my proxy at the ceremony. Later on, I was able to sign the church register myself. Some of the Italian officials who knew about it apologized to me and explained about the squeeze from the Americans.

"Ever since then, I keep in touch with my godson, Francesco. There's one thing I try to impress upon that kid, that he shouldn't grow up like me. Every once in a while, I see him lookin' at me like I was some kinda tin god and I want to reach over and knock that look right off his face. One time we was talkin' and I told him he hadda become some kind of professional man. He asked me, did I mean a lawyer? And I said, 'Not on your life. Lawyers are nothin' but crooks.' I said he's gotta be a doctor, which is the best thing because he can make a good livin' and at the same time he can help people."

In 1973, Francesco Lucanía was, indeed, following his godfather's advice. He was enrolled in the medical college of Bologna University.

30.

Through the rest of 1949 and into 1950, the Villa Igea in Palermo was home to Luciano and Igea. It was a place both had come to love, where they had been happy in the past. Still, he fretted under the constant surveillance, under the eight o'clock curfew, under the other restrictions designed to curtail his movements and activities, and so, when necessary, he tried with some success to evade his watchers. "Naturally, I couldn't meet nobody in Palermo, so I always found ways to slip across the island to Taormina in case it was somethin' important, like meetin' my friends from America."

As there had been since his arrival in Italian exile, a steady parade of couriers and emissaries arrived from America, bringing money and messages and seeking advice and counsel. Now, instead of meeting him in Rome or Naples, they trooped to Taormina and talked in the warm sun and vacation atmosphere of the resort.

One day, his old friend Meyer Lansky arrived. He was taking the grand tour of Europe, both as a delayed honeymoon with his second wife, Thelma — she had been his manicurist in Miami before his divorce from Anna and their marriage in 1948 — and as a way to avoid for the moment some of the heat arising from the opening stages of the Senate crime investigating committee under Estes Kefauver.

At Taormina, Lansky filled Luciano in on the status of the

organization. "He said things was goin' very good with all our gamblin'. He told me he was goin' to Switzerland to open up some new bank accounts for a few of the guys, like Joe Adonis and our good friend Batista." The conversation turned to the ambitious Vito Genovese. "Meyer said that Vito and Carlo Gambino was makin' it look on the outside like they wasn't gettin' along too good, but under the table they was like two fingers together." That, both Lansky and Luciano agreed, could only mean trouble in the future. Together with Frank Scalise, Gambino had risen high in the Mangano organization in Brooklyn, run then by Phil and Vince Mangano, and had become one of the most trusted lieutenants to Albert Anastasia, heir apparent in that family. "Meyer said it wouldn't surprise him if one of these days, Albert took care of the Manganos and took over that outfit. [In 1951, a year later, Philip Mangano was murdered and Vincent disappeared; Anastasia became the new boss.] When that happened, Carlo was liable to get very ambitious. So Lansky asked me to send a message back to Vito and Carlo to tell 'em I knew what they was doin' and to cut it out immediately, that I wouldn't sit still for Vito tryin' to muscle in on Anastasia. I also sent back a little private side message to Gambino. I told him I thought he was one of the best leaders in New York and maybe in ten or fifteen years, he could be head of it all. But he oughta keep his pecker down and be patient. That helped put a clamp on Vito for a few more years."

Lansky also brought up the subject of an expansion of the organization's gambling empire to Europe. He told Luciano he planned to stop in London for a scouting trip on his way back to New York. "I told him when the time was right, I would manage to slip up there and meet him and we could make some decisions personally.

"It was a nice visit. Meyer had his new wife along, Teddy, and she really surprised me. She was no Igea but she was a damn good-lookin' girl and really bright."

Soon after Lansky's visit, Luciano was back in the news. During one session of his organized crime committee's hearing, Senator Kefauver, echoing the constant refrain of Harry Anslinger, called the exiled gangster "the head of a phantom government which enforces its own laws and carries out its own executions." Luciano,

348

he said, was "the brains in an international drug ring running between Italy and the United States," and he demanded that Italian authorities take some action. Luciano responded at a press conference with scorn and derision. And the Italian police were circumspect and somewhat less than compliant. "The Italian police are excellent in detecting and enforcing the law, but the laws are not adequate and sentences are not strict enough," said one official. There was a problem with France, he said, where legal production of narcotics was permitted without government supervision. "We must now have legislation which will legally outlaw unsupervised narcotics distribution and choke off the source of illegal supply." Luciano's name was nowhere mentioned. But the surveillance and the pressures on him seemed to increase, for a time.

Then, in the summer of 1950, they relaxed and his enforced absence from the Italian mainland came to a sudden end. With the United States embroiled in what would turn out to be a long and frustrating war in Korea, and convinced that general war in Europe was imminent, President Truman reversed the direction of American foreign aid. Under the Marshall Plan, it had been mainly for the economic recovery of Western Europe; now the President ordered a deemphasis on the economic aspects and a sharp increase in the military, to arm the allies for the struggle ahead. In Italy, by then beginning to make a substantial recovery from the ravages of World War II, that announcement was greeted with anything but pleasure and the Italian government began to resist some of the all-pervasive American influence.

Luciano was one beneficiary. "One day, it was sometime late in the summer of '50, a few big muckety-mucks come over to see me at the Villa Igea. They was very polite fellas that I never seen before, but I knew about 'em and I'd been tryin' for months to find some bagman who could put me in touch. But it seemed they wouldn't take no dough. Now here they was, out of a clear blue sky, without even a phone call in advance and they tell me and Igea that we can live in Naples. It didn't cost me a cent. They said I had been behavin' myself all that year while I was in Palermo and they had no reason to keep me tied up in Sicily forever.

"So we packed up everythin' and we headed back for Naples. Only this time, I'm feelin' that all this freedom could blow up again, knowin' about the way my Italian countrymen operate, and I figure these very nice fellas will be right on my ass as soon as somethin' big happens anyplace in Italy or the States. Igea wanted to find an apartment and bring the furniture down from storage in Rome, but I said no, on account of who knows what's gonna be tomorrow. So we moved into a hotel, and you know where we moved to? Right into the Hotel Turistico in Naples. You know why? Because it's right across the street from the Caserna Zanzur, the military barracks of the Guardia di Finanza, the guys who are in charge of investigatin' junk. I said to Igea, 'If those guys wanna keep a watch on me like they've been doin', I'm gonna make it easy for 'em. I'm gonna live right across the street so they can see me from their goddamn windows every time I come in or go out."

Luciano's permission to return to the mainland had its restrictions. He could travel freely in the south, but he could not go north of Rome. And this was distressing. "Back in the States, I learned to play golf pretty good. I figured I could take it up again and maybe Igea could learn and we could both play together. But the nearest golf course was up in Fiuggi, which is a little bit north of Rome. Them Italian bastards wouldn't let me go up there. Then one day a messenger from Frank Costello in New York shows up with a beautiful set of golf clubs, complete. Frank had 'em made special to my measurements by the pro shop at the West-chester Country Club, perfectly balanced and made by hand, and they must've set him back at least six, seven hundred. Frank knew I was barred from every golf course in Italy, because all of 'em are north of where I can go, so he sends me a set of clubs for a present, the dirty cock. Some sense of humor." Almost as a reminder, Luciano, though he was never to use those clubs, kept them standing in a corner wherever he lived and had them polished and cleaned every week.

In the spring of 1951, another present arrived from New York, this time one he could make use of. "When Lansky was over, he noticed I was drivin' a little Italian car and that bothered him. So when he got back to New York, he told the fellas to look around and they arranged for me to get a brand-new 1951 Buick — Lan-sky looked all the cars over and decided the Buick was the best car in the States to use the kind of gas they have in Italy. A tourist

350

brought the car with him on a boat trip and when the ship stopped in Naples, this guy was kind enough to leave the keys with me."

In his new car, Luciano was often on the road, speeding across southern Italy, usually just for the pleasure of driving. It was too conspicuous, though, for those times when necessity, as it often did, demanded that he break the travel ban and head north. Many of those trips were to Milan, to visit the Lissonis, and then he would use one of the small Italian cars he had at his disposal.

"There was only one time we had any trouble. Most of the time we took the back roads so I wouldn't be spotted, because on the main *autostrada* you had to stop at the toll booths and any one of them guards could've known who I was. But this particular trip, it was in the spring of '51, we had to go on the *autostrada* because it was rainin' like hell and all the side roads was flooded. When we got there, I was a damn fool. While Igea was seein' her folks, I decided to go to the San Ciro racetrack and bet a few bucks on the ponies. That's where I must've been spotted.

"The next day, it was still rainin' hard, so I decided to leave the car in Milan for somebody to drive back for us when the roads was clear, and take the train. When we got to the station, there was a million cops waitin' for us. As soon as our taxi pulled up they surrounded me like I was John Dillinger. A dozen of them plainclothesmen got on the train with us and rode all the way back to Naples. I don't know what they thought I was gonna do while the two of us was cooped up in that little compartment. When we got to the Termini in Rome, them cops wouldn't even let us off the train to stretch our legs. If it hadn't been so damn uncomfortable, it would've been funny. But the whole thing was rotten for Igea. She never said a word; all the way back, she just kept smilin' and once in a while, she'd reach out and pat me on the arm and say, 'Don't think about it, it's not important.'

"About this time, we met a guy from Rome by the name of Giuseppe Dosi. I guess he was my enemy because he was head of the Rome branch of Interpol. He met Igea one time with me in Naples and when I saw him the next day, he looked at me and he said, 'Luciano, there has to be some good in you, because that girl is one of the finest women I've ever met. If I hear that you ever do

351

anything unkind to her, I will personally see to it that you spend the rest of your life in the Regina Coeli prison.' "

Late in 1950, a visitor arrived in Naples with some unpleasant news. The visitor was Carlo Gambino, and he had come to talk about Luciano's old friend Willie Moretti. The New Jersey mobster was in the advanced stages of syphilitic deterioration. "Just like it happened with Capone, Willie's brain was bein' affected and he couldn't control himself half the time. He hadda be watched whenever he went out, because nobody knew what he might say in public. There was a vote in the council that Willie had to go — for his own good and everybody else's. At that point, I guess the whole idea of killin' anybody began to make me sick. I had a lifetime of it and now I hadda vote on whether to kill a guy who had been one of my best friends. I told Carlo I wanted the hit held up. I gave Carlo the orders to tell the council absolutely no on Willie, unless there was no way he could be helped by the right kind of doctor, and I didn't mean one of our bullet-hole specialists. I said, let 'em take him to a guy on Park Avenue, the Mayo Clinic, or anywhere to try to save him."

But Moretti's deterioration had progressed too far to be reversed or even arrested. On October 24, 1951, Willie Moretti was shot twice in the head, from the front, in a restaurant near Cliffside Park, New Jersey.

The attitude of the Italian police in these years was a strange and variable one toward Luciano. If they wanted to restrict his travel inside the country, fearing that free scope would lead to illegal deeds, they nevertheless had no compunction about permitting travel abroad. In October 1950, only a few months after he returned to the mainland, he was once more issued an Italian passport, with visas good for travel to Switzerland, Belgium, France, Spain and England.

"I didn't ask for it at that time and I didn't pay to get it. I wanted it, but I didn't think I'd get one if I applied. It was just that one day a guy from the Caserna across the street drops over to the Turistico and asks me if I'd like to have my passport back. I tell him, sure, you bet. So they give it to me, just like that. I think the Italians was tryin' to stick the needle into Uncle Sam for tellin' 'em that American loans would have to go for military defense and never mind the food. Shit, at that point the Italian people just wanted to eat and they didn't give a fuck about buildin' a new army."

With passport in hand, Luciano quickly became a European traveler. "I never used the visas for Belgium or Spain, but I did go to England and France and Switzerland. Lansky had opened an account for me in Zurich when he was up there on his honeymoon and I wanted to see what it was all about. I didn't have too much in the account, maybe a couple hundred thousand, but at least I wanted to make sure nobody was foolin' around with that nest egg.

"Another time, I went up to see the races at Longchamps, outside of Paris. I went all by myself and nobody bothered me and I came back in a couple of days. I had never been to Paris before, and even though I was only there for about forty-eight hours, it took me two months to tell Igea every little detail. The first question she asked me when I got home was did I go to the ballet. I burst out laughin' and she started to cry and wouldn't talk to me for a whole day.

"The first trip I made to London was to meet Meyer there. I stayed at a quiet little hotel next to a park. It was called the White House — can you imagine Lucky Luciano sleepin' at the White House? I even thought about maybe sendin' a bunch of picture postcards to all the guys in the outfits in the U.S.A. to let 'em see where I was stayin'. So I spent a few days up there just before Christmas in 1950 and I bought some presents for Igea, looked over the territory that Meyer and me figured we might move in on, and so forth. That was the time gamblin' still wasn't legal in London, but it didn't hurt none to get a feel for the place. Then I bought a lotta cloth for suits and I went to that famous French store on Bond Street, Sulka, and I got a dozen bolts of material for shirts. I had all that stuff made up in Italy, but Sulka made ties to order and they sent 'em to me by airmail."

In the next few years, until his passport was lifted in 1955, Luciano traveled often. He would go to London a few times a year, "just to listen to the Limeys talk English and get clothes. Also about the weather up there. I never liked the cold weather when

I was in New York, and I'd always head for Florida in the winter when I could. But once you've been livin' in Italy, you miss everythin' about New York, the weather included. Then I found that the cold in London was just like New York. There was days I used to stand on the street corner in London and just let the wind blow across my face, stand there freezin' and lovin' every minute of it. There was people walkin' by, speakin' a language I could understand, and the cold — it was great."

He went to Paris, too, to see shows, specifically the Folies-Bergère. "And they had some movie houses where you could hear American actors in English, not dubbed in Italian like in Italy. Just to sit in a damn movie house and listen to the original sound was worth the dough for the trip."

Sometimes Igea would go with him, on rare occasions to London, for she did not like that city, and more often to Paris, where she would attend the ballet while Luciano was at the movies or the racetrack. "She used to get real sore at me when I told her I would do anythin' for her but watch a bunch of fairies jump around in tights with their balls showin'."

But on all his trips he studiously avoided the private gambling clubs. "All I hadda do was walk into one of them joints and somebody'd recognize me like a shot and four minutes later Scotland Yard or the French police or Interpol and every cop on duty would be givin' me a free ride back to the airport. So I figured, it's not worth it; besides, maybe I'd drop a bundle and that was somethin' I didn't need."

31.

Despite his freedom in the years after 1950 to travel outside Italy and, to a limited degree, within the country, Luciano never was far from feeling that he was teetering on disaster. His occasional sudden and unexplained absences almost invariably brought the police down upon him on his return, brought more harassment and interrogation, and his silences led only to increased suspicion. The conviction of American and Italian authorities continued that he was the dominant figure not only in the organized rackets in the United States and Italy, but more particularly in the illegal narcotics trade around the world.

Then, early in 1951, Charles Siragusa arrived. He had been working as a narcotics agent for the United States Treasury Department in Paris, but he convinced Anslinger that his background, his ability to speak fluent Italian, both Neapolitan and Sicilian dialects, and his knowledge of the underworld ambience, would suit him ideally for work as an undercover agent in Italy, would permit him to get Luciano. The Guardia di Finanza and Italian authorities in Rome agreed to cooperate, but local police officials in Naples were not advised, because they were considered eminently corruptible.

Siragusa initially centered his activities in Naples, posing as a well-to-do American narcotics buyer. Wherever he went and to whomever he talked, he tried to turn the conversation to Luciano, to develop evidence. But his efforts failed repeatedly.

Unfortunately for Siragusa, within hours of his arrival in Naples, Luciano's informants advised him of the agent's presence. "He no more'n opened his mouth in Naples when I knew all about it. I thought to myself, when the hell is that fuckin' Asslinger gonna leave me alone? Then, a couple days later, I heard that Siragusa's propositionin' guys to say that they bought from me, and he was tryin' to have me planted with packages. That was too much. So I arranged to have word reach the *questura* and they picked up the bastard and tossed him in the clink. They didn't know who he was, only that he was an American in Italy tryin' to buy dope. They interrogated him all night long, and that dumb son of a bitch was caught in the middle. If he opened up and told 'em who he was, that meant he blew his cover; if he kept his mouth shut, they could keep him under wraps for Christ knows how long. After a few hours, the shitheel broke and told 'em who he was. But the funny part was the Naples cops didn't believe him, and it took a helluva lot of wires and calls back and forth to Rome before the Guardia di Finanza in Naples got a confirmation. Siragusa went back to Rome with his tail between his legs, his face as red as a beet and showin' a yellow streak a mile wide. After that, he hated me worse than Asslinger. Every few days, I kept gettin' reports from different sources that he was tryin' to nail me. As far as I was concerned, all he was gonna dig up was his own dirt."

Siragusa, as it happened, already had reason enough for antipathy toward Luciano. They had battled at least once before, only then it had been at long range, before the narcotics agent's arrival in Naples.

In 1950, Eugenio Giannini was a minor American hoodlum, a member of Tommy Lucchese's outfit, an occasional courier to Europe and, often, a dope peddler for Vito Genovese. He was something else, too: for years he had been an informant for the narcotics bureau.

"After I got to Naples in 1950, this guy Giannini come down to see me one day from Rome. He brought me some money from New York and a couple messages from Tommy Lucchese and other guys. Then he gives me a proposition. He asks me to handle some black market money. I told him I'd think about it and I let him cool his heels for a couple days while I made some contacts. Somehow, this guy just didn't sit right."

While Giannini was waiting, he was picked up by Italian police for smuggling penicillin into Italy. "They didn't give a shit about the black market in money, but when it come to medicine and some son of a bitch was tryin' to gouge a guy's eyes out for a dose of penicillin, that really got 'em sore. Then, the minute Giannini landed in the clink, he started screamin' for help, and the guy he starts screamin' for is Siragusa. It didn't take me long to add it up. Siragusa would've used Giannini to frame me. So I sent back word to New York that Giannini was a fink and they should get him when the Italian cops threw him outa the country. There was no question to me that Siragusa was plannin' to use that idiot Giannini to get me if he could."

On September 20, 1952, Giannini was shot in the head in East Harlem.

Lack of success did not prevent Siragusa from sending back a report to Washington on his findings. "Ever since his arrival here," he wrote, "Luciano has been in touch with the most notorious delinquents of the United States in various ways. Especially through the chiefs of the underworld who visit Italy. We can prove that Luciano has received big sums of money from these visitors."

And he kept searching for a break. In April of 1951, he thought he had found one. An Italian police captain named Giulano Oliva received a tip that a plane from Milan to Palermo, with several stops, would contain a passenger named Frank Callace, whose luggage would contain three kilos — a little over six and a half pounds — of pure heroin, bound for America. When the plane landed at Rome, police removed an American named Frank Callace. They found nothing in his luggage, and then became a little suspicious, for the tip had said Callace would be in his fifties; the man they had taken into custody was in his thirties. Wires were sent to the next stop, Naples, and as the passengers debarked, the police spotted a man answering the original description. They detained him. He was traveling under the name Nick Cappo, but almost immediately he admitted that he was the real Frank Callace and the man arrested in Rome was his nephew. Trapped, Callace began to sing, and his song was that he had received the heroin found in his suitcase from a Frenchman named Cheveaux during a visit to Milan. He was taking it to Palermo to sell to a friend. An investigation could turn up no Cheveaux and revealed that Callace's Sicilian friend had been dead for two months. Callace was tried, convicted, and sent to jail for two years; on his release, he disappeared, turning up in New York in 1954 in a parked car with three bullets in his head.

There was nothing in the case to indicate any tie to Luciano, except vague word from the original informant that Callace's source of supply had been an old friend of Luciano's named Joe Biondo. This did not deter Siragusa. He declared that Luciano must be involved, demanded that he be arrested and his suite at the Turistico be searched. The Naples police did as asked, but when nothing incriminating was found and no ties to Callace could be developed, Luciano was released. As he left the Guardia di Finanza, one of the officials mentioned Siragusa and pointed to his head, saying he had become "*pazzo*" when it came to Luciano.

But still Siragusa was determined to have some satisfaction, however slight. He had noticed Luciano's Buick and now he demanded that police investigate to see if he had any right to own it. Luciano was soon haled into court and charged with failure to register his new automobile with its New Jersey license plates. He was fined thirty-two thousand lire — fifty dollars.

"These things was doing terrible things to Igea. After they searched our place, I sat down with her and told her that this kind of life was not for her. She was entitled to peace and a decent way of livin' and she could never have it with me. I pleaded with her to go back to Milan; I told her she would never have to worry about money for the rest of her life. It was like talkin' to the wall; she just ran over to me and held me so tight that I finally stopped talkin'.

"That's when I decided to do somethin' radical. I decided to go to the source of my problems, to Mr. Harry Asslinger. Around the end of April, I sent him a proposition in writing. I had somebody write it for me, in good English. I told him I would agree to solve his whole goddamn narcotics problem, or at least a fuckin' good part of it, if he would pull the wires that could get me back to the States. I said even though he knew that I didn't deal in junk, that I had the reputation for bein' the head of it because of the publicity he and Kefauver and the rest of them guys was givin' me. So I would use that position to do somethin' that he never had the brains to think of and that I was probably the only guy in the world who could do. I explained that the United States narcotics business was strictly import, with all the stuff comin' out of Europe and the Middle East. So, I agreed to go to the source, as the only way to shut off the supply to America. I said I would round up and organize the suppliers, which nobody had ever thought of doin', maybe because they was so spread out in different countries. Naturally, I didn't tell Asslinger that every one of them pipelines had been tied together by Vito and all I hadda do was step in and talk to them bums. Once I had the suppliers together, I told him, I would go to the States and tell all the guys in the outfits around the country that I was gonna burn the junk unless they got out of the business.

"The worst thing that could've happened to me was they would knock me off. But I figured such a drastic thing on my part would make the guys in the States realize I was serious and later on they'd all respect me for helpin' all of 'em, the whole outfit. As far as the Narcotics Bureau in Washington was concerned, the rest would be up to them; they would have the biggest part of that fuckin' business in their hands; they wouldn't have to worry about the States if they had the right kind of moxie to force all the countries where the supply was comin' from to clamp down on what I would organize. It sounds wild but I just felt inside me that I could make it work.

"I didn't tell Igea about all this. What was the use of gettin' her excited? I know my offer got to Washington and I know Siragusa knew about it. But I never received no answer from neither one of 'em. The only thing I could figure was that either Asslinger and his boy Siragusa was fruity on the subject of Luciano and didn't want to hear nothin' good from me, or somebody in Washington figured they'd rather have the narcotics business keep goin' instead of Lucky Luciano settin' foot in the United States again."

Luciano not only failed to receive a reply to his offer, but he also found himself, in the aftermath, the object of increased pressure from Siragusa. The surveillance was tightened, his telephone tapped, his visitors photographed by telephoto lenses. And then Siragusa found a staunch ally in Naples, the new police chief, Giovanni Florita.

"I was warned the day Florita was appointed that he was gonna be trouble for me. Only a couple days later, Siragusa shows up and I get the word that him and Florita are together like two peas in a pod. One of the guys from the Guardia meets me in secret and he tells me that I gotta watch out for Siragusa, because he made a deal with Florita to work together to get me for bein' the head of junk. Both of 'em figure if they can get me they'll become big men in one jump."

For the next eighteen months, Florita and Siragusa labored, fruitlessly, to trap Luciano. "They pulled a lotta stupid things. One time, there was a countess in Naples whose husband had a good title, only he didn't have no money to go with it. She was really good-lookin'. It was durin' the time of the Callace mess and Igea and I had a fight about me gettin' out of the rackets and I felt rotten about it because it's the first time we ever had an argument. I left the hotel and I'm walkin' over toward the piazza when a fella walks alongside me and hands me a note and then runs like hell. It's in a lady's handwritin' and it was signed by this contessa. She invited me over to the Hotel Londres to have an aperitif with her. I walk into this little bar and she's sittin' there waitin' for me. Right away, I figure this has to be a plant, but I don't say nothin' and I wait for her to make the move. In a couple minutes, after we do a little chitchat, she comes up with the proposition. She says that everybody in Naples knows I'm the head of the black market and she's been runnin' money and cigarettes, helpin' certain guys, back and forth between Naples and Tangier. She says there ain't enough dough in this and she's gotta make more money.

"Then she comes out with it. She says she's willin' to take some risks if I could use her services. When she says the word 'services,' I know she means I can take her right upstairs and lay her as a kind of goodwill down payment. I don't bat an eye and finally I says to her, very polite, 'Contessa, I've been lookin' at you from far away with the greatest desire. I can't hold back no more.' She practically pulls me to my feet and drags me over to the elevator and we wind up in a nice room overlookin' the piazza. As soon as I lock the door, I turn to her, grab her dress by the neck and tear it right off.

"And then I clipped her right on the jaw and knocked her across the bed. Her eyes almost popped. I was so mad I could've torn her apart. She was practically naked, but it didn't mean a thing to me. I said to her, 'I got a girl who's worth a thousand of you. I wouldn't touch you with Florita's prick. Tell me why you're tryin' to set me up.' Well, I finally convinced her to tell me the truth. She said that Florita and Siragusa give her the money to stage this little play and she was supposed to let me carry some junk for her."

Still the attempts to embroil Luciano continued. Late in 1953, Mayor Lorenzo Rago of the town of Battipaglia, on the coast near Naples, disappeared, and Siragusa and Florita were off and running once more. In addition to his official duties, which paid little, Rago's ostensible business was manufacturing tomato sauce. But it was discovered that Rago had an annual income in excess of twenty million lire — fifty thousand dollars — which is a lot of money from a small spaghetti-sauce company. It seemed that the money was coming from the black market; Rago was running contraband between Italy and Tangier. And then the rumors began to spread that he was doing more than just trading in nylons and cigarettes; he was, it was whispered, in the narcotics business.

The search for Rago intensified, and then a decomposed body was discovered in a rowboat, trussed up like a turkey. The police were convinced this was the body of the missing mayor. Police Chief Florita promptly arrived at Luciano's door and had him hauled away in handcuffs. Siragusa arrived at the police barracks, was installed in a nearby office, and there helped guide the interrogation. Luciano was informed that he was under suspicion of having murdered Mayor Rago. The motive: he and Rago had been partners in narcotics smuggling, Rago had obviously doublecrossed him and just as obviously Luciano had meted out retribution. Luciano was held without bail, to await the results of a pathological examination of the corpse. When the results arrived, the case collapsed. The body was not that of Mayor Rago — it was, in fact, never identified.

That did not stop the investigation or the suspicion of Luciano. Then there was a new turn, with the appearance of Francesco Scibilia, a seedy, out-of-work occasional hoodlum who scrounged the Naples waterfront. As it happened, Scibilia was an American deportee; he had been arrested in Florida for trafficking in narcotics and for forgery, had served fifteen months in Lewisburg Penitentiary, and then was shipped abroad. On his arrival in Naples, he had offered his services to Siragusa, and had been hired to infiltrate the Luciano organization. "For chrissake, we spotted the guy five minutes after he showed up. I threw him out on his ass and told him to go back to Siragusa and ask for a better job."

Scibilia told a different story. He said that Luciano had given him fifty million lire (two hundred forty thousand dollars) to pass on to Mayor Rago. It was to be used to finance Rago's narcotics operation. As proof, Scibilia displayed a business card with the name Antonio Rago on it, his signature and handwritten notation: "48,000 lire." This Rago, said Scibilia, was a relative of Mayor Rago; he ran a small boat that carried wine legally out of the coast town of Trapani. But, Scibilia claimed, that boat was used as well for the narcotics operation of Luciano and the missing mayor, and one dark night the mayor's body had been dumped from it into the sea for permanent burial.

Once more, the police descended upon Luciano. Now, they declared, they had the evidence they needed. Once more, the case collapsed. Antonio Rago, an investigation soon revealed, indeed had a boat, but that boat was too small ever to have made trips into open water and it never left the waters around Trapani and the nearby islands. Further, Antonio Rago was no relation of the missing mayor and had, in fact, never even met him. As for the business card Scibilia had flourished, Antonio Rago had, indeed, given it to him and made the notations. But that had happened during a chance meeting on a train when Rago had sold Scibilia a watch for forty-eight thousand lire (eighty dollars) and had given him the business card as a receipt.

So Luciano was free again (the body of Mayor Rago never did turn up). As for Scibilia, he was brought before the court, fined, and given a three-year prison sentence for having slandered a citizen of Naples, one Salvatore Lucanía.

This failure no more deterred Siragusa and Florita than had any of the others, and when the biggest narcotics scandal of postwar Italy erupted, they were after him once more. The scandal involved three major chemical and medical laboratories that produced legal heroin for medical uses under license from the government — the Schiaparelli Laboratories, SAIPOM Corporation and a company called SACI. During a three-year period, the laboratories had diverted more than nine hundred pounds of heroin into the illicit market — heroin worth $30 million wholesale in the United States, and on the streets at retail, more than $200 million. A number of executives and scientists of the three companies were incriminated. Behind the whole conspiracy, declared Charles Siragusa, was Charlie Luciano. As proof, there was his relationship with Egidio Calascibetta, the head of SACI, and with his old friend, Joe Biondo.

"Sure, I knew this guy Calascibetta. He was a *commendatore*, a big shot up in Milan with medals and all kinds of honors for helpin' his country. I met him once in Capri; he was there with his family and Igea liked 'em. We rented a little summer place in Capri and one time Calascibetta was a guest in our house. Does that mean we was in business together? Hell, I knew Hutton real good in New York, but was I in the brokerage business with him?

"And of course I knew Joe Biondo; we was good friends from the old days. He was with me that time when we all got picked up in Cleveland when I went to see Moe Dalitz about the Masseria-Maranzano problem, and he used to come up to see me at Dannemora and bring things to me, little things that counted. So Joe come over from New York and he dropped in to see me in Naples. He had some dough, he carried a lotta dough for me from the States. But this particular time he says he has a deal in New York to buy some chemicals and he asks me to introduce him to somebody in Italy who has a plant. Am I supposed to say to him, after all these years, 'I'm sorry, Joe, I can't do nothin' for you'? We was goin' to Milan anyway, because Igea's sister Daria was sick, so I took Joe along to introduce him to this guy I met in Capri, Calascibetta."

That introduction was made, but no sooner did Luciano and Biondo leave the plant than they were picked up by the police, taken to the barracks, and questioned about the reason for being at SACI. Luciano's explanation was simple: He was simply bringing two people he knew together so that, perhaps, they might come to terms on a business deal. The authorities seemed satisfied.

Then the scandal broke and that meeting took on a new significance. "Siragusa got on a soap box and he started screamin' that Lucky Luciano was a friend of them big-shot junk dealers, and that Joe Biondo was the go-between on account of he was connected with me in the States. As far as I'm concerned, Siragusa knew less arithmetic than I ever learned in grammar school. He could add two and two and wind up with nine and then Asslinger would pat him on the back for bein' such a smart boy and doin' his homework so good on Lucky Luciano."

Siragusa's charges were unavailing. In the wake of the revelations, several companies, including SACI, were closed down and some of the individuals involved were jailed and fined. But not Calascibetta; he was merely denounced publicly. And not Luciano; an intensive investigation by the Guardia di Finanza and other Italian authorities failed to turn up any evidence against him, and so he was absolved.

32.

With the authorities constantly after him, fear was never far from Luciano that one day all his freedom would be lost. Igea urged him repeatedly to turn away from his past, to make a sharp break with the world of illegal business. He took some steps to comply at least partially. At her suggestion, he purchased some land in the small town of Santa Marinella, and it was turned into a productive farm under the guidance of a younger cousin and namesake, Salvatore Lucanía. He looked, as well, for new opportunities in legitimate enterprises.

The candy business, by then, was almost at an end. Though Calcedonia Lucanía had run it at a steadily increasing profit, the rumors spread by authorities that it was merely a front to ship narcotics across the Atlantic proved disastrous. "That's when I really got to hate Charlie Siragusa. He was so crazy blind that he lost every sense of decency. He was a U.S. law enforcement officer and he had no orders to be a monster. But all he wanted to do was stick it into me, right or wrong, as long as he knew I would hurt. Nobody never found nothin' in none of them boxes but candy, but that didn't stop him or them other guys. We had gotten a contract to export our candy to the States, to a lotta stores in the Little Italys in Chicago, Philadelphia, New York, all the big cities. Because of Siragusa's muscle, they started investigatin'. They practically ruined our shipments by breakin' open and testin' half the boxes. The candy had to go through a laboratory for examination and the rest of the shipment sat out there on the dock. By the time the lab report came back, it would all be ruined. So finally we hadda sell, and I dropped forty grand. Because them guys made up their minds that I shouldn't be allowed to do nothin' legit."

Still, Luciano persisted in a search for a legitimate business that would pay off. He promised Igea that he would find one.

And he promised her that he would quit the rackets, at least those in Italy. "But I explained to her that I hadda be just as careful about gettin' outa things as I was when I was in 'em. All them years after I become the boss, people all over the world thought of me as the head of somethin'. If it became public that I decided to be the head of nothin', then everybody in Italy would believe that Igea talked me out of the rackets. In Italy, a thing like that can ruin a guy, because in this country a man has to be the head of the house. A guy who's led around by the nose by any woman gets a fast reputation for bein' a *castrato*. So Igea agreed with me that I hadda keep up the front; I hadda still be the big gangster, Charlie Lucky, whether I was or not."

Then Luciano began his second legitimate venture. He opened an electrical appliance store in Naples. He sold both major appliances, like washers and refrigerators, and small ones that had not been seen in Italy in years, like irons, toasters and mixers. Had he desired, he could have tapped his American Army contacts for U.S.-made appliances, but that would have been to flaunt the black market openly, and he was determined to keep this business legitimate. So he specialized in Italian-made products and those from Germany and other countries on which he could get import licenses and win franchises. And he brought to the business an American selling technique — installment buying.

At first, it looked as though he had found success. But then American-made appliances began to appear on the Italian market in increasing numbers, and Luciano's business started to suffer. It dipped into the red and within a few years, he closed the store, with a loss of fifty thousand dollars mostly in the form of unpaid installments. In the old days in the United States, no one would have welshed on debts to Lucky Luciano, and he was determined that the same thing would be true in Italy. Luciano sent for a collector. He was an old relative, Momo Salemi, who had come out of hiding in the Sicilian mountains and, through the intervention of other relatives, had managed to convince Luciano to use him again. This time, Salemi was completely loyal. He scoured the back alleys of Naples and, with a little bit of muscle, managed to collect at least part of the debts outstanding.

So, Luciano began once more to seek a business, a legitimate one that, if not paying as well as the rackets, at least would not collapse around him. If he did not find one immediately, he at least discovered another occupation, and a worthy one, to divert him. His old friend Father Scarpato arrived one day from Mount Vesuvius and insisted that Luciano and Igea return with him to his parish at San Sebastian al Vesuvio. Midway up the lava-strewn slope, the priest stopped and pointed to a vacant lot. "Here, my friends," he said, "you see the Clinic of Our Lady of Lourdes."

"Igea and I looked at each other and I could see that we was thinkin' the same thing, that this little round butterball with the cigarette ashes all over his front had finally blown his top. But, as it turned out, he had a terrific idea. There was no hospital for miles around and if anybody in one of them villages all over Vesuvius got sick, they hadda go to Naples. Most of 'em didn't have cars and it was a pretty long hike by donkey cart to a doctor. They could die by the time they got to Naples.

"Don Cheech said he was gonna build a hospital with more than a hundred beds, the best modern equipment and the best doctors. All he wanted to know was would I help him. Of course, I said I would, and I got involved in somethin' that gave me more satisfaction than anythin' I ever did."

Father Scarpato was filled with plans and he had the technical ability to design and blueprint his dream. To Luciano fell the task of organizing the project and raising the money. It was slow and difficult and, because of its nature, one to which he would not lend the old techniques. Later, he would remember the times when he returned home after being spurned by those he had approached for money and Igea would mock him. "She'd say to me, 'Maybe for the next three or four days I forgive your promise. Go and make protection for a few big *milionarios*. You can play the part of Robin Hood and maybe someday they will talk about how you raised the money for the clinic for the poor by giving protection to the rich.'"

These may have been happy days, but Luciano had a persistent and nagging concern. His finances were not in good shape. His Swiss bank account was being depleted rapidly by the losses in the candy and appliance businesses, his own continued high standard of living, and his personal charities. He was approached daily by the poor, by out-of-luck deportees, by a horde of people with hard-luck stories, and almost always he would pass over a few bills. There were those, too, who had once been on his payroll in the black market or who were still on his payroll, and to each he paid fifty or seventy-five dollars a week. He was still getting about twenty-five thousand a month from the States, from those interests administered by Meyer Lansky, but he was spending almost all of it.

He began to give some heed to something Lansky had told him in Taormina, something the underworld treasurer had called his "laundry business." It was a simple operation. Money was skimmed off the top of gambling and other American operations and sent to Switzerland for deposit in numbered accounts. Then Lansky would arrange for some of the underworld's legitimate operations — in real estate, legal gambling in Nevada, hotel-building and more — to borrow that money. "It was all nice and legit. We'd borrow money from ourselves and pay interest on that dollar right into our own pockets, only the interest was a business expense we could write off on American income taxes. It was like Lansky always said, 'A lot of dough is nice, but it don't do no good just lyin' around. We have to work it the way the bankers do. They got money out, other people's money, workin' for 'em to make more money.'

"Of course, our way was better. It helped us take over legit businesses and get guys in hock to us. Meyer was sendin' money from the outfits to Switzerland like an avalanche and bringin' it back in loans and then sendin' the interest back to Switzerland as part of the nontaxable profits. It was like we had a printin' press for money. Back in '51, it was just beginnin', but you could see where it was goin'.

"Meyer told me I oughta get in on the system, take some of my dough that was comin' in regular and whatever I could put aside from what I was makin' in Italy and put it into one of them laundry accounts in Zurich. I said, okay, and that's the way it started.

"Then I got word that Joe Adonis was comin' with some money for me and I should meet him at the airport in Zurich where we could both do our bankin'. They got branches right at the airport and all you have to do is step off the plane and walk right into your bank; you don't even have to go through customs. This was the time when Joe A. was startin' to have trouble; he got called in front of Kefauver, like Costello, Longie Zwillman and the rest of 'em, and then they started lookin' into his gamblin' in Jersey and his payoffs to the politicians, and then they even started to investigate where he was born; the fuckin' idiot told 'em he was born in New York. He figured he had that covered pretty good but he wasn't takin' no chances that they might find out he wasn't even a citizen. So that's why he was goin' to Zurich, to sock away a bundle nobody could find just in case he had to leave the States.

"I went to Zurich and hung around the airport until Joe's plane come in from New York. He was still the same guy, standin' on the ramp, combin' his hair and posin' like some movie star. It was the first time we seen each other since Havana and the meet was all happy and friendly. Joe'd been my pal for maybe thirty years, and between him and Frank and Meyer, they're representin' my outfit and tryin' to keep a lid on that greedy pig, Vito.

"We walk over to one of the banks and Joe hands me an envelope for me to deposit. There's a hundred grand in it, which I didn't figure to be a helluva lot, not with the kind of business we was doin' in the States. I maybe'd retired in Italy, but I was still the chairman when it came to the outfits in the States. Then Joe made out his own deposit. You know how much he dropped into the account? Three million bucks, that's how much. It's all sittin' in this suitcase he's got. He opens it up, counts it, and deposits it — three million. And I'm puttin' in a measly hundred grand.

"I took him into a private room they have for personal depositors, and I was so fuckin' mad I could've gone through the wall. I said to him, 'Joe, what the hell's goin' on here? I get a hundred grand and you're puttin' in three million? You better explain that to me.'

"Joe A. says, 'That's the way it is, Charlie. The three million's the dough I socked away all over the years. It's my own personal money.'

"I said, 'Joe, that's bullshit. You live just as high as me and you spend whatever you get. I'm gettin' a net of twenty-five grand a month from the States, besides this envelope you brought me that's been skimmed off the top of my own share. You guys are mintin' money over there and you're shortchangin' me.'

"Joe says, 'Listen, Charlie, the Little Man makes out all the sheets and he figures what everybody's share of the pot is. If you got a complaint, take it up with Meyer.'

"Well, I was gettin' madder and madder, not only because I know I'm bein' rooked but even more because I know that this old pal is gonna get on the plane and go back to the States, to New York, to the Copa with all them beautiful broads around him, and the best I can do is go back to Naples and once in a while go to a crummy nightclub like the Snake Pit or the San Francisco, which are so dirty they have to keep the lights low so the customers won't get a good look and vomit. And here's a guy who's got a big mansion over in Jersey and he's a big American patriot who's always talkin' about how his kid's gonna go to West Point, just like Meyer was talkin' about his kid, and I couldn't help but think about how Igea and me're livin', how we can't have kids because I'm supposed to be the big boss and they watch me twenty-four hours a day, while Joe A. is shakin' hands with senators and congressmen and all the big shots every night at the Copa.

"So I tell Joe that he oughta split that three million with me. I explain to him about me and Igea, how we wanna set up a decent life and it's the first time I ever cared for anybody like that. I said to him, 'Joe, if it hadn't been for me, you wouldn't have a fuckin' quarter. I started you, all the way back from the time I took you down to Philly and put up the dough for you to buy that Scotch from Waxey Gordon. Your memory stinks, Joe. Don't you know I made you?'

"You know what he said? He said, 'Maybe you did, Charlie, but you can't break me.'

"Thirty years of friendship went right down the crapper, then and there. I never trusted the son of a bitch again.

"When I got back to Naples, I sat down and wrote a letter to Lansky askin' what the fuck was goin' on. I let Meyer know, quiet and easy, that I wanted some good accountin', right away. Meyer sent word that he would come to see me, personal, and he did. He said that what Joe A. told me at the Zurich airport was right. For a couple years he had been worried that he was gonna get deported, so he'd been savin' every nickel and bankin' it all for the rainy day. Even though I still trusted Meyer in them days, and I figured maybe there was some truth in what he explained, I still wasn't happy about it. I didn't buy the whole story and it never changed the way I felt about Joe A. after that time."

For the next few years, Luciano made regular trips to Zurich to deposit more money in that laundry account (later, he would be forced to withdraw it, when his funds ran short and the supply from the United States dried up). "But every time I went up there, I remembered that time with Joe A. and I would get mad at the bastard all over again."

Then suddenly, in 1955, those trips — and all foreign travel — were over. Siragusa had become the European director of the United States Bureau of Narcotics. One day, he called in the press to issue another denunciation of Luciano and another demand that something be done about him. This time there was a response. Luciano was ordered to appear before the Naples Warning Commission, a kind of municipal morality board. The hearing was scheduled for November 5, and he was told to be prepared to answer all questions and give a detailed accounting of his sources of income.

In the weeks before the hearing, American and Italian authorities began to feed the press with a variety of stories about Luciano. He was, it was said, a potential danger to American military security, a danger that grew from his wide contacts with sailors and officers of the fleet anchored in Naples and his seemingly free access to goods from the PX and to APO mail channels. Naples Police Chief Florita joined the chorus with a ringing denunciation of Luciano, saying that recent investigations had turned up a variety of nefarious deeds that could be traced to him. Siragusa offered his congratulations and added, "I collaborated with the Naples police at their request." The demands that the commission, when it met, do something about Luciano even came from across the Atlantic. New Hampshire's Republican Senator Charles Tobey, a member of the Kefauver committee, declared, "There are men whose conduct offends the nostrils of other American citizens, and in my judgment, Lucky Luciano heads the list."

The commission met, heard Luciano in his own defense and the authorities against him, and then retired. Within a few months, it announced its decision. Luciano, it said, was "socially dangerous," and as such was, for the next two years, to be barred from leaving his home between dusk and dawn, from traveling more than sixteen miles outside Naples, and from frequenting places such as nightclubs and the Agnano racetrack. Certain minor exceptions, however, were made: he and Igea were allowed to go to the beach resort at Ostia outside Rome for a vacation, and he was permitted to go to his farm at Santa Marinella, forty miles northwest of Rome.

33.

His life had become a frustrating cycle, spinning endlessly between times of limited freedom and times of stringent restriction, between moments of power and moments of impotence. What was worse, for a man who once believed he controlled his destiny and the events around him, he seemed prey to the whims of others, he had little ability to influence the forces that moved around him, to shift the tide.

In the early 1950's in Italy, Luciano could only sit before his television screen, or in the darkness of a movie theater, and watch with horror the same scenes that were fascinating television viewers in America — the sudden light shining brightly on the organization he had created, as his old friends were dragged from the dark corners where they had hidden, from behind the respectable fronts they had assumed, and exposed as the masters of the organized underworld. Unlike honest American citizens, Luciano found nothing enthralling in Estes Kefauver, the drawling Tennessee senator some called a Rhodes Scholar in a coonskin cap, or his touring Senate crime investigating committee as it opened a few windows on the underworld's corruption and control of American cities. He was not amused at the shocked incredulity of the aging Senator Tobey who castigated the "rats" testifying before the committee and demanded of their attorneys an answer to his question why any self-respecting lawyer would represent such "scum." He was not fascinated or captivated by the sharp questions and lisping voice of committee counsel Rudolph Halley.

Americans may have been hypnotized, but Luciano was sickened at the sight of the nervously clenching and unclenching hands of Frank Costello (he refused to permit his face to be televised), his rasping voice barely audible as he refused to answer questions on advice of counsel, one of Luciano's old lawyers, George Wolf. Costello was the star of the show, the heavy, along with Virginia Hill, the comic relief, good for a laugh (though not from Luciano) with her self-portrait of an innocent, dumb, naïve blonde who knew nothing about anything. There was the long parade of his old friends, their faces suddenly no longer anonymous — Joe Adonis, Longie Zwillman, Meyer Lansky (with Moses Polakoff, another Luciano lawyer, at his side), Willie Moretti, Albert Anastasia, the whole underworld hierarchy — professing shocked surprise at being called and questioned, feigning ignorance of any wrongdoing, alternating with sullen silence, devious evasion and outright refusal to answer. There was even former New York City Mayor William O'Dwyer, by then United States Ambassador to Mexico, sweating, fidgeting, attempting to minimize the import of his relationship with Costello, Luciano and others that was being laid before him and the public. Perhaps the only satisfaction for Luciano was the portrait of New York Governor Thomas E. Dewey arrogantly refusing to testify in public before the committee about the release of Luciano or about the open gambling at Saratoga.

"For me, it was like a nightmare. Them investigations, when they was all over, didn't make a dent in nothin' back in the States, except puttin' the spotlight a little brighter on some of the guys. But, for me, every time my name got mentioned, the Italian cops kept pullin' me in for questionin', makin' my life miserable. I was already out of all the rackets in Italy, tryin' to live up to my word to Igea, but that didn't stop 'em. Siragusa was in there pushin' every fuckin' day and pushin' Florita to keep roustin' me.

"It just didn't let up, and things came to a kind of head around '54. There was an election for governor in New York and the Democrats was throwin' a lotta stuff at Dewey about makin' a deal with me to let me go and Dewey was sayin' he let me go because of the secret work I done for the government durin' the war, which he couldn't talk about. Things got so hot that the Italians set up an open court in Palermo to find out whether I really helped the United States and they took me down there to testify. I knew nobody wanted to hear the truth; they just wanted me to stand up and tell all the lies, so I put on an act for 'em. You'd have thought I was General Eisenhower, the way I told 'em what a big American patriot I'd been, how I got all the Italians and Sicilians in the States workin' to knock out the Nazis and how I got everybody in Sicily helpin' the Americans during 1943, which is why the invasion was such a big success. It was all shit, but it was what they wanted to hear and they loved it. I was so good on that witness stand, I could've won an Academy Award."

But there was more to Luciano's decision to perpetuate and expand the fictions. He knew that had he told the truth, he could have inflicted some wounds on Dewey and thus earned a measure of revenge. But such revenge would not have come cheap. The rumors of his contributions to the war effort had won him considerable popularity with ordinary Italians and had brought him the assistance of many reputable and influential Italian politicians and businessmen. While the truth might have hurt Dewey, it might also have dissipated Luciano's popularity and lost him some of his powerful friends. He was not willing to take that risk.

Luciano's testimony was widely reported in the Italian press. It combined with the publicity about his romance with Igea Lissoni and the rumors of his many beneficences to the poor of postwar Italy to far outweigh, with the Italian public at least, the unceasing pressures, hostility and publicity about his criminal activities that poured from Siragusa and Florita.

By then, Luciano had abandoned almost all hope of a return to the United States and had begun to accept as reality that Italy would remain his home for the rest of his life. His return to

America, he had always felt (despite his offer to Anslinger), hinged on election of Thomas Dewey as President. That was no longer even a faint possibility. In 1952, Dwight D. Eisenhower had won a landslide victory; his reelection in 1956 appeared inevitable, and by the time his term was up, a new generation of American political leaders would certainly have emerged. Tom Dewey would then be little more than an elder statesman, without a political future and with neither national office nor much national influence.

So Luciano bowed to Igea's long-held wish for a permanent home. They rented an apartment on the Via Tasso, halfway up the hillside overlooking the Bay of Naples. Igea's furnishings were brought from storage in Rome, and Father Scarpato, in his spare time, installed bookshelves and wood paneling. A middle-aged Sardinian housekeeper named Lydia was hired and Luciano bought two miniature Manchester terriers who soon were accompanying him everywhere.

He even found a new legitimate business, one he was sure would be a success and one that would do little harm to the image he was trying to develop as a man of good works. He opened a store in the Hotel Royal, specializing in X-ray machines, fluoroscopes, electrocardiograph machines and other medical equipment. Through that store, too, could be channeled the equipment Father Scarpato would need once his clinic was finished.

Still, he remained under twenty-four-hour surveillance and was restricted by the dusk-to-dawn curfew, and his telephone was tapped. On occasions, though, he managed to slip away, usually for meetings in secret with couriers and other important visitors from the United States. In 1958, most of these meetings began to take place in Taormina; his friend and confidant Rosario "Chinky" Vitaliti was then spending much of his time away from his home in the United States at a villa he bought in that Sicilian resort, and that house was put at Luciano's disposal.

There was, however, one important arrival from America whom Luciano studiously avoided. Joe Adonis had finally abandoned his fights with the police and courts in New York and New Jersey, with federal tax men and with immigration authorities. Rather than go to prison and then face deportation, he voluntarily agreed

374

to leave the United States forever. After a riotous round of fare-well parties, Adonis boarded the Italian luxury liner *Conte Biancamano* on January 3, 1956, and set sail in a style befitting a millionaire; he had the most expensive suite on the ship, a sitting room, bedroom and bath, costing $740.

It was Adonis's announced intention to settle in Milan. But his ship's first Italian port was Naples. He was due January 17. Would he meet Luciano, his old friend, when the ship docked? "I'm not going to look him up," Adonis told reporters, "and I hope he doesn't look me up."

In Naples, reporters who descended upon Luciano in his medical supply store got the same answer. "No, I'm not gonna meet no boat. I got nothin' in common with types like him. If he wants to look me up, that's his business. But I got no reason to go to him." Then Luciano began to lecture the press about Father Scarpato's clinic and his work with the priest.

"For one of the few times in my life, I really zippered my mouth. I knew Joe was comin' in on the *Conte Biancamano* and that he was travelin' in the bridal suite, all by himself. Every day that boat was sailin' nearer to Italy it made me think of my trips across on the *Laura Keene* and that rat-infested Turkish freighter, the *Bakir,* that smelled of nothin' but sweat and piss and vomit. And here was this son of a bitch comin' over to smell the beautiful perfume of his three million bucks in Zurich. And me, I'm not even allowed to go out at night to a restaurant for dinner. It got so bad for me durin' that week that if I hadn't had Igea with me, I think I'd've done somethin' real drastic."

The ship docked. Luciano stayed far away. Adonis debarked and that afternoon boarded a train for Milan.

But both men fully intended to meet, and a week later, Luciano and Igea drove secretly to Milan. While she visited her family, Luciano and Adonis met at a small, out-of-the-way hotel that rarely saw a tourist. There was little warmth between them. The meeting was strictly business and brief. Adonis had some messages for Luciano and some reports on the state of the underworld in the United States. Then they parted. They would not meet again until Christmas.

Just before that next meeting with Adonis, Luciano finally received some good news. In November, some of the restrictions on him were lifted by the Naples police; the two-year sentence had run out. Almost the first move he made, in concert with other deportees, was to send a formal appeal to President Eisenhower requesting readmission to the United States. It was denied. He was not surprised. "I never expected it. So somethin' you don't expect, when it don't happen, it also don't disappoint you. Of course, I know that Asslinger give Eisenhower's staff a whole file of lies about me that Siragusa had been sendin' to Washington. He was dreamin' up them charges in his head, what they call a 'paper case' because it's strictly crap that got put on paper when one of the agents wrote it into the files. The funny thing, though, was that when I got turned down, Igea was very happy. She never looked forward to goin' to the States with me. She just felt that I would get back into the rackets and big trouble would really start up all over again."

Hopeful that Luciano could now settle into a normal and peaceful existence, Igea talked often with him about buying a home — a villa somewhere or an apartment, something they could own. Luciano agreed. As they began their search, a friend named Gino Cuoma came to their assistance. He had been born in Italy, had emigrated to the United States where he had made a small stake in the restaurant business and then, in late middle age, had returned to Naples, hoping to open a restaurant. But he lacked sufficient capital. When Luciano met him and heard his story, he advanced the necessary funds (and was later repaid when the restaurant began earning a profit). Cuoma opened his restaurant in 1957 on the Partenope, the roadway paralleling the Bay of Naples and a short walk from the Excelsior and other hotels that catered to American tourists and naval personnel. He called it the California, and with Luciano as a frequent patron, it became an immediate attraction for Americans anxious to catch a glimpse of the notorious gangster. So proud of his friendship with Luciano was Cuoma that he decorated the walls of the restaurant with pictures of Luciano and visiting celebrities. Even today, they remain, though one, showing Luciano in conversation with Frank Sinatra, was removed a few years ago: Cuoma was visited one day by "some men I did not know" and requested to remove that photograph. He complied.

The California was still in the construction stage at the end of 1956 when Cuoma learned that his friends were looking for a place to buy. He volunteered his services and discovered a cooperative penthouse atop a five-story building on the exclusive Parco Comola, just off the Via Tasso where Luciano and Igea were living. It was spacious and surrounded by a huge red terrazzo veranda. Luciano quickly bought it for twenty-five thousand dollars with the deed made out in the name of his brother Bartolo in order not to complicate or delay the legal transfer. (Six years later, Bartolo would sell it, and all its furnishings, for thirty-two thousand dollars, less than half its value then, according to Naples real estate dealers.) The penthouse, with its view over the bay to Vesuvius, was everything Igea wanted, and she spent her days cajoling gardeners to fill the terrace with flowers, bartering with furniture dealers and cabinetmakers, employing the sisters at a nearby convent to embroider the linens with the initial "L" — and then teasing Luciano that if they ever separated, he must promise to let her take the linens with her since they both had that same initial.

"It was just about the time we bought the apartment that I started to change businesses. I found the medical supply setup was goin' to hell because I spent more time with Don Cheech up on Mount Vesuvius than in the store. I had a very nice secretary by the name of Dora De Negris, but she couldn't run the business all alone, even though she sure tried. That's when Father Scarpato came up with the plan to start a small factory to make furniture for Catholic schools. The idea was that a little plant could turn out plenty of desks and things like that and we could also use it to make furniture for the clinic. He was no dope, Don Cheech; he knew the only way I was gonna help him every day was for him to be my partner. So I got into the furniture business and we started to sell everything we could turn out. There wasn't a church that didn't have a school and there wasn't one of them schools that didn't need new desks and chairs and that type of stuff. I thought to myself that I'd finally hit on an honest business that was gonna pay off. Was I wrong! But I didn't find it out for a few years. We sold everything we made, but that didn't mean we collected our money. It seems there's some kinda law that makes it almost impossible to sue a church in Italy. So my furniture business wound up with a million accounts receivable and I was back where I was before I brought Momo Salemi over from Palermo to try to locate the deadbeats that never paid me for the appliances. Sometimes I would go home at night and want to hit my head against the wall, because every time I turned my hand to somethin' in Italy, either it got chopped off or I lost a bundle of dough.

"I put Momo to work again, only this time it was tougher, to try to collect at least some of the bills from the churches. He couldn't put the muscle on 'em, of course, like he did with a few of them appliance buyers. All he could do was go to see some priest or monsignor and ask very nice for a little dough on account. Ninety-nine per cent of the time, he got the same answer, that the church was too poor to pay. He'd come back to me and say, 'Charlie, what am I gonna do? You want me to hit the priest or steal the collection?' Then we'd laugh and write in another zero on the ledger."

One day, Luciano had a surprising visitor to his new home, a United States senator. "If you want to see some real crooks, take a look at our senators and congressmen in America. They call somebody a gangster, a racket guy or a crook because he's doin' somethin' against the law, when they're the worst kind of thieves, within the law. The United States was lendin' a lot of money to Europe, most of the time puttin' it into partnerships with the foreign country where there was plenty of profits. The dough would sit in Europe and pile up and they called the account 'counterpart funds.' It came to billions of lire in Italy and it was controlled by the American Embassy. So a senator and his family and his friends and his staff would arrive in Rome on a U.S. government plane, which they got the use of free, and somebody from the embassy would meet 'em and hand 'em a big bagful of lire from that counterpart fund; it happened all over Europe the same way. And these guys from Washington would spend the dough like it was dishwater, payin' their expenses, buyin' presents for the family, fur coats and jewels for their wives, you name it.

"This one senator who come to see me in Naples, he drank more booze, took out more airline stewardesses and embassy secretaries, and spent more counterpart funds than any nine congressmen put together, and to top it, he had a yen to be in the White House. He also had a yen to meet me. So we met, and I found out he would steal a red-hot stove. He talked about tryin' to fix up a way for me to come back to the States. He said he knew my record, but he also knew that Asslinger was way off base where I was concerned; he said he'd asked the American Embassy guys, includin' Siragusa, to show him proof that I was connected with the drug traffic in Italy, and he said they come up empty.

"Just before he left my apartment, he happened to look at this ring I wear on my pinky [a star sapphire and diamonds set in platinum] and he said to me, 'That's a beautiful ring. I've always wanted one like that.' I could've thrown that hayseed right off the roof. Instead, I said, 'Senator, you can have it and a lot more the day I set foot in New York — permanent.' We shook hands and he left and that's the last I ever saw of that chiselin' son of a bitch."

(Off to one side of the room during this conversation sat an Italian friend of Luciano's who spoke no English. But he remembered the meeting clearly, for when it was over Luciano told him the man was an important United States senator. He was not told the visitor's name, but recently he described him as "a tall, thin man. He wore glasses and he had a very prominent nose. What I remember best about him is his enormous capacity for drinking.")

During these years of the middle fifties, Luciano appeared relaxed and contented much of the time. With Fernando Alotti, the chauffeur-bodyguard he hired when Naples police chief Florita lifted his driver's license, he tinkered often with the Alfa Romeo Giulietta, a modest and relatively inexpensive sedan Alotti had persuaded him to buy in place of his customary American cars. They retooled the engine and occasionally out on the *autostrada*, where there is no speed limit, Luciano would take the wheel and push the car over 120 miles per hour. "He may have been a gangster in America," Alotti said, "but he was one of the nicest men I have ever known — kind, considerate and very brave. Sometime there would be people who would try to approach Mister Sharlie at the racetrack or someplace in public, to do something wrong or maybe to try to make some publicity for themselves. It was then that I could see him turn to steel. Nothing ever bothered him and he never lost his nerve. But la Signora [Igea] worried about him all the time."

By then, Luciano had become the most famous tourist attraction of Naples. Visiting Americans and sailors from the naval base invariably made the California a place to stop in order to see him. "Them kids would come up and ask for my autograph, and we'd talk about the States, what was happenin' back there. I found out if I give 'em an autographed picture made out to, let's say, their captain or some officer on the ship, it was good for a three-day pass."

With the curfew no longer hampering his movements, Luciano and Igea often went to the Agnano racetrack in Naples in the evening. "I even bought a horse. Back in the States I never could've done that; everybody would've figured that I'd fixed the race he was in. But in Italy, nobody give it a thought. And, you know, that horse of mine never finished in the money, not once. I sometimes thought I could walk faster than that fuckin' nag could run."

With Igea he dined out often at favorite Naples restaurants such as the Transatlantico, the Giacomino and the Zi Teresa, and they spent frequent weekends on Capri, renting again the small house they had occupied two years before.

None of his problems then seemed insurmountable. Though Father Scarpato's plans for his clinic were being obstructed by the Communist leader Ivan Montoni, the support and financial backing Luciano was giving openly to the priest seemed to help win the allegiance of the townspeople. The furniture business, at the end of 1956, seemed to be prospering, too, with the only apparent problems those of obtaining the necessary supplies and personnel.

"I was only sorry that this wasn't all takin' place in New York, where I could come home every night on the subway with the *World-Telegram* and have Igea meet me at the door, kiss me like a regular wife and the first thing I'd ask her would be, 'What're you makin' for dinner?' "

But any dreams Luciano had for a life as a suburban husband with a good legitimate business were not to last long. During the Christmas holiday, he and Igea received special permission to drive to Milan to visit her family. There Luciano met with Joe Adonis, their second meeting since Adonis's arrival in Italy earlier in the year. The first had been brief and in secret in Milan, in June. This time, there were urgent matters to discuss. Both Luciano and Adonis had received news from New York that a major struggle was about to erupt, with Vito Genovese the focal point.

34.

Under the guidance of Igea Lissoni, Luciano had spent many of his evenings when under curfew reading the books that he had ignored all his life. In his apartment on the Parco Comola one day in 1961, he motioned to the bookshelves and asked, "You know anythin' about Shakespeare? When I went to grammar school, they didn't teach Shakespeare. But I've been readin' him for the last few years." He reached into a bookcase and pulled out a worn copy of the collected plays and opened it.

"Well, in *Julius Caesar,* you remember a guy by the name of Cassius? He was a pain in the ass. It seems like everybody's got a Cassius in his life. And I got one, too — only his name is Vito Genovese." He paused for a moment. "Come to think of it, I even had two Cassiuses in my life, the other one bein' a guy by the name of Meyer Lansky. But I didn't get on to him for a long time."

By Christmas of 1956, when Luciano met with Adonis in Milan, the ambition of Vito Genovese had reached the stage where it had become an urgent matter. Any checks on Genovese seemed to have vanished with the decision by Adonis to abandon his fight to remain in the United States and instead to return to Italy, and with Frank Costello's multiplying problems — with the Bureau of Internal Revenue over charges of tax evasion, with his appeals from jail sentences for contempt of the Kefauver committee.

"I figured that at least my good friend Meyer Lansky was still around and that he would be lookin' after things for me and keepin' a leash on that greedy pig. I knew Vito was burnin' with ambition to be the Boss of Bosses and someday he was gonna make a try for it. From what Joe A. told me, I could see that Vito'd already been at work. He'd replaced some guys who'd been loyal to me and moved up other guys like Tommy Eboli who was willin' to give him loyalty over anybody. Then Joe told me that Eboli had moved up Tony Bender as his first lieutenant, and that could mean only one thing: Vito was gonna make his try now.

"But outside of Joe tellin' me that trouble was brewin', all I got from him at that meet was doubletalk without no details. He knew how I felt about him ever since that time at the Zurich airport and I knew he didn't have no more love for me. But I thought when it came to stuff in the States, we was still partners. But he just wouldn't mention Vito's name and I even had the impression he was sidin' with Vito. If that was so, it hadda be against me. So I decided to wait until I got word from New York direct about what was goin' on."

That word was brought in the first week of February 1957, by Genovese's newly appointed chief aide, Tommy Eboli. A sometime prizefight manager under his own name and the alias Tommy Ryan, Eboli was a man with a quick and volatile temper (he was later barred from handling fighters after leaping into the ring to dispute a decision and assaulting the referee). He had served as a courier to Luciano once or twice before, but the exiled gang leader did not know him well and what he knew he did not particularly like.

"I guess he'd been told by Vito to watch his mouth with me, because when he come over he showed me a lotta respect. Eboli said there'd been a meet of the council to discuss Frank Costello, because Frank told Vito and the rest of the guys a few months before that he wanted to get out. He was in so much hot water that he didn't hardly have no time left over for the Unione's business or nothin' else. He just wanted to retire with honor. Of course, there ain't no such thing as retirin' from the outfit; once you're in, you're in, and the only way out is in a box. But, hell, Frank had been part of it since the beginnin'; he helped me set the fuckin' thing up and he'd been with me all the way. So I didn't see no reason why an exception couldn't be made in his case.

"Eboli told me that the council had already met and voted and he'd come to Italy to get my vote. I asked him how the council voted and he said it was unanimous — everybody agreed that Frank oughta be allowed to step down. All they needed was my vote to make it official. Naturally, that means that Anastasia, Tommy Lucchese, Joe Bananas and all the other guys, includin' Joe Adonis, okayed it. So I began to think to myself, why the hell did Adonis doubletalk me on the details? I asked Tommy whether Adonis had voted before me, and he said, 'Yeah, he went along with everybody.' I began to wonder why Adonis didn't send word to me when he was asked for his vote before Eboli showed up in Naples. I can't come up with no answer except my nose tells me somethin' stinks."

Though disturbed by his growing suspicions, Luciano nevertheless sent Eboli back to New York with the word that he had no objections to Costello retiring to the home he had bought at Sands Point on Long Island, or anyplace else he wanted. But that night, Luciano sent a short note to Costello through the APO address to which he had access. "I couldn't trust nobody to carry that note personally, but I knew that Uncle Sam would get it to Frank without no questions. All I wanted to know was would Frank send me word by messenger what was up and gimme the whole story."

About a month later, a new courier arrived with Costello's reply. He was Pasquale "Pat" Eboli, sometimes known as Pat Ryan, the younger brother of Tommy Eboli; in recent years, he, too, had served as a courier from the States, carrying money and messages. But unlike his older brother, he and Luciano had instantly become close friends, a friendship that created a schism between the two Ebolis.

Costello had called Pat Eboli to a meeting at the Waldorf-Astoria and given him the reply to take to Luciano. "First, Frank said Joe A. was right, that trouble was really gettin' ready to blow up. Joe Bananas come to Frank a couple weeks before this and told him that Vito had been goin' around on the sly, talkin' to the heads of the different families. Vito didn't say nothin' direct; he was tryin' to find out in them little private meets who would be loyal to who if the goin' got tough and a showdown come. He didn't say who the showdown was gonna be with, Joe told Frank; he just let that hang. Knowin' Vito, he probably figured that since Bananas was very big in junk and was buyin' from him, Vito had nothin' to worry about Joe backin' him all the way. The only thing was, Vito was so stuck on himself he thought he could muscle everybody to his way of thinkin'. He always made that kinda mistake. He could never read guys right. That's why Joe Bananas went to Costello; he was smart; he knew that if Vito tried to shut me out, he'd have to climb over a lotta guys, especially Anastasia and Tommy Lucchese.

"So, readin' between the lines of what Pat Eboli told me, I realized that Costello was also on the spot because he wanted to retire. I asked Pat whether Frank had made any comment about his retirement and Pat told me that Frank wanted him to use the exact words to me: 'Tell Charlie I'm gonna retire even if it kills me.' Well, that gimme the whole answer to everythin'. All the rest was just words and Costello knew that I'd understand it. He was simply tellin' me that Vito didn't really give a shit about no decision by the council or nobody else. He was gonna make his move and get where he's been wantin' to reach all along, no matter who got killed."

It was a very disturbed Luciano who came away from the meeting with Eboli. For the next several days, he spent much of his time away from Igea and his apartment, telling her nothing of what had happened so as not to worry her. And during the next weeks, he began to learn more and more about events in the United States.

At the time of Costello's decision to retire, his major interests — aside from attempting to stay out of jail — were in gambling and real estate. He owned points in the Beverly Club, the Beverly Hills Club and three Las Vegas hotels, interests that were administered for him by Meyer and Jake Lansky and Phil Kastel. He personally supervised his real estate portfolio — owned in his own and cover names — consisting of parcels in Wall Street and along Park Avenue. He had proposed to his associates on the council that if he were permitted to retire, he would surrender all his decision-making powers and even withdraw from active participation in gambling. He wanted only to continue receiving the income from gambling and real estate.

To most members of the council, Costello's proposal seemed reasonable. But not to Genovese. Despite his earlier agreement to Costello's retirement, he began to oppose it. "When I heard about that, I was sure that Vito had started to make his move by beginnin' a real squeeze on Frank. He got up at the last meet I was told about and said there was only one way a guy could get out. Frank couldn't quit and live. Then I heard that Lansky got up and said, 'Frank should have the right to live in peace after all he's done for everybody.'

"That give Vito the openin' he was lookin' for. He said that if Frank got out and retired, he would have to throw everything he had into the pot for the city, for all the families in the city, and then the New York bosses would decide what kind of a pension he should have. Of course, that was a lotta shit. Vito couldn't have cared less about Frank's interests goin' into a pot. I realized there hadda be somethin' else — that little son of a bitch was out to get Costello because he never forgot that time when Costello insulted him back in the Claridge Hotel when he objected to me bringin' Dutch Schultz into our outfit. I just knew that was in the back of Vito's mind like a fire all them years and he'd been tryin' to figure a way to pay off Frank for talkin' to him like a piece of shit. Now, he got a chance to do it, and with the council's okay, because they didn't know what was really behind it.

"Then my brother Bart come over to Naples with some money and with a message from Albert. There had been another meet just two days before Bart left New York. Albert said that things was comin' down to a choice between Vito and Costello. Vito finally opened up and said he was gonna be the boss. Albert told him that he was boss of nothin'. He said that I set up everything back in 1931 so that no one guy could run nobody else's outfit. If Vito thought he was gonna change that way of operatin' and try to become another Maranzano, Albert would personally make sure that Vito would be very, very sorry.

"Then, Albert said, Lansky tried to calm everybody down by sayin' that Costello might end up in stir for a long stretch and that could solve a lotta problems. He asked Vito, 'After all, how much of a danger could Frank be if he's in jail?' When Vito seen that Lansky's question was havin' an effect on everybody else, he said, 'Okay, maybe you're right. Maybe what we oughta do is just let him take the rap, just let him fight his own fight and not help him out at all.' What Genovese was doin' was tryin' to go against everythin' we always did when a guy got into trouble; everybody helped him out, and if he went away for good, we would help out his family. It was like a law with us. Now, that dirty prick was tellin' the council we oughta forget the rules anytime they got in his way to the top.

"I didn't wanna involve my brother. Things was gettin' too complicated in New York in the early part of 1957 and the less he knew about it the better. Besides, I had a feelin' in my guts that Albert's little speech to Vito was gonna bounce back and hit him bad. I didn't want Bart connected with that, neither. I sent him back to New York and told him to stick to his garment business and not talk to nobody at all. I was about to send word to Chinky Vitaliti to see Albert in Brooklyn when I got word that the council had gone against Vito. They ruled exactly the way I suggested, that Frank should be allowed to quit with honor, that he could keep all his interests and just give up his vote on the council."

But Luciano was convinced that Genovese would not be deterred by the council's decision. Not only would Genovese continue his campaign against Costello and Anastasia, Luciano was sure, but he would also direct his fire at Lansky for having attempted to interfere with his plans at the council session. "You know, there's a very simple difference between the Jews and the Italians; the Jews, they kill *for* each other; and the Italians, they kill each other. But the fuckin' Neapolitans, they kill each other in the back."

What Luciano did not know, and what he was never to learn, was that Genovese had already set in motion plans to kill him. Luciano, in fact, had been marked as Genovese's first major victim on the road to the top, and a killer had been dispatched from New York in 1956 to accomplish that deed. At Luciano's funeral in 1962, his cousin Calcedonia Lucanía began to talk to several people near the open coffin, remarking on his own relationship. "One of the men," he said, "took me aside and we talked. I said to him what a shame it was that Charlie had died so young. The man, he was an Italian-American whose name I did not know, but he was medium-sized with glasses and I could tell he was from America, he said to me, 'Yes, it is a shame, but then Charlie had more years than some people might realize. He almost died in 1956.'

"I said to him, I was so amazed, 'No, that isn't so. He was very well then. He only had a bad back.' This man answered, 'I know he wasn't sick. I came over here in 1956 to kill him. I had orders to kill him. But how could I kill a man who had once saved my life and who had saved me from starvation many times?'

"I was so shocked that I blurted out, 'Well, if you were ordered to do this thing and you did not do it, how is it possible that you are still alive?' The man shrugged his shoulders and told me, 'Well, I managed. I just couldn't do such a thing, not to Charlie Lucky.' After the funeral the man went away and I never saw him again."

Unaware that he himself was a target, Luciano waited to see in what direction Genovese would strike in defiance of the council. The obvious target was Costello. With Adonis and Luciano in Italy, Costello, even in retirement, remained a symbol of the old days and so stood in the way of Genovese's assumption of absolute control over the Luciano family, central in the underworld. By disposing of this remaining co-custodian of Luciano's American interests, Genovese would stand supreme.

The council had given Frank Costello his life and a rich retirement. Genovese secretly decreed his death. Luciano later learned that Genovese gave the orders for Costello's murder to Tommy Eboli, by then so high in the upper echelons that he would not carry it out himself. He turned the contract over to Tony Bender. But Bender was a devious man who always tried to stay on the good side of all bosses and would-be bosses, and he was squeamish about taking on such an assignment that might put him in peril.

He farmed out the contract to a three-hundred-pound former prizefighter and small-time hoodlum whose multiplicity of quivering chins gave him his nickname: Vincent "The Chin" Gigante.

On May 2, 1957, Frank Costello as usual dined out in the evening. He had a few drinks at Peacock Alley with Frank Erickson, his gambling partner, who was also suffering from overexposure by the Kefauver investigation, and Little Augie Carfano, an old-time member of the Luciano outfit. Later in the evening, Costello joined some other friends at an upper East Side restaurant. About eleven, he excused himself, saying he was expecting an important telephone call from one of his Washington lawyers, Edward Bennett Williams. As his cab let him off at his apartment, the Majestic at 115 Central Park West on the corner of Seventy-second Street, a large black Cadillac stopped behind; a huge man got out and hurried into the building. Costello strolled in behind him without haste. When Costello was halfway into the lobby, Vincent Gigante, the fat man, stepped out from behind a pillar, a .38-caliber revolver in his hand. He shouted, perhaps with a last-second nod to the old tradition that a leader deserves to meet death from the front, "This is for you, Frank." Then he fired one shot.

At the sound of the voice, Costello turned, and that movement saved his life. The bullet creased the right side of his scalp, tearing it open just above the ear. But Gigante assumed that his mission was a success; he raced out to the waiting Cadillac and sped away.

Bleeding and groggy, Costello was rushed to a hospital for emergency treatment. Unfortunately for him, while the doctors worked over him, New York City police went through his coat pockets and discovered eight hundred dollars in cash and a slip of paper that read: "Gross casino win as of 4-26-57 — $651,284. Casino win less markers [IOU's] — $434,695. Slot wins — $62,844. Markers — $153,745." Costello refused to discuss that slip of paper and said he had no idea how it had gotten into his pocket. But the totals, an investigation revealed, matched exactly the officially reported gambling revenues of the Tropicana Hotel in Las Vegas, in which Costello had an interest. As a result of this discovery and Costello's refusal to talk about it, he was given a short prison term for contempt of court and for income tax evasion.

Costello also would not identify his would-be assassin, saying he had not seen or recognized him. The doorman at the Majestic, however, did describe the fat man and police began a search for Gigante. A couple of months later, Gigante reappeared, blandly saying he had only just discovered that the law was looking for him. During those months he had slimmed down, and by the time he was put on trial, the doorman could no longer positively identify him. When Costello continued to maintain his silence, Gigante went free.

For Genovese, whose repudiation of the council's ruling was now in the open, the aborted attempt on Costello was a dangerous moment. He sealed himself inside his palatial home in Atlantic Highlands, New Jersey, protected by more than forty armed men, and proceeded to summon all the lieutenants in the Luciano family for a show of support for his actions. He could use such unanimity before the council to lend legitimacy to his action and avoid retribution. All but one of those lieutenants answered the summons, though some still loyal to Luciano did so out of fear for their lives. The only absentee was Little Augie Carfano; within two years he would be shot to death on orders of Genovese.

And from outside the Luciano family, another voice was raised in protest, that of Frank Scalise, second in command to Albert Anastasia in that Brooklyn family. A month later, Scalise was killed. (Mafia informer Joe Valachi would later say that Scalise had been shot by Vincent Squillante, who within three months also cut the throat and dismembered the body of Scalise's brother, Joseph. Valachi claimed the deaths of the Scalises had been ordered by Albert Anastasia. But according to Luciano, Anastasia had nothing to do with them. The orders had come from Vito Genovese, who saw the death of Frank Scalise as the removal of a major rival within the Anastasia organization.)

"After Gigante blew the hit on Costello, Genovese and Costello had a private meet at Longie Zwillman's house in Jersey. Frank sent me word about it later. Vito proposed a compromise because they had each other over a barrel after what happened. He told Frank, 'Don't do nothin'. Don't complain to nobody. And most of all, don't go to Charlie Lucky with this thing, because if you do, you're gonna start a war. In that case, I promise that you'll be the first guy dead.' So they made a deal. What choice did Frank have? He said he would drop the whole thing and Vito agreed to let him retire like he wanted, with all his gamblin' and real estate. Of course, about that time, Frank was convicted on income tax evasion and had to do a couple years in the can. But after he got out, he went out to his place in Sands Point and started to clip coupons."

The attempt on Costello, the first open use of guns against an underworld leader since the early thirties, was a shock to Luciano. "I was up at a health spa in Montecatini with Igea. I had somethin' wrong with my back and the baths up there was very good for it. It was the mornin' of May 3 when the Guardia and the Mobile picked me up and took me in. One of the inspectors at the barracks asked me why I tried to have Frank Costello killed. I'm sure they must've believed me because my reaction was absolutely straight. I told 'em I didn't know nothin' about it until that minute. One of the inspectors said, 'But, Signor Lucanía, you must know what happened?' I said to him, 'All I know from what you tell me is that the guy who done it must've been a lousy shot.'

"Of course it was all over the newspapers, with pictures showin' Frank bein' attended by the doctors in the hospital. From that minute on, Igea wouldn't let me outa her sight. As for me, I was so fuckin' pissed off that if Florita hadn't lifted my passport, I'd've been on the next fuckin' plane to Switzerland or someplace where I could set things up to get back into the States in secret and straighten out that little bastard Vito. But without a passport, with the cops watchin' me so close, and with Igea hangin' on my neck twenty-four hours a day, it wasn't possible.

"So I drove down to Rome and sent a letter to Meyer through the APO of a friend of mine and told him to send somebody over right away. Before Meyer even got that letter, who shows up in Naples but Tommy Eboli. He didn't beat around the bush; he tells me he's comin' straight from Vito and Vito says there's gotta be peace and I shouldn't start nothin'. Then that stupid Eboli throws me a little thought of his own; he advises me to take it easy and everything's gonna be fine. I told him to go fuck himself with his advice and run back to Vito and tell him the day hasn't come yet when he can take me in no kind of a fight. Eboli looks at me with his eyes wide open and he says, a little nervous, 'Charlie, are you sure you want me to tell that to Vito?' So I looked at him and laughed. Then I went to the door and held it open for him and told him, 'Tommy, you ain't a bad kid, but your trouble is that you're not like your brother. You're the one who has to learn to take it easy.' "

Now Luciano's attention was focused solely on what Genovese might do next; he waited anxiously, too, for a reply from Lansky. To protect himself, he avoided most vulnerable public places and went nowhere without Fernando Alotti, Joe Di Giorgio or Momo Salemi, turning away abruptly the advances of any but his closest friends. Finally a message came, from Paul Gambino, brother of Carlo, requesting an urgent, private meeting. Within a few days, the two were together at Luciano's farm at Santa Marinella.

"Paul told me exactly what happened about Vito's attempt to eliminate Frank and the deal Vito and Frank made afterwards. Then he tells me that the ways things are goin', it looks like Anastasia is gonna have 'serious trouble very soon.' I was sure he was actin' in the interest of Albert because his brother was Albert's solid right hand, or so I thought. So I told him to get back to New York right away and have Albert call the council together — everybody except Vito. Albert was to tell 'em that I approved a hit on Vito. I suggested that in order to keep the meet a secret they should go someplace private, like Atlantic City, where they could look like a bunch of tourists and nobody would know why they was there. I emphasized for Gambino to tell Albert that in this particular case he was actin' for me and to do it exactly like I said."

The next day, Paul Gambino was on his way back to New York. "I figured Albert got my message right away and I'm waitin' to hear that he's called the council and they've okayed what I suggested. I couldn't see no reason for them not to approve it, because it was the unwritten rule that if any head of a family ever put the rest of us in real danger, he hadda go. But if Albert did get my message, that stupid hotheaded bastard must've decided not to follow it, because the next thing I hear is that he's goin' after Vito himself, on his own. By that point, Anastasia was really off his rocker and he just wanted to kill anybody who came to his

391

mind that he got mad about. He was startin' to see himself like some guy in the old gangster movies, like Jimmy Cagney. For chrissake, he even had that kid Arnold Schuster knocked off because he seen him braggin' on television about how he spotted that bank robber Willie Sutton and tipped off the cops."

But Luciano heard something even more unsettling than Anastasia's apparent decision to ignore his orders and go it alone. "About the beginnin' of June, I heard that Vito had a contract out on me. At first I couldn't believe it, but when I started to analyze it, I hadda admit that deep inside I always knew this day was gonna come. I got this word from Longie Zwillman when one of his boys was on a trip to Europe for his 'health' and dropped in to see me in Naples first. So at that point, I hadda outmaneuver Vito. Knowin' that little bastard like the back of my hand, there was one thing I was sure of — he wouldn't be comin' at me from the front. It would have to be some kind of angle, some guy sneakin' up from behind.

"I spent a couple days tryin' to wear Genovese's shoes, and then it comes to me, nine chances out of ten, how he's gonna do it. The son of a bitch knows how much I love cars and that I'm always foolin' around with motors. So if he's gonna get me, then the easiest way would be somethin' connected with my car."

At the bottom of the Via Tasso escarpment was a service station. Luciano had become friendly with the owner and together the two had periodically worked with meticulous care over Luciano's Alfa Romeo. "Once I figured out how Vito was gonna come at me, we began goin' over the car every day, from the front bumper to the rear bumper, real careful, because I thought that some night Vito's guys would try to plant a bomb in it. If it'd been anybody but Vito, I never would've thought to look for a bomb; a shotgun in the back, maybe, but not a blowup. Then I tried to set a regular pattern which anybody who was watchin' me could've fixed their clocks by. At the same time every day, I'd go down to the service station with Salemi and Fernando and the three of us and that mechanic'd go over the car. Then Fernando'd take the car out and drive me wherever I hadda go, and then at night, before we put the car away, the four of us would check it out again in my garage at the rear of my apartment building.

"This one night, it was at the end of June, Igea wasn't feelin' too well and I went out to dinner at the Zi Teresa with John Raimundo. I left my car in the garage and John picked me up in a taxi; it was a big treat for Cockeye when I took him to dinner in a swell place and I enjoyed watchin' him eat, though I wasn't too hungry in them days, what with tryin' to second-guess Vito. After dinner, Fernando and Salemi came by the restaurant in Salemi's car. We dropped John off at the Torino Hotel where he lived and they drove me home. The mechanic was waitin' for us there. I opened up my garage, which was a private stall with its own door and lock, and the three of us start to check over the car, when suddenly I hear a noise behind me, and I could feel somethin' comin' at me. It was kinda instinctive, and it went through my mind in a half a second that I was gonna get it then and there and I could already feel the slug goin' between my shoulder blades. I must've ducked and that's what saved me. Just as I looked around, there was two guys, I never seen 'em before, and they was comin' at us with lead pipes. The first guy takes a swipe at my head, but he missed me and hit the car — the son of a bitch put a terrible dent in the fender. The other guy went for Salemi and caught him across the shoulders, but didn't knock him out.

"We didn't give 'em a second chance. The mechanic was a skinny little runt who weighed about seven pounds soakin' wet, so he was no good to us. But Fernando tackled them two guys like a pro football player and knocked 'em both right on their ass. And then we went to work on 'em. They both had guns, but I guess they didn't drill me because they knew the police was keepin' watch on me and a lotta noise was the last thing they wanted. What I never knew was where the hell them cops was, anyway; they always followed me like shadows and this one night when I could've used 'em, they wasn't even around.

"Anyway, we beat them two guys into a bloody pulp. I tried to get 'em to tell me who they was or what town in the States they came from, whether they was independent or in somebody's outfit, and especially if Vito sent 'em. They wouldn't open their mouths except to say, 'Don't kill us. We're Italians.' We found phony passports on 'em — they must've had real ones stashed away someplace — so that didn't help none. The way I felt then, I was ready

393

to kill 'em without blinkin' an eye; I was ready to knock somebody off for the first time with my own hands. But then I began to cool off and think a little bit. Finally, I decided to keep 'em alive and send 'em back to Vito with a message. We threw some water on 'em, got 'em up on their feet, and I told 'em to go back to New York and tell Vito that if he wanted to start a war with me, he would get to know what it feels like to have somebody drop an atom bomb on him. I said to tell the little bastard he would never be the boss as long as I was alive and that I intended to live for a long time. Then we tied 'em up and locked 'em in the garage overnight."

The next morning, the two would-be assassins were driven from Naples directly to Rome Airport, put in first-class seats aboard a TWA Constellation, and sent back to the United States. What happened to them when they arrived, Luciano never learned.

For a moment, Luciano considered dealing directly and finally with Genovese, then rejected that idea. "I set up the outfit and I made the rules, so I couldn't be the one to break 'em. If Vito was gonna go, like I told Albert after the hit on Frank, it'd have to be by order of the council, all legal, accordin' to our rules."

35.

Igea was never told of the attempt on Luciano, for he was determined to protect her from that side of his life. Further, he had begun to notice a growing listlessness and increasing pallor about her, which he attributed not to illness but to concern for him during a time when much of his attention had been directed elsewhere. When Pat Eboli arrived in Naples with money from New York a few weeks later, Luciano decided to take him and Igea for a short holiday to Taormina. Chinky Vitaliti, now back in the United States, had extended the use of the house he had bought there to Luciano.

"We had a little boat down there and Pat and I took it out a little ways and anchored it. At first he was kinda hedgy, sorta beatin' around the bush about the trouble back in the States. He was in a helluva spot because everything that was goin' on right at that time with Vito involved his brother Tommy right up to the eyebrows, and I didn't want to bring no pressure on Pat to be a stool pigeon about his own brother. But Pat told me the situation between Vito and Albert was gettin' worse every day, especially since Cheech [Frank Scalise] got knocked off. After a day or so, I sent Patsy back to New York, without no messages. The kid was already in a fight with Tommy over loyalty to me and I didn't have the heart to get him involved no further.

"Then I got a hunch that maybe Albert never got my message, which could mean only one thing; the Gambinos was on Vito's side and didn't pass on the instructions. Then it all began to make sense, because after all, I done the same kind of thing myself years before. Carlo was willin' to wait on the sidelines in the fight between Anastasia and Genovese, just figurin' the odds that Albert was so crazy in the head Vito would take him sooner or later. When that happened, Mister Carlo Gambino winds up head of the Anastasia family. After Albert knocked off Phil and Vince Mangano in the early part of '51 and took over that outfit, he made it a hundred times bigger. So, if my hunch was right, the minute Gambino gets control, he or Paul will be comin' over to Naples again to make peace with me."

Luciano, though, was not willing to abandon his old friend Albert Anastasia. Through his APO contact, he sent a direct message to Anastasia at a secret post office box in Fort Lee, New Jersey, alerting Anastasia to what Luciano considered very real and imminent danger. No acknowledgment was ever received. All Luciano could do was wait.

On October 25, 1957, Albert Anastasia was driven by his chauffeur-bodyguard out of the electrified gates of his estate in Fort Lee into Manhattan, arriving at ten-fifteen in the morning at the barbershop in the Park Sheraton Hotel on West Fifty-fifth Street. Anastasia entered, hung up his jacket, and sat down in his customary chair number four. Hardly glancing at barber Joseph Bocchino, he said, "Haircut," and then settled back. Indeed, he needed a haircut, for his black hair was shaggy and uneven. Bocchino draped a towel and cloth around Anastasia's chin and went to work with scissors and clippers. Suddenly, the front door opened and two men, with scarves masking their faces and pistols in their hands, walked in. "Keep your mouth shut if you don't want your head blown off," one of them said to Arthur Grasso, the shop's owner. Then they quickly stepped up behind Anastasia's chair and opened fire. Anastasia leaped forward out of the chair at the first shot, landing on his feet, weaving. Apparently disoriented, he lunged toward the reflection of the gunmen in the mirror. Another volley of shots smashed into and around him, sending him reeling into the mirror and the shelf under it. As he fell, bottles of hair tonic crashed to the floor with him. Then two more shots were fired, one smashing into the back of his skull. Ten bullets were fired at Anastasia; five hit him — one in the left hand, one in the left wrist, one in the right hip, one in the back and the final one in the head that killed him.

It was over in less than a minute, and the two gunmen were out of the shop and around the corner into the Fifty-fifth Street entrance to the BMT subway, dropping their guns as they raced away — one was found in the corridor leading from the shop to the hotel lobby, the second two blocks away at the end of the Fifty-seventh Street BMT platform. Just who the killers were has been the subject of rumors and speculation for years. According to Luciano, however, he was told they were "Crazy Joe" Gallo, a young Brooklyn hoodlum who owed his allegiance then to Carlo Gambino, Joe Profaci, and Joe Biondo, once part of the Luciano family and now devoted to Genovese. (Fifteen years later, Joe Gallo met the same sudden fate in a restaurant in Manhattan's Little Italy.)

"I was sittin' at home when I got a phone call from the Caserna Zanzur, which was across the street from where I used to live at the Hotel Turistico. The man callin' said his name was Andrea Speziale and he's an important inspector with the Guardia di Finanza. He says they want to see me down at the Caserna right away. It was late in the afternoon and I just figured it was another one of them things, another roust about nothin' in particular. Fernando drove me down here and I go into Speziale's office and he tells me to sit down. He's very polite and quiet-spoken, nothin' like that prick Florita. He looks at me for a minute, then he says that over in the United States a gangster just got killed and what do I know about it? I kinda shrugged, but inside I was thinkin' that Albert finally done what he was supposed to do. So I said, 'I don't know nothin' about no American gangster gettin' killed today. How the hell could I? I'm sittin' here in Naples about five thousand miles away. I don't even know who you're talkin' about.'

"I'm expectin' Speziale to tell me that the guy he's talkin' about is Vito Genovese. He gives me another one of them looks, with a kind of smile, and he says, 'The gangster I have in mind was a friend of yours — named Albert Anastasia.' Then he gives me all the details. I almost fell over. I couldn't figure out how it could've happened. I had warned Albert weeks and weeks before. How could he have been so stupid to get caught alone in a closed-in place like a barbershop? I was sure in that second Vito was behind it, and he must've been responsible for knockin' off Frank Scalise, too. I think Speziale must've seen I was tellin' the truth because I was so staggered, so he didn't press me. He got up and put his hand on my shoulder and walked me to the door.

"When I left the Caserna, I started to think. I realized I hadda get in touch with my friends in New York, the guys I could still depend on." During the next days, messages flew back and forth across the Atlantic between Luciano and his allies in the Unione. He learned almost immediately that Genovese was about to make his final push for the top. He had sent out a call to his peers throughout the underworld for a general conference of all leaders of the Unione Siciliano in mid-November, only three weeks after the Anastasia murder. To that summons he had added the statement, "Charlie Lucky wants the meeting held to set things straight."

"It was like the shit hit the fan all over the country. A lotta guys really didn't know how bad things was between Vito and me at that time, but I think a lot of 'em must've smelled a rat. After all, the word was around that Vito and I wasn't on the best of terms, so why would I send a notice for a national council meet through Vito? When they began to ask me, I answered 'em all, by letters, couriers and cablegrams under other names, that I didn't know a fuckin' thing about no council meet. Besides, I would never've been such an idiot to call a wholesale conference of all the leaders at one time. Maybe if I'd been in the States, I'd've gotten a few guys together in small groups in an open public place where we could still have some privacy, like we used to do on the beach at Atlantic City. But that wasn't Vito. He just hadda have a big meet, with everybody sittin' around and bowin' to him, like he was Maranzano's Messiah. He even had the fuckin' guts to tell all the council members to bring envelopes. I think he had it in mind to have himself named king, because I don't think he would've settled for the title *capo tutti capi;* that wouldn't've been big enough for that little round, fat bastard."

In the weeks before Genovese's scheduled meeting, personal agents from many of the American leaders arrived in Naples to seek Luciano's advice. Among the arrivals was Carlo Gambino himself, who had assumed control of the Anastasia operations. With that goal reached, he now pledged his loyalty to Luciano again.

"I told Carlo to go to the meet, but not to bring no envelope. He took my advice, because as it turned out, he only had some travelin' money with him and, he told me later, that if things had come to a showdown, he was gonna stand up and tell Vito to go to hell, that he didn't have the chance of a snowball in hell that the council would name him top *capo.*

"A few other guys was smart enough to pass up the meet. Frank Costello got out of it by coppin' a plea that he had so much heat on him and maybe he was bein' tailed everywhere, so that if he went it might cause a lot of trouble. Little Meyer had a different excuse. He said he had a sore throat and laryngitis and leavin' Florida in November would be too risky for his health."

On November 24, 1957, about a hundred top- and middle-level underworld leaders from all over the United States — most of them Italians — gathered at the estate of an outwardly respectable Buffalo businessman named Joseph Barbara in the rural Sullivan County community of Apalachin. The parade of so many big black limousines containing so many obviously unrural gentlemen, however, aroused the suspicions of New York State Police Sergeant Edgar Cresswell. With the three state troopers he had under him, he set up roadblocks immediately around the Barbara estate. The roadblocks were spotted as the meeting was just getting under way, and the alarm was raised.

Then, in one of the most ludicrous scenes in the history of organized crime in the United States, the leaders of the American underworld, dressed in their hand-tailored silk or imported woolen suits, went scurrying out windows and doors, crashing through the woods and underbrush in a frantic effort to escape. Many did. But Cresswell and his troopers, aided by reinforcements, rounded up sixty. It was a haul that bewildered law enforcement officials for the moment, for into their net was swept a galaxy — Genovese; Barbara; Joe Bonanno; Joe Profaci; John Scalise, the Cleveland leader; Louis Trafficante, Jr., from Florida; Joe Zerilli from Detroit; Frankie Zito from downstate Illinois (other Midwestern leaders, including Chicago's Sam Giancana, managed to escape); Joe Ida of Philadelphia; Colorado's James Coletti; Dallas boss James Civello, and many more. For some, the raid was an almost fatal blow, for it destroyed the cover of respectability they had labored for years to erect. One of these was John C. Montana, a Buffalo taxi operator who only the year before had been named Man of the Year in Buffalo by the Erie Club, the police department's official social organization.

Not one of those picked up would explain the reasons for his presence in such company at Apalachin, and so a number were tried, convicted, fined and sent to prison for conspiring to obstruct justice by their silence. All the convictions were upset on appeal.

For Genovese, the raid and resultant publicity were serious blows to his ambitions and his pride. For years he had been a shadowy figure about whom there were only rumors while attention was focused on more famous and colorful leaders like Luciano, Adonis, Costello and Anastasia. Now he was out in the open, the light full on him, where it would remain for the rest of his life. And, for him, even worse was the embarrassment he had suffered in the eyes of his colleagues.

"The way Vito organized the Apalachin thing only proves the worst part about him — that he was stupid. He never learned. He always put his greed in front of common sense. The last thing you wanna do is call attention to yourself. What the hell did Vito think would happen when a bunch of guys from all over the country, dressed in fancy city clothes, come drivin' up some country road in their big Cadillacs like it was a fuckin' parade?

"I was sittin' in Naples, waitin' to hear the results of the meet that day. Mostly, I was wonderin' how Vito would take it when the majority of the guys told him to go fuck himself. I felt like celebratin' in advance, so I took Igea and Joe Di Giorgio out to dinner at the Transatlantico on the bay. I'd just finished a plate of good spaghetti with butter and cheese, just the way I liked it, when Cockeye comes rushin' in. He takes me aside and says, all excited, 'Charlie! Did you hear what happened?' He tells me it's all over the radio and the newspapers got it out on the streets already, and then he gives me the whole mishmash about what happened at Apalachin, about them overfed fat guys runnin' through the woods for their lives. I'll bet not one of 'em had been off the city streets before and I could just picture 'em, bein' lost for days in the woods, maybe even starvin' to death and probably freezin' their balls off.

"Joe drove Igea and me home, and all the way up the hill to the Parco Comola I can only think about the outfit that I designed and made and built up from nothin', and in less than an hour that dirty fuckin' pig Genovese practically threw it down the shithouse. When I got back to the apartment, I went into the bathroom and vomited. Everything I had to eat and all the bile I'd been swallowin' all through the years in Italy come up at the same time."

36.

Rage burned deep inside him, and so did despair over the spectacle of the underworld as the object of buffoonery after Apalachin. No one seemed able to penetrate his isolation as his mind dwelt only on the need for quick revenge against Genovese.

Within days, however, an outside event brought Luciano out of himself, forced him for the moment to dismiss Genovese from his mind. He was alone in the penthouse one afternoon when he received a visit from the family physician, Professore Dottore Matteoli. Igea had done more than shopping that day. Dr. Matteoli had just given her a complete physical examination, the second within a matter of a few weeks. She had gone to him complaining of persistent fatigue, and of soreness around several small lumps in her left breast. On the first visit, the doctor said, he had tried to aspirate the lumps, but when Igea returned, the lumps and soreness had reappeared. It was essential, Dr. Matteoli told Luciano, that Igea have an immediate exploratory operation.

"The doc assured me there was no reason to believe them little bumps hadda be malignant. He said maybe they was just little tumors that could be taken out and that would be that. But the big problem, and the doctor knew this as well as me, was how we could get Igea to agree to an operation. Igea had tried to be everythin' to me, all kinds of women, for more than ten years. She was so proud of her body and she gave herself to me with such openness that it was like glue for us and held us together closer than I could ever dream of bein' with anybody. I knew the first thing she would think about was that havin' an operation might give her some kinda physical defect and turn me away. The doctor tried to explain to me that this is a thing medical people call 'preoperative trauma.' I didn't understand the fuckin' words, but I got the idea, and in Igea's case, he was two hundred per cent right. If only it could've been me. I had enough scars on me that another one would be like drinkin' a cup of coffee. Dr. Matteoli told me to think about how we oughta go about it, but not to wait too long."

When the doctor left, Luciano waited anxiously for Igea's return, wondering what he would say to her. But when she came through the door, she was laden with packages from a pre-Christmas shopping trip and she was radiant, all the pallor and listlessness gone. Luciano watched her carefully, but the radical change continued for the next months and she seemed to be herself once again. But Luciano wanted to be reassured. He called on Dr. Matteoli and the doctor told him that another examination of Igea had revealed a diminishing of the lumps. But, the doctor warned, this was not uncommon and Igea should be watched constantly for any change, though perhaps the operation could wait.

"This was some load off my mind, because just then I had plenty of troubles. Father Scarpato was workin' like an animal up at his clinic and he needed help almost every day. And on top of everythin' else, that was when we started tryin' to collect some of the bills for the furniture we sold to church schools and found out it was impossible. I began to feel like I was behind one great big eight ball. But as long as Igea was well, there was only one problem that really ate into my guts — how to take care of my dear friend, Don Vitone.

"Then I got a terrific idea. Why should I put out a hit on Vito, even though he deserved it? It could only put me in danger, and besides, I'd been away from the States a little too long to be a hundred per cent sure of the guys who might get the job done exactly right. The idea I got really appealed to me. For a long time, Vito had been tryin' to set me up, tryin' to prove to me he could frame me as easy as rollin' off a log. Well, I decided the best and easiest way to get Genovese out of everybody's hair without knockin' him off was to let the U.S. government do the job. All we hadda do was frame the evidence and we could hand Vito over on a silver platter. If we could work it right, we could get him tied in with narcotics on a personal basis, and that meant a federal rap good for fifteen years minimum. When he got out, nobody'd even think twice about him. But we hadda send him to a federal prison, because in a state pen that little bastard would be runnin' things in a week.

"First, I worked out the details with Costello and Lansky, and after it was all put together, I asked my new-old friend Carlo Gambino to meet me at Santa Marinella."

Gambino arrived early in 1958. Before leaving New York, he had discussed the plan fully with Costello and Lansky and had developed ideas of his own for its expedition. He agreed that letting the American government take care of Genovese was the only sensible approach; to kill him would be a mistake, bringing down a great deal of unwanted publicity on the organization. But, Gambino said, Genovese should not be the only fish thrown into the government's net; some of his aides should go with him.

Gambino then began to explore his approach with Luciano. He suggested that the services of Longie Zwillman and Tony Bender be utilized by the plotters. At the name of Bender, Luciano balked, until Gambino explained that he had very recently had a private meeting with Bender, who apparently had become convinced that Gambino was the man of the future and so had sworn loyalty to him. As for Zwillman, he had no love for Genovese. The Internal Revenue Service was after Zwillman, claiming he owed more than seven hundred thousand dollars in back taxes. Seeking financial help, Zwillman had turned to Genovese, whose estimated thirty-million-dollar fortune in bonds, mortgages, negotiable securities and cash was no little the result of operations developed by his partnership with Zwillman and Luciano during the twenties and thirties. Genovese, however, was notoriously parsimonious, his only extravagance the money he spent on his ex-wife, Anna. (She had told the full details of Genovese's life, business and financial dealings a few years before in her petition for separate mainte-nance. To the surprise of every one of his associates, Genovese had not dealt with her in the usual manner prescribed for stool pi-geons; he had only ordered the murder in 1953 of Steve Franse, her constant escort and cover for her bisexual activities.) So Genovese spurned Zwillman's plea and in so doing earned his bitter enmity.

"Carlo'd been pretty clever. He had all the actors ready to play their parts and it looked like it couldn't miss. The deal was this: Vito knows that Longie don't have nothin' to do with junk, so Longie tells him that he has a guy who come to him lookin' for a way to get rid of some pure heroin for a hundred grand that's worth a million on the street. The pusher is just as hard up as Zwillman, so he's willin' to sell it to Longie or any guy Longie puts him in touch with for sixty or seventy grand. Longie tells Vito all he wants for himself is a commission, ten or fifteen thou-sand, to tide him over for a while."

Genovese's greed, and his conviction of his supremacy in the underworld despite Apalachin, overcame any suspicions he might have had, and he agreed to make the buy at a stipulated spot along a back road in New Jersey. According to Luciano, Bender was supplied with the package of narcotics and sent out to meet Geno-vese at the appointed time and place and collect one hundred thousand dollars on the spot. Federal narcotics agents were tipped off and were supposed to be waiting to arrest Genovese once the transfer had been made.

"Would you believe it? The federal idiots blew it. They was supposed to be waitin' down the road, only nobody was there and that little prick Vito got away with it. I heard he made over seven hundred grand out of that buy, net. When I heard about it two days after, I damn near went through the ceiling. I sent word to Carlo that he was responsible for the fuckup; it was his play and he muffed it. So, no matter what it cost him, he hadda make good. And I told him I still didn't trust Bender, that he was always for sale to the highest bidder, so I wanted Bender on ice until Carlo put Vito away."

Gambino had a secondary plan, already rehearsed and prepared, in case the original one failed. Serving a narcotics sentence in Sing Sing was a minor Puerto Rican hoodlum named Nelson Cantellops. At various times during his career, Cantellops had worked for Sam Giancana in Chicago and as a messenger for Meyer Lansky. It was Gambino's idea to use Cantellops to get Genovese. "Of course, we hadda grease him pretty good. He got a hundred grand stashed away for him in cash, half from Gambino and half from me, which Lansky paid into the kitty, plus the best legal service. Of course, Costello put up half of my end, just to have fat Gigante nailed tight along with Vito."

The Narcotics Bureau Strike Force in New York received an anonymous tip that Cantellops was willing to make a trade: information about the narcotics racket and Genovese in return for a suspended sentence from Sing Sing. John Ray Enright, head of the Task Force under the chief of the federal Narcotics Bureau's New York office, George Gaffney, interviewed Cantellops and came away with what he had long sought.

"Cantellops told Enright and his boys that he had been an eyewitness to Vito's makin' buys, and he also ties in Carmine Galante and Big John Ormento, two of Vito's best guns, and a few other guys, includin', of course, Gigante, who was all handlin' junk for him. Ray Enright had it handed to him on a plate, because as far as I know, Cantellops never set eyes on Vito until they got into the courtroom almost a year later. I don't know whether the Narcotics Bureau really knew that Genovese was a gift, and I don't give a shit. The point is, we helped 'em land a big fish and they helped us by puttin' the little rat away. Carlo wanted Cantellops to put the finger on Tommy Eboli, too, because the whole idea was to try and break up Vito's personal muscle and Gambino was sure Tommy would cause trouble sooner or later, especially when Vito got sent up. I blocked that. I was sore at Tommy all right, but I couldn't do that to his brother Pat."

In mid-1959, Cantellops was the star witness for the government against Genovese and twenty-four others, including Gigante, for narcotics conspiracy. On the basis of his testimony, all were convicted. Genovese was sentenced to fifteen years in federal prison. He served the first years in Atlanta, was then transferred to Leavenworth, and, in 1969, died of heart failure at the federal medical facility in Missouri.

But there was retribution for some of those involved in the plot against him. Nelson Cantellops was released from Sing Sing, and for a time enjoyed freedom and his hundred-thousand-dollar payoff. In 1965, he was slain in a nightclub brawl.

In 1959, soon after Genovese was sentenced, Abner "Longie" Zwillman was found hanging by a wire in the cellar of his New Jersey mansion. The official verdict was suicide; the reason: Zwillman's almost insoluble tax problems with the federal government. "That's bullshit. They murdered Longie. He tried to put the arm on Carlo after Vito got his sentence; what the hell, the poor guy was part of us for a long time and there was enough money around to give him a hand. But the guys in Brooklyn was afraid he'd do a Reles. So they beat him up and trussed him up like a pig and hung him in his own cellar.

"It was when Longie got it that I began to get a feelin' inside about Lansky. Why didn't Meyer put up for him? The question started to nag at me and I began to watch out for things that didn't fit together where he and I was concerned. Money makes people do strange things that sometimes you can't predict, and of all the fellas from way back, the one guy who loved dough more than anybody else was the little walkin' addin' machine.

"Anyway, for me and Costello and Lansky, at least we had Vito put away in a federal jug. The best he could do from there was give a few orders, but that didn't mean they'd be followed. Tommy

Eboli had too many ambitions and Jerry Catena is a guy who just wants to live good; he don't look for power or trouble. So, I still had to watch out for any moves.

"Then I got clobbered by somethin' I couldn't do nothin' about."

37.

Early in 1958, with Luciano absorbed in the plot against Genovese that was reaching fruition, he was suddenly diverted by a more urgent demand for his time and attention. Once more, Igea's energy and good humor were being drained and the pains and suspicious lumps in her left breast returned.

"This time, I took her to see Dr. Matteoli myself, and I went right in his office while he examined her. There was no question about it, she was really in pain. But he wouldn't let on nothin' to her, he just said, 'Well, young lady, I think we should put you into the hospital and take out those little bumps.' He was very cheerful and said she had nothin' to worry about. He just called 'em tumors and she wasn't to be frightened. Then he turned to me and said, 'Listen, Charlie, why don't you stay and let me give you an examination?'

"So I stayed behind and as soon as Igea left the office, I said to the doc, 'All right, tell me, what's wrong with her?' He said, 'I think she has cancer. It looks bad and I'm sorry we waited so long.'

"I almost got sick right there in the office. I said to him, 'Are you sure?' He said, 'No, I can't be sure. But she has too many symptoms and we have to do an exploratory operation.' I said to him, 'But if she's got cancer, does that mean she's gonna die?' He said, 'Not necessarily. If we reach it in time, she'll live a long life. But if the tumors are cancer, we'll have to remove her breast.' I said to him, 'I don't care what you gotta do, just save her life.' "

The next day, Igea was taken to the hospital and the following morning, when the pathology revealed carcinoma, her left breast was removed; the cancer had spread deep and so the excision was extensive.

The operation took several hours and Luciano paced the waiting room with an almost unbearable anxiety, waving away even the close friends who came by. "I just couldn't stand to have nobody even near me. I smoked one butt after another and prayed. I promised God anythin' if only He would make her better. Then Dr. Matteoli came out and told me it looked like the operation was a success. They hadda remove her breast, but he was hopeful they got all the cancer. One thing was sure. We had the best surgeons we could get in this part of Italy.

"They let me go into the recovery room and I sat down by Igea's bed. She was still out and her face looked so little and pale that I felt like breakin' my hand against the wall. As I looked at her, I just couldn't help but feel that maybe it was my fault, my fault for meetin' her ten years before, for gettin' her tied up with me. The more I looked at her, layin' there so helpless, knowin' she was gonna wake up and find out that what she was scared of really happened, the more I realized how much I cared for her. I once said that I didn't know what love is, but at that minute it come to me that I knew all along — love and Igea was the same thing for me.

"After about an hour, Igea woke up a little bit and asked me what happened. She was so groggy from the anaesthetic she could hardly open her eyes. I told her the surgeons said everythin' was okay and that she was gonna get better. She went back to sleep again and I kept sittin' there by her bed. Every couple minutes, the nurses come in and tried to get me to eat somethin', but I couldn't get it down; I just had a little coffee.

"Then Igea woke up again. She was a little more conscious this time and the first thing she noticed was all the heavy bandages around her chest, especially on the left side. She asked me, 'They took off my breast?'

"All I could do was nod my head. My throat was so tight I couldn't talk and when she asked me, 'I have cancer, isn't that right?' she said it like it was a death sentence and then she started to cry. What could I say? What could I do? I just told her the surgeons said they got it all and that she'd be okay. But the words stuck in my throat and she shook her head, like she knew it was a lie."

When Igea returned to the penthouse after a few weeks, she was withdrawn and morose, shying from Luciano's touch, apparently convinced that now she was less than a woman and no longer attractive to him. Himself filled with fear and concern, he tried without much success to raise her spirits, to make her feel needed and wanted. And he was helped from outside; the story of Igea's illness reached the press and soon the apartment was filled with flowers from people all over Italy, from strangers.

In the midst of Igea's illness, however, there was some good news. In early February, one of Italy's most famous lawyers, Giovanni Passeggio, telephoned Luciano from Rome. He had become intrigued by Luciano's almost endless problems with Italian and American authorities and suggested that perhaps he might be of some help. A meeting was arranged for the following day in Naples.

At that session, Passeggio told Luciano that during a recent trial he was handling in Rome, he had learned that John Cusack, head of the U.S. Treasury Department's Narcotics Bureau in Rome and immediate superior to Charles Siragusa, was still pressuring Italian authorities to do something about the exiled gangster, and that pressure seemed to be mounting in the wake of the sympathetic stories in the press about Igea. It had reached a point, Passeggio said, where police magistrates in Naples had been issued orders to summon Luciano before them to reopen inquiries about his activities. If Luciano desired it, Passeggio concluded, he would be willing to appear as his counsel.

"I could hardly believe my ears. This guy was one of the most important legal brains in Italy, with plenty of muscle in the government, and he comes to me first without even bein' approached. It seemed to be a sign of good luck."

The hearing on Luciano opened on February 24 before a police magistrates' tribunal headed by Judge Attilio Zanotti. On the bench were two other magistrates, the Naples police chief and a *carabinieri* official. It was not a friendly group. Pointed questions were asked about Luciano's business, about his income, about whether he might, in fact, be "socially dangerous." Judge Zanotti seemed particularly displeased with reports that since the partial lifting of restrictions and curfew, Luciano had been spending his evenings in nightclubs and at the Agnano racetrack; it was, the court suggested, "beneath the dignity" of a supposedly retired gangster to be seen at public places where there was gambling and seminude entertainment. It might be a good idea, the tribunal said, if investigators dug deeply into Luciano's finances and activities to see whether there was anything to the demands from the American Embassy in Rome that he was so dangerous he ought to be exiled from a major city such as Naples.

Passeggio was indignant. Instead of judging Luciano by his past, he said, the court ought to be concerned with his present. Luciano was an honest businessman and his work was all for the benefit of society; he was selling medical supplies, heading a company that produced equipment for schools, and devoting his spare time to the construction of Father Scarpato's desperately needed Clinica di Lourdes.

When Passeggio had finished, Judge Zanotti declared that the matter would remain open and under investigation. "Giovanni," Luciano said to his lawyer, "do you think they'll ever leave me alone?"

"Be patient," Passeggio said, putting his hand on Luciano's shoulder. "We have only now begun to fight." He smiled. "That's a famous expression from your American history, no?"

"I wouldn't know who said it," Luciano answered, "but I sure like the sound of it comin' from you about me."

The tribunal's investigation lasted nearly a month. On March 20, it reconvened to announce the results of its thorough examination of Luciano's activities since his deportation in 1946, an inquiry that had dealt with his circle of American friends, his knowledge of and whereabouts at the time of the Anastasia murder, his legitimate business interests in Italy, and reports that "dear friends" in America provided him with a "comfortable" but not a "luxurious" living. The Italian authorities and the court said that while Luciano was seen from time to time in the company of Italian-American "undesirables" who had been deported from the United States — something he freely admitted — there was nothing harmful to the state or to the Italian people in such relationships. The government's prosecutor, Antonio De Franciscis, told the court that there was no evidence to warrant any further prosecution, though he asked permission to continue the investigation of the sources of Luciano's income — and it was granted. Then the court announced its decision. Luciano, it said, was "a free citizen who, as has been proved, conducts a perfectly regular life which gives no grounds for censure."

Under normal circumstances, the decision might have been cause for celebration. But Igea was still ill. She had, however, rallied enough to permit limited travel, so Luciano immediately took her to Capri, back to the small house by the sea. There, for a time, some happiness seemed possible. Then, one morning in the middle of April, Luciano awoke to find Igea sobbing bitterly. For a moment he thought she might once again be in pain from the operation. But she lowered the right side of her nightgown and pointed to her breast — there were several small but visible red lumps on it.

"One of our little dogs was named Bambi. Igea loved that Walt Disney picture about Bambi, so she named the dog after it. He was never out of her sight; Bambi even slept on our bed no matter where we was. Well, Igea started huggin' that dog and cryin'. Of course, I realized why she was so upset. It was the fear of another operation and that maybe they would have to remove her right breast, too. I put my arms around her and I said all that mattered was for her to be well, that was all that counted to me."

Luciano hurried Igea back to Naples, back to the hospital where, as both had feared, her right breast was removed. "Dr. Matteoli came out after they finished and he just kind of shook his head at me. He couldn't talk. Then he finally gimme the bad news. After they opened her up they found the cancer had spread too far and they couldn't get it all. I said to him, 'Are you tryin' to tell me that Igea is gonna die?'

"He said, 'Yes, Charlie, there's nothing more we can do. There is cobalt, but I don't think it will have much effect. The disease is spreading all the time.'

"I asked him how long she had and he said he didn't know; she could die in a couple weeks or maybe she could last a few months, but not longer than that. At that minute, I had the feelin' that he was the most thoughtful man I ever knew. He never stopped tryin' to help. After I took Igea back to the apartment, there wasn't a day he didn't come there and spend some time with her or do everythin' he could to keep her from havin' pain, like she was part of his own family and not just another patient. Finally, though, the pain got so bad that even the big shots of morphine didn't help.

"Don Cheech came all the time and prayed. Sometimes there would be a dozen friends in our livin' room, all of 'em hoodlums, deportees, the roughest kind of guys you could think of, accordin' to the police, and they'd get down on their knees and cry as they prayed along with Father Scarpato. Everybody loved Igea. I thought Johnny Cockeye would go out of his mind; every time he saw me, he'd look deep into my face and then run away. He told me later he couldn't stand to look into my eyes, they was always so full of tears."

During the brief periods when pain abated enough so that she could talk with a smile, she would insist that Luciano not sit around the apartment, that he get out and be with people. He would go to the California, but return quickly. "When Igea and I could talk, what made me so sad was that all she ever wanted to think about was how I was gonna make out after she died. It was like a knife in me and I would tell her not to worry about that. I ordered her not to die; I ordered her to get better. But she was too smart to buy that crap. About the middle of the summer, she said she wanted to see Giovanni Passeggio the next time he come to Naples. I brought him about a week later. What do you think she said to him? She wanted him to arrange with the police so that I could go up and live with her folks in Milan after she died. Jesus Christ. He told her that he'd arrange anythin' she wanted if she promised not to think such thoughts. And I told her that she'd been with me, like a wife, for ten years and I just couldn't think of bein' nowhere without her. Near the end, she told me she wanted to be buried at the Cimiterio di Musocco in Milan, in the family plot. I made her that promise."

411

In September of 1958, Igea fell into a coma. She lingered for several days. On the advice of the doctors, Luciano telephoned her father, Giovanni Lissoni, and he immediately flew to Naples. In those final days, Luciano rarely left Igea's bedside, sitting next to her, watching her intently for hours. He ate nothing and the lines in his face were etched deeper.

Early in the morning of September 27, Igea awoke briefly from the coma. She recognized Luciano, moved her hand slightly toward her father. She tried to form some words, then said distinctly, *"Caro mio."* She lapsed into unconsciousness again and within an hour, at the age of thirty-seven, Igea Lissoni was dead.

The body was taken to Milan for burial, and in the obituary section of the *Corriere della Sera* of Milan on September 30, a black-bordered notice appeared:

Solaced by religious comfort, after a trying illness, her soul given to God, IGEA LISSONI, 37. Advising of the sad news are her Papa, her adored Charlie, sister Daria with her husband, niece Danila, uncles, aunts, cousins, and all relatives. Funeral will take place Wednesday, Oct. 1, at 14 hours, leaving the house at Via Rosalino Pilo, 14. Everyone who will attend the ceremony is thanked in advance. Milan, 27 September, 1958.
> Participating in this notice:
> The Manna uncles and aunts,
> the Carrera family.

The official ban on northern travel by Luciano was lifted so that he might attend the funeral. He walked directly behind the hearse drawn by eight plumed horses, on a dreary, rainy day. Igea's body, with a gold wedding band on her finger, rested in its coffin on a huge bed of roses, her favorite flower. Across her chest was a silk sash embroidered with the name "Charlie."

Long after everyone else had left the cemetery, Luciano stood at the graveside, his glasses misted by rain, his face pale and strained as the gravediggers covered the coffin.

Then he returned to Naples. Igea was gone and in the penthouse there were only the housekeeper, Lydia, and the two small dogs, who darted here and there searching for their mistress. Igea's clothing and personal possessions were given to her sister,

412

with Luciano retaining only a mountain of photographs and memories.

"Everybody I knew come around to try to get me outa the house. Chinky Vitaliti was back in Taormina by then and he wanted to come and stay with me for a while, and all the guys tried to make me understand that life was for the livin', as they put it. I was so damn lonely that nothin' seemed to matter, and even my friends, really good friends, couldn't help me. It was my insides that was empty."

For weeks, Luciano mourned, wearing the traditional black tie and black ribbon in his lapel. He was morose, uncommunicative. Eleven weeks after Igea's death, on December 13, he was suddenly forced back into the world.

The Italian Court of Appeals was ready to hand down a decision based on the investigations of Prosecutor Franciscis. With Giovanni Passeggio at his side, Luciano arrived at the court promptly at two in the afternoon, dressed in a gray suit, overcoat and felt hat. The proceedings lasted less than an hour, and when they were over, Luciano was a free man. The decision, read by Judge Zanotti, restored to him all the privileges that had been taken away four years before; he had his driver's license again and his identification papers, even a passport. Luciano, the court declared, "has nothing to do with murder, narcotics or illegal rackets." It was a complete victory and a complete vindication. And, perhaps, it revealed how little the court really knew, how little the investigation had really uncovered.

Part Five

The Last Years
1959-1962

38.

By the turn of the year, into 1959, Luciano's season of outward mourning was at an end. Events in the world outside continually intruded and he could no longer ignore them.

The plot against Vito Genovese was reaching its climax in the United States — that would come in the spring, with the trial, conviction and sentence of the mob leader. But as long as Genovese was free, and, indeed, even after the prison gates closed behind him, his ambitions remained unchecked. His forces were encroaching ever more openly into the Brooklyn domain of Joe Bonanno and bloody warfare appeared inevitable. Other members of the council appealed to Luciano to intervene and help restore peace.

There was trouble in Cuba. Fidel Castro and his revolution had swept out of the Sierra Maestra mountain stronghold, routed the government forces of dictator Fulgencio Batista, and seized control of the country. Batista had been forced to scurry for his life, fleeing to sanctuary in Florida, and the resident American gamblers had hurried after him. Lansky's casino empire in Havana collapsed as Castro's puritanical regime shuttered the city and the country.

As the disaster approached, Lansky had begun a search for alternatives and replacements. He found them. In the Bahamas, gambling was legal and officials could be corrupted to provide easy entrée for the underworld. And in Las Vegas, Bugsy Siegel's dream of a new Eldorado was coming true. Americans, infected by gambling fever, were pouring into the city in ever-increasing numbers to try their luck at the tables. Everywhere new hotel-casinos were springing up. No matter the names on the real estate deeds and state licenses, the vast majority were controlled by the Mob, often in partnership with legitimate interests. For even honest businessmen in Nevada seemed to feel that only the under-world could operate a casino at a profit — a profit that was enormous even after the racketeers had skimmed twenty per cent or more off the top of the casino's income for their own private, nontaxable use. Under Lansky's supervision, and with the approval from Italy of Luciano, the underworld poured millions into Las Vegas and took out even more.

But even as Cuba and his gambling empire there were falling, Lansky did not abandon his old friend Batista. He helped the Cuban dictator, he told Luciano, transfer more than three hundred million dollars into Swiss numbered accounts, in the names of Batista and his family, particularly his two sons. Under Lansky's guidance, some of Batista's fortune would wind up as investments in gambling enterprises in Nassau, Beirut, London and later even in Communist-controlled Yugoslavia, where Tito seemed to find no objection to wooing currency with American casino-operating expertise.

All these matters required Luciano's personal attention and so he was forced to emerge from his shell. His personal life began to take on a familiar pattern. He was dining again at the California, the Zi Teresa and other old favorites, was spending time with his friends, and was beginning to seek out girls. His only personal problem seemed to be a sacroiliac condition which had started some years before, and now appeared to be worse.

One unusually warm day in January 1959, Luciano was having an open-air lunch on the patio of the Santa Lucia Restaurant in Naples with some friends when a young, plump Neapolitan shop-girl named Adriana Rizzo strolled by. "I knew Adriana for a couple years. She worked in a store where they sold trusses and medical belts and them things; when I first had trouble with my back, the doc sent me to this store around the corner from the Santa Lucia Hotel, and that's where I met her. This particular day, my back was botherin' me again. Adriana waltzed through with her bouncy little walk and as she passed my table, she said hello to me. I reached out and kind of gave her a little pinch on the fanny. I didn't mean nothin' nasty by it; with Italian girls, it's kind of a compliment. Adriana stopped and she said she'd heard about Igea and how sorry she was, and one thing led to another. I went back to the shop with her to get a new belt support for my back, and that's the way it started.

"Adriana had a little trainin' as a nurse and after a few times takin' her out to dinner and seein' her, I suggested that maybe she oughta move into my apartment and look after me. By then we wasn't exactly strangers. The only problem was, she was half-engaged to some guy. I talked her outa that, and she became the new lady in my apartment. She knew how I felt about Igea, but she seemed nice and sincere and we was comfortable together, so it worked out just fine. And this time, there was no kickback from her family. Her father was a taxi driver and they was real Neapolitans; they understood there was no point in talkin' about marriage. As long as she was happy with the situation, they didn't interfere — and I helped 'em out once in a while. And Adriana got along with Lydia, so everythin' settled down to peace and quiet."

Luciano may have had peace and quiet at home, but there was little of that outside, particularly in the United States. Internecine warfare was erupting in New Jersey, in Manhattan, in Brooklyn. Lansky was shuttling back and forth around the Caribbean, supervising the growing gambling operations there, and worrying intensely about the results of the Castro takeover in Cuba. "It seemed like all over the world we was makin' a fortune in spite of the fact that everythin' was gettin' fucked up."

It was time, he thought, to take some kind of hand himself. So despite his personal animosity, he drove secretly to Milan for a meeting with Joe Adonis. "When I tried to discuss the New York situation with Adonis, it was like talkin' to the wall. He didn't give a shit about what was goin' on noplace except where he was concerned in Milano. As he put it, he had his socked away and he also had a nice thing goin' with import and export as a legitimate front for his old business of hot jewelry. He was into that again up to his neck. There must've been somethin' about him from childhood; I don't know what it was, but he liked flashy things. He always thought of himself as an elegant guy, which I guess is why he was attracted to sparklin' jewelry. The thing that bothered me the most about my meet with him was his not askin' me if there was anythin' I needed or wanted — I was right, he was a no-good selfish cocksucker."

The meeting with Adonis, then, resulted in nothing concrete. Before he could do anything more, he himself was stricken. Adriana may have been good for his back, but the sexual demands this twenty-three-year-old girl made on a sixty-two-year-old man were draining. A month after she moved into the apartment, Luciano had a heart attack. Though it was a mild one, Dr. Matteoli called in a cardiologist, Dr. Di Martine.

"Now I had two doctors hangin' on my neck, warnin' me to slow down, that I was pushin' too hard. Dr. Di Martine said if I kept on goin' like I'd been doin', that I could have a real bad attack and maybe even drop dead. That scared the shit out of me. Adriana made me stay in bed; she wouldn't even let me go to the bathroom. After a couple of weeks, when I was feelin' better, I made a grab for her a couple times and she gimme such a whack over the head that it raised a lump. That's when I knew I was lucky to have found her."

Within a few weeks, though, Luciano was well enough to tour the restaurants and nightclubs again and to watch the trotters at Agnano racetrack — and watch the horses he bet on invariably finish out of the money, costing him two or three thousand dollars an evening. He was feeling well enough, too, to spend time at his office desk, trying to do something to rescue the rapidly collapsing furniture business. And he began to travel up to San Sebastian al Vesuvio in his spare time, to help Father Scarpato with the construction of the clinic, at times even taking with him prospective investors and suppliers to watch the building rise — the foundation had been laid by 1959 and the shell of the building had been erected.

Luciano was, in fact, acting as though nothing had happened. He even resumed his lovemaking with Adriana. It was all too much. Late in the spring, he was stricken with a massive coronary occlusion.

"When you're laid up in a hospital for a month, you really have a chance to do a lot of thinkin' about yourself. The first thing I realized was that Dr. Di Martine was right when he told me the little attack I had before had been a warning. I would be a goddamn fool not to understand that the second attack, which almost killed me, was somethin' I couldn't fuck around with. The first couple days I was in the hospital, they didn't have to tell me I was a case of touch-and-go. I knew it and, let me tell you, I was really scared of dyin'. I began to understand that I wasn't no kid no more. I was sixty-two years old, and who needs all the trouble in the States that the doctor claimed was really the cause of the attack? I said to him one day in the hospital, 'I thought you believed that what I done with Adriana was what made me keel over.' But he explained that the pressures had been buildin' up and takin' such a big toll on my heart so that finally one long session in bed with Adriana was what pulled the trigger. In a nice way he was tellin' me I could live a long time if I would retire, get rid of my problems, and spend the rest of my life just enjoyin' the fact that I was alive.

"I thought it over for a long time and then I decided to send for Chinky Vitaliti to consult with him about my decision. Dr. Di Martine wouldn't let me have no visitors until I told him it was a meetin' that would relieve me of all the pressures. So he let Chinky come to see me in the hospital. I told Chinky I was gonna take myself out of the Unione and his eyes almost popped. I explained that it was really necessary if I wanted to save my life. So I asked him to get word back to New York that if Frank Costello could retire, why not Charlie Luciano?

"I told Chinky to tell 'em all I wanted was for 'em to keep on sendin' my dough, like it was a pension, and they shouldn't ask me for nothin' else. I just wanted to step down from bein' the chairman of the board, which is the way I liked to think of it, and turn it over to whoever the council would select. In my own mind, I figured it'd wind up in Carlo Gambino's lap. One or two of the younger guys might want to fight him for it, but it was my opinion, and I told it to Chinky, that Carlo would be able to take care of himself. I said to Chinky, 'Just tell 'em to send me my dough and leave me alone.' I said he should make sure Lansky got the message first, because he was handlin' the money."

But Luciano's associates in the United States did not believe the message, could not believe that he really meant it. "The dough kept comin', but so did guys with questions that needed answers, with messages and information. They just didn't let me alone. To be honest about it, it made me feel good. After all, when a hundred guys say to you that you can't retire, that they need you, well, what the hell, I have to admit I wasn't strong enough to stick to my decision.

"So it went along just like before, except for one thing. I never could lay my hands on a big hunk of dough; there always seemed to be some reason, some excuse why Lansky couldn't arrange it. There was this friend of mine from the old neighborhood when I was a kid, the guy Coppola who lived with me in the cold-water room. When his wife died and his two kids moved away and he was alone and too old to work — the guy was always legit — I thought it would be a nice idea to bring him over to Naples and set him up in a little store like we used to have down on the East Side, the Two Cents Plain kind of candy store. I started to look around for a spot in Naples where I could put up a nice place to sell good candy and homemade ice cream, American style. By the time I got through, it would've cost me fifty, sixty thousand bucks, and I just didn't have that kind of dough to lay out in one hunk. It was drivin' me crazy. I had already tapped the laundry account in Zurich for a load of money. Igea had been sick for almost a year and the bills for the hospital and the doctors and surgeons and nurses was sky-high, but I wanted her to have the best."

For months, Luciano sent back urgent messages to his friends in New York, by mail and through the couriers who regularly came to him, that he wanted a large sum of money, in one payment, for the personal reasons he laid out. But the money did not come. So Luciano began to turn away the couriers without answering the questions they brought to him, with refusals to send along any advice. "All I did was send back the word that I was retired and to leave me alone. But those bastards in America still wouldn't believe me.

"But you know who did believe me? The Italian police. And my lawyer, Giovanni Passeggio, he believed me, too." (Passeggio, who would later become a close adviser to Italian President Giovanni Leone, talked privately to Italian authorities in Luciano's behalf and helped convince them that he was just as inactive in American affairs as he had been for years in Italian ones.)

"Some of the newspaper guys believed me, too, and some of 'em even began to talk about me as a kind of Bernie Baruch, like I was a senior citizen doin' nothin' but sittin' on a park bench. One guy from the New York *Herald Tribune* named Barrett McGurn wrote a very nice and honest thing about me bein' retired and it was printed all over Italy and the States. It helped things ease up for me, helped me get over that bad heart attack and start livin' again. But I was always burnin' up about the sixty grand I wanted to open a store for Coppola in Naples. That's how the whole thing about a movie of my life got started."

During all the years he had been in Italy, Luciano had received an endless series of offers from European and American motion picture producers seeking his cooperation and approval for a film on his life. He had spurned them all. But at this moment in 1959, he began to reconsider. That summer, he was introduced to a producer from New York who made a proposal of the kind Luciano had heard so often in the past. Initially, Luciano turned him away.

"By September of 1959, I was still feelin' pretty lousy. The pinch on my money from New York was causin' me a lot of tension and the doc said that it was aggravatin' my heart condition. I began to have what he called angina pains in my chest and I was takin' a lot of nitroglycerin pills for that and other kind of pills because my blood pressure was goin' up. Everything was pretty rotten. So this producer hit me again at the right time. I guess he must've understood that I needed money, so he made me a proposition that sounded okay. He would get a script started right away and as soon as they began to start filmin', I would get a hundred thousand dollars, cash on the barrelhead. Then I was also supposed to get ten per cent of the profits. And if I didn't like what he was doin', I had the right to call the whole thing off." On Capri at the beginning of October, Luciano signed a contract giving an option to make his life story, with the provision that the picture had to be completed within three years.

If the movie was started, Luciano would have the money he wanted. Meanwhile, the pressures on him from New York mounted. In mid-October, Luciano's close friend Pat Eboli arrived as a courier with money and a number of messages. The council in New York wanted Luciano's views on how to handle what seemed like an impending war in Brooklyn, revolving around the aging and ill Joe Profaci. Then, there was still a problem with Vito Genovese. In his cell in Atlanta, he had apparently come to the conclusion that Luciano had been in some way responsible for his predicament, and so he had dispatched orders to Tommy Eboli and Gerry Catena to "do something about Charlie Lucky." Genovese, Pat Eboli said, was openly insisting that he would get Luciano if it was the last thing he ever did.

But what was perhaps the most important news brought by Pat Eboli dealt with the organization's response to a new campaign in the press, supported by Washington, against the so-called American Mafia. "Pat told me that a plan was bein' worked out all around the country to do somethin' about a television program called *The Untouchables*. It was a big hit and all it did was use some of the newspaper files about the old Chicago mob in the Capone days and maybe change a couple names. The program was really goin' over with the public, and the sponsor, Chesterfield cigarettes, was as happy as a kid with a new toy. So the council had a meet about it and one of the guys in Profaci's outfit, named Joe Colombo, come up with the idea of formin' a legitimate association of Americans with Italian backgrounds to start a campaign against usin' just Italian names for them gangsters in the TV shows and movies. The whole idea was to try to get *The Untouchables* off the fuckin' air. Pat was told to get my point of view and see if I could recommend the right guy to head up the new association.

"I thought about the whole thing for a day or so, while Pat was still there, and I couldn't see nothin' wrong with the idea, on condition that nobody connected with any outfit have his name involved. It had to be strictly legit on the surface or it would fall into the shithouse before it ever got off the ground. I looked over the list of names they sent me and finally I agreed on Santangelo." Congressman Alfred Santangelo, New York Democrat, was soon named New York State president of the Federation of Italian-American Democratic Organizations and headed a nationwide campaign to force *The Untouchables* off the air through a boycott of the sponsor, Liggett & Myers Tobacco Company. That campaign

finally paid off on March 14, 1961, when the cigarette manufacturer announced it was withdrawing its sponsorship because of the
pressures. According to Luciano, "Santangelo knew from the
beginnin' that the whole thing was dreamed up and supported by
the outfits.

"After we got all through talkin' about that, I asked Pat about
why the envelope he handed me was a little short inside. He
looked kind of embarrassed and he said, 'The Little Man didn't
have everything in order when I was ready to leave, so he told me
to bring what he gave me.' That's when I knew — I mean, when
I was sure — that Lansky was the only one in the States who took
me seriously when I said I wanted to retire. So the dirty son of a
bitch was startin' to slice me into a fuckin' two-bit pension. I
didn't say nothin' to Pat about it. I just let it ride, to see what
would happen the next time somebody come with my dough. And
I was dead right. A few weeks later, I get an envelope with a little
bit less — I think it was down to about ten grand. Only this time,
there was a message from Lansky that was a load of shit. He said
things was goin' bad in the States and everybody was tightenin'
their belts. Castro had taken over Cuba, which was knockin' our
treasury out of about six million a year, and there wasn't nothin'
to replace it yet.

"That little bastard knew goddamn fuckin' well that London
was already runnin' good and that the second new casino in the
Bahamas was jammed every night; even after the British government's taxes and the private payoffs, the profits was beautiful, up
in the millions. So all my partners was cuttin' up the numbers
high up in the seven figures and I'm sittin' on my ass in Naples
without enough dough to open a goddamn candy store."

There was something else, closer to home, that bothered Luciano, too. Siragusa had been transferred out of Italy, which was
good news for Luciano, even though he began to get a fill-in on
exactly what Siragusa had been doing for nearly a decade. "Guys
I knew in the Guardia di Finanza and the *carabinieri* told me all
kinds of little stories about how this son of a bitch had tried to
nail me."

The departure of Siragusa, however, did not mean that the
Americans had abandoned their attempts to nail Luciano. It

merely indicated a change in tactics. The new chief of the campaign was another Italian-American, this time attached to the Central Intelligence Agency, named Henry Manfredi. "He was a lot smoother than Siragusa, and he had plenty of savvy. He took it easy and he wasn't gonna be a wise guy to run down to Naples wearin' dirty old clothes and tryin' to make believe he was a drug buyer. He was too smart for that. Instead, he used a guy who called himself Mike Cerra, only I was told that wasn't his real name. Cerra was a big, good-lookin' guy in his thirties and he passed himself off as a major in the U.S. Air Force. I was tipped off about him the day he arrived in Naples and my contacts suggested that maybe this time I oughta string him along, let him think I believed him, maybe even let him get little things from the PX for me. That way, he wouldn't get no ideas that I was on to him, and we could use the guy. If he didn't get wise, we figured we could feed him all kinds of crap and really screw things up back in Rome and Washington, which is what we did. Every once in a while, me and Momo or Joe Di Giorgio would cook up a little scene and let Cerra think he was on to somethin' big. Boy, would I like to see the crap he wrote up in his files from the stuff I was throwin' him.

"To tell the truth, though, I kinda took to this Mike Cerra, or whatever his real name is. He was a likable fella even though I know that everythin' he tells me is strictly bullshit. Actually, we had some nice talks and a couple times I invited him to the farm at Santa Marinella and to my apartment, but never when Adriana was around; I told her about him and she couldn't hide things, so I think she would've spit in his eye."

Playing with Cerra was an amusing game. But there were other problems not quite so frivolous. Luciano was greatly worried about his health and his finances. He was concerned, too, about Adriana. He even suggested to her that she leave him and return to her family and her old boy friend when doctors advised him to abstain from sex. But Adriana, even with Luciano's promise to provide for her, would hear none of this. Instead, she became ever more attentive to his needs, and she attempted to serve as a buffer between him and the mounting outside pressures.

39.

By the fall of 1959, Luciano was growing increasingly disenchanted with the movie project. The producer seemed unable to come up with a script to Luciano's liking; all the ideas were merely reprises of old gangster movies from the 1930's. "It looked like I made a bum decision. I told him if he couldn't do better right way, we might as well forget the whole thing. I needed the money and I didn't want to fool around no more."

In Madrid to make another film, the producer met Martin Gosch, one of the authors of this book, a former Hollywood producer and screenwriter who was then running his own production company in Spain. Gosch agreed to try his hand at a new screenplay and then to work as coproducer of the film, conditional on a meeting with Luciano and securing his approval and agreement to cooperate.

A meeting was arranged. In October, Gosch and his wife detoured from a trip to New York to call on Luciano in Naples. Gosch's idea of a film on the years in exile appealed to Luciano. Furthermore, during the early 1940's, Gosch had produced and had been one of the writers on the Abbott and Costello radio program. "When I was in the can up at Great Meadow in 1943," Luciano told him, "I used to love to listen to that program every Thursday night, even though I knew that fat bastard Costello was a no-good prick. He come from over in Jersey and all the guys in the outfit over there knew him. The minute he made it big, he started to act like his shit was gold. I figure anybody who could make a nice guy out of a shit like Lou Costello should certainly be able to handle me and tell my story fair and decent."

Before leaving Naples, Gosch gave Luciano an outline of the script he proposed: it would be almost wholly fictionalized, based on the relationship between an exiled American gangster and an

Italian girl he falls in love with, and centering around attempts by the American underworld to gain possession of a diary in which the gangster, supposedly Luciano, had recorded all the secrets of his life; of necessity, there would be scenes dealing with major and well-publicized events in the United States, such as the attempt on Frank Costello and the assassination of Albert Anastasia.

"Your contract gives you the right to turn down anything I prepare for any reason whatever," Gosch told Luciano. "That's a big gamble for me, in time, effort and money."

"It's a good gamble, Marty," Luciano said. "I think you should take it."

So Gosch went off to work on the screenplay. To collaborate with him, he hired an English writer named John Cresswell, for he had been told that nobody in America would be willing to do a script that would deal even partially sympathetically with a man of Luciano's notoriety.

While Gosch and Cresswell worked, Luciano's money was still coming from New York, but each courier seemed to bring less than the one before. There was enough, barely enough, for his own needs, but now he found himself unable to hand out the weekly allotments to the army of deportees and impecunious Italians who depended upon him. Among them seemed to be every needy prostitute in Naples. "All over the world I was the big white slaver, the guy who beat up broads and made 'em whores. So here I am in Naples givin' 'em money just so's they can eat. I'd like Tom Dewey to know about that. But when the dough got so short, I couldn't face all them people. I began to spend more and more time up on the farm in Santa Marinella so I wouldn't have to see 'em and tell 'em there was no money this week or next week. I really felt lousy that I hadda go and hide.

"One day, Pat Eboli come up with another one of them short envelopes. I told Patsy that when he got back to New York, he was to tell Lansky and the rest of the guys that I was gettin' into the picture business, that I signed a deal to have a picture made that was supposed to be about my life, but I had the last word and I was gonna make sure it didn't hurt nobody. In a little while, I got word back to go ahead, that they didn't have no objections."

In December, Gosch returned to Naples, this time with Cresswell, to outline the script in more detail. Luciano was entranced, and was even more excited when Gosch told him that he had worked a way for Luciano to return, at least briefly, to New York, though he would explain no details until the script had been finished and approved.

By February, the screenplay was done, and on February 18, 1961, Gosch sat in the living room of Luciano's Naples penthouse and for three hours read the script aloud. Then he handed a pen to Luciano and said, "Here, sign it." Luciano signed his approval on the first and last pages and initialed each of the 175 pages in between.

Then Luciano looked up. "Okay, wise guy," he said. "Now let's have that secret about gettin' me back into New York."

Under the terms of his movie contract Luciano had given the producer the right to sue others in his name in case of any legal infringements. However, under New York State law, in cases of defamation and invasion of privacy, a suit could only be brought by the injured party. At that moment, the Columbia Broadcasting System was televising a weekly series called *Your Witness* that dealt with mock trials of underworld figures. The initial show, in 1960, had concerned Luciano. The dialogue spoken by the actor portraying the gangster had never been shown to Luciano for his sanction and so, according to a legal opinion Gosch had secured, Luciano could sue for invasion of privacy and such a suit "would be impregnable against dismissal" and Luciano "would be entitled to his day in court." This meant that permission would have to be granted for Luciano to appear personally at the hearings in New York. That Luciano's stay in Manhattan would be a brief one, during which he would be closely guarded and his movements tightly restricted, and that the suit would undoubtedly be thrown out of court seemed certain. Nevertheless, he would get his chance, however short, to return.

It was an idea that Luciano embraced enthusiastically. He talked about it with animation as he drove Gosch back to the airport, and talked, too, about the plans for the movie. Gosch asked him if he had any ideas about the casting of the title role. After a moment's thought, Luciano said, "Cary Grant." It was such a strange choice that Gosch was stunned. "Okay — you got any ideas?" Luciano asked.

Gosch's choice was the singer Dean Martin, who had begun to do some straight acting in films. But Gosch added that he did not know Martin and so it might be difficult to get a script to him.

"Don't worry about that," Luciano said. "I'll take care of it right away." Luciano took two copies of the script, one for himself and the other to be airmailed immediately to Hollywood. Later, he told Gosch that he had sent a copy directly to Frank Sinatra, who had delivered it to Martin.

Then Gosch was off, first to Madrid for a brief stopover, and then on to London and Paris to arrange both financing for the movie and a newspaper syndication of a Luciano life story, to be ghostwritten from old clippings.

On February 20, as Luciano was waiting for word from Gosch, he had another visitor. It was not a courier with the money he was expecting, however reduced the sum might be, nor his friend Pat Eboli. "I went to the airport and it turned out to be Tommy Eboli. He was lookin' kinda sour." Instead of money, Eboli brought orders — from Genovese in Atlanta, from Gambino, Joe Bonanno and even from Luciano's close friend, Tommy Lucchese; from, in fact, the entire leadership of the American underworld, including Lansky. The pressures on Chesterfield cigarettes had so far failed to move the sponsor from backing *The Untouchables*. Therefore, the council had decided, that pressure would be increased, to include a boycott. The last thing the Unione wanted at this moment, Eboli informed Luciano, was a motion picture based on the life and times of the Sicilian-born underworld leader, which would put the light once again on a galaxy of Italian criminals.

"Tommy told me that this was not a request from nobody; he was givin' me orders. He talked to me like I was some young punk. The more he opened his mouth, the madder I started to get. I told him to his face that I saved him from goin' to the can, that if it hadn't been for me, he would be in Atlanta with his dear friend, Don Vitone. It was like talkin' to the wall. He told me not to get sore at him, because he was only deliverin' a message — that if I didn't give up the picture, I was gonna be cut off complete. Or

430

maybe I wouldn't even be around to enjoy the profits. That's how strong it was.

"When I realized that Meyer Lansky was right in the middle of this, that's when I knew he had us all by a string. Why should Lansky, bein' a Jew, give a shit whether or not some fuckin' movie had a bunch of Italian names in it? Because he was pullin' the wires and everybody was dancin' to his tune on the other end, like a bunch of puppets. Lansky held the purse strings, too; he was the treasurer and he was really tryin' to be the boss of everythin'. It was just as clear as crystal to me what that little bastard was doin'. He was so hungry for power behind the scenes he'd kiss anybody's ass and do anythin' he had to do so that in the end, he — Meyer Lansky, my old partner and a Jew — would wind up the real boss of bosses of all the Italians and the Jews — and without a single fuckin' vote on the council. I never really knew what it meant when we was kids and I used to call him the Genius. But at the age of sixty-four, I finally got wise."

Despite his rage, Luciano had no choice at that moment but to bow to the demands. He sent Eboli back to New York with the word that he would abandon the film.

In Naples the next day, however, Luciano came to two decisions. The first was to call Martin Gosch back from London, tell him there would be no film, and make him a counterproposal — to become the repository of the life and secrets of Charles Lucky Luciano, a life story Luciano felt might not have much longer to run because of the second decision. That was to emerge from his self-proclaimed retirement and challenge the powers across the Atlantic. A decade later, Adriana Rizzo would say, "Charlie said, 'They're tryin' to cut me off and push me around like I'm some kid. They don't even lemme retire, like they done with Costello. Now they wanna start this crap with me. Well, screw 'em. I'm gonna teach 'em a lesson.' "

40.

At Rome airport on February 26, 1961, Luciano and Gosch reached their agreement. Then Luciano revealed his plans for the months ahead. "All these years," he said, "I've been accused of bein' the king of narcotics for the whole fuckin' world. It was all bullshit. It's been almost forty years since I got a quarter out of junk. But all that's gonna end right now. Once I offered the United States government to really head up narcotics so I could help squash it, but they wouldn't listen. Now I'm gonna do that, what they said I've been doin' all along. I'm gonna take over the supply of narcotics once and for all. It's the only way I know to teach my 'friends' in the United States that they can't order me around, that I won't sit still for it. But you're not gonna know nothin' about it, Marty. I'm gonna tell you the story of my life as far back as I can remember, but what I do from this point on has nothin' to do with you and you're out of it. What I do from now on may succeed or it may get me bumped off, but then at least one person in this world will know the whole truth."

As soon as Gosch had left, Luciano began to implement his plan to organize the multitude of independent and disorganized growers, shippers, processers and sellers. A decade earlier, his proposal to do that to shut off the supply of narcotics had been ignored. Now he would do it to create an empire that would enable him to squeeze his onetime associates in the United States whom he had now come to see as his enemies. They would be forced to come to him for their supplies. He would make himself so indispensable to the heads of the drug traffic in the United States that his life and safety would be insured, that they would not dare attempt any reprisals.

"If they wanted to make a buy, they was gonna have to come to me. All them guys like Vito found it so easy to buy junk that they never gave a thought to organizin' anything but the sales; they always figured the suppliers couldn't live without 'em. That's the first lesson I was gonna teach 'em — that without the supply they could have all the demand in the world and it wouldn't do 'em no fuckin' good. That was my version of Lansky's Law.''

Immediately, Luciano closed out his "laundry" account in Zurich, taking half of the remaining balance of fifty thousand dollars and depositing it in the Naples branch of the U.S. Bank of America. The other half, twenty-five thousand dollars, he held in cash in his apartment, as a fund for his agents who began to fan out to France, Germany, Turkey and other areas. They talked to poppy growers, small-boat owners, drug refiners, carrying the message that Charlie Lucky wanted to organize, that those who created the supply should have the same protection and bargaining strength as those who created the demand. Reports back to Luciano indicated that after initial suspicion, there was considerable enthusiasm.

"I was spendin' money hand over fist, wherever I could dig it up, but I was makin' a lot of progress. One of the things that gimme a big kick was that most of them European suppliers was the same guys who'd been Vito's original contacts as far back as the thirties, before the war when he was in Italy. Half my life, the name Charlie Lucky was supposed to carry a lotta weight, but I never gave it much thought. This time, the guys kept reportin' back that the minute my name was mentioned, them guys in Turkey and Italy and Egypt and Germany practically scraped the ground. I figured I'd have the whole thing all set up and workin' by the end of summer."

With his goal in sight, Luciano sent back word to his associates in New York that he had taken steps to make their purchases of narcotics a more simplified and organized operation. Henceforth, they would have to deal only with him, and, he said, any attempt by them, individually or as a group, to bypass him he would take most unkindly.

It took only a few days before Luciano had his first response. He began to receive what he called "poison pen letters" from all over the United States. "Them letters all looked like they was written by me. I mean, with lousy grammar, like I have. Maybe I don't know how to use good grammar and that stuff, but I sure can recognize it when it's written right. All them letters said the same thing, that I was makin' a big mistake and that if I knew what was good for me, I would just keep my nose clean. Naturally, none of this advice had no return addresses and they wasn't signed, and they didn't say what it was all about. The postmarks was from weird little towns in the States where I never knew nobody and there was just no way to trace 'em. I mean, what cop could find out that Joe Profaci sent me a letter if it was postmarked Marion, Ohio?"

At first, Luciano was amused. With the arrival of each piece of hate mail, he would turn to Adriana and say, "Let's see where the Black Hand is this week." Even his health seemed to improve.

But late in the spring, the fun died. Pat Eboli arrived in Naples. "He had only a couple grand for me from New York, but he had plenty of messages. He told me when the word got back that I was gonna tie up the junk supply in Europe, everybody really got violent. He said when Tommy brought the news down to Vito in Atlanta, Genovese practically had a hemorrhage right in the visitors' room and demanded that I was to get hit right away, without no delay. I told Pat if that kind of threat come from Joe Profaci, I'd take it serious. But I knew that little pig too goddamn well, and the way his mind worked. He was gonna try to do somethin' different. All I hadda do was figure out what it meant by different."

As he had done often in the past, Luciano tried to put himself into Genovese's mind. He came to the conclusion that the reprisal against him would be of the same kind he and the others had used to send Genovese to prison. It would be totally apart from whatever moves the other leaders of the organization might take, for Genovese, Luciano was certain, would want his own revenge. And Luciano concluded that it would probably entail an attempt to get Charlie Lucky on a narcotics charge.

Now Luciano began to worry, convinced that two major adversaries were about to descend upon him — the combined forces of the American underworld bent on his murder, and the forces of Genovese determined to see him imprisoned for the rest of his life. Luciano went into partial seclusion in his penthouse. His chest pains returned, more severe than ever, his blood pressure rose, and he began taking increasing quantities of medicine. He would sit for hours staring out the window, his body sagging, his face drawn and ashen. He saw no one but his closest and most trusted friends.

On his frequent visits, Gosch became aware of the deepening depression, as Luciano talked of a sudden yearning to see his family. He had even sent for his sister Fannie and she was due to arrive within a few days. During one of these sessions, Gosch made a proposal that he hoped would turn Luciano from his current drive and would, at the same time, provide him with the money he needed. He told Luciano that he had recently been approached in Madrid with a proposition to develop the Algarve coastline in Portugal into a major resort area, complete with hotels and gambling casinos. Gosch had arranged for options on beachfront land where a luxury hotel, marina and casino would be built. Perhaps Luciano might be interested in acquiring a percentage of the casino operation. Luciano told Gosch he would, indeed, give the matter some thought and let him know later.

During the next several days, Luciano tried to relax and assume an optimistic front while his sister was visiting. Once she and her family returned to the United States, he sent for his friend and adviser Chinky Vitaliti, who had been informed of all Luciano's moves. He told Vitaliti that while it was obvious that his plans to organize the narcotics traffic in Europe were on the verge of success, it was just as obvious that these plans were going to boomerang, and he was convinced that his health could not stand up under the pressures and anxieties.

"Charlie," Vitaliti told him, "give up the junk. It's nothing you ever wanted and you must stop it, now, today. Tell them immediately. As far as Vito is concerned, I think you are right and we must watch carefully."

Once more, Luciano sent a message to his associates in New York. He was abandoning his plans for narcotics, he said, returning once more to a life of retirement. He would devote some of his energies, he said, to a new opportunity that had been presented to him to help develop the Portuguese Algarve.

435

Luciano had become, almost without comprehending it, an old man losing his grip. A few years before, he would have met the demands and challenges from his old friends in the States — if they would even have dared issue dictates and threats then — without hesitation. Then, as he had done so often, he would have conceived a devious plan to defeat them and gone on to accomplish his aim. But now he was isolated, weakened by age and personal afflictions — the loss of Igea Lissoni, his heart attacks and more. The power that had once been his over organized crime had vanished, and now he knew it. The self-confidence that had once radiated from him, the conviction that nobody and nothing could stand up before him — they, too, were gone. And he began to realize that he no longer even had the ambition that had once driven him and carried him so far. He seemed governed by whim, sometimes idle, drifting from one plan to another, one project to the next, never able to see any through to the end.

His message reached New York early in September. About ten days later, a courier arrived in Naples with an envelope filled with cash. It was not back up to the old twenty-five thousand dollars, but close to it. Through the ensuing weeks of the year, the flow of funds continued, and even improved. Just before Christmas, extra money was sent and Luciano used some of it to buy Adriana a fur coat for the holidays.

But it was never quite enough to meet all his needs. There were all those people in Naples, Rome and Sicily who were still dependent on his generosity. The furniture business was going under rapidly, taking with it nearly a hundred thousand dollars of Luciano's money.

What worried him most, however, was the potential fallout from his move into European narcotics. His agents may have been reliable, but he had no way to control anyone they might have talked with. Sooner or later, he was certain, the Italian authorities would learn of his intentions without necessarily realizing that he had abandoned them. This would send them down on him once again.

Then, during the fall, he received news that portended major trouble. Two New York gangsters, Vincent Mauro and Frankie "The Bug" Caruso, once part of the Luciano family but latterly tied closely to Genovese, had been arrested and indicted in New York on narcotics charges. They had been released on $100,000 bail — and promptly vanished.

"When the hell is this ever gonna end? Now I'm gonna be blamed for that." He was right. He was summoned to the headquarters of the Guardia di Finanza in Naples and questioned closely about the disappearance of Mauro and Caruso. It was even suggested by Italian narcotics authorities that his money had been used to finance their bail and flight.

Though the matter was not pressed, Luciano was once more under suspicion. The surveillance on him was resumed and so were the telephone taps. And there were increasing demands from Henry Manfredi and American narcotics officials in Rome that the Italians do something drastic about Luciano.

In the midst of this mounting trouble, Father Scarpato arrived from Mount Vesuvius with problems of his own that needed Luciano's help. As his clinic neared completion, there was need for a great deal more capital to buy all the necessary technical equipment. The priest had discovered a possible way to get that money. He had made some inquiries and learned that a municipal law permitted the importation and use of slot machines for charitable purposes. What could be more charitable, he asked, than helping to complete and equip his new hospital? Indeed, he had learned that Naples authorities would grant him an import license if the machines were used solely for that purpose.

Luciano was horrified. "I told him that he was just askin' for trouble. I pointed out that guy Montoni who had been fightin' with him for years had been made a judge because the Communist Party put a lotta pressure on to get him the job. If Don Cheech got himself mixed up with slot machines, Montoni would probably try to come down on him like a ton of bricks. But he gave me a good argument. He said that with me bein' sick and with money bein' so short, there was no other way to raise the dough to get the hospital open. So I finally said okay, that I would arrange for him to get money to bring in the slots, and for him to go and get his licenses for the import and the right to run 'em as a benefit for the church and the hospital, like they do in the States with bingo games. I arranged for a whole bunch of slot machines to be trucked down from Germany and over to Mount Vesuvius and he stored 'em in the basement of his church, all crated up just the way they was delivered. How the hell did I know that he was gonna be insane enough to put them slots into the bars and nightclubs and stores all over the slope of Vesuvius, figurin' the license would permit that, and he'd make a quick killin' to get the hospital opened right away?"

After Luciano's death, Father Scarpato was arrested for operating the slot machines illegally and sentenced to a prison term by his old enemy, Judge Ivan Montoni. The people of his parish held public demonstrations in his behalf and the Vatican eventually intervened. After six months, he was released and permitted to return to his parish. But during his incarceration, his clinic was declared bankrupt and was seized by creditors who would later operate it without his assistance. And upon his return, Don Cheech discovered that vandals had destroyed his home and desecrated his church.

Early in December, Luciano suffered severe heart failure. For a few minutes, he was sure he was going to die, the attack catching him at the base of the throat and blocking his ability to breathe. He was rushed to the hospital, where it was discovered that the attack, though nearly fatal, had not been a coronary and had done no further damage to his heart. Within a week, he was home. But almost overnight, it seemed, he had aged. His once-black hair was almost completely gray. He stooped a little when he walked, and behind his steel-rimmed glasses his face was deeply lined and almost benign. He looked like a retired clerk or schoolteacher, and he looked his age, sixty-four.

He had not been home long before he received two visitors from New York, Henry and Theresa Rubino. Luciano had known Rubino for some years, as a member of the Genovese outfit back in New York and as an occasional courier to Naples. He was, too, often involved in deals with Mauro and Caruso. In 1957, Rubino had approached Luciano with a narcotics proposition and had been abruptly spurned. Nevertheless, he had kept up his contacts with the exiled racketeer whenever he was in Italy. In the late fall of 1961, Rubino and his wife arrived in Rome again and telephoned Luciano at his Naples apartment, using the private number reserved strictly for friends. Luciano ordered him not to use it again. But Rubino explained that he and Theresa were in Europe only for a vacation, not for business, and they would like to pay Luciano a visit. Christmas was approaching and they had no other friends with whom to spend the holidays. After some hesitation, Luciano invited the Rubinos to accompany him and Adriana to Taormina.

On New Year's Eve, Luciano and Adriana gave a small party at La Giarra nightclub in Taormina and were joined by the Rubinos, Vitaliti and the club's owner, Francesco Scimone and his wife. As Adriana remembers that party, "It was a pleasant, quiet evening to see the New Year in. The only bad thing was when I overheard Rubino trying to persuade Charlie not to retire. He wanted him to keep on with his plans. But I heard Charlie tell Rubino that he was too old and didn't want to fight any more. I leaned over and I said to this Henry, 'Please leave my Charlie alone.' Chinky heard it, too, and he told Rubino to shut his mouth."

The next morning, Luciano told Vitaliti that he had a feeling Mauro and Caruso had not jumped bail in New York just to stay out of jail. His instinct told him that it was part of Genovese's vendetta. He had mentioned Mauro and Caruso to Rubino, he said; Rubino had flushed and denied instantly any knowledge of their activities or whereabouts. "It don't add up," Luciano said. "We better be careful."

After the holidays, Luciano and Adriana returned to Naples while the Rubinos went on to Rome. On January 17, Pat Eboli arrived. It was a sorrowful Eboli this time; he had come as a friend and not as a courier, though he had messages from New York. Luciano, he said, had been the subject of council discussions and the feeling was that he had become a danger to the organization he had founded. He was no longer considered trustworthy and there was a strong belief that as long as he lived, nobody was safe. Luciano's execution, Eboli told him, was imminent.

There was a finality to Eboli's statement. But then he added that during the council meeting, there had been considerable discussion of the motion picture about Luciano's life. Eboli suggested that if Luciano could obtain the original copy of the script, which he had signed and approved, and send it back to New York, it might serve as a sign of goodwill on Luciano's part and might save his life. As long as that signed script was in existence, the council's theory went, there was a danger that the movie might yet be made.

Luciano agreed. Knowing that Gosch had the original script, he placed a call to Madrid on Wednesday evening, January 24, to ask Gosch to bring the script to Naples immediately.

It is one of the ironic coincidences of these final days that only a few days earlier, Gosch had written to Luciano to sound him out about reconsidering the decision to back out of the film. Cameron Mitchell, the actor, had been a visitor in Gosch's home shortly before. He had recently arrived in Spain from Naples, where he had met Luciano and had come away with a determination to portray him on the screen.

"This accidental meeting with Cam Mitchell," Gosch wrote, "now brings us back to life again — if you give the word. If you give me the word that circumstances are such that we can go forward, I will come to Rome to meet with you. It is entirely up to you and I would appreciate your writing to me at once with the answer. I know how you hate to put a pencil to paper, but please, Charlie, take an extra pill and write to me as soon as you receive this."

When Gosch had not received a reply after five days, he picked up the phone in his home in Madrid to call Luciano in Naples. The two calls crossed. For the first several minutes, neither Luciano nor Gosch could hear each other — their conversation, though they did not know it, was being monitored at both ends, by the Guardia di Finanza in Naples and the Brigada Criminal in Madrid.

Finally, with both men shouting, their voices became intelligible. "Marty," Luciano said, "could you come here?"

Hearing those words — the same words that had brought him from London to Naples nearly a year before — Gosch realized that Luciano was calling him. "Why, Charlie?" he shouted. "What's wrong?"

Luciano ignored the questions. "Could you come here and bring the script?"

"Why in the world do you want the script?"

Luciano was insistent. "If you can't come here, I'll send some-body around to your house to pick it up."

Luciano's tone was hard, almost menacing to Gosch, the first time in their relationship that the producer had felt even an im-plied threat. "Don't bother, Charlie," he said quickly. "I'll come to Italy. Besides, there's something I want to talk to you about anyway."

"Okay, that's good. When are you gonna come?"

"I'll see if I can get a flight tomorrow. I'll send you a cablegram tonight."

Gosch checked the airline schedules and found that he could make a flight from Madrid via Iberia to Rome that connected with an interior Alitalia flight to Naples, so he sent Luciano an over-night cable giving him the flight information, adding, "Bringing script."

What Gosch did not know was that the flight schedules had been revised by Iberia and the Thursday flight to Rome now departed on Friday. As soon as he discovered this, he sent a second cable to Luciano advising of the twenty-four-hour delay.

But that initial cable had been intercepted in Naples by the police, and it set off the final scenes in Luciano's life. Luciano was under closer surveillance than ever before. The telephone con-versation with Gosch had been monitored, and it was thought to have hidden meanings; the words "bringing script" in the cable were assumed to be a code involving narcotics. The separate strands of Luciano's life and works were merging at the end.

41.

Over the years, Luciano had given explicit instructions to all his associates, from the United States and in Italy, that no business calls of any nature were ever to be made to his home. Taps on his phones had always disappointed listeners, for his orders had always been obeyed and the calls into and out of the apartment were invariably innocent, innocuous and personal.

But in January 1962, after his return from Taormina, those orders were ignored, and ignored repeatedly. Rubino called several times from his hotel in Rome and argued openly about Luciano's decision to retire. Despite heated injunctions from Luciano not to call again, Rubino persisted. Luciano became convinced that behind Rubino's open disobedience lay Genovese's plan to ensnare him in a narcotics conspiracy.

Then, just after the middle of the month, almost coincident with the arrival in Naples of Pat Eboli, another call came in on the apartment phone, this time from Vince Mauro in Spain.

Mauro and Caruso, together with an accomplice named Salvatore Maneri, had arrived in Spain by a devious route. After jumping bail in New York, they had fled south with a hundred thousand dollars in cash, turning up in Nassau, where they basked in the sun, chased girls, toured the night spots, and spent money with abandon. After a couple of weeks, they left for Canada, picked up fake passports made out in the names of actual Canadians, and departed again, one step ahead of the police. For three Canadian girls they had met in Nassau recognized their photographs in a Toronto newspaper after their return home and notified the Royal Canadian Mounted Police. They were too late. Mauro, Caruso and Maneri turned up in rapid succession in the next weeks back in the Bahamas, in Jamaica, in Caracas and then across the Atlantic, in London and later Nice. Nowhere did they attempt to hide. They traveled openly, visited casinos and gambled heavily, stayed at the best hotels; and Mauro, trying to enhance his reputation as the greatest underworld lover since Joe Adonis, made a pitch for every woman he came across.

By mid-January, they were in Barcelona, from which they made several calls to Italy. One was to the Rubinos in Rome, who immediately hurried off to Spain to meet them. After a brief talk in Barcelona, they all made their way to Madrid, where Mauro, Caruso and Maneri checked into the Palace Hotel. The Rubinos stayed for a few days more and then went back to Rome.

On both January 14 and 15, Mauro placed calls from the Palace to Luciano in Naples, directly to his home at the number given him by Rubino. He made no attempt to hide his identity, or the reason for the calls. He reminded Luciano of his loyalty in the past and then said that since Luciano was "moving big into the junk business," Caruso and Maneri and he had come to Europe to offer their services, for whatever use Luciano could make of them.

Before Mauro could finish, Luciano cut him off. When Mauro called again the next day, Luciano hung up on him after the first words. When Luciano put down the receiver, he turned to Adriana, his face white with rage. He told her the call was going to make a lot of trouble and he was sure it was part of Genovese's plot to frame him on narcotics. "The easiest thing in the world," he said, "is to frame somebody as long as the guy you're trying to get is wide open for a frame."

Suddenly, Luciano slumped to the floor, agonizing pain in his chest. Convinced he was having a heart attack, Adriana rushed to the phone to call an ambulance. Luciano stopped her. "Let's see if the pills work first," he said weakly. Within a few hours, he was feeling better; it had only been an angina attack.

Like all the calls into and out of the penthouse on the Parco Comola, that call from Mauro had been monitored by the Guardia di Finanza. It had also been overheard by the Brigada Criminal in Madrid, for the Spanish police had spotted Mauro and his friends soon after their arrival in Barcelona and had been watching them closely ever since. Interpol and American narcotics authorities were notified by both Italian and Spanish police, and the watch on all the suspects was tightened.

On the evening of January 24, the authorities decided to move. At the request of Washington, forwarded through Clark Anderson, an FBI undercover agent at the U.S. Embassy in Madrid, the Spanish police descended on the Palace Hotel and arrested Mauro, Caruso and Maneri. In Mauro's possession, they found $11,730 in cash and the keys to a hotel safety deposit box; in that box was another $43,759 in cash. For more than a week, the three were interrogated and then turned over to American authorities for extradition. (On the same plane, a TWA flight from Rome to New York with a stop in Madrid, was Pat Eboli; but no communications were exchanged.) In New York, they stood trial for narcotics conspiracy and bail-jumping, were convicted, and were sentenced to fifteen years in prison. In the spring of 1972, after serving nine years, all were released.

In Italy, meanwhile, the authorities waited. The interception of the cable from Gosch — the police assuming that the words "bringing script" indicated that he was part of the conspiracy and would be arriving with narcotics or illegal currency — sent them into motion. In Rome, the police moved in on the Excelsior Hotel and picked up Henry and Theresa Rubino. They were held for several days of questioning and then, because they were American citizens and had committed no provable crime, were released and sent back to the United States. In the early summer of 1972, Henry Rubino was shot and killed while playing golf in Miami. His murderer was never found.

Almost simultaneously with the actions in Rome, the Guardia di Finanza and the *questura* moved in Naples, prodded by the American Embassy's Luciano-watcher in Rome, Henry Manfredi. At one o'clock in the morning, a troop of police burst into Luciano's penthouse. He was not completely surprised, for he had been alerted earlier in the evening that Mauro, Caruso and Maneri had been picked up in Madrid, and that police were aware of the calls to him. But Adriana became nearly hysterical. She screamed at the police that Luciano was seriously ill, that his heart was weak, that they were killing him. Wearing only a sheer nightgown, she leaped at one of the taller officers and beat him about the chest, then raced out of the apartment and pounded at the door of a neighbor, begging for helping, screaming that the police were assassins torturing a sick man.

The police ignored her. While Luciano watched, dazed by the sleeping pills he had taken a few hours earlier, they meticulously searched the apartment, looking for money, narcotics, anything incriminating. They found only the usual household possessions, keepsakes and mementos — photographs of Luciano, Adriana, Vitaliti, recent ones taken of them and the Rubinos at Taormina on New Year's Eve, a photo of Mike Cerra in his Air Force uniform, autographed to Luciano, a gold cigarette case engraved "To my dear pal, Charlie, from his friend, Frank Sinatra." In the apartment were only the relics of a long life.

Luciano was permitted to dress under the eyes of the police and then, in the darkest hour of the morning, while Adriana called down the saints on their heads, they took him to the barracks for questioning. Captain Speziale and his staff pounded away on the subject of narcotics and Luciano's involvement. Though his strength was rapidly failing and he was seized by almost constant chest pains, he fought them off, denying as he always had any knowledge of or complicity in a narcotics conspiracy. He insisted he was retired from all business of any kind. He was asked about the call from Mauro in Spain; he admitted receiving it but said that the police knew, since they must have been listening in, that he had spurned any suggestion of a meeting, of any business deals and had ordered Mauro not to call again. They pressed him about the call to Gosch in Madrid, about the demands for the "script" and Gosch's cable. Luciano insisted that the call dealt only with negotiations about a movie of his life; it was as simple as that. The police were skeptical. Luciano invited them to accompany him to Capodicino Airport the next day to see for themselves.

Gosch's second cable, arriving in the morning, postponed that trip, for a day. The police armed themselves for that eventual meeting, securing a warrant for Gosch's arrest with the right to seize and search his property.

By late in the afternoon of January 25, Luciano was permitted to return home under police guard. All his energy and reserves were gone and he slept until late the following morning. Then he rose, dressed, and, accompanied by his guards and with their permission, went to his favorite barbershop for a shave. As he relaxed in his chair, Pat Eboli entered. They had a hurried conversation, Luciano telling Eboli what had occurred and complaining that he had no dollars readily available. Eboli managed to pass him a five-hundred-dollar bill as they shook hands goodbye. Just before leaving the barbershop, Luciano put the bill in his wallet; that evening, it would be missing when his wallet was searched.

At mid-afternoon, Maresciallo (Marshal) Cesare Resta of Captain Speziale's Guardia staff arrived at the penthouse to take Luciano to the airport to meet Gosch's five o'clock flight, to see if Luciano was really telling the truth and if the "script" was really nothing more than a screenplay.

Luciano had eaten nothing all day. At the airport, he had a

small glass of orange juice, then waited anxiously for the plane to arrive.

The flight was a few minutes early. As Gosch came down the ramp, he saw Luciano and another man he didn't know, Resta, standing just inside the terminal at the observation window. He waved; Luciano waved back. Gosch walked into the terminal, and was stunned when he saw Luciano. The man seemed to have aged twenty-five years since they had last met in November; he seemed shrunken, his skin almost parchment, his voice weak.

"Hello, Charlie," Gosch said, "how are you?"

"I'm pretty lousy," Luciano said.

Gosch handed Luciano a paper bag containing a bottle of his favorite Spanish brandy and a box of chocolates for Adriana. "Maybe this will make you feel better."

Luciano thanked Gosch, then pointed to Resta. "This guy's a pal of mine. He don't speak too much English." Gosch and Resta shook hands, Gosch assuming that Resta was one of Luciano's Italian associates.

The three men started to walk through the airport building toward the parking lot. They walked slowly, Luciano maneuvering himself so that Gosch was between him and Resta. Immediately, Luciano began to speak to Gosch in a low, halting voice. Resta made several attempts to listen, but Luciano was speaking too quietly, brokenly, and in English.

"I fucked myself, Marty. They're gonna kill me."

"Who's going to kill you?"

"All of 'em, all of 'em. I only got one friend in the world, Pat Eboli. He's a good kid and you can trust him. . . . Please remember the promise you made me, but use it all. Don't hold back. . . ." The words were coming with great effort, Luciano pausing and gulping for breath. "I couldn't even go through the narcotics bit . . . and I'm not even gonna end up the king of junk. . . . Lansky's gonna wind up the boss of everything . . . and all the money. . . . They wouldn't let me out. . . . It was dead or nothin'. Some choice, huh? Two hoods, they're tryin' to trap me for Vito. . . ."

As Luciano was speaking, they reached the edge of the parking lot and Gosch saw Luciano's Alfa Romeo Giulietta in the middle. Gosch stopped, put his hand on Luciano's arm, and said, "Wait a minute. I have to get my suitcase." He reached into his topcoat pocket and pulled out a stub. They came to a halt near the baggage claim area. Luciano held tightly to the paper bag.

Suddenly, he lurched against Gosch and started to sag to the ground. "Marty . . ." His eyes rolled up as he gasped for breath. With the help of Resta, Gosch lowered Luciano to the pavement, quickly loosened his tie, unbuttoned his shirt and knelt astride him to administer artificial respiration.

Luciano was gasping for breath, unable to speak. As Gosch cried out for help, he noticed the large clock above the terminal door; it was eight minutes after five. Then he felt Resta's hand in his pocket, trying to get the baggage check, taking it and starting for the claims area. "For God's sake, never mind the damn suitcase. Get a doctor, you idiot; call an ambulance; get some oxygen."

Resta was at his side again, saying to him, *"Pilloli, pilloli,"* and pointing to Luciano's trouser pocket. Gosch nodded and motioned for him to get the gold pillbox. A half-dozen nitroglycerin tablets were placed under Luciano's tongue.

In the distance, Gosch heard the sound of the ambulance. Just as it pulled into sight, Luciano shuddered, his chest stopped heaving, his gasping stopped. His eyes opened, staring at nothing. Gosch glanced once more at the terminal clock. It was 5:26 in the afternoon of January 26, 1962.

The ambulance, a battered American jeep with a red cross on its side, pulled up a moment later. Two men in white jackets jumped out and hurried to Luciano. In a mixture of languages and gestures, Gosch tried to make them understand they should inject adrenaline immediately. A long hypodermic needle was driven directly in Luciano's chest. When it was withdrawn, there was no sign of blood. One of the attendants put a stethoscope to Luciano's heart, looked at his eyes, checked his pulse. It was too late.

Gosch turned to Resta. "He's dead." Resta paled, staggered against Gosch and, with effort, held himself upright. Then Gosch turned to the attendant. "Do you know who this man is?"

The attendant shook his head.

"This is a man that you probably do know. *Egli è famoso.* He is Charlie Lucky Luciano."

447

The ambulance attendant stared in disbelief. The few onlookers who had remained to watch also heard the name and stared.

Once Luciano had said that he would end up on a cement slab.

Now, in tailor-made navy blue blazer and gray flannel slacks, the collar of his white shirt open, his striped blue tie pulled down, he lay on the cement pavement of the airport parking lot. Someone brought out a bilious green-yellow slicker and threw it across the body. It did not cover the face. For several hours, until an official could be found to authorize release of the body to the Naples morgue, the remains of Lucky Luciano lay in the middle of the parking lot, covered by the slicker, staring sightlessly into the night sky.

42.

The end had been sudden and unexpected. When Pat Eboli, in his hotel room in Naples, heard the news, he could not believe it and rushed to the morgue to make sure. The body had not yet arrived, and so Eboli was convinced it was all a mistake. Then he was told it was true, the body was there. But he would not be assured until he had seen it. "I had to bribe that dirty fuckin' guy at the morgue to get a look," he said later. Convinced, he went to the cable office and sent a message back to the United States: Charlie Lucky was dead, not of a bullet but of the ills of age, of a heart attack.

Three days later, those who could or who cared gathered at the Holy Trinity Church in Naples to celebrate the requiem mass for the dead man. Father Scarpato came down from Mount Vesuvius to eulogize his friend's passing. Giovanni Passeggio and other friends from the world of respectability were there, and so were the friends who had labored close to his side in the good old days in New York and in the days of exile in Italy. They were men grown old now, like Joe Di Giorgio and John Raimundo, and with his death, they were bereft and uncertain in their own exile. The central figure in their lives was gone.

Joe Adonis received permission from Italian authorities to attend. He arrived with a mournful expression, tears in his eyes and a final tribute to his old friend — a massive floral wreath with a black band on which, in gold letters, was inscribed the ancient gangland farewell: "So Long, Pal."

Pat Eboli remained a few days more to help with the disposal of Luciano's goods. Of his family, only his brother Bartolo made the trip. Of his friends, associates, comrades, followers in the American underworld, none appeared, though Lansky sent a floral offering and so did many others, most of them anonymously. There was no word from Vito Genovese in Atlanta, though some said that on that day he was smiling, effusive and more generous than was his habit.

More than three hundred people — many of them watchful police officers from Italy, the United States and Interpol, not mourning but on duty — sat through the mass and then, on foot, followed the flower-bedecked coffin in its silver-and-black funeral carriage, drawn by eight prancing black horses with floral plumes, and the other flower-laden carriages; they walked on as the procession wound slowly through Naples to Poggio-Réale's English Cemetery where the body was placed in the chapel to await a final decision on the place of interment.

In life, Luciano's desire had been to return to the place he had always thought of as home, the United States. That was not to be. But if not in life, he had hoped that at least in death, when no one could any longer consider him a danger, his body would be permitted burial there. He had made plans for that day; in 1935, he bought ground and for twenty-five thousand dollars built a small vault, large enough for sixteen coffins, in St. John's Cathedral Cemetery in Queens. His mother, father, an aunt and an uncle were already buried there. Now the request was made to the United States Embassy in Rome to permit Luciano to join them.

The question was debated for some days. During those days, the estate left by Luciano was settled. There was the penthouse on the Parco Comola in Naples, registered in Bartolo's name. He quickly sold it for less than half its value and evicted Adriana, though at the intervention of Pat Eboli, he reluctantly gave her three thousand dollars in lire and allowed her to take away her clothes and other personal possessions. There was the farm at Santa Marinella; that, too, was sold for less than its real worth. A search of all Luciano's papers and records, in Naples and elsewhere, turned up no loose money and only the records of a single bank account, in the Banco Americano in Naples, containing sixteen thousand dollars. If there was anything else, it was never discovered.

Early in February, American authorities in Washington and Rome decided there would be no peril in permitting Luciano's remains to return to New York for burial. On February 7, the body arrived on a Pan American Airways cargo plane. It was met by a score of reporters, fifty FBI men, narcotics agents and New York City and state police — and two mourners, Luciano's brothers, Bartolo and Joseph.

The coffin, with a simple silver plate on its lid bearing only the name Salvatore Lucanía, was placed in a hearse and driven at high speed to St. John's Cemetery and there placed into the vault with its simple Grecian columns and the legend LUCANIA. Only about a hundred feet away was another vault, with the legend GENOVESE. There, within seven years, Vito Genovese would come to his final rest.

It was all over in minutes. There was no graveside ceremony. As the bronze doors were closed, some of those watching noticed a stained-glass window in the vault, depicting a bearded saint leaning on a shepherd's staff. Bartolo Lucanía was asked who the saint was. "I don't know," he said. "I'm not acquainted with saints."

Index

458

459